"This is a superb book. Jeffrey and Maillet are skilled guides, well-versed in Scripture, Christian theology and literary history, and to travel in their company is to be delighted and instructed. None of the questions raised in this book deserve simple answers, least of all the initial one: 'What does Jesus Christ have to do with English literature?' And no simple answers will be found here, but rather a deep exploration, by turns sober and festive, of the possibilities that arise when Christian thought bears on great writing."

Alan Jacobs, Clyde S. Kilby Chair Professor of English, Wheaton College

"Truth is at the very heart of fiction. It is the invisible yet palpable force that infuses the fictional narrative with the lifeblood of meaning. As such, Christianity and literature are inseparable. This fine volume guides the Christian lover of literature through the panoramic panoply of the literary landscape. It's a monumental achievement that serves as a testament to the beauty of truth, and the truth of beauty."

Joseph Pearce, Writer-in-Residence and Associate Professor of Literature, Ave Maria University

"*Christianity and Literature* provides a brilliant assessment of Christian theological aesthetics, at once based on a biblical foundation and an understanding of the world of the ancient literature and philosophy that has influenced both the ways Christians have and should read literary works and the literary forms they have taken. Historically informed, critically astute, eminently valuable as is, but delightfully pregnant with hints that today's Christian scholars can and should heed to develop an aesthetic they can own. More than fifty years ago when I began serious literary study, I combed libraries for such a book. None was even on the horizon. What a leg up for today's students and budding scholars!"

James W. Sire, author of *The Universe Next Door*

"In language almost as unapologetic as that of the Bible itself, David Lyle Jeffrey and Gregory Maillet set forth the value of Christianity for the study of literature and vice versa. At every turn in this bold, wonderfully learned manifesto I gained some new insight or experienced the illumination of something I knew already if somewhat dimly. But don't read this book for knowledge alone. Throughout, it breathes a prophetic passion—bracing, salutary and sometimes uncomfortable—that transcends mere academic discussion and leaves the reader interrogated as well as taught."

Dennis Danielson, Professor of English, University of British Columbia, Vancouver, and editor of *The Cambridge Companion to Milton*

"This is a very useful book for anyone interested in the field of religion and literature, and it is especially illuminating for Christian scholars, be they fledgling or seasoned. With its graceful organization, thoughtful judgments and capacious scope, *Christianity and Literature* will provide a welcome resource for university English classes. Students and their teachers will come away from this book with a keener understanding of the way the Christian tradition—grounded in metaphysical and critical realism—animates enduring literature. In the book's consistent exploration of the ways literature integrates the true, good and beautiful, readers will also emerge with renewed confidence in their vocations as literary scholars."

Paul J. Contino, Professor of Great Books, Pepperdine University, and editor of the journal *Christianity and Literature*

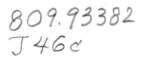
Christianity *and* LITERATURE

Philosophical Foundations

and Critical Practice

DAVID LYLE JEFFREY &
GREGORY MAILLET

IVP Academic
An imprint of InterVarsity Press
Downers Grove, Illinois

InterVarsity Press
P.O. Box 1400, Downers Grove, IL 60515-1426
World Wide Web: www.ivpress.com
E-mail: email@ivpress.com

InterVarsity Press® is the book-publishing division of InterVarsity Christian Fellowship/USA®, a movement of students and faculty active on campus at hundreds of universities, colleges and schools of nursing in the United States of America, and a member movement of the International Fellowship of Evangelical Students. For information about local and regional activities, write Public Relations Dept., InterVarsity Christian Fellowship/USA, 6400 Schroeder Rd., P.O. Box 7895, Madison, WI 53707-7895, or visit the IVCF website at <www.intervarsity.org>.

All Scripture quotations, unless otherwise indicated, are taken from the Holy Bible, Authorized (King James) Version.

Parts of chapter nine are taken from David Lyle Jeffrey, "Communion, Community, and Our Common Book: Or, Can Faustus Be Saved?" Christianity and Literature 53, no. 2 (2004): 233-46; and also from David Lyle Jeffrey, "Tolkien and the Future of Literary Studies," Tree of Tales: Tolkien, Literature and Theology, ed. Trevor Hart and Ivan Khovacs (Waco, Tex.: Baylor University Press, 2007), pp. 55-70. Both are used by permission.

Design: Cindy Kiple

ISBN 978-0-8308-2817-3

Printed in Canada ∞

Library of Congress Cataloging-in-Publication Data

Jeffrey, David L., 1941-
  Christianity and literature: philosophical foundations and critical
practice / David Lyle Jeffrey and Gregory Maillet.
      p. cm.—(Christian worldview integration series)
  Includes bibliographical references and index.
  ISBN 978-0-8308-2817-3 (pbk.: alk. paper)
  1. Christianity and literature. 2. Christianity in literature. I.
Maillet, Gregory, 1965- II. Title.
  PN49.J44 2011
  809'933823—dc22
                                                                    2010040594

P   20   19   18   17   16   15   14   13   12   11   10   9   8   7   6   5   4   3   2   1

Y   28   27   26   25   24   23   22   21   20   19   18   17   16   15   14   13   12   11

CONTENTS

Life's short and we're all busy. If you're a college student, you're *really* busy. There's your part-time job (which seems full time), your social life (hopefully) and church. On top of that you're expected to go to class, do some reading, take tests and write papers. Now, while you are minding your own business, you hear about something called "integration," trying to relate your major with your Christianity. Several questions may come to mind: What is integration, anyway? Is it just a fad? Why should I care about it? And even if I do care about it, I don't have a clue as to how to go about doing it. How do I do this? These are good questions, and in this introduction we're going to address them in order. We are passionate about helping you learn about and become good at integrating your Christian convictions with the issues and ideas in your college major or your career.

What Is Integration?

The word *integrate* means "to form or blend into a whole," "to unite." We humans naturally seek to find the unity that is behind diversity, and in fact coherence is an important mark of rationality. There are two kinds of integration: conceptual and personal. In conceptual integration, *our theological beliefs, especially those derived from careful study of the Bible, are blended and unified with important, reasonable ideas from our profession or college major into a coherent, intellectually satisfying Christian worldview.* As Augustine wisely advised, "We must show our Scriptures not to be in conflict with whatever [our critics] can demonstrate about the nature of things from reliable sources."[1] In personal integration we seek to live a unified life, a life in which we are the same in public as we are in private, a life in which the various aspects of our personality are consistent with each other and conducive to a life of human flourishing as a disciple of Jesus.

The two kinds of integration are deeply intertwined. All things being equal, the more authentic we are, the more integrity we have, the more we should be able to do conceptual integration with fidelity to Jesus and Scripture, and with intellectual honesty. All things being equal, the more conceptual integration we accomplish, the more coherent will be our set of beliefs and the more confidence we will have in the truth of our Christian worldview. In fact, conceptual integration is so important that it is worth thinking some more about why it matters.

SEVEN REASONS WHY INTEGRATION MATTERS

1. The Bible's teachings are true. The first justification for integration is pretty obvious, but often overlooked. *Christians hold that, when properly interpreted, the teachings of Holy Scripture are true.* This means two things. If the Bible teaches something relevant to an issue in an academic field, the Bible's view on that topic is true and thus provides an incredibly rich resource for doing work in that academic field. It would be irresponsible to set aside an important source of relevant truth in thinking through issues in our field of study or vocation. Further, if it looks like a claim on our field tends to make a biblical claim false, this tension needs to be resolved. Maybe our interpretation of Scripture is mistaken, maybe the Bible is not even talking about the issue, maybe the claim in our field is false. Whatever the case, the Christian's commitment to the truth of Scripture makes integration inevitable.

Adolfo Lopez-Otero, a Stanford engineering professor and a self-described secular humanist, offers advice to thinking Christians who want to have an impact on the world: "When a Christian professor ap-

---

[1]Augustine *De genesi ad litteram* 1.21, cited in Ernan McMullin, "How Should Cosmology Relate to Theology?" in *The Sciences and Theology in the Twentieth Century*, ed. Arthur R. Peacocke (Notre Dame, Ind.: University of Notre Dame Press, 1981), p. 20.

proaches a non-believing faculty member . . . they can expect to face a polite but condescending person [with a belief that they possess] superior metaphysics who can't understand how such an intelligent person [as yourself] still believes in things which have been discredited eons ago."[2] He goes on to say that "[Christian professors] cannot afford to give excuses . . . if they are honest about wanting to open spiritual and truthful dialogue with their non-believing colleagues—that is the price they must pay for having declared themselves Christians."[3] While Lopez-Otero's remarks are directed to Christian professors, his point applies to all thinking Christians: If we claim that our Christian views are true, we need to back that up by interacting with the various ideas that come from different academic disciplines. In short, we must integrate Christianity and our major or vocation.

2. Our vocation and the holistic character of discipleship demand integration. As disciples grow, they learn to see, feel, think, desire, believe and behave the way Jesus does in a manner fitting to the kingdom of God and their own station in life. With God's help we seek to live as Jesus would if he were a philosophy professor at Biola University married to Hope and father of Ashley and Allison, or as a political philosopher at Baylor University married to Frankie.

Two important implications flow from the nature of discipleship. For one thing the lordship of Christ is holistic. The religious life is not a special compartment in an otherwise secular life. Rather, the religious life is an entire way of life. To live Christianly is to allow Jesus Christ to be the Lord of every aspect of our life. There is no room for a secular-sacred separation in the life of Jesus' followers. Jesus Christ should be every bit as much at home in our thinking and behavior when we are developing our views in our area of study or work as he is when we are in a small group fellowship.

Further, as disciples of Jesus we do not merely have a job. We have a vocation as a Christian teacher. A job is a means for supporting ourselves and those for whom we are responsible. For the Christian a vocation (from the Latin *vocare*, which means "to call") is an overall calling

---

[2]Adolfo Lopez-Otero, "Be Humble, but Daring," *The Real Issue* 16 (September-October 1997): 10.
[3]Ibid., p. 11.

from God. Harry Blamires correctly draws a distinction between a general and a special vocation:

> The general vocation of all Christians—indeed of all men and women—is the same. We are called to live as children of God, obeying his will in all things. But obedience to God's will must inevitably take many different forms. The wife's mode of obedience is not the same as the nun's; the farmer's is not the same as the priest's. By "special vocation," therefore, we designate God's call to a [person] to serve him in a particular sphere of activity.[4]

As Christians seek to discover and become excellent in their special vocation, they must ask: How would Jesus approach the task of being a history teacher, a chemist, an athletic director, a mathematician? It is not always easy to answer this question, but the vocational demands of discipleship require that we give it our best shot.

Whatever we do, however, it is important that we restore to our culture an image of Jesus Christ as an intelligent, competent person who spoke authoritatively on whatever subject he addressed. The disciples of Jesus agreed with Paul when he said that all the wisdom of the Greeks and Jews was ultimately wrapped up in Jesus himself (Col 2:2-3). For them, Jesus was not merely a Savior from sin; he was the wisest, most intelligent, most attractive person they had ever seen.

In the early centuries of Christianity the church presented Jesus to unbelievers precisely because he was wiser, more virtuous, more intelligent and more attractive in his character than Aristotle, Plato, Moses or anyone else. It has been a part of the church's self-understanding to locate the spiritual life in a broader quest for the good life, that is, a life of wisdom, knowledge, beauty and goodness. So understood, the spiritual life and discipleship to Jesus were seen as the very best way to achieve a life of truth, beauty and goodness. Moreover, the life of discipleship was depicted as the wisest, most reasonable form of life available so that a life of unbelief was taken to be foolish and absurd. *Our schools need to recapture and propagate this broader understanding of following Christ if they are to be thoroughly Christian in their approach to education.*

---

[4]Harry Blamires, *A God Who Acts* (Ann Arbor, Mich.: Servant Books, 1957), p. 67.

3. Biblical teaching about the role of the mind in the Christian life and the value of extrabiblical knowledge requires integration. The Scriptures are clear that God wants us to be like him in every facet of our lives, and he desires commitment from our total being, including our intellectual life. We are told that we change spiritually by having the categories of our minds renewed (Rom 12:1-2), that we are to include an intellectual love for God in our devotion (Mt 22:37-38), and that we are to be prepared to give others a reasonable answer to questions others ask us about why we believe what we believe (1 Pet 3:15). As the great eighteenth-century Christian thinker and spiritual master William Law put it, "Unreasonable and absurd ways of life . . . are truly an offense to God."[5] Learning and developing convictions about the teachings of Scripture are absolutely central to these mandates. However, many of Jesus' followers have failed to see that an aggressive pursuit of knowledge in areas outside the Bible is also relevant to these directives.

God has revealed himself and various truths on a number of topics outside the Bible. As Christians have known throughout our history, common sense, logic and mathematics, along with the arts, humanities, sciences and other areas of study, contain important truths relevant to life in general and to the development of a careful, life-related Christian worldview.

In 1756 John Wesley delivered an address to a gathering of clergy on how to carry out the pastoral ministry with joy and skill. In it Wesley catalogued a number of things familiar to most contemporary believers—the cultivation of a disposition to glorify God and save souls, a knowledge of Scripture, and similar notions. However, at the front of his list Wesley focused on something seldom expressly valued by most pastoral search committees: "Ought not a Minister to have, First, a good understanding, a clear apprehension, a sound judgment, and a capacity of reasoning with some closeness?"[6]

Time and again throughout the address Wesley unpacked this re-

---

[5]William Law, *A Serious Call to a Devout and Holy Life* (1728; reprint, Grand Rapids: Eerdmans, 1966), p. 2.
[6]John Wesley, "An Address to the Clergy," in *The Works of John Wesley*, 3rd ed. (Grand Rapids: Baker, 1979), p. 481.

mark by admonishing ministers to know what would sound truly odd and almost pagan to the average congregant of today: logic, metaphysics, natural theology, geometry and the ideas of important figures in the history of philosophy. For Wesley study in these areas (especially philosophy and geometry) helped train the mind to think precisely, a habit of incredible value, he asserted, when it comes to thinking as a Christian about theological themes or scriptural texts. According to Wesley the study of extrabiblical information and the writings of unbelievers was of critical value for growth and maturity. As he put it elsewhere, "To imagine none can teach you but those who are themselves saved from sin is a very great and dangerous mistake. Give not place to it for a moment."[7]

Wesley's remarks were not unusual in his time. A century earlier the great Reformed pastor Richard Baxter was faced with lukewarmness in the church and unbelief outside the church. In 1667 he wrote a book to meet this need, and in it he used philosophy, logic and general items of knowledge outside Scripture to argue for the existence of the soul and the life to come. The fact that Baxter turned to philosophy and extrabiblical knowledge instead of small groups or praise hymns is worth pondering. In fact, it is safe to say that throughout much of church history, Scripture and right reason directed at extrabiblical truth were used by disciples of Jesus and prized as twin allies.

In valuing extrabiblical knowledge our brothers and sisters in church history were merely following common sense and Scripture itself. Repeatedly, Scripture acknowledges the wisdom of cultures outside Israel; for example, Egypt (Acts 7:22; cf. Ex 7:11), the Edomites (Jer 49:7), the Phoenicians (Zech 9:2) and many others. The remarkable achievements produced by human wisdom are acknowledged in Job 28:1-11. The wisdom of Solomon is compared to the wisdom of the "people of the east" and Egypt in order to show that Solomon's wisdom surpassed that of people with a long-standing, well-deserved reputation for wisdom (1 Kings 4:29-34). Paul approvingly quotes pagan philosophers (Acts 17:28), and Jude does the same thing with the noncanonical book *The*

---

[7]John Wesley, *A Plain Account of Christian Perfection* (London: Epworth Press, 1952), p. 87.

Assumption of Moses (Jude 9). The book of Proverbs is filled with examples in which knowledge, even moral and spiritual knowledge, can be gained from studying things (ants, for example) in the natural world. Jesus taught that we should know we are to love our enemies, not on the basis of an Old Testament text but from careful reflection on how the sun and rain behave (Mt 5:44-45).

In valuing extrabiblical knowledge our brothers and sisters in church history were also living out scriptural teaching about the value of general revelation. We must never forget that God is the God of creation and general revelation just as he is the God of Scripture and special revelation.

Christians should do everything they can to gain and teach important and relevant knowledge in their areas of expertise. *At the level appropriate to our station in life, Christians are called to be Christian intellectuals, at home in the world of ideas.*

4. Neglect of integration results in a costly division between secular and sacred. While few would actually put it in these terms, faith is now understood as a blind act of will, a sort of decision to believe something that is either independent of reason or makes up for the paltry lack of evidence for what one is trying to believe. By contrast, the Bible presents faith as a power or skill to act in accordance with the nature of the kingdom of God, a trust in what we have reason to believe is true. Understood in this way, we see that faith is built on reason and knowledge. We should have good reasons for thinking that Christianity is true before we completely dedicate ourselves to it. We should have solid evidence that our understanding of a biblical passage is correct before we go on to apply it. We bring knowledge claims from Scripture and theology to the task of integration; we do not employ mere beliefs or faith postulates.

Unfortunately, our contemporary understanding of faith and reason treats them as polar opposites. A few years ago I (J. P.) went to New York to conduct a series of evangelistic messages for a church. The series was in a high school gym and several believers and unbelievers came each night. The first evening I gave arguments for the existence of God from science and philosophy. Before closing in prayer, I entertained several questions from the audience. One woman (who was a Christian) complained about my talk, charging that if I "proved" the existence of God, I would leave no room for faith. I responded by saying that if she were right, then we should pray that currently available evidence for God would evaporate and be refuted so there would be even more room for faith! Obviously, her view of faith utterly detached it from reason.

If faith and reason are deeply connected, then students and teachers need to explore their entire intellectual life in light of the Word of God. But if faith and reason are polar opposites, then the subject matter of our study or teaching is largely irrelevant to growth in discipleship. Because of this view of faith and reason, there has emerged a secular-sacred separation in our understanding of the Christian life with the result that Christian teaching and practice are privatized. The withdrawal of the corporate body of Christ from the public sphere of ideas is mirrored by our understanding of what is required to produce an individual disciple. Religion is viewed as personal, private and a matter of how we feel about things. Often, Bible classes and paracurricular Christian activities are not taken as academically serious aspects of the Christian school, nor are they integrated into the content of "secular" areas of teaching.

There is no time like the present to recapture the integrative task. Given the abandonment of monotheism, the ground is weakened for believing in the unity of truth. This is one reason why our *uni*versities are turning in to *multi*versities.[8] The fragmentation of secular education at all levels and its inability to define its purpose or gather together a coherent curriculum are symptoms of what happens when monotheism, especially Christian monotheism, is set aside. At this critical hour the Christian educator has something increasingly rare and distinctive to offer, and integration is at the heart of who we are as Christian educators.

5. The nature of spiritual warfare necessitates integration. Today, spiritual warfare is widely misunderstood. Briefly, spiritual warfare is a conflict among persons—disembodied malevolent persons (demons and

---

[8]See Julie Reuben, *The Making of the Modern University* (Chicago: University of Chicago Press, 1996).

the devil), human beings, angels and God himself. So far, so good. But what is often overlooked is that this conflict among persons in two camps crucially involves a clash of ideas. Why? The conflict is about control, and persons control others by getting them to accept certain beliefs and emotions as correct, good and proper. This is precisely how the devil primarily works to destroy human beings and thwart God's work in history; namely, by influencing the idea structures in culture. That is why Paul makes the war of ideas central to spiritual conflict:

> For though we live in the world, we do not wage war as the world does. The weapons we fight with are not the weapons of the world. On the contrary, they have divine power to demolish strongholds. We demolish arguments and every pretension that sets itself up against the knowledge of God, and we take captive every thought to make it obedient to Christ. (2 Cor 10:3-5 NIV)

Spiritual warfare is largely, though not entirely, a war of ideas, and we fight bad, false ideas with better ones. That means that truth, reason, argumentation and so forth, from both Scripture and general revelation, are central weapons in the fight. Since the centers of education are the centers for dealing with ideas, they become the main location for spiritual warfare. Solid, intelligent integration, then, is part of our mandate to engage in spiritual conflict.

6. *Spiritual formation calls for integration.* It is crucial that we reflect a bit on the relationship between integration and spiritual/devotional life. To begin with, there is a widespread hunger throughout our culture for genuine, life-transforming spirituality. This is as it should be. People are weary of those who claim to believe certain things when they do not see those beliefs having an impact on the lives of the heralds. Among other things, integration is a spiritual activity—we may even call it a spiritual discipline—but not merely in the sense that often comes to mind in this context. Often, Christian teachers express the spiritual aspect of integration in terms of doxology: Christian integrators hold to and teach the same beliefs about their subject matter that non-Christians accept but go on to add praise to God for the subject matter. Thus, Christian biologists simply assert the views widely ac-

cepted in the discipline but make sure that class closes with a word of praise to God for the beauty and complexity of the living world.

The doxological approach is good as far as it goes; unfortunately, it doesn't go far enough in capturing the spiritual dimension of integration. We draw closer to the core of this dimension when we think about the role of beliefs in the process of spiritual transformation. Beliefs are the rails on which our lives run. We almost always act according to what we really believe. It doesn't matter much what we say we believe or what we want others to think we believe. When the rubber meets the road, we act out our actual beliefs most of the time. That is why behavior is such a good indicator of our beliefs. The centrality of beliefs for spiritual progress is a clear implication of Old Testament teaching on wisdom and New Testament teaching about the role of a renewed mind in transformation. Thus, *integration has as its spiritual aim the intellectual goal of structuring the mind so we can see things as they really are and strengthening the belief structure that ought to inform the individual and corporate life of discipleship to Jesus.*

Integration can also help unbelievers accept certain beliefs crucial to the Christian journey and aid believers in maintaining and developing convictions about those beliefs. This aspect of integration becomes clear when we reflect on the notion of a plausibility structure. Individuals will never be able to change their lives if they cannot even entertain the beliefs needed to bring about that change. By "entertain a belief" we mean to consider the *possibility* that the belief *might* be true. If someone is hateful and mean to a fellow employee, that person will have to change what he or she believes about that coworker before treating the coworker differently. But if a person cannot even entertain the thought that the coworker is a good person worthy of kindness, the hateful person will not change.

A person's plausibility structure is the set of ideas the person either is or is not willing to entertain as possibly true. For example, few people would come to a lecture defending a flat earth, because this idea is just not part of our common plausibility structure. Most people today simply cannot even entertain the idea. Moreover, a person's plausibility structure is largely (though not exclusively) a function of beliefs already held. Applied to accepting or maintaining Christian belief, J. Gresham Machen got it right when he said:

> God usually exerts that power in connection with certain prior condi-
> tions of the human mind, and it should be ours to create, so far as we
> can, with the help of God, those favorable conditions for the reception
> of the gospel. False ideas are the greatest obstacles to the reception of
> the gospel. We may preach with all the fervor of a reformer and yet suc-
> ceed only in winning a straggler here and there, if we permit the whole
> collective thought of the nation or of the world to be controlled by ideas
> which, by the resistless force of logic, prevent Christianity from being
> regarded as anything more than a harmless delusion.[9]

If a culture reaches the point where Christian claims are not even part of its plausibility structure, fewer and fewer people will be able to entertain the possibility that they might be true. Whatever stragglers do come to faith in such a context would do so on the basis of felt needs alone, and the genuineness of such conversions would be questionable, to say the least. And believers will not make much progress in the spiritual life because they will not have the depth of conviction or the integrated noetic structure necessary for such progress. This is why integration is so crucial to spirituality. It can create a plausibility structure in a person's mind, "favorable conditions," as Machen put it, so Christian ideas can be entertained by that person. As Christians, our goal is *to make Christian ideas relevant to our subject matter appear to be true, beautiful, good and reasonable to increase the ranking of Christian ideas in the culture's plausibility structure.*

7. Integration is crucial to the current worldview struggle and the contemporary crisis of knowledge. Luther once said that if we defend Christ at all points except those at which he is currently being attacked, then we have not really defended Christ. The Christian must keep in mind the tensions between Christian claims and competing worldviews currently dominating the culture. Such vigilance yields an integrative mandate for contemporary Christians that the Christian Worldview Integration

---

[9]J. Gresham Machen, address delivered on September 20, 1912, at the opening of the 101st session of Princeton Theological Seminary, reprinted in *What Is Christianity?* (Grand Rapids: Eerdmans, 1951), p. 162.

Series (CWIS) will keep in mind. There is a very important cultural fact that each volume in the series must face: *There simply is no established, widely recognized body of ethical or religious knowledge now operative in the institutions of knowledge in our culture.* Indeed, ethical and religious claims are frequently placed into what Francis Schaeffer called the "upper story," and they are judged to have little or no epistemic authority, especially compared to the authority given to science to define the limits of knowledge and reality in those same institutions. This raises pressing questions: *Is Christianity a knowledge tradition or merely a faith tradition, a perspective which, while true, cannot be known to be true and must be embraced on the basis of some epistemic state weaker than knowledge? Is there nonempirical knowledge in my field? Is there evidence of nonphysical, immaterial reality (e.g., linguistic meanings are arguable, nonphysical, spiritual entities) in my field? Do the ideas of Christianity do any serious intellectual work in my field such that those who fail to take them into consideration simply will not be able to understand adequately the realities involved in my field?*

There are at least two reasons why these may well be the crucial questions for Christians to keep in mind as they do their work in their disciplines. For one thing, Christianity claims to be a knowledge tradition, and it places knowledge at the center of proclamation and discipleship. The Old and New Testaments, including the teachings of Jesus, claim not merely that Christianity is true but that a variety of its moral and religious assertions can be known to be true.

Second, knowledge is the basis of responsible action in society. Dentists, not lawyers, have the authority to place their hands in our mouths because they have the relevant knowledge—not merely true beliefs—on the basis of which they may act responsibly. If Christians do little to deflect the view that theological and ethical assertions are merely parts of a tradition, ways of seeing, a source for adding a "theological perspective" to an otherwise unperturbed secular topic and so forth that fall short of conveying knowledge, then they inadvertently contribute to the marginalization of Christianity precisely because they fail to rebut the contemporary tendency to rob it of the very thing that gives it the authority necessary to prevent that marginalization, namely, its legitimate claim to give us moral and religious knowledge. Both in and out of the church Jesus has been lost as an intellectual authority, and Christian intellectuals should carry out their academic vocation in light of this fact.

We agree with those who see a three-way worldview struggle in academic and popular culture among ethical monotheism (especially Christian theism), postmodernism and scientific naturalism. As Christian intellectuals seek to promote Christianity as a knowledge tradition in their academic disciplines, they should keep in mind the impact of their work on this triumvirate. Space considerations forbid us to say much about postmodernism here. We recognize it is a variegated tunic with many nuances. But to the degree that postmodernism denies the objectivity of reality, truth, value and reason (in its epistemic if not psychological sense), to the degree that it rejects dichotomous thinking about real-unreal, true-false, rational-irrational and right-wrong, to the degree that it believes intentionality creates the objects of consciousness, to that degree it should be resisted by Christian intellectuals, and the CWIS will take this stance toward postmodernism.

Scientific naturalism also comes in many varieties, but very roughly a major form of it is the view that the spatiotemporal cosmos containing physical objects studied by the hard sciences is all there is and that the hard sciences are either the only source of knowledge or else vastly superior in proffering epistemically justified beliefs compared to nonscientific fields. In connection with scientific naturalism some have argued that the rise of modern science has contributed to the loss of intellectual authority in those fields like ethics and religion that supposedly are not subject to the types of testing and experimentation employed in science.

Extreme forms of postmodernism and scientific naturalism agree that there is no nonempirical knowledge, especially no knowledge of immaterial reality, no theological or ethical knowledge. *The authors of the CWIS seek to undermine this claim and the concomitant privatization and noncognitive treatment of religious/ethical faith and belief.* Thus, there will be three integrative tasks of central importance for each volume in the series.

HOW DO WE ENGAGE IN INTEGRATION? THREE INTEGRATIVE TASKS

As noted earlier, the word *integration* means "to form or blend into a whole," "to unite." One of the goals of integration is to maintain or increase both the conceptual relevance of and epistemological justification for Christian theism. To repeat Augustine's advice, "We must show our Scriptures not to be in conflict with whatever [our critics] can demonstrate about the nature of things from reliable sources."[10] We may distinguish three different aspects of the justificatory side of integration: direct defense, polemics and Christian explanation.

1. Direct defense. In direct defense we engage in integration with the primary intent of enhancing or maintaining directly the rational justification of Christian theism or some proposition taken to be explicit within or entailed by it, especially those aspects of a Christian worldview relevant to our own discipline. Specific attention should be given to topics that are intrinsically important to mere Christianity or currently under fire in our field. Hereafter, we will simply refer to these issues as "Christian theism." We do so for brevity's sake. Christian theism should be taken to include specific views about a particular area of study that we believe to be relevant to the integrative task, for example, that cognitive behavioral therapy is an important tool for applying the biblical mandate to be "transformed by the renewing of your mind" (Rom 12:2).

There are two basic forms of direct defense, one negative and one positive.[11] The less controversial of the two is a negative direct defense where we attempt to remove defeaters to Christian theism. If we have a justified belief regarding some proposition P, a defeater is something that weakens or removes that justification. Defeaters come in two types.[12] A rebutting defeater gives justification for believing not-P, in this case, that Christian theism is false. For example, attempts to show that the biblical concept of the family is dysfunctional and false, or that homosexuality is causally necessitated by genes or brain states and that

---

[10]Augustine *De genesi ad litteram* 1.21.
[11]See Ronald Nash, *Faith and Reason* (Grand Rapids: Zondervan, 1988), pp. 14-18.
[12]For a useful discussion of various types of defeaters, see John Pollock, *Contemporary Theories of Knowledge* (Totowa, N.J.: Rowman & Littlefield, 1986), pp. 36-39; Ralph Baergen, *Contemporary Epistemology* (Fort Worth: Harcourt Brace, 1995), pp. 119-24.

therefore it is not a proper object for moral appraisal are cases of rebutting defeaters. An undercutting defeater does not give justification for believing not-P but rather seeks to remove or weaken justification for believing P in the first place. Critiques of the arguments for God's existence are examples of undercutting defeaters. When defeaters are raised against Christian theism, a negative defense seeks either to rebut or undercut those defeaters.

By contrast, a positive direct defense is an attempt to build a positive case for Christian theism. Arguments for the existence of God, objective morality, the existence of the soul, the value and nature of virtue ethics, and the possibility and knowability of miracles are examples. This task for integration is not accepted by all Christian intellectuals. For example, various species of what may be loosely called Reformed epistemology run the gamut from seeing a modest role for a positive direct defense to an outright rejection of this type of activity in certain areas; for example, justifying belief in God and the authority of Holy Scripture. *The CWIS will seek to engage in both negative and positive direct defense.*

2. Polemics. In polemics we seek to criticize views that rival Christian theism in one way or another. Critiques of scientific naturalism, physicalism, pantheism, behaviorist models of educational goals, authorless approaches to texts and Marxist theories of economics are all examples of polemics.

3. Theistic explanation. Suppose we have a set of items that stand in need of explanation and we offer some overall explanation as an adequate or even best explanation of those items. In such a case our overall explanation explains each of the items in question, and this fact itself provides some degree of confirmation for our overall explanation. For example, if a certain intrinsic genre statement explains the various data of a biblical text, then this fact offers some confirmation for the belief that the statement is the correct interpretation of that text. Christian theists ought to be about the business of exploring the world in light of their worldview and, more specifically, of using their theistic beliefs as explanations of various desiderata in their disciplines. Put differently, we should seek to solve intellectual problems and shed light on areas of puzzlement by using the explanatory power of our worldview.

For example, for those who accept the existence of natural moral law, the irreducibly mental nature of consciousness, natural human rights or the fact that human flourishing follows from certain biblically mandated ethical and religious practices, the truth of Christian theism provides a good explanation of these phenomena. And this fact can provide some degree of confirmation for Christian theism. *The CWIS seeks to show the explanatory power of Christian ideas in various disciplines.*

WHAT MODELS ARE AVAILABLE FOR CLASSIFYING INTEGRATIVE PROBLEMS?

When problem areas surface, there is a need for Christians to think hard about the issue in light of the need for strengthening the rational authority of Christian theism and placing it squarely within the plausibility structure of contemporary culture. We will use the term *theology* to stand for any Christian idea that seems to be a part of a Christian worldview derived primarily from special revelation. When we address problems like these, there will emerge a number of different ways that theology can interact with an issue in a discipline outside theology. Here are some of the different ways that such interaction can take place. These represent different strategies for handling a particular difficulty in integration. These strategies will be employed where appropriate on a case-by-case basis by the authors in the series.

1. The two-realms view. Propositions, theories or methodologies in theology and another discipline may involve two distinct, nonoverlapping areas of investigation. For example, debates about angels or the extent of the atonement have little to do with organic chemistry. Similarly, it is of little interest to theology whether a methane molecule has three or four hydrogen atoms in it.

2. The complementarity view. Propositions, theories or methodologies in theology and another discipline may involve two different, complementary, noninteracting approaches to the same reality. Sociological aspects of church growth and certain psychological aspects of conversion may be sociological or psychological descriptions of certain phenomena that are complementary to a theological description of church growth or conversion.

3. The direct-interaction view. Propositions, theories or methodologies in theology and another discipline may directly interact in such a way that either one area of study offers rational support for the other or one area of study raises rational difficulties for the other. For example, certain theological teachings about the existence of the soul raise rational problems for philosophical or scientific claims that deny the existence of the soul. The general theory of evolution raises various difficulties for certain ways of understanding the book of Genesis. Some have argued that the big bang theory tends to support the theological proposition that the universe had a beginning.

4. The presuppositions view. Theology may support the presuppositions of another discipline and vice versa. Some have argued that many of the presuppositions of science (for example, the existence of truth; the rational, orderly nature of reality; the adequacy of our sensory and cognitive faculties as tools suited for knowing the external world) make sense and are easy to justify given Christian theism, but are odd and without ultimate justification in a naturalistic worldview. Similarly, some have argued that philosophical critiques of epistemological skepticism and defenses of the existence of a real, theory-independent world and a correspondence theory of truth offer justification for some of the presuppositions of theology.

5. The practical application view. Theology may fill out and add details to general principles in another discipline and vice versa, and theology may help us practically apply principles in another discipline and vice versa. For example, theology teaches that fathers should not provoke their children to anger, and psychology can add important details about what this means by offering information about family systems, the nature and causes of anger, and so forth. Psychology can devise various tests for assessing whether a person is or is not mature, and theology can offer a normative definition to psychology as to what a mature person is.

In this volume, authors David Lyle Jeffrey and Gregory Maillet explore the relationship between Christianity and the study of literature. Given the nature of our faith—one in which the Word of God plays an authoritative role in our communities and the Word made flesh is our sovereign King—the proper way by which Christians approach the written word is essential to the development of intellectual and spiritual powers. The Great Books of the West—from the pre-Christian Homer to Shakespeare to Solzhenitsyn—simply cannot be understood without seeing their place in forming or being formed by Christianity and the civilization it produced. Recent trends in the study of literature and literary theory suggest ways to interpret texts that challenge the way in which Christians have traditionally read Scripture as well as other literature. For these reasons, this book is a valuable resource for students of literature who want to think intelligently and rigorously about their Christian faith.

We hope you can see why we are excited about this book. Even though you're busy and the many demands on your time tug at you from different directions, we don't think you can afford not to read this book. So wrestle, ponder, pray, compare ideas with Scripture, talk about the pages to follow with others and enjoy.

A FINAL CHALLENGE

In 2001 atheist philosopher Quentin Smith published a remarkably insightful article of crucial relevance to the task of integration. For over fifty years, Smith notes, the academic community has become increasingly secularized and atheistic even though there have been a fair number of Christian teachers involved in that community. How could this be? Smith's answer amounts to the claim that Christians compartmentalized their faith, kept it tucked away in a private compartment of their lives and did not integrate their Christian ideas with their work. Said Smith:

> This is not to say that none of the scholars in their various academic fields were realist theists [theists who took their religious beliefs to be true] in their "private lives"; but realist theists, for the most part excluded their theism from their publications and teaching, in large part because theism . . . was mainly considered to have such a low epistemic status that it did not meet the standards of an "academically respectable" position to hold.[13]

---

[13]Quentin Smith, "The Metaphysics of Naturalism," *Philo* 4, no. 2 (2001): 1.

Smith goes on to claim that while Christians have recaptured considerable ground in the field of philosophy, "theists in other fields tend to compartmentalize their theistic beliefs from their scholarly work; they rarely assume and never argue for theism in their scholarly work."[14]

This has got to stop. We offer this book to you with the prayer that it will help you rise to the occasion and recapture lost territory in your field of study for the cause of Christ.

Francis J. Beckwith
J. P. Moreland
Series Editors

---

[14]Ibid., p. 3. The same observation about advances in philosophy has been noted by Mark A. Noll in *The Scandal of the Evangelical Mind* (Grand Rapids: Eerdmans, 1994), pp. 235-38.

Authors' Preface
and Acknowledgments

The last thing the authors of this book imagine is that it should be taken as an authoritative guide to the study of literature—even of the English literature we are primarily concerned with. Even where of necessity we have focused our attention in more detail, we were nonetheless obliged by the limitations on our task to leave out much more than we would wish. Rather, we have seen our job as that of suggesting ways that a Christian worldview can provide a pertinent and fruitful approach to literary study as an academic discipline. We offer here no universal template, therefore, but merely a rough map and some possible strategies for negotiating the terrain. We hope that our readers will find it both interesting and encouraging that while the authors are linked by intellectual friendship, we are of two generations and two distinct Christian traditions. David Lyle Jeffrey is a senior scholar and lifelong evangelical Protestant Christian with deep, equally abiding Catholic sympathies. Gregory Maillet is a mid-career scholar, a committed Catholic with deep evangelical sympathies. Our joint purpose in this project is to bring our shared love for Christ and the church to bear on our intellectual work in such a way that we are able to offer something of potential value to serious Christian students of literature in both traditions.

Our volume was written primarily for Christian students of literature in both secular and Christian universities and colleges. Can a non-Christian student find anything of value here? We think so. As the great historical critic Basil Willey has put it, "if we admit that literary judgments are often disguised (or undisguised) ethical judgments, or that they presuppose such judgments, then we ought to be enquiring into the nature and history of moral ideas."[1] Literary judgments, as theorists on all sides agree, are *never* value-free. For our part we do our best here to show, period by period, how literary texts and judgments about them are invariably subtended by ethical (or counterethical) presuppositions. To the degree that we have been accountable in this effort, that demonstration, we think, will in itself be of value to any serious student. Yet as our title suggests we wish to indicate something more, namely, that full appreciation of literature in English requires a curriculum that acknowledges the persistent presence of Christ in the literary imagination down through the centuries, even while candidly confirming the evident complexity of response to that presence by individual writers. Moreover, as the initial chapters of this volume will argue, an elucidation of biblical or Christian inspiration in a literary text also requires a critical framework that distinguishes itself from many secular approaches by its effort to ensure (among other things) respect for the biblical lineage of many English literary achievements and attentiveness to the very language of literary expression. It is our view that study of the history of the English language (itself profoundly influenced by its formative encounter with the Bible) is crucial to a discerning study of English texts.[2] In practice, literary study may also necessitate learning unfamiliar languages, tracing some elements back into classical literature and incorporating important encounters with non-Christian culture.

Space does not allow for our method to be exegetical or to express itself frequently in close readings of individual literary works. For the authors we address, key historical contexts are briefly outlined, especially Christian ideas and institutions of their time, but our discussion is above all intended as an invitation to explore the riches of individual literary works, first in their own terms and then also in the light of a Christian worldview. Briefly noting the pattern of these texts' aesthetic

---

[1]Basil Willey, *The English Moralists* (New York: W. W. Norton, 1964), p. 11.
[2]For a keen sense of the pertinence of such study the student may profitably begin with C. S. Lewis, *Studies in Words* (Cambridge: Cambridge University Press, 1960), and Owen Barfield, *History in English Words* (Grand Rapids: Eerdmans, 1967).

forms, metaphysical assumptions and moral imperatives, we also provide, at the end of each chapter, bibliographical suggestions to help guide further reflection. For authors we do not address—and there are many excellent ones—we encourage students to consult other, more compendious surveys and author-specific accounts.[3]

Tolkien once noted, in a wonderful 1948 letter to C. S. Lewis, "the only just literary critic is Christ, who admires more than does any man the gifts He Himself has bestowed."[4] Actually, without saying so, it seems that Tolkien was here paraphrasing correspondence from Gerard Manley Hopkins to his friend, the Anglican priest and poet Robert Watson Dixon, published posthumously in 1935.[5] Acknowledgment of Hopkins's letter is explicit in the American poet John Berryman's poem, "Eleven Addresses to the Lord" (1968), in the tenth of which he writes, "Father Hopkins said the only true literary critic is Christ. Let me lie down exhausted, content with that."[6] The repetition of this crucial insight by a range of Christian writers is instructive. Tolkien's own poetic manifesto, "Mythopoeia," famously calls for the Christian writer to see his or her work as that of a "sub-creator," creatively responding with "refracted light" that is "splintered from a single White."[7] Retrospectively, many of our finest poets, playwrights, essayists and novelists seem to have envisioned their art in much this refractory way, proving perhaps, as Tolkien says, that "we make still by the law in which we're made."[8]

---

[3]Among notable Christian poets of the modern period we would like to have included here are W. H. Auden, Richard Wilbur, John Betjeman, Donald Davie, R. S. Thomas, Jack Clemo and Denise Levertov.

[4]J. R. R. Tolkien, "Letter 113: To C. S. Lewis," *The Letters of J. R. R. Tolkien*, ed. Humphrey Carpenter (Boston: Houghton Mifflin, 1981), p. 128.

[5]"Fame whether won or lost is a thing which lies in the award of a random, reckless, incompetent, and unjust judge, the public, the multitude. The only just judge, the only just literary critic is Christ, who prizes, is proud of, and admires, more than any man, more than the receiver himself can, the gifts of his own making" (Gerard Manley Hopkins, *The Correspondence of Gerard Manley Hopkins and Richard Watson Dixon*, ed. C. C. Abbott [Oxford: Oxford University Press, 1935], p. 8).

[6]John Berryman, *Love and Fame* (New York: Farrar, Straus & Giroux, 1970).

[7]J. R. R. Tolkien, "Mythopoeia," *Tree and Leaf* (London: Grafton, 1992), p. 98; also, Kirstin Johnson, "Tolkien's Mythopoesis," in *Tree of Tales: Tolkien, Literature and Theology*, ed. Trevor Hart and Ivan Khovacs (Waco, Tex.: Baylor University Press, 2007), pp. 25-38.

[8]Tolkien, "Mythopoeia," p. 99.

We do not dispute that to some considerable degree Matthew Arnold saw the future of Christian culture in the West when in "Dover Beach" (1867) he described "the Sea of Faith . . . retreating, to the breath of the night wind." But we affirm yet more strongly the faith of Gerard Manley Hopkins in "God's Grandeur," namely, that there is always a sense, for faithful Christians, in which

> morning, at the brown brink eastward springs—
> Because the Holy Ghost over the bent
> World broods with warm breast and with ah! bright wings.

Holy creativity is never spent, though some may wish it so; as with the Benedictine communities in early medieval Europe, so it may be for Christian colleges and universities in the twenty-first century: these are among the institutions in our era which, perhaps more than any other, have the opportunity to cherish and nurture a great literary heritage through forgetful and unstable times.

We also hope this book offers a view of Christian culture that can help orthodox Christians to remain invested in the artistic realm and through that effort meditate more commensurably upon the mysteries of God. Though that is not our primary task, we think this stewardship is crucial to the health of the universal church. As brothers in Christ from two traditions we wish to encourage Protestant Christian students of literature to be "people of the Book," capable of creating a literary culture grounded in scriptural revelation; equally, we wish to encourage Roman Catholic Christians to foster the "fruitful dialogue" between the gospel and the arts which John Paul II saw as a crucial element of the twenty-first-century "springtime of evangelization."[9] Whatever your spiritual roots, we invite you to consider our menu for a literary feast sure to offer both pleasure and fulfillment, not least because so many of its *chefs-d'oeuvres* are textured and flavored by the Word through whom "all things were made" (Jn 1:3), and in whom "are hid all the treasures of wisdom and knowledge" (Col 2:3).

Readers will note that the translation of the English Bible we have used, unless otherwise specified, is the King James Version (1611). Our

---

[9]John Paul II, "Letter of His Holiness Pope John Paul II to Artists," 1999.

reason for this choice is predetermined by the overwhelming preference of English authors from the later seventeenth century to the present (even modern writers from James Joyce to Wendell Berry still quote the KJV in preference to other versions), and our concurrence with the conviction of many contemporary scholars who write on the Bible from a literary point of view (Jewish scholars included) that this historic translation, about to celebrate its four-hundredth anniversary, still has the greatest pertinence for literature in English.

Our thanks are hereby extended to our forbearing colleagues and even more forbearing families. We acknowledge with gratitude our debts to those innumerable colleagues from whom we have been so glad to learn, especially Phillip Donnelly, who read the first draft of chapter one and offered valuable suggestions, as also did Jim Hoover, our editor. Most especially we are abidingly grateful for the keen eye and discerning judgment of Katherine B. Jeffrey, professional editor and sterling accomplice. For any errors and distortions that may remain, the authors bear sole responsibility. With one of our greatest inspirations, Geoffrey Chaucer, we nonetheless pray that the inevitable lapses and unfinished business will be attributed to our "unkonnynge" and not our "wyl." We would gladly have written better if we could.

PART ONE

CHRISTIAN FOUNDATIONS

"The only just judge, the only just literary critic, is Christ."

GERARD MANLEY HOPKINS

LITERATURE AND TRUTH

*[Fiction is] a single-minded attempt to render the highest kind of justice
to the visible universe, by bringing to light the truth.*

JOSEPH CONRAD

What has Jesus Christ to do with English literature?" For at least
three reasons, this particular adaptation of St. Jerome's famous, ancient question—"What has Horace to do with the Psalter? Or Virgil
with the Gospel? Or Cicero with the Apostle"[1]—is a reasonable way
of formulating the contemporary academic question this book seeks to
answer. The initial, most obvious answer is historical reality: one cannot deny (except by extreme revision of the canon) that the library of
English literature includes an exceptionally large number of influential Christian authors. Just understanding their work often requires
awareness of Christian teachings and the often complex means by
which, in practice, these writers express and explore the meaning of
Christian faith.

Second, as Erich Auerbach showed in his landmark book *Mimesis*, the
influence of a religious worldview upon literature is never reducible simply
to historical information of the sort that can be listed in footnotes; rather,
faith often determines aesthetic form, and literary form in turn "represents" reality, engaging its readers in a fashion preconditioned by the

---

[1]St. Jerome, "Epistle 22," in Philip Schaff, *The Nicene and Post-Nicene Fathers*, 2nd series (Grand
Rapids: Eerdmans, 1954), 6:29.

form of discourse experienced as a distinctive way of seeing the world.[2] Thus, features critical to imaginative placement of a particular struggle, quest or journey toward new awareness are often, as Jesus said concerning his parables, available only to those with "ears to hear" (Mk 4:9).

Third, Christian literature often requires of its readers not only an interpretative response that attempts to understand textual meaning accurately, but also an evaluative response that calls one, in the light of the gospel, to an aesthetic, moral or intellectual transformation—effectively a conversion of one sort or another.[3] Evaluative response may lead the reader in turn to contemplate whether a particular work of art presents beauty, goodness and truth, or is in fact marked by their absence. As with any coherent literary approach, therefore, a Christian literary theory should be guided by clear philosophical principles and methodology appropriate to a faithful interpretation and evaluation of literary texts. For a serious engagement of those texts in their intellectual and cultural dimension, we need a sound appreciation of traditional as well as contemporary reflection in the area of Christian philosophy and theology of literature, or what some now call "theological aesthetics."[4]

This is certainly a larger task than an introductory book such as this can undertake. Yet even an effort to offer a rather modest Christian approach to literature that would seek in some measure to guide interpretation, encourage a balanced critical evaluation and coherently outline some rudiments of Christian literary aesthetics poses a considerable challenge. As T. S. Eliot saw so clearly early in the twentieth century, the vast increase in our scholarly information and resources does not necessarily lead to clear, confident knowledge claims, and still less does it provide any shared sense of catholic, universal wisdom.[5]

---

[2]Erich Auerbach, *Mimesis: The Representation of Reality in Western Literature* (1953; reprint, Garden City, N.Y.: Doubleday, 1957).

[3]For a theologically developed approach to the nature and variety of Christian conversion, see Bernard J. F. Lonergan's *Method in Theology* (1972; reprint, Minneapolis: Seabury, 1979).

[4]See Hans Urs von Balthasar, *The Glory of the Lord: A Theological Aesthetics*, 7 vols. (San Francisco: Ignatius, 1982-1989); see also, Gesa Elsbeth Thiessen, *Theological Aesthetics: A Reader* (Grand Rapids: Eerdmans, 2005); and David Bentley Hart, *The Beauty of the Infinite: The Aesthetics of Christian Truth* (Grand Rapids: Eerdmans, 2003).

[5]T. S. Eliot, *Choruses from "The Rock": The Complete Poems and Plays of T. S. Eliot* (1934; reprint, London: Faber & Faber, 1969), p. 147.

Postmodern intellectuals reflect an awareness that the project of Enlightenment rationalism has now pretty much run off the rails, with destructive consequences. As was most clearly and influentially prophesied by Friedrich Nietzsche—on the strength of his observation that, at least in the intellectual culture, "God is dead"—the vacuum created by a loss of confidence in rational progress has been culturally charged not only with uncertainty but, in its most cynical manifestations, with much explicit nihilism.[6] The space thus emptied of shared meaning has tended to be filled by dynamic manifestations of the will to power by strong individuals or groups, usually without much regard for the ethical principles, religious convictions, personal happiness or suffering of others less powerful.

Yet despite widespread general awareness of this pattern, and the confirming commentary in writings as diverse as Yeats's "The Second Coming" (1921), C. S. Lewis's *The Abolition of Man* (1943) and Tolkien's *The Lord of the Rings* (1954-1955), much twentieth-century literary criticism has carried on its own business without sufficient regard for the implications of a fundamentally changed intellectual terrain. Many critics and teachers of literature have either continued to adopt the philosophical assumptions of Enlightenment rationalism, attempting a supposedly "value free" or "objective" literary criticism, or, once postmodernist critics had revealed the project of modernity to be "value laden," opted instead for Nietzschean views that denied any objective reference whatsoever to historical fact and moral value, let alone to spiritual truth.[7] Given these incoherent and contradictory tendencies, and certain attendant follies in public utterance and behavior of some practitioners, literary criticism has in the last two decades lost prestige as an intellectual discipline.[8] Worse, general cultural confidence in literature itself as a source of meaning and value has likewise diminished;

---

[6]Friedrich Nietzsche, *The Gay Science*, trans. Walter Kaufmann (1882; reprint, New York: Vintage, 1974).

[7]See Camille R. LaBossiere, "Nietzsche," *Encyclopedia of Contemporary Literary Theory*, gen. ed. Irena R. Makaryk (Toronto: University of Toronto Press, 1993).

[8]See, e.g., Andrew Delbanco, "The Decline and Fall of Literature," *New York Review of Books* 46, no. 17 (1999), and the seven books on the subject he there reviews; also *MLA Newsletter* 41, no. 4 (2009).

the tendency to regard literary works generally as merely diversionary entertainment rather than as a source of cultural wisdom has gained momentum in many quarters, even as, in and beyond the arts, much of liberal democracy continues in a correlative political effort to eliminate the idea of a higher or divine wisdom from the public square.

Despite the high technical quality and popularity of much contemporary writing, beneath a good deal of it despair concerning enduring and shareable meaning has grown so extreme as to merit the dark judgment of Flannery O'Connor that, wherever one lives in the West, "nihilism" has become "the gas you breathe."[9] One of the consequences of breathing this gas, obviously, is a general loss of concern for truth.[10] Yet, for any Christian literary criticism, having a nose for truth and a capacity to sniff out its opposite is the least dispensable of the qualities upon which both intellectual rigor and spiritual health depends.

MATTERS OF FACT—AND FICTION

So then, to pursue our inquiry a step further: What has *truth* to do with literature—which, after all, is "fiction"? It should be apparent that this is analogous to asking the heuristic question we began with. But let us consider this second and potentially more naive question, at least at first as if it does not depend (though for a Christian, in fact it does) on the givenness of divine creation and the preeminence of Christ. Literature, whether poetry, stories or plays, has by customary definition an imagined, that is, fictive character. It is not therefore "true" in the conventional sense that it necessarily records some historical fact. As Aristotle observed,

> The work of Herodotus might be put into verse, and it would still be a species of history, with meter no less than without it. The true difference [between history and poetry] is that one relates what has happened, the other what may happen. Poetry, therefore, is a more philosophical

---

[9]Flannery O'Connor, "Letter to Elizabeth Hester," *The Habit of Being: Letters of Flannery O'Connor*, ed. Sally Fitzgerald (New York: Farrar, Straus & Giroux, 1979), p. 97.

[10]Jean Daniélou, in his very helpful book *The Scandal of Truth* (Baltimore: Helican, 1962), observes that when "nothing is less loved than truth" it is a sign that intelligence is in crisis (p. 2). See especially pp. 49-60, "Poetry and Truth."

and a higher thing than history: for poetry tends to express the universal, history the particular.[11]

In much the same vein we suggest that any work of art that offers itself as worthy of intellectually serious consideration has usually earned a place in the curriculum because it has been regarded as giving us exemplary truth, whether as in a true insight, a truer understanding or a valid interpretation of the world. Intellectually worthy poetry or fiction, most of us think, will provide us a means of grasping basic truth by abstracting a plausible insight from divergent probable particulars. There are, of course, related aesthetic matters to consider: fiction typically fabricates, but necessarily in such a way (to borrow from Horace) that it delights; a successful work of literary art is captivating, winsomely drawing our imagination. Yet, again recalling Horace, it delights in order to teach.[12] When that which is to be taught is itself good and true, then fiction has generally been recognized as an ethically accountable means of providing insight into a general truth and human wisdom.

Another way to think about this relation is via the distinction between true and false analogy; creative literature usually implies some analogous phenomenon or experience in which we recognize a persuasive, credible correspondence. Fantasy writers such as George MacDonald, C. S. Lewis or Ursula Le Guin can with propriety be said to write truth in this sense of the term, as may Lewis Carroll in *Through the Looking Glass* or William Steig in his wonderfully illustrated children's book *Rotten Island*, even though what they picture is not in the world of our physical experience thoroughly "factual." Mythopoesis, in the hands of Homer or Virgil, is intended to give us an order of truth about lived human experience as we may know it less colorfully, but in the light of their high coloration we may come to understand it better than we ever had before. Very young readers grasp this intuitively. Thus, in the children's story of Little Red Riding Hood an intelligent child is not long deterred by the fanciful prospect of a talking wolf from

---

[11]Aristotle *Poetics* 9.2-4, ed. Francis Ferguson (New York: Hill & Wang, 1961), p. 68.

[12]"Poets aim at giving either profit or delight, or at combining the giving of pleasure with some useful precepts for life" (Horace *Ars poetica* [numerous online translations of this poem are available, some in prose]).

the everyday practicality of the story's embodied warning. As with Jesus' parable about hireling shepherds and his remarks about wolves in sheep's clothing (Jn 10:1-17; Mt 7:15), we readily see lived reality beneath an engaging cortex of imaginative analogy and say of the extended metaphor or fiction, "Aha! That rings true."

While we cannot long detain ourselves with the pertinence of analogy, it is important that students of literature recognize how basic it is to the way we use language itself as a primary tool in our coming to understand the world. This is a much richer phenomenon than we may at first grasp, but literary students employ it, even if unconsciously, all the time. When a child is taught to identify in a book of children's poems a four-legged creature she has never seen before as a "lamb," she acquires not only a univocal term for the wooly little animal that tags along after Mary on her way to school, but she locates the lamb's relationship to Mary in an analogy to similar relationships between persons and pets or other animals. It need hardly be added that the lamb's affection for Mary in this little poem humanizes the lamb, as Mary's "friend." But the principle illustrated here extends very far indeed where our learning through language is concerned. As the philosopher Willard Quine has suggested, it may be that all language acquisition depends on recognizing analogous contexts for a word.[13] It would certainly seem to be the case that, at any level of sophistication, poetry in particular depends upon it.[14]

Our apparently hard-wired human instinct for analogizing makes possible later, polysemous (many-layered) uses of an analogy, which depend upon a profound reconception of the first experience we have of a correspondence between the word we speak and that which it refers to: for example, "Behold the lamb of God, who takes away the sins of the world" (Jn 1:29 NASB). We should recognize that the second statement is not less poetic than the first, but actually more so. This is what the great Renaissance poet Petrarch was getting at when he asked the rhe-

---

[13]Willard Van Orman Quine, " A Postscript on Metaphor," *On Metaphor,* ed. Sheldon Sacks (Chicago: University of Chicago Press, 1979), p. 160.

[14]See Paul Ricoeur, *The Rule of Metaphor: Multi-disciplinary Studies of the Creation of Meaning in Language,* trans. Robert Czerny et al. (Toronto: University of Toronto Press, 1977).

torical question, "What is theology, if not poetry about God?" He need not have known the opinion of theologian Thomas Aquinas, that "poetic knowledge is of things which on account of a defect of truth cannot be grasped by reason and that is why reason must be seduced by certain likenesses"; it would have been sufficient for a poet to consider the preferred teaching method of Jesus. Marilynne Robinson, in her essay on Dietrich Bonhoeffer, writes in a similar vein that "great theology is always a kind of giant and intricate poetry, like epic or saga."[15]

Here is an example of what they all mean. When the most poetic of biblical prophets, Isaiah, writes, "All we like sheep have gone astray; we have turned every one to his own way; and the LORD hath laid on him the iniquity of us all," he has invoked an analogy that confronts our humanity, "prone to wander," as the old hymn says. When Isaiah immediately adds, "He was oppressed, and he was afflicted, yet he opened not his mouth: he is brought as a lamb to the slaughter, and as a sheep before her shearers is dumb, so he openeth not his mouth" (Is 53:6-7), he invokes a further analogy that raises our conception of humanity to a transcending level of our sense of the possible content in "human."

When John the Baptist, imbued with the prophetic poetry of Isaiah (Lk 3) sees Jesus coming toward him and says, "Behold the Lamb of God, which taketh away the sin of the world" (Jn 1:29), the ultimate predicate for the now familiar analogy is revealed: the ultimate Lamb, to paraphrase William Blake, is he who made all lambs; it is the Son of Man, the Suffering Servant born of Mary who is our God himself, Creator and Redeemer. In this way we may say, as did Augustine, that the truth of the language of Scripture corresponds to the truths of creation and redemption, or, as Aquinas argued, to the nature of Being itself in such a way as to make possible our recognition that the correspondence operates at many levels. When we say of "Mary Had a Little Lamb," *Little Red Riding Hood* or Jesus' parable about the wolves in sheep's clothing and hireling shepherds, "Aha, that rings true!" we do so by way of integrating analogies. Moreover, while existentially we may consider the idea of God to be derived

---

[15]Marilynne Robinson, *The Death of Adam: Essays on Modern Thought* (Boston: Houghton Mifflin, 1998), p. 117.

analogically from finite beings, as Aquinas has shown, we will also learn from Scripture, as Augustine and Aquinas both remind us, that our knowledge of finite beings, by reason in the light of Scripture, is itself finally predicated on the divine archetype "in whom," as St. Paul says, "we live, and move, and have our being." "As certain also of your own poets have said" he adds, for the benefit of his Athenian audience (Acts 17:28). It is this truth of analogy (or analogical predication) that makes the language of poetry *necessary* to a properly Christian understanding of the world. The best place to learn how this works, as we shall attempt to show in chapter three, is from the Bible itself. The second best place to learn it is from the work of theologically literate, biblically informed Christian poets.

Many cultural "texts" in our own day, be they novels, television commercials, political speeches or legal documents, may, for various reasons, "ring false." Even when fiction masquerades as reality, as in some prime-time television programs, or when advocacies of various kinds dress up as ostensibly "nonfiction" books or documentaries, we are wise to be discerning about where truth lies. Such offerings contribute to the widespread diminishment of concepts such as reality and truth—even to skepticism that truth exists at all or is worth pursuing. For a reader of the Bible it may be useful to recall that the situation is not peculiar to our time, but that the biblical response to it differs markedly from the rather more laissez-faire attitude common to our contemporaries. Consider the comment of St. Paul in his letter to Titus regarding the inhabitants of Crete: "One of themselves, even a prophet of their own, said, the Cretians are always liars." Paul then wryly adds, "This witness is true" (Tit 1:12-13). He does not, however, at that point just shrug his shoulders and say, "Well, that's Cretan culture for you," or "Well, that's just life in the Mediterranean." Rather he tells Titus to rebuke this habitual disregard for truth along with other forms of self-indulgent behavior to which the Cretan converts are apparently prone, such as gluttony and sloth. The apostle's sense of congruence among these three vices is itself worth pondering; a sloppy regard for truth may be a form of intellectual self-serving or outright laziness. But most of us, if we are mentally healthy, want to be at least a little like Diogenes with his lantern, on the lookout for truth, even when reluctant to admit it in some social settings. And if we are students of poetry or the Bible (either will do for this point) we will be aware that sometimes the truth we are looking for is to be found disguised as a fable, parable or "harmless tale." We recognize a serious purpose in the fanciful tale; the warning to little girls (and maybe not only little ones) embodied in *Little Red Riding Hood* is a nontrivial warning.

Thus, to quest for truth by the means of fiction, as almost all serious literary readers come to appreciate, is to be engaged in the pursuit of discernment and wisdom. Often such a tale embodies a corrective political, social or ethical realism which, to be successfully achieved, may most naturally engage the services of a gifted fabulator such as Jonathan Swift (in *Gulliver's Travels*), George Orwell *(1984; Animal Farm)*, Aldous Huxley *(Brave New World)*, C. S. Lewis *(That Hideous Strength)* or Mikhail Bulgakov *(The Master and Margarita)*. Moreover, we may find that on occasion a journalist, news anchor or professional political commentator may be much less successful at conveying a sense of truthfulness than a good satirist.

Concern for the truth transcends any facile sense of the boundary between fiction and nonfiction. It can hardly be stressed too strongly that in *every* genre discernment is required of the reader. Not least this is because we are obliged to recognize that truth does not reside in words themselves. Additionally, it is important to see that the truth of the reference of words to reality does not reside, as Descartes seems to have thought, in a "thinking self" who is somehow apart from the world.[16] Rather, and at several levels, a Christian thinker must openly confess that he or she is very much *in the world*, even when aspiring to be not *of the world*. Neither is there enough evidential warrant to sustain the argument of Ferdinand de Saussure against St. Augustine that language is an artificially enclosed system, referring only to itself as a system and not functionally to an external world.[17] Language, as Augus-

---

[16]John A. Macmurray, *The Self as Agent* (1957; reprint, London: Faber & Faber, 1967), pp. 74-79; also Paul Ricoeur, *Oneself as Another* (Chicago: University of Chicago Press, 1992), pp. 4-16.

[17]Ferdinand de Saussure, *Cours de linguistique générale* (Paris: Gallimard, 1916); cf. Augustine *On Christian Doctrine* 1.2-9; see also from a different point of view Jacques Derrida in *Speech and Phenomenon*, trans. David Allison (Evanston, Ill.: Northwestern University Press, 1973), p. 140.

tine representatively argued in his *On Christian Doctrine*, is, as sign, a system of intersubjective agreements that functions accountably in reference to an external world, and the fact that meaning resides not only in that external world, as itself a system of signs referring to transcendent Being, does not alter but amplifies the mind-independent character of external reality.

For literary criticism to acknowledge the perspective of an individual knower is not accordingly to yield to a protean subjectivism or to give in to moral relativism; rather, such a way of speaking necessarily assumes the objective reality of a *shared* world in which various locations can be inhabited and, as a consequence of individual choices, in which various points of view arise. All perspectives, all theories, are thus debatable, all open to confirmation or disconfirmation in terms of the common external realities. This certainly includes the truth many of us find most clearly expressed in biblical or, as we may say, orthodox Christianity; Christian truths may, like all truths, be tested: we are invited, for example, to "taste and see that the LORD is good" (Ps 34:8).

Telling the truth in any ordinary context is a matter of representing reality as it is, whether descriptively, logically or by that form of analogical speech we may in the broader sense call "poetry." This principle can be abused, of course, even passively. Sadly, it is all too common for nominally intelligent people to receive propagandistic journalism or "historical" accounts as factual truth, when in many cases such accounts should more probably be recognized by historically informed and critically acute readers as a morally culpable sort of *deceptive* fiction. This point is made memorably by Czech writer Milan Kundera on the deliberately historical first page of his pertinently titled novel *The Book of Laughter and Forgetting* (1979):

> In February, 1948, Communist leader Klement Gottwald stepped out on the balcony of a Baroque palace in Prague to address the hundreds of thousands of his fellow citizens packed into Old Town Square. It was a crucial moment in Czech history—a fateful moment of the kind that occurs once or twice in a millennium.
>
> Gottwald was flanked by his comrades, with Clementis standing next to him. There were snow flurries, it was cold, and Gottwald was

bareheaded. The solicitous Clementis took off his own fur cap and set it on Gottwald's head.

The Party propaganda section put out hundreds of thousands of copies of a photograph of that balcony with Gottwald, a fur cap on his head and comrades at his side, speaking to the nation. On that balcony the history of Communist Czechoslovakia was born. Every child knew the photograph from posters, schoolbooks, and museums.

Four years later Clementis was charged with treason and hanged. The propaganda section immediately airbrushed him out of history and, obviously, out of all the photographs as well. Ever since, Gottwald has stood on that balcony alone. Where Clementis once stood, there is only bare palace wall. All that remains of Clementis is the cap on Gottwald's head.[18]

Kundera here is connecting his novel, a fiction, to national history in a way that clarifies a crucial point about truth and falsehood in either species; he here exposes the literal erasure of a signal moment in recent European history by a propaganda machine, so as to show how a "fact" presented by public "history" may be itself a lie. He also hints at the symbolic character of the redefinition of potentially redemptive social virtues such as charity and mercy under the duress of coercive power. The eponymous gesture of Clementis (Lat. "of mercy"; "clemency"), giving away the hat off his own head, is brutally removed from the record by his adversarial political boss and executioner: the "man of clemency" receives no mercy and is written out of the story—until Kundera, thirty years later, "remembers" and bears him witness.

TRUTH AND CONSEQUENCES

Truth is a matter of importance not only for disciplines such as science, forensics and theology, but also for the interpretation of literary texts. As we have already seen, this sort of truth includes, invariably, truth about others and ourselves. At a deeper level truth is one of the three transcendentals with which aesthetics in the Christian intellectual tradition has always been concerned, and in crucial respects it proves to be foundational to a coherent approach to the others (being, love, the

---

[18]Milan Kundera, *The Book of Laughter and Forgetting*, trans. Michael Henry Heim (New York: Penguin, 1981).

good, the beautiful). The way we understand all of the transcendentals recognized by both classical and medieval philosophy incurs profound implications for the way we think about worldview questions, whether we consider them in the context of metaphysics (the nature of reality), epistemology (how we can be said to know) or ethics (what we take to be good). For our purposes in this book we must be content to refer the reader to theologians such as Aquinas, Calvin and Karl Barth regarding questions of being.[19] For the more evidently pervasive literary explorations of the nature and operation of love we can refer the reader for primary discussion to Augustine and also to writers as diverse as Dante and C. S. Lewis (especially in his *The Four Loves*). However, the remaining triad (the true, the good and the beautiful), in our own context of literary criticism, is of immediate concern. In particular, as these opening remarks should make clear, we believe a sound conception of truth is indispensable for a specifically Christian literary criticism. Accordingly, it may be helpful to identify succinctly three received academic theories of truth, two of which have had a profound impact on literary theory and criticism more generally.

THREE THEORIES OF TRUTH

Correspondence theory. Historically, the predominant way of looking at truth is the one that occurs first to common sense. According to the *correspondence theory* of truth, a verbal claim is true only if it corresponds to pertinent fact or external reality.[20] If there is no correspondence (e.g., if I claim that the sky is falling and some of my students run outside to check and confirm, sensibly, that it is not), the claim is evidently false at the literal level. On this view, if a speaker or writer claims that the earth is flat or that it will come to a catastrophic end in Y2K (A.D. 2000) or that drinking a certain beverage will make us irresistible to the opposite sex, there are ways to investigate the veracity of each claim.

---

[19]Aquinas *On Being and Essence*; John Calvin, *Institutes of the Christian Religion* 1.13; Karl Barth, *Church Dogmatics* 4.1; see Colin Gunton, *Becoming and Being: The Doctrine of God in the Theology of Charles Hartshorn and Karl Barth* (London: SCM Press, 2001).

[20]George Englebretsen, *Bare Facts and Naked Truths: A New Correspondence Theory of Truth* (Aldershot, U.K., and Burlington, Vt.: Ashgate, 2006) is a reliable guide and comprehensive standard worthy of a serious student's acquaintance.

Even when we account for variance in the way people see things, this theory tends to apply to most situations quite serviceably. In each case of this sort, actuality (or as we might say, reality) takes precedence and is indispensable to the claims made regarding it, as well as to the plausibility of inferences that may be drawn or actions recommended in consequence. In a famous example from the New Testament, St. Paul insists that if Christ did not literally rise from the dead, then all discussions of the event and our faith in it are meaningless and a waste of time (1 Cor 15:12-20). The poetic commentary of John Updike in his "Seven Stanzas at Easter" (1960) is thus both historically and logically on the mark when he says:

> if he rose at all
> it was as His body;
> if the cells' dissolution did not reverse, the molecules
> reknit, the amino acids rekindle.
> the Church will fall.[21]

Updike is in this poem uncompromisingly biblical in his insistence on a correspondence theory of truth; no soft metaphorizing of the resurrection, given the explicit factual claims of Scripture and the church, can be other than a lie—especially if created, as Updike says, "for our own convenience, our own sense of beauty." Updike was in this poem reacting to common liberal theological platitudes and, in the fashion recommended by Paul to Titus, giving such revisionary constructions a stiff rebuke. To turn the *essential* truth given in historical event into an evasive and naturalistic trope is here to pervert the proper business even of poetry, especially for the poet who wants to think like a Christian.

Not incidentally, for a poet thinking as a Christian, beauty properly understood is not, any more than truth, simply subjective—construed as merely an impression in the eye of the beholder. Beauty in the ultimate Christian sense does not depend any more than does truth upon our taste for it: remarking on the habit of scholastic philosophers such as Thomas Aquinas to use words such as *splendor* and *claritas* to de-

---

[21]John Updike, "Seven Stanzas at Easter," *Telephone Poles and Other Poems* (New York: Alfred A. Knopf, 1964), pp. 72-73.

scribe beauty, Jacques Maritain observes that "it is a Cartesian error to reduce *absolute* beauty to beauty *for us*. Such an error," he continues, "produces academicism in art and condemns us to such a poor kind of beauty as can give only the meanest of pleasures to the soul."[22] To this we may add that a just appreciation of beauty is certainly not to be had by means of eliding beauty and truth, any more than by failing to refer the beauty of creational variety to its Source (cf. Eccles 3:11). This is a point clarified in a Christian way by Gerard Manley Hopkins in his well-known poem "Pied Beauty" (1877):

Glory be to God for dappled things—
For skies of couple-colour as a brinded cow;
    For rose-moles all in stipple upon trout that swim;
Fresh-firecoal chestnut-falls; finches' wings;
Landscape plotted and pieced—fold, fallow, and plough;
    And áll trádes, their gear and tackle and trim.

All things counter, original, spare, strange;
Whatever is fickle, freckled (who knows how?)
    With swift, slow; sweet, sour; adazzle, dim;
He fathers-forth whose beauty is past change:
Praise him.[23]

"Is there no truth in Beauty?" asks George Herbert elsewhere:[24] the Christian answer will be yes, but also that to preserve it without idolatry one must be careful not to conflate them with each other in such a way as to confound the particularity of either truth or beauty.[25] What Hopkins shows us is that beauty is not restricted to the idealized human form on a classical Grecian urn. To apply his point in a contemporary way: the airbrushed, erotic female nudes of the pornographer are not from a Christian perspective more beautiful than the freckled face of an ordinary little "Mary"; indeed, they are less so. Pornography is the

<hr>

[22]Jacques Maritain, *Art and Scholasticism* (London: Sheed & Ward, 1930), p. 23.
[23]Gerard Manley Hopkins, *The Poems of Gerard Manley Hopkins*, ed. W. H. Gardner and N. H. Mackenzie (London: Oxford University Press, 1967), p. 69.
[24]George Herbert, "Jordan I," *The Temple* (1633), in *George Herbert and Henry Vaughn: The Oxford Authors*, ed. Louis L. Martz (Oxford: Oxford University Press, 1992).
[25]Cf. John Keats, "Beauty Is Truth, Truth Beauty," in his "Ode on a Grecian Urn." See the discussion in chap. 7.

sort of lie that denies creational good by making self-referential and sterile what was intended to be an independent and fruitful otherness. All such perversions of the good of creation are a form of lie because they fail to preserve the referential character of their derivation from the One who is their source.

In its strongest form the correspondence theory of truth holds that a valid correspondence is likewise objective and mind independent. Metaphysical realism as expressed in traditional Christian theology asserts that neither Christ's resurrection (which to be true depends on a fact that, as the Gospels show, may in a variety of ways be tested) nor the earth's revolving on its axis around the sun (the truth of which has consistently been confirmed by independent observation and rational inference from that evidence) requires our own perception or consent to count as truth. The claims of Scripture, like most claims of science, are each in their own way open to a correspondence verification. Each depends, it is important to note, on analogy (scientists sometimes call this "modeling") for progress in understanding. There is, of course, also a crucial difference. As Jean Daniélou has put it, "A mind that habitually associates certitude with scientific procedures is disconcerted by the techniques proper to metaphysics and to faith, and is tempted to deny them the rigor that alone elicits the unreserved adherence of the intellect."[26] As he goes on to say, to such a mind, or one convinced of the superiority of science to religious insight or philosophical reflection, science will seem to provide a superior truth. Yet among scientists there is now far more skepticism about the truth claims of science than this common prejudice allows, and within certain scientific disciplines, such as theoretical mathematics and physics, an appreciation that we are necessarily working with contingencies beyond our ken and thus dependent on a language of metaphor and symbol more akin to poetry, and indeed on a metaphysic more akin to theology, is now fairly widespread.

Whether we choose to verify or, as often is in practice necessary, to accept that rational testimony of those who have in the past done so, is

---

[26]Daniélou, *Scandal of Truth*, p. 2.

our call. Faith, for a Christian, is to some degree like faith that the scientist puts in the laws of nature and the work of other good scientists; as the scientist cannot possibly repeat all the experiments for him- or herself and must rely for progress on the authority of others, and above all on nature itself, so too the Christian must accept as reliable the knowledge tradition of the church and ultimately of Scripture itself. This does not mean that either the scientist or the Christian intellectual in any discipline fails to test by such experimental means as appear to be pertinent to the general hypothesis. That is, faith in either species most certainly does not entail a blind disregard for evident matters of truth; rather, it is a matter of conviction placed in a body of knowledge derived from credible testimony and tested by personal experience, both our own and that of others, against and across time.

For Christians, in whatever walk of life, this experimentation includes data from that community we call the church. It answers thus to a correspondence theory of truth in which, as Daniélou puts it succinctly, we come to recognize that "the thing that is sovereignly real is God."[27] Sadly, Christians in the West are sometimes uneasy about this type of transparent expression of the actual basis of their worldview, hemmed in perhaps by a desire not to seem intolerant, or bound by a culture-conforming deference to political correctness of one kind or another. They should, in our view, get over it. One way to begin is by considering the double standard typically inherent in the attempted suppression of Christian views by those who claim to represent a more liberal perspective. Although religious certitude is indiscriminately attacked by postmodernists as inherently intolerant, where religious conviction is expressed candidly and with personal humility this charge is unwarranted, even self-contradictory. Terry Eagleton, a literary theorist with a strongly Marxist perspective, grasps the nettle more firmly than many Christians: "In a pluralistic age, conviction is thought to be at odds with tolerance; whereas the truth is that conviction is part of what one is supposed to tolerate, so that one would not exist without the other."[28] Making such points will hardly grant one immunity from

---

[27]Ibid., p. 7.
[28]Terry Eagleton, *Reason, Faith and Revolution: Reflections on the God Debate* (New Haven,

prejudice, but it constitutes a form of truth-telling about the world which is obligatory for faithful Christians.

Coherence theory. It is important to recognize that the correspondence theory is not the only theory of truth the Christian critic must deal with. According to a second philosophical view, the *coherence theory*, there is a kind of truth that pertains less to physical realities or events than to a set of propositions within which a claim may be regarded as true if found to be logically consistent—or coherent—with the rest of the data set. Mathematicians are familiar with this kind of verification principle, as were medieval metaphysicians. On such a theory, which works especially well in the realm of pure number, there may be no need for a specific correspondence to observable physical reality. (String theory, a branch of post-quantum theoretical physics, offers several incommensurable but internally self-consistent models of the universe—and parallel universes—as coherence theories of truth.)

As an expression or function of coherence within a set, coherence truth involves a criterion of appropriate relationship of reasonableness given certain presuppositions. Non-Euclidean geometry, particularly of the type developed by the great mathematician Henri Poincaré, can appear to create a self-consistent non-Euclidean universe. Poincaré's extended thought experiment offers an example of this kind of coherence truth; while non-Euclidean geometry doesn't work consistently in the "real world" (neither, on a large scale, does the geometry of Euclid), it works satisfactorily in its own theoretical context, more or less as a system of descriptive logic. In the relevant and analogous philosophical terms, a statement in such a context may be considered as true if it is logically consistent with other hypotheses we hold on good logical grounds to be true; a belief that is inconsistent with these same premises and yet postulated within the set is likely to be false. Both classical and medieval philosophers (one might consider the *De musica* of Boethius as a *locus*) thought that the arts of the quadrivium offered pertinent insight. If we may vernacularize: in music a high C doesn't

---

Conn.: Yale University Press, 2009), p. 136. A helpful excursus into such matters by a Christian philosopher and spiritual writer is Dallas Willard's *Knowing Christ Today: Why We Can Trust Spiritual Knowledge* (San Francisco: Harper, 2009).

evidently correspond to any object in the real world; it is, however, a fixed point in a chromatic scale which has twelve intervals. (There are other discrete systems, such as the rather more complicated one found in Chinese classical music.) But with respect to our traditional Western scale, if we are at a concert in which the soprano fails to hit that high C, we will wince with discomfort. We call this a false note. Similar self-contained systems are the stuff of both modern and ancient game theory: in chess, for example, where the rules are rigid and the possibilities complex, there is no necessary correspondence between the roles and geometrical privileges of a knight, bishop, king or queen and their real-life medieval counterparts. The parallel universe of the chessboard seems like an analogy, but it is actually both less and more than analogical.

Something rather like coherence criteria for truth might perhaps be thought to apply to texts in which a writer creates, in effect, an imaginative, self-consistent universe different from but parallel to our own. This is what some critics believe J. R. R. Tolkien attempted in *The Lord of the Rings*. In the hands of such a master of mythopoesis and, not incidentally, of theoretical linguistics, a certain coherence is established within an imagined universe in remarkably precise philological as well as figural detail. Readers tend to have a high degree of agreement about the coherence of meaning in such a rigorously executed alternative universe. In Tolkien's fictive Middle Earth, invented languages make sense; we may even come to accept certain characters such as Tom Bombadil and Goldberry as unfallen, innocent in a way unlike any postlapsarian innocence we know, and yet as true by reason of their compelling coherence within the artwork as Tolkien has created it. In the hands of a lesser writer than Tolkien (many are the examples), we are likely to notice disjuncture, points at which something seems out of place; we may find ourselves at such a moment becoming doubtful about the work as a whole, and we are at the least likely to complain that such and such an element "does not ring true." Coherence truth is thus something we may *think* we recognize analogically as a factor in the appreciation of fantasy and space fiction. In practice, however, even here the sense of truth created resembles in the end more closely the realm of correspondence theory pretty much as it works in parable, as we shall see.

But here we must, as readers and critics, acknowledge an issue more basic than that of genre or even of analogy: if we are honest with ourselves, is truth always what we are looking for? Clearly not. This acknowledgment brings us to the heart of the issue as it presents itself to literary studies in a politically charged, often polarized environment. In such circumstances it may well be that, as the Roman playwright Terence long ago observed, *veritas odium parit*—truth engenders hatred.[29] This is obvious enough almost to need no commentary: there are occasions in almost everyone's life when an exposure to the light of some unacknowledged truth about the self will produce a moment of self-rebuke and quite possibly also resentment of those who have exposed the truth we would rather have remained hidden. Though a healthy person will repent of this reflex and try to deal with the truth constructively, we all know that an unhealthy person may strike out at the messenger or retreat more deeply into strategies of deception, even to a pathological degree. Whole societies may do this, if such self-deception becomes acceptably normative; that is St. Paul's point about the Cretans, and it is also the point of a very useful book for students of literature and criticism, written by the psychologist Scott Peck, called *People of the Lie*.[30] That such evasion of truth at the personal level will conduce to evasion at the level of textual interpretation will be evident to anyone who has considered the problem either in a religious or an academic context. Christians today are not exempt any more than were the new converts of Crete whom Titus was obliged to correct.[31] Indeed, sophis-

---

[29]For an extended discussion of this point, including especially the analysis of St. Augustine in his *Confessions*, see David Lyle Jeffrey, *Houses of the Interpreter: Reading Scripture, Reading Culture* (Waco, Tex.: Baylor University Press, 2003), pp. 227-40.

[30]M. Scott Peck, *People of the Lie: The Hope for Healing Human Evil* (New York: Touchstone, 1993); for an in-depth philosophical and theological treatment see Paul J. Griffiths, *Lying: An Augustinian Theology of Duplicity* (Grand Rapids: Brazos, 2004). Additional useful perspectives may be had in Bernard Williams, *Truth and Truthfulness: An Essay in Genealogy* (Princeton, N.J.: Princeton University Press, 2002); Frederick Buechner, *Telling the Truth: The Gospel as Tragedy, Comedy and Fairy Tale* (San Francisco: HarperCollins, 1977); and Alan Jacobs, *Shaming the Devil: Essays in Truth Telling* (Grand Rapids: Eerdmans, 2004).

[31]See, e.g., David F. Wells, *No Place for Truth, or, Whatever Happened to Evangelical Theology* (Grand Rapids: Eerdmans, 1993).

tical defenses of theological confusions, many of which argue from a neo-Baconian assurance that something is true if enough people think so, abound among people who describe themselves as Christians. This is the ethos that Updike, in his "Seven Stanzas at Easter," is challenging. Spokespersons for temporizing views often get such disproportionate airtime that some people in the pew may become confused about how to understand the truths of Scripture. Others may conclude that, as St. Peter suggested (citing the case of Balaam, the postmodern prophet of Num 22), even a dumb ass may more likely speak the truth than the religionists (2 Pet 2:15-21).

At an apparently less insidious level, of course, people in any walk of life may simply become tired of truth—or at least tired of trying to think about truth as mind independent, historically contingent and open to verification. A disposition to skepticism, which, it must be said, may be the outward form either of rigorous intellectual honesty or of intellectual laziness, is likely to develop; in the lazy case more often than not skeptics will be tempted to cite boredom or distaste (cf. Lord Henry in Oscar Wilde's *The Picture of Dorian Gray*) as an excuse for "moving on." This is not an exclusively postmodern, but rather, as literary history shows, a universal human temptation: Samuel Johnson, the brilliant eighteenth-century writer and critic, once quipped to an interlocutor, "Truth, sir, is a cow which, when skeptics have found that it will give them no more milk, they have gone to milk the bull." Some of the "bull," as Johnson well knew, could nevertheless be well disguised.[32]

Pragmatic theory. This is certainly a potential criticism of some modern and postmodern philosophers who have done much of the theorizing behind the third major theory of truth we now need to consider, the *pragmatic theory*. In respect to motive, this position does not at first seem so bad: the pragmatists have much in common with the latitudinarian theologians and philosophers of the Enlightenment in Britain; commendably, they seek to blunt the sharp edge of absolutizing truth claims, especially in religion, so as to minimize unwelcome social conflict. With this motive, at least, we must be sympathetic. Associated in

---

[32]Jeffrey, *Houses of the Interpreter*, pp. 233-34.

its more modest form with the American philosopher William James, whose notion is that "true ideas are the ones we can assimilate," the pragmatic theory can initially seem to some degree akin with "common-sense" ideas about the nature of truth.[33] There is in fact a decisive difference. In the pragmatic theory, something may be held to be true if believing it somehow "works" in a political or social sense. A more assertive form of this view, associated with the late Richard Rorty, among others, holds that (1) there are degrees of truth, and (2) what is true for one person or group may not be true for another, to the degree that the truth of a proposition may not in fact be determined or even clarified by testing and debate. Debate becomes for Rorty a species of therapy, a more or less synchronous bypass of what he calls "incommensurable discourses," determining nothing.[34] Politically and culturally this has become an attractive idea for many in our time: though there is not space for it here, one might well consider the rhetoric in debates over abortion and marriage laws as providing illustrative material. Truth in such contexts is by definition always *relative,* a subjective term employed to refer to an idea in the mind of an individual perceiver. In the reflexive lingo of a famous female talk-show host, you may have "your truth" and, regarding identical phenomena, I may have "my truth": truth for me need not be the same as truth for you.

However, we have seen that the "truth" of some may come in time to be regarded as a consensus social construction, then pragmatically agreed upon by a powerful community of perceivers and legislatively imposed. In this second case, consensus develops expediently, as when a social group decides that it is in their political interest to assert as true what works for them, or, as, in our context, literary theorist Jonathan Culler has said, "gets us what we want." Unsurprisingly, what counts as true then changes according to various interests or agendas to which it becomes conveniently a tool. To take an extreme but actual example, according to one historical agenda of the twentieth century the so-called *Protocols of Zion,* an anti-Semitic forgery, are true, and the his-

---

[33]William James, *Pragmatism* (Cambridge, Mass.: Harvard University Press, 1978), p. 6.
[34]Richard Rorty, *Philosophy and the Mirror of Nature* (Princeton, N.J.: Princeton University Press, 1979).

tory of the Holocaust false. For practical purposes the term *truth* eventually becomes in such usage a buzzword, anesthetically therapeutic for some, but logically useless, conceptually empty of meaning.

Less extreme examples from the everyday work of science may further clarify. On the pragmatic account, although sunspot correlation recorded over several centuries might seem to a practicing meteorologist to be a relevant factor in much of the variation in global temperature cycles (such as the medieval warm period or the little ice age that followed), the record of these phenomena, the correlations and correspondence, might by others pragmatically come to be marginalized as evidence. Such a reconfiguration of the historical record might be prompted by something as mundane as a desire for government funding. For politicians working for geopolitical control and redistribution of wealth from "have" to "have-not" countries, and strategically deploying a case for recent unprecedented and potentially catastrophic anthropogenic global warming as rationale, recorded evidence that pretty good burgundy wine grapes were being grown in Gloucestershire between A.D. 1000 and 1200 is not a helpful fact, and might not therefore count as true *for their purposes*. Advocates for political change, or scientists dependent on the funding, might accordingly seek a means of discounting such evidence, even striving for it to be somehow airbrushed out of history, like Clementis from the photographs of that balcony in Prague.[35] To take another example: some HIV-infected men in certain parts of Africa appear to believe (however tragically) that sex with a virgin will cure them of HIV-AIDS.[36] When a large body of people believe a "truth" which they think "works for them," even of this dreadfully misguided sort, it is nonetheless regarded as a pragmatic or "consensus the-

---

[35]For an article that addresses the erasure of the "inconvenient" medieval warm period (and also affords a useful caution about the use of certain online sources), see Lawrence Solomon, "How Wikipedia's Green Doctor Rewrote 5,428 Climate Articles," *Financial Post*, December 19, 2009 <http://network.nationalpost.com/np/blogs/fpcomment/archive/2009/12/18/lawrence-solomon-wikipedia-s-climate-doctor.aspx>.

[36]The myth of "virgin cleansing," investigated by (among others) a joint study of the Nelson Mandela Foundation and South Africa's Human Sciences Research Council, has been shown to be widespread, so much so that some African governments (e.g., Zambia) have launched billboard campaigns to dispel it. See Suzanne Leclerc-Madlala, "On the Virgin Cleansing Myth: Gendered Bodies, AIDS and Ethnomedicine," *African Journal of AIDS Research* 1, no. 2 (2002): 87-95.

ory" of truth. In this last example we see that a consensus truth (even if it derives from superstition rooted in folk medicine) can confound the practical application of verifiable correspondence truth—in this case the means of curbing the spread of sexually transmitted disease.

The educated reader should not be deceived into thinking these examples are not formally analogous: the AIDS example might rather too readily seem clear enough to most who read this book, because our readers are likely to be informed about the pertinence of the corresponding science. Much the same will likely be true in respect of Holocaust denial and some of the other sad facts of history. Yet other perhaps equally unwarranted consensus convictions of what counts as truth may well go unchallenged by most of us, for we too are disposed to accept our own kinds of prevailing social consensus as the truth. It is uncomfortable to be a doubter in a time of political enthusiasm, and quite possibly dangerous. Few citizens of Prague questioned the revised photograph of the politicians on the balcony. We should on this evidence be inclined more to self-examination than to judgment. More innocuously, but not irrelevantly, many among us are inclined to read *The New York Times* or watch a morning news program so as to learn what to think. A well-managed and yet ultimately distorted and partial media consensus may even prevail as public "truth" unless there are contrarians willing to observe and declare the actual state of whatever imperious antirealism may be involved.

Why are these three theories pertinent in an elaboration of a Christian approach to literary theory and textual criticism? Well, precisely because the third, pragmatic, version of truth has come to dominate literary theory in our time to a greater degree than any other. It should be evident that such protean approaches to truth questions, whether starkly as tools of manipulation in the hands of a propagandist or more subtly as an assertion of the indeterminacy of meaning enabling arbitrary redefinition (defended as "playfulness" by a deconstructionist like Jacques Derrida), are *fundamentally incompatible* with a Christian worldview.[37] While correspondence and coherence theories of truth

---

[37]David Lyle Jeffrey provides an extended discussion of deconstruction, with particular reference to Derrida and Harold Bloom, in his *People of the Book: Christian Identity and Literary*

can each find their place in a Christian philosophy of textual interpretation, a pragmatic theory effectively invalidates the very facts and propositions most necessary to a cogent and coherent understanding of truth itself, and hence, ultimately, of the ground of Christian belief. Formally, pragmatic theories are utterly incommensurable with central Christian claims about the veridical, mind-independent character of creational and revealed truth. Theologically, they render unintelligible the words of the One who said, "I am the way, the truth, and the life: no man cometh unto the Father, but by me" (Jn 14:6).

Accordingly, we recommend caution with respect to certain varieties of poststructuralist literary theory. There are theorists of merit, however, who are not shaped by structuralism and poststructuralism in predictable ways: one of those of value for Christians, for example, is Mikhail Bakhtin. Bakhtin's early association with Russian formalism inclines him to a respect for the text and a close reading practice not unlike that of the New Critics in the United States, yet his interest in dialogue in literature (rather than dialectic) makes him alert to "otherness" in a way germane to a Christian worldview, while his concept of *heteroglossia*—the multiplicity and multivalence of language use within any culture—makes him a fruitful partner where ethical and theological criticism is contemplated.[38] In short, there is truth value in his approach. What we hope for our Christian readers is that they will strive in their own work to be, as St. Augustine says, "true from the Truth." As he goes on to clarify: "The Truth, then, could not speak contrary to the true man, or the true man contrary to the Truth."[39]

A BIBLICAL ILLUSTRATION

The story of the demise of King Ahab in 1 Kings 22 is as charged with the mystery of truth and consequences as any of the tragedies of Sopho-

---

Culture (Grand Rapids: Eerdmans, 1996), chap. 1, also an exposition of Augustine's theory of language and signification, contrasting it with Saussure, in chap. 2.

[38]See Mikhail Bakhtin, "Discourse in the Novel," in *The Dialogic Imagination* (Austin: University of Texas Press, 2001); also Alan Jacobs, *A Theology of Reading* (Boulder, Colo.: Westview, 2001), for a briefer introduction.

[39]Augustine *Homilies on the Gospel of John* 5.1, cited from Philip Schaff et al., eds., A Select Library of Nicene and Post-Nicene Fathers of the Christian Church, Series 1 (reprint, Peabody, Mass.: Hendrickson, 1994), 7:31.

cles. If an ancient Greek had written it, it might well have had the
theme "Whom the gods would destroy, they first make mad." But this
is a biblical text, so there is quite a bit more to it than simply the *hubris*
and *nemesis* of Greek tragedy.

We sincerely recommend that readers stop at this point and read this
remarkable chapter for themselves. Here are the highlights: Ahab,
whose lust for pleasure and power has already made him an antithesis
of all that constituted righteousness in the Jewish worldview, wants to
expand his holdings into Ramoth-gilead in Syria. He needs allies, so he
invites the king of Judah, Jehoshaphat, to join him (vv. 1-4). Jehoshaphat, whose name means "God judges" (repeated thirteen times, it
serves as an ironic leitmotif in this chapter), demurs, asking that Ahab
consult the word of the Lord first.[40] Ahab gathers his court prophets,
four hundred of them, and asks them if he should go to war or not. The
prophets are shrewd; they know that their job is to tell the king what he
wants to hear, and they do just that. But Jehoshaphat sees this display
of craven consensus for what it is and asks, skeptically, if there is not a
legitimate "prophet of the Lord" who may be consulted (vv. 5-7). Sure,
says Ahab, "There is yet one man, Micaiah the son of Imlah, by whom
we may enquire of the Lord: but I hate him; for he doth not prophesy
good concerning me, but evil."

It is evident that Jehoshaphat is looking for truth in a way Ahab is
not. So Ahab sends for Micaiah by a messenger well aware of the prophetic consensus, who advises Micaiah to vote with the majority for his
own good (v. 13). Micaiah announces his intention to speak the truth
as God declares it (v. 14). Once in the court, however, he says to the
king, "Go, and prosper: for the Lord shall deliver [Ramoth-gilead]
into the hand of the king," echoing the four hundred. Whether by Micaiah's tone of voice or by previous experience of his unpleasant but
authoritative prophecies, the king knows he is being toyed with and
demands "nothing but that which is true in the name of the Lord" (v.
16). So Micaiah, now in a different grammatical mood and tone, replies: "I saw all Israel scattered upon the hills, as sheep that have not a

---

[40]See the discussion in Peter Leithart, *1 and 2 Kings* (Grand Rapids: Brazos, 2006), pp. 158-
64.

shepherd: and the LORD said, These have no master: let them return
every man to his house in peace" (v. 17).

Ahab tries to interrupt, but Micaiah continues:

> Hear thou therefore the word of the LORD: I saw the LORD sitting on
> his throne, and all the host of heaven standing by him on his right hand
> and on his left. And the LORD said, Who shall persuade Ahab, that he
> may go up and fall at Ramoth-gilead? And one said on this manner, and
> another said on that manner. And there came forth a spirit, and stood
> before the LORD, and said, I will persuade him. And the LORD said unto
> him, Wherewith? And he said, I will go forth, and I will be a lying
> spirit in the mouth of all his prophets. And he said, Thou shalt persuade
> him, and prevail also: go forth, and do so. Now therefore, behold, the
> LORD hath put a lying spirit in the mouth of all these thy prophets, and
> the LORD hath spoken evil concerning thee. (vv. 19-23)

The word of the Lord as it comes from Micaiah makes it clear that
though the unseen court of heaven is in some respects analogous to the
court of Ahab, there is also a profound difference: the heavenly court is
presented with a God who has already judged Ahab, and who asks for
opinions about how Ahab may be deceived regarding the truth of that
just judgment into ironically helping bring it to pass, by his own pig-
headed resistance to the word of the Lord or truth in any form.

Micaiah, of course, is rebuked for failing to toe the party line; indeed
he is condemned to prison and the truth with him (vv. 26-28). Or so
Ahab thinks. Going out to battle, Ahab dissembles, wearing the garb
of an ordinary soldier, in his cowardice ironically confirming that he is
no true king (vv. 29-30). Understandably, given that the Syrian king
has his sights set on Ahab alone, his soldiers surround Jehoshaphat, the
only evident Hebrew king in the field. But when Jehoshaphat shouts
his war cry (one may imagine a southern accent) they realize they have
the wrong man and become confused (vv. 31-33). Suddenly, an unnamed man "drew a bow at a venture, and smote the king of Israel between the joints of the harness" (v. 34)—a very small target, hit perfectly, by a random shot. It is clear enough that what appears the most
improbable of chances owes in fact to the precision of someone other
than the archer. Ahab wants to flee, but his men, fearful of a loss of

morale, strap him up in his chariot as the now chaotic battle unfolds through the day, until by evening Ahab has bled to death while watching all Israel scatter, as "sheep without a shepherd." In a grim denouement the blood-drenched chariot is washed by the pool of Samaria, the dogs licking the blood while (according to the Septuagint text) the prostitutes wash in it, "according unto the word of the LORD" (v. 38).

Here is a biblical narrative that clearly presents us with two of our theories of truth, and hints at the third in a way that has unsettled many a reader. That Ahab and his court are devoted to an age-old version of pragmatic or consensus truth, while Micaiah and the narrator, and even Jehoshaphat, each view events in the light of correspondence of word to reality, is clear enough. But what Micaiah reports about the word of the Lord and the court of heaven hints at a "parallel universe." This universe, though not without contact with our own, has its own internally consistent, coherent reality. In the heavenly court the Holy Spirit himself may propose to infect sinful beings in our universe with a lying spirit and so confirm a will to power that has already usurped the will to truth. This characterization suggests that there are a number of things about both God himself ("No man hath seen God at any time" [Jn 1:18]) and his heaven ("eye hath not seen, nor ear heard, neither have entered into the heart of man, the things which God hath prepared for them that love him" [1 Cor 2:9]) that may not be adequately accounted for by a correspondence theory of truth. But this story also suggests that the truth of heaven, if we may call it that, is internally self-consistent and equally distinct, as truth, from the subjective distortions of any consensus view, which are inevitably to be disclosed as lies. When the writer to the Hebrews speaks of the "immutability" of God's counsel, adding that it is "impossible for God to lie" (Heb 6:17-18), he points us to the mysterious story of Melchizedek, who had no known parentage, indicating in his presentation of Melchizedek ("King of righteousness") as a type of Christ that there is, apart from our temporal reality *(chronos)*, a distinct order of spiritual reality *(kairos)* which nevertheless interpenetrates our own. This does not mean that we grasp the principles by which the truth of the divine reality co-inheres. We do know from Scripture, however, that it does, that its truth is real truth, even if now we only "see through a glass darkly" or in brief glimpses (1 Cor 13:12). Each sacrament of the church, though it has its signature temporal history, is likewise charged with a mystery proportional to an unseen order of reality. Christians regard such reality as nonetheless actual, just as the theoretical physicist does when he treats as real an invisible matrix.

CONCLUSION

We shall say something more about the evolution and practice of pragmatic postmodern approaches to literary studies in our last chapter, but for now it will serve us well enough to summarize these opening remarks with a few consequent practical suggestions. First, Christian intelligence requires knowledge of reality as it is. Christians may and should conjure with the fact that both self-referential and consensus versions of pragmatic theory of truth undergird much postmodern literary and social theory. We should come to understand empathetically the occasion of the genesis of such approaches so we may better empathize with the thinking of persons who hold these views. But the ordinary Christian will necessarily also identify, if not with Micaiah, then at least with the little boy who blurts out a correspondence view of the truth about the emperor's new clothes. Saying so, of course, will not often win immediate acclaim. In our academic context we are more likely to discover that when we are interacting with those who hold to a pragmatic view of truth they may well reveal themselves to be in practice intolerant of deviation from the prevailing consensus.

It is all the more imperative that Christian intellectuals understand on the basis of revealed truth that persons who hold values intrinsically alien to Christianity are to be respected as persons and actually *loved* as neighbors—whether they love us or not—even as we love ourselves. To be authentically Christian, however, a critic cannot love truthfully while acceding silently to any view of truth, literary or otherwise, which is effectively a species of lie. The informed and thoughtful Christian student of literary criticism will have recognized that postmodern pragmatism often disdains consideration for the worldview and language of particular *authors* as well as readers, hence violating the Christian sense that each author, too, is a sort of neighbor who is to be loved and listened to attentively for what he or she is actually saying. The Christian will also, because of an integrated worldview, come to recognize that any antirealist view of what counts as truth ultimately prevents authentic appreciation of the beautiful and pursuit of the good, including inevitably what we call the common good. A cascade of further implications follow, reaching to the possibility of our gaining an understanding of love and ultimately of being.

It is not our place in this series to reflect on political theory, science or law. It may be helpful to the literary student to reflect nonetheless on the relationship between law and literature. Historically, correspondence theory, when prevalent, has tended to make evident as a dominant concern of law the pursuit of *justice.* In a text such as *On the Laws and Customs of England* (c. 1260), by the first British scholar of law, Henry de Bracton, the derivation of first principles from divine revelation, such as the law given to Moses, is explicit: human justice makes every effort to correspond to its exemplar in divine justice, and it does so in part by relating culpability to intention. Coherence theory (whether in the theory of a contemporary philosopher such as Willard Quine or the legal commentary of F. W. Maitland and William Blackstone two centuries ago) tends to privilege a pursuit of "reasonableness" in juridical determination rather than justice strictly speaking; given that the ultimate standard is human reason rather than the law of God, justice is much more difficult than rationality to articulate. Under a now prevalent pragmatic theory, especially where deconstructionist criticism is applied to the body of constitutional and case law, we have tended to produce an environment in which advocacy or, we might say, the advantage to be gained by rhetorical subversion and lexical redefinition, typically goes to the highest bidder, with too little concern for what may appear as a clear meaning of the law or facts of the case, let alone anything like transcendent principles.[41] The theory of truth we operate with thus has conse-

---

[41]The literature of legal theory on this issue is voluminous, but from a journal both of literary and legal theory it is possible to get a sense of the trajectory that has produced legal theorists such as Andrea Dworkin, Catherine McKinnon and others: see Ronald Dworkin, "Law as Interpretation," *The Politics of Interpretation,* a special issue of *Critical Inquiry* 9, no. 1 (1982): 179-200. In law *originalism* or "strict constructionism" is now regarded as a conservative de-

quences in many spheres, obviously, not just in the library or laboratory, but also in everyday inquiry in almost any discipline.

Part of the benefit of a sound literary education in a Christian liberal arts curriculum should be the acquisition of critical discernment sufficiently acute to parse rhetoric, determine presuppositions and distinguish between legitimate and illegitimate analogies. Coupled with this there ought to be a clear sense of the importance of a sound conception of what counts as truth. This should be evident in the quality of writing that Christian students learn to produce: no less for us than for Horace it should be evident that "the foundation and fountain-head of good composition is a sound understanding" *(Ars Poetica)*. No such soundness can develop without a sincere dedication to grasping truth.

A final point, to which the whole history of literature in English bears abundant witness, deserves notice here: historically and literarily, denial of the existence of veridical truth follows inexorably upon denial of the existence of God. For reasons that should by now be apparent, a refusal to accept the existence of mind-independent truth typically, in its first effect, makes a god of the ego itself. In its next effect it raises the ego of some self-made demigod to exercise what our forebears since Augustine have called *libido dominandi*, a passion for power over others, and to have what we wish to be true accepted consensually or coercively as true. As the cultural consequences of the denial of God have become increasingly evident, some Christian artists and theologians have commented prophetically on the consequences, offering hope for redress, for restoring cultural and spiritual communion by considering in ways both new and old the presence of God still offered by the gospel of Christ. Some non-Christian critics have observed that postmodernism, in its rejection of the same Enlightenment rationalism that Christians also find suspect, has nevertheless often adopted a version of the self-referential hubris that characterized Enlightenment thinking itself.[42] This should remind us of the vulnerability all of us have to succumbing to intellectual temptations such as are represented by a very old story

---

fense analogous to correspondence theory of truth as it might pertain to evidence.

[42]This observation, made by Marxist critic Terry Eagleton in his book *After Theory* (London: Basic Books, 2003) among others, will be discussed further in our last chapter.

told simply in Genesis 1–3, and retold magnificently in Milton's *Paradise Lost*, Marlowe's *Doctor Faustus* and C. S. Lewis's *Perelandra* and *That Hideous Strength*. As these texts make clear, painful consequences follow from rhetorical subversion of the word of God, as from even the cleverest attempts to have godlike knowledge apart from communion with God. By contrast, the triumph of the gospel over the temptation to violate truth so powerfully retold in Milton's *Paradise Regained* restores hope that a much happier re-creative story is always being written as part of an eternal "book of life" to be read one day in paradise (Rev 21:27) by the Author of all.

SUGGESTIONS FOR FURTHER READING

Auerbach, Erich. *Mimesis: The Representation of Reality in Western Literature*. 1953. Reprint, Garden City, N.Y.: Doubleday, 1957.

Balthasar, Hans Urs von. *The Glory of the Lord: A Theological Aesthetics*. 7 volumes. Edited by Joseph Fessio and John Riches. Translated by Andrew Louth, Francis McDonagh and Brian McNeil. 1961. Reprint, San Francisco: Ignatius, 1982-1989.

Beckett, Lucy. *In the Light of Christ: Writings in the Western Tradition*. San Francisco: Ignatius, 2006.

Brown, Frank Burch. *Religious Aesthetics*. Princeton, N.J.: Princeton University Press, 1989.

Buechner, Frederick. *Telling the Truth: The Gospel as Tragedy, Comedy and Fairy Tale*. San Francisco: HarperCollins, 1977.

Daniélou, Jean. *The Scandal of Truth*. Baltimore: Helicon, 1962.

Farley, Edward. *Faith and Beauty: A Theological Aesthetic*. Aldershot, U.K.: Ashgate, 2001.

Girard, René. *I See Satan Fall Like Lightning*. Translated by James G. Williams. 1999. Maryknoll, N.Y.: Orbis, 2005.

Griffiths, Paul J. *Lying: An Augustinian Theology of Duplicity*. Grand Rapids: Brazos, 2004.

Harris, Richard. *Art and the Beauty of God: A Christian Understanding*. London: Geoffrey Chapman, 2000.

Hart, David Bentley. *The Beauty of the Infinite: The Aesthetics of Christian Truth*. Grand Rapids: Eerdmans, 2003.

Hass, Andrew, David Jasper, and Elisabeth Jay, eds. *The Oxford Handbook of*

English Literature and Theology. Oxford: Oxford University Press, 2009.

Jacobs, Alan. *Shaming the Devil: Essays in Truth Telling.* Grand Rapids: Eerdmans, 2004.

Maritain, Jacques. *Art and Scholasticism.* New York: Scribner's, 1962.

Ricoeur, Paul. *Oneself as Another.* Chicago: University of Chicago Press, 1992.

———. *The Rule of Metaphor: Multi-disciplinary Studies of the Creation of Meaning in Language.* Translated by Robert Czerny et al. Toronto: University of Toronto Press, 1977.

Schmidt, Thomas. *A Scandalous Beauty: The Artistry of God and the Way of the Cross.* Grand Rapids: Brazos, 2002.

Shanks, Andrew. *"What Is Truth?" Towards a Theological Poetics.* New York: Routledge, 2001.

Sherry, Patrick. *Spirit and Beauty: An Introduction to Theological Aesthetics.* Oxford: Clarendon, 1992.

Thiessen, Gesa Elsbeth. *Theological Aesthetics: A Reader.* Grand Rapids: Eerdmans, 2005.

Vaught, Carl G. *Metaphor, Analogy, and the Place of Places.* Waco, Tex.: Baylor University Press, 2004.

Wells, David F. *No Place for Truth, or, Whatever Happened to Evangelical Theology?* Grand Rapids: Eerdmans, 1993.

Willard, Dallas. *Knowing Christ Today: Why We Can Trust Spiritual Knowledge.* San Francisco: HarperOne, 2009.

Williams, Bernard. *Truth and Truthfulness: An Essay in Genealogy.* Princeton, N.J.: Princeton University Press, 2002.

Wolterstorff, Nicholas. *Art in Action: Toward a Christian Aesthetic.* Grand Rapids: Eerdmans, 2005.

THEOLOGICAL AESTHETICS AND CHRISTIAN LITERARY CRITICISM

Faith and Reason are like two wings on which the human spirit rises
to the contemplation of truth; and God has placed in the human heart
a desire to know the truth—in a word, to know Himself—so that,
by knowing and loving God, men and women may also
come to the fullness of truth about themselves.

JOHN PAUL II

While many acknowledge that the proper nourishment of literary learning is in the primary texts themselves rather than in much of the criticism and theory occasioned by them, far fewer agree on how best to approach, interpret, evaluate or even to establish a canon of merit among the authors available for study. As students often first discover in courses on contemporary literary theory, we now have a wide diversity of approaches to literature, yet little consensus regarding the relative validity or comparative utility of these approaches to a wider educational purpose, let alone any constructive sense of their relationship to the work of great critics from earlier periods. Structuralism, deconstruction, psychoanalytic criticism, Marxism, feminism, New Historicism, postcolonialism and other currently fashionable approaches might all be deemed interesting, and can even empower one to publish or pursue postgraduate studies within the postmodern literary and academic culture. Many literature majors, however, graduate without any clear sense of whether literary theory enables them to find—to employ venerable but still crucial terms—any truth, goodness, beauty or even meaning in literature. The young Keats's certainty that objects of aesthetic beauty offer eternal joy (a conviction that still draws a substantial number of students to the discipline) is not on the curricular radar of most contemporary theory courses. On a practical level many find it difficult to navigate the relationship of the more recent critical approaches to the linguistic tools of literary analysis once popularized by the New Criticism, and now more typically maintained by diverse studies in philology, linguistics, rhetoric, composition studies or creative writing. While the entertainment, diversity and traditional wisdom offered by literature itself is likely to ensure its continued study in some measure, the knowledge claims and broad intellectual values of literary criticism (within the university, a discipline little more than a century old) appear to have less certain enduring merit and can often deter rather than inspire young intellectuals—Christian or otherwise—to pursue literature as an academic study. Considering literary study from the point of view of hermeneutic assumptions is thus one important venue for the Christian student to approach an integration of faith and understanding.

The questions raised by literary theory, though complex and often adversarial to Christian thought, need to be faced by all serious students of the discipline. This is especially the case for Christians, however. For example, it is abundantly clear that one can misinterpret even overtly Christian literary texts in ways that evade the actual religious ideas of their authors. It is equally clear that even readers who consider themselves Christians can do this, often unintentionally. The timing for reassessment of the way literature is studied is propitious, not least because of a general discovery of the "religious dimension," as recently noticed by Stanley Fish and others. The full value of texts of recent religious interest, however, cannot be appreciated without a method that explores their theological meaning, which is why we agree with Kevin Hart that "those of us involved in the 'turn to religion' in literary studies need to spend some time not only with phenomenology after the 'theological turn' but also with theology itself."[1] It is surely the case that Christians of all persuasions, even in the academic world, tend now to be severely underformed theologically.

In its brief history as a university academic discipline, English literary studies has seen a shift away from the early attempt, broadly speaking, to be a science whose methods proceeded independently of a critic's own beliefs. Today, by contrast, ideological and political advocacies are commonly foregrounded, and there is now almost an expectation that personal beliefs *must* shape one's interpretations of literary texts. If every reader brings foundational assumptions to the reading of texts, there can be no purely neutral or value-free approach to literary criticism; rather, a central task of literary theory is to expose, analyze and debate these assumptions. Christians today are therefore less likely to be accused of imposing their beliefs on a text than of suppressing presuppositions that need to be deconstructed. However, because of its prevalent contradiction of a traditionally Christian normative respect for truth, ultimate good and beauty, the epistemological and moral relativism of postmodernism generally is not, as we have suggested already, a coherent option for Christians. While Christians can certainly adopt some of the insights of contemporary critical theory and many of the linguistic tools of analysis from earlier critical schools, the underlying conflict between the presuppositions of the postmodern project and the central tenets of a biblically informed worldview cannot be entirely evaded without a grave risk of intellectual dishonesty.

Nor is it sufficient for Christian interpreters simply to critique other approaches. Rather, fundamental philosophical issues must be addressed if we are to provide a coherent foundation for a distinctively Christian approach to literary criticism.

A CHRISTIAN PHILOSOPHY OF LITERATURE

For literary studies to constitute a coherent body of knowledge and an academic discipline that can be taught, practiced and expected to progress, the discipline must be able to address the central questions within

---

[1]Kevin Hart, "Afterword," *Christianity and Literature* 38, no. 2 (2009): 299.

the major branches of philosophy. In *epistemology*, How does one know? In *metaphysics*, What reality does one thereby know? In *ethics*, What good does this knowledge allow one to achieve? The central questions of *aesthetics* are also essential: In what *form* is the art expressed, and how does this form create an experience of beauty, the traditional partner of truth and goodness? The answers to such questions determine how specific literary theories are substantively constituted and practically proceed. And, as in every other field of study, it is in relation to such questions that the crucial distinctions between different schools of literary interpretation may most profitably be debated. In general, therefore, *philosophy of literature* is perhaps a better term for our purposes than *literary theory;* a specifically Christian philosophy of literature may well be understood under the term *theological aesthetics*, provided that *aesthetics* is seen not as a limiting term but one that reflects an interdependent relationship with the other relevant branches of philosophy.[2]

One cannot posit a distinctively Christian philosophy of literature, however, without tracing its foundations to divine revelation. Nothing should make a greater presuppositional difference than whether or not one believes in God and, if so, what kind of God. Given the historical character of Christian revelation, there is no way of discerning the difference between an essentially atheistic philosophy and the approach or approaches followed by Christians except by an appeal to history, including the unfolding of sacred Scripture and its historic interpretation through the centuries. Despite elements of division among believers today, there remains a common substance or deposit of faith, what C. S. Lewis calls "mere" (or essential) Christianity, whose common truths are of central significance to all those who choose to think about reality in the light of Christ. Although we "know in part" (1 Cor 13:12), to be cogent we must affirm that part which we know. The specific nature and character of the triune God revealed in the Bible must be acknowledged, rather than some vague, philosophically generic conception of deity. Again, with Kevin Hart:

---

[2]See Hans Urs von Balthasar, *The Glory of the Lord: A Theological Aesthetics*, 7 vols. (1961; reprint, San Francisco: Ignatius, 1982-1989). Also Gesa Elsbeth Thiessen, *Theological Aesthetics: A Reader* (Grand Rapids: Eerdmans, 2005).

The word "God" in Christianity . . . *means* in part that God has the right and power to give himself on his own terms: in the reading of scripture, in the proclamation of the word, in prayer, in moral action, and in the sacraments. We understand how the word "God" functions in Christianity only when we recognize that God is irreducible, that he transcends his various phenomenalities.[3]

While the biblical foundations of our approach will be traced more fully in chapter three, it should be immediately apparent that there are some crucial, interdependent epistemological and ethical elements that a Christian approach to literary criticism must accept in order to warrant the adjective *Christian*. These elements we might categorize under the heading "theistic realism."[4]

THEISTIC REALISM

Very briefly, as with other human creatures, literary critics are made in the image of God; this does not mean, however, that we are entitled to think of ourselves *as* gods—or to behave as though we had divine prerogatives. We live in a created universe that precedes our thinking about it, and it precedes and thus to some degree constrains our acts of naming reality as we find ourselves living and thinking within it. We accept that human nature was designed for a fullness of life in loving communion with the triune God—Father, Son and Holy Spirit—and that the very essence of the Fall is the rebel angel's attempt to convince humanity that we can "be as gods" ourselves (Gen 3:5). According to Genesis, Adam and Eve's decision to experience evil mars the communion God intended, making the human race that descends from them incapable of fully knowing and living the moral good (Gen 2:17). Theirs was the first confusion concerning whether it is we who are made in the image of God or whether our notion of God is to be some projection of our own image: the *agon*, or conflict, here represented is one of the great themes in literature down the centuries. Our very words *protago-*

---

[3]Hart, "Afterword," p. 298.
[4]This term, coined by Phillip Johnson in his 1995 book *Reason in the Balance: The Case Against Naturalism* is useful shorthand for a scripturally based worldview, in which true knowledge begins with acknowledgment of God and his revealed truths.

nist and *antagonist* reverberate with this great question. The Genesis story of the Fall explains why most of us "naturally" perceive life in a materialistic, self-centered way that fails to acknowledge spiritual reality, especially the existence and authority of God, until the destiny of our own souls becomes a serious question for us. In this life, Christians believe, we cannot understand our own human nature except through the restored unity, the at-one-ment created by the life and sacrificial death of the incarnate Son of God, the Christ—Jesus of Bethlehem, Nazareth and Calvary. Eternal salvation is offered by Christ and, through his grace, received by believers, who must still undergo a process of sanctification, or continual conversion toward a full restoration of the divine image.

All human creatures, including those who become literary critics, can expect to acquire knowledge through two distinct but related sources: those matters available through revelation must be apprehended by faith; other matters, because of the created nature we participate in, may be apprehended through reason. Both reason and faith, in the Christian view, are necessary. Since the European Enlightenment, they have frequently been forcibly separated, with reason often set up as the singular light by which empirical science has forged the technology of the modern world, while faith (sometimes termed *blind faith*) is reduced to a lingering emotional carryover from a less mature understanding of human potential, a relic of the "Dark Ages." (That the typical post-Enlightenment appeal to reason often masks unacknowledged assumptions or biases that have none of the empirical proof supposedly intrinsic to scientific method is one of the ironies of this split.)

Theistic realism depends on historical evidence as well as revelation; to put this another way, religious faith requires a trust in the authority and credibility of those teachers and saints whose recorded words now warrant the category of sacred Scripture. Christian Scripture is not, however, primarily concerned with material knowledge in the manner of post-Enlightenment science; rather—whether through narrative, drama or poetry—it is more often focused on moral and spiritual knowledge, the kind of learning some still term *wisdom*. In a famous biblical definition faith is both "the substance of things hoped for" and "the evidence of things not seen," pointing us beyond the merely physical to spiritual reality (Heb 11:1). Recorded in Scripture, graven in the human heart and accessible in the still light of prayer, the teachings of faith allow God's revelation to reach both the simple and the learned, in part by becoming, in Blake's phrase, a "great code of art."[5]

Faith offers literary criticism knowledge in a variety of ways, but none are incompatible with reason. That is to say, faith is itself a means of knowing, and the content of faith constitutes in itself a body of knowledge. Moreover, the capacity of our reason to recognize and, accordingly, to know the truth, a capacity demonstrated in countless concrete situations, is regarded by Christian theology as part of the divine image imprinted upon us. As fallen creatures, however, our ability to reason in moral and spiritual situations depends greatly on our communion with the One who is the way, the truth, and the life (Jn 14:6). To put this in the terms of the Christian Scriptures and theological tradition, for Christians who follow their Shepherd as naturally as do sheep, that very intimacy fosters an awareness of our sins and biases, even the collective biases absorbed from the prevailing culture. Given the destructive force of such inevitable errors, the corresponding need for reason as the companion of faith becomes all the more obvious. Reason must critically question personal and societal assumptions, not doubting for doubt's sake, but rather from a deep desire to know truth. Used accountably, in harmony with faith, reason is a gift from God that enables humans to examine the reality of any given situation, gather information, form intelligent insights and then ask reflective questions that attempt to judge a given proposition as true or false. As Aristotle argues in the opening line of his *Metaphysics*, humans by nature desire to know[6] and, contrary to the more extreme examples of Nietzschean skepticism fashionable in some parts of the academy, our senses and our capacity for reflective questions do permit us to know certain truths; it is possible for one to be deceived or uncertain for a time, sometimes a

---

[5]William Blake, "The Laocoön" (1820), *Blake Complete Writings*, ed. Geoffrey Keynes (London: Oxford University Press, 1969), p. 777.
[6]Aristotle *Metaphysics* 1.1, trans. Hippocrates G. Apostle (Bloomington: Indiana University Press, 1966), p. 12.

long time, but with thorough, free investigation, normally the truth will out. There are, moreover, certain truths that one cannot *not* know except by a willful resistance to the givens of human experience.[7] Such commonsense judgments are an important part of how humans transcend the finite limitations of individual subjectivity and confirm reality in everyday life.

Of course, there are also scholarly questions that require much further, labor-intensive investigation, and it can be helpful to seek correction within communities of similarly interested investigators; in this sense, the "communities of interpretation" suggested by some reader-response literary theorists can be useful to Christian critics.[8] Such communities must employ a common methodology (or at least commensurable methodologies) and be guided by valid philosophical principles; as enjoyable as it is to be among friends, one needs something more than companionability or even mutual accountability, though these are indispensable: one thinks of the words of Feste the fool in Shakespeare's *Twelfth Night*, "my foes tell me plainly I am an ass, so that by my foes, sir, I profit in the knowledge of myself" (5.1.16-17). For truth as such, as we have seen, is not narrowly a matter of consensus or conformity, but rather of the correspondence between perception and reality. Over time, many forms of false religion, false science, false propositions must shatter and fall. Ultimately, however, it is folly to attempt a holistic philosophy merely "after the tradition of men," for a full knowledge of any subject can be reached only by tracing it back to divine purpose and intention. In this sense Christians strive to bring "every thought" captive "to the obedience of Christ" (2 Cor 10:5), seeking thus the path of truth which transcends any individual or particular interest; if we truly desire the mind of Christ Jesus (Phil 2:5), we will seek the objective, catholic, lasting truth revealed by him. Our rational intellect plays a crucial role, for Christ himself adds to the great commandment of Deuteronomy 6:5—to love God with all of our "heart . . . soul . . . [and] might"—the injunc-

---

[7]See J. Budziszewski, *What We Can't Not Know: A Guide* (Dallas: Spence, 2003).

[8]The locus classicus argument for American literary theory is Stanley Fish, *Is There a Text in This Class? The Authority of Interpretive Communities* (Cambridge, Mass.: Harvard University Press, 1980).

tion that we should also love him "with all of [our] *mind*" (Lk 10:27, emphasis added).

There is, then, no enduring conflict between the substance of faith and the horizons of reason; without denying their distinct natures, faith and reason can pursue the same goals while being aided by different sources of knowledge. Just as the one God of faith offers his children many gifts of truth, goodness and beauty, so too our souls in the image of God can use reason, guided by faith, to come to know the nature, purpose and value of these gifts. The mirroring process here recalls the mysterious saying of Heraclitus, that "the way up and the way down are one and the same,"[9] along with his further observation that "although the *logos* is common to all, most people live as though they have a wisdom of their own." T. S. Eliot uses both sayings as epigraphs for *Four Quartets*, his brilliant, postconversion poems on the relationship of time and eternity, reflecting that it is only by the Logos stepping "down" into time, becoming Christ in the flesh (Jn 1:14), that we are able to understand those elements of our created human nature by which God had always intended to lead us "up" again to be united with him. In the poetic words of John Paul II, faith and reason are "two wings" that lift us toward knowledge of the truth about God and ourselves. Both wings require human will, work and time, but despite

> all the toil involved, believers do not surrender. They can continue on their way to the truth because they are certain that God has created them "explorers" whose mission it is to leave no stone unturned, though the temptation to doubt is always there. Leaning on God, they continue to reach out, always and everywhere, for all that is beautiful, true, and good.[10]

CRITICAL REALISM

While it is thus possible to propose a Christian philosophy based on the harmony of faith and reason, it remains to be seen how such thought

---

[9]Heraclitus Fragment 60: ὁδος ἄνω κάτω μία καί ὡυτη. T. M. Robinson, *Heraclitus: Fragments: A Text and Translation with a Commentary* (1987; reprint, Toronto: University of Toronto Press, 1991), p. 41, has "A road up <and> down <is> one and the same <road>."
[10]John Paul II, *Fides et Ratio*, p. 33.

can be systematically applied to literary criticism. Although the gifts of grace proper to faith retain preeminent significance in many ways, contributions to the academic discipline of literary criticism are made by people with diverse beliefs and even by some with no apparent metaphysical stance at all. To "walk in wisdom toward them that are without, redeeming the time" (Col 4:5), and to enjoy dialogue, mutual correction and the community of literary critics, Christians can first outline some common terrain which a rational analysis of the available literature can then explore. It seems preferable to begin by using reason to argue for some of the elements on which critical realism—as distinct from theistic realism—would seem to insist.

In particular, reason is necessary for coming to terms with the nature of literature. The vast diversity of literature makes definition complex, but not impossible, and traditional aspects of Aristotelian definition can clarify the subject; in particular, the basic question of any subject's nature, "what is it?" can generally be answered in two distinct ways: what it does—or the constitutive elements and differentiating features of the subject—and what it is for—the initial causes and ultimate purposes for which it exists.

The question concerning what literature does has traditionally received at least three common answers. First, literature presents independent aesthetic structures with objective forms; not merely words or black letters housed within bound paper, these forms are coherent artistic structures that create what Aristotle called *mimesis*, by which the elements of literature creatively represent or imitate diverse aspects of human life.[11] Aristotle argues that in drama, for example, the *plot* forms a related set of events; portraits of *character* distinguish the story's key individuals; the emphasis of ideas suggested or stated by these characters form the text's *thought;* the words of the text are its *diction;* finally, the performance of the play presents a *spectacle* for the physical eye.[12] Not merely copying or representing material elements of life, literature as an independent, mimetic universe has features that must be considered by

---

[11]Aristotle, *Poetics. The Critical Tradition: Classic Texts and Contemporary Trends*, ed. David H. Richter (Boston: Bedford St. Martin's, 1998), pp. 59-61.
[12]Ibid., pp. 63-64.

all fair interpreters, and a self-enclosed internal structure that does not necessarily answer to external questions. This view of art can apply to painting, sculpture or even a sheet of music, yet is also suggested by any completed novel or script, or by the theme of Keats's "Ode on a Grecian Urn" (1819) or the apparent lack of historical reference in a poem like Coleridge's "Kubla Khan" (1798). Perhaps the best-known single statement of this view of literary art is Archibald MacLeish's "Ars Poetica." To cite just three of the poem's twelve rhyming couplets:

> A poem should be wordless
> As the flight of birds . . .
> A poem should be motionless in time
> As the moon climbs . . .
> A poem should not mean
> But be. (7-8, 15-24)[13]

The justly famous final dictum confirms literature's independent existence as a distinct, real entity whose being must be investigated as such. To further describe what literature does, those who focus on art's objectivity have also turned to Aristotle to define what differentiates literature from, most notably, philosophy on the one hand or history on the other. As Sir Philip Sidney argues in his Renaissance "The Defence of Poesy" (1595), literature provides concrete forms and examples for the precepts of philosophy, but the poet is not bound by the facts of history in deciding to illustrate these precepts.[14] Yet contrary to the popular view of literature as purely imaginative fiction, Aristotle in his *Poetics* differentiates literary writing from other forms of discourse only by the freedom with which it mingles empirical or historical fact, ethical principle and imaginative speculation; creatively selecting whatever one deems important to the subject at hand, the mimetic poet can represent things "either as they were or are, or as they are said or thought to be or to have been, or as they ought to be."[15] Within the freedom of

---

[13] Archibald MacLeish, "Ars Poetica," *Collected Poems 1917 to 1982* (Boston: Houghton Mifflin, 1985), p. 106.

[14] Philip Sidney, "The Defence of Poesy" (1595), *Sir Philip Sidney: The Oxford Authors*, ed. Katherine Duncan-Jones (Oxford: Oxford University Press, 1989), pp. 212-50.

[15] Aristotle, *Poetics*, p. 79.

this artistic license, poets form new worlds of literature, "subcreations" that enable delight even while suggesting or elucidating important truths also studied in the other human sciences. While philosophy can surely be illustrated through story, and history can teach by both abstract principles and concrete examples, literature is distinguished by the versatility of its *mimesis*. In a sense literary art becomes a vessel for human perceptions and understanding in which the ingredients of learning may be distilled and made into a new elixir.

Reading a literary masterpiece for not only the first but even the hundredth time can also be compared to discovering a new world, and is often accompanied by something like the wonder of Keats who, "on first looking into Chapman's Homer," felt "like some watcher of the skies / When a new planet swims into his ken" (9-10).[16] Repeated exploration does not entirely diminish such wonder; the complexity of any truly great literary work exceeds the capacity of any individual observer or critic fully to grasp it. Almost inevitably, then, literary scholarship will be to some degree interdisciplinary, even though very often an extrinsic insight leads to new questions rather than simple answers. Moreover, within this process of exploration the experienced literary critic is likely to discover that MacLeish is only partially correct; precisely because literature is not "wordless" but, rather, composed of complex, fascinating words with multiple references, it can mean, must mean, will always mean much more than criticism can fully describe or even than the writer can fully control. Following Horace, Sidney says that a *mimesis* is "a speaking picture," but whereas one picture may prove to be worth a thousand words, a thousand words can yield an even greater number of pictures.[17] This capacity to express multiple layers of meaning through artistic forms and mimetic references is the third and perhaps most important thing that literature does, for it allows literature to affect readers in a variety of different ways according to the plenitude of experience and taste they bring to it. It may be, for example, that one of the distinctive readerly attributes Christian readers

---

[16]John Keats, "On First Looking into Chapman's Homer" (1816), *John Keats: Selected Poems and Letters*, ed. Douglas Bush (Boston: Houghton Mifflin, 1959), p. 18.
[17]Sidney, "Defence," p. 217.

bring to a text is a circumspection formed by having learned to read the Bible and Christian literature not as a means of achieving mastery but rather, in a self-examining spirit, in a willingness to *be interpreted by* the text. Christian literature typically offers, in the words of Bunyan's "Apology" for *The Pilgrim's Progress*, the opportunity to "read thy self . . . and know whether thou art blest or not."[18] Devotional reading, as Liam Corley has recently argued, is normative for Christians, for it implies "a crucial reliance upon the plenitude of meaning in a text"; while certainly there is a Christian tradition of reading the Bible prophetically (one thinks of William Blake), "the principal mode of devotional reading is self-critique,"[19] a habit creating what Jeffrey has called elsewhere the receptive disposition of "the broken-hearted reader."[20]

The meaning of meaning and the means of achieving artistic meaning are accordingly two of the central questions that critical realism needs to explore. The capacity of words to mean through both literal, empirical identification and a wide variety of figurative suggestion creates a vast complexity of reference, but not the abyss of undecidable "aporia" often asserted by postmodern critics seemingly unaware of the history of rhetoric.[21] Tropes, or language in which the literal meaning is precisely not what is meant, must be understood according to the specific figure's form and function, whether metaphor, metonymy, personification, paradox and the like; even schemes or artistic arrangements of words can suggest much depth of meaning, as the tireless classifications of rhetoricians regularly reveal.[22] Similarly, literal and especially colloquial language commonly used in literature requires extensive historical research; here, the evolution of critical editions for major authors and of historical dictionaries like the *Oxford English Dictionary* have proven invaluable for students. Whether a given reference

---

[18]John Bunyan, "The Author's Apology for his Book," *The Pilgrim's Progress*, ed. W. R. Owens (1678; reprint, Oxford: Oxford University Press, 2003), p. 9.

[19]Liam Corley, "The *Jouissance* of Belief: Devotional Reading and the (Re)turn to Religion," *Christianity and Literature* 58, no. 2 (2009): 255, 257.

[20]David Lyle Jeffrey, *People of the Book: Christian Identity and Literary Culture* (Grand Rapids: Eerdmans, 1996), pp. 353-74.

[21]See Mario J. Valdes, "Aporia," *Encyclopedia of Contemporary Literary Theory*, gen. ed. Irena R. Makaryk (Toronto: University of Toronto Press, 1993), p. 507.

[22]See here Paul Ricoeur, *The Rule of Metaphor* (Toronto: University of Toronto Press, 1981).

is literal or figurative, it is also helpful to distinguish between the intra-textual meaning within the literary universe of the text in question and extratextual meaning that speaks more directly to and about the world outside the text.

Briefly, to clarify the distinction between these two realms, within literature one discovers many words whose reference is intratextual or related primarily to the internal universe established by the form of the literary work. For example, events within the plot follow from or are foreshadowed by other events; characters respond to these events; actions create consequences for those within the story. On the other hand, Aristotle himself argues that people "find pleasure in viewing representations because it turns out that they learn and infer what each thing is"; whereas, "if one has not happened to see the object previously, he will not find any pleasure in the imitation qua imitation but rather in the workmanship or coloring or something similar."[23] In other words, words can have an intratextual meaning but also an extratextual reference that points readers to what they may or may not recognize as elements in their own experience. In the latter case the literary work may be beyond the reader's initial horizons, and education must close the gap. In the former the recognized reference may be to a purely material object or a historical event; it may be a likeness or similitude of history; it could relate to other words or ideas in politics, philosophy or, in the case of a great deal of English literature, Scripture; it may represent human emotions or ethical acts that move our hearts and minds. As St. Augustine explains in his discussion of biblical exegesis in *On Christian Doctrine*, figurative tropes can refer to extratextual realities, and accurate interpretation often depends on knowledge of the extratextual reference.[24] Similarly, even clearly fictional characters can portray ethical dilemmas related to extratextual historical events or judgments.

In pursuing the interpretation of both intratextual and extratextual meaning, the literary critic's job is primarily descriptive. While there are critics who regard their work as creating rather than discovering

---

[23]Aristotle *Poetics*, p. 61.

[24]See especially Augustine *On Christian Doctrine*, bk. 3, trans. D. W. Robertson Jr. (1958; reprint, Upper Saddle River, N.J.: Library of Liberal Arts, 2006).

meaning, such an emphasis is not consistent with critical realism. Initially, of course, the two relevant parties who must be considered are the text's author and implied audience, both subjects of much contemporary theoretical debate. Without elaborating the wide variety of possible relationships between these parties, one can state that it is simply an unintelligent, antirealistic denial of extratextual meaning *not* at least to investigate how one's understanding of a text can be influenced by the real author or audience from the historical period the text originated in. Often, in fact, historical evidence related to these parties can confirm or at least corroborate references within the text. It can also rule out radically false interpretations such as would, in effect, slander real persons. Just as a reasonable judge throws spurious claims out of court, the reasonable reader rejects spurious assertions that would influence his or her interpretation of a work of art. In an analogous but imaginative way the same standard of reasonable judgment applies to the interpretation of intratextual meaning or of the characters living within the literary text in question. Casual readers or critics of *Hamlet*, for example, might be prepared to damn Ophelia and agree that she must be buried outside of hallowed ground; other readers, attentive to her mental state within the play and aware of the traditional Christian teaching on suicide and mortal sin, will with Laertes rebuke the "churlish priest" and look to angels to protect Ophelia's eternal soul.[25]

Such radically divergent interpretations cannot be held by the same reader at the same time, and yet judgment on the matter deeply affects how one reacts to Ophelia's death. Just as a judge in a court of law assesses evidence and then passes reasoned judgment, it is possible that for the literary critic the weight of argument and evidence will eventually shift interpretation away from a judgment that one decides is simply false, or that one or more possible contradictory readings will finally be rejected. As in life, some questions are more easily resolved than others. Critical realism, however, refuses to validate the ignoring of evidence and embracing of arbitrary judgment—an approach that becomes ready prey to current cultural bias, no matter how lacking in

---

[25]William Shakespeare, *Hamlet* (1602), *William Shakespeare: The Complete Works*, gen. ed. Stanley Wells and Gary Taylor (Oxford: Clarendon, 1988), pp. 654-90.

pertinence or respect for the literary text in question. It is not critical realism, for example, to try through ingenious means to make an avowedly naturalistic poem into some sort of Christian parable, any more than it is to try to reduce a parable of Jesus into a case for atheistic libertarianism.

Nevertheless, it is also true that some literary texts do seem designed, as Keats argued of *King Lear*, to build "negative capability," the capacity to accept "uncertainties, mysteries, doubts without any irritable reaching after fact & reason."[26] Yet here too fact and reason enter into any sustained, coherent interpretation of both intratextual and extratextual meaning. The great variety of relationships between authors, literary texts and their audiences accounts for astonishingly diverse forms of literature, and immense learning from many different fields is required before one can begin to grasp even a basic level of reference in some of the world's great literary masterpieces. A reading of *Hamlet* or *King Lear* by a student at twenty is not likely to be nearly as rich as that by the same student twenty years later, or twenty years after that. While a critic's own beliefs may influence what he or she is able to perceive at any point, from the standpoint of critical realism the accuracy of interpretative arguments will depend on empirical evidence, whether intra- or extratextual, and on logical argument consistent with that evidence. To proceed otherwise is potentially to make literary criticism not a field of progressive knowledge but rather, as some postmodernists seem to wish, an exercise in personal creativity that in the long run likely comes to little more than either self-adulation or the imposition on texts of cultural assumptions that distort rather than illuminate the unique mimetic world contained within them. By contrast, those committed to critical realism in literary criticism should seek in every reading to develop a credible interpretation of the literary work, one which reflects awareness of both the literary conventions and artistic structures employed to create meaning within the intratextual, self-contained mimetic universe. They should also endeavor to draw upon a wide range of pertinent interdisciplinary scholarship in a candid effort to trace the

---

[26]Keats, "To George and Thomas Keats" (1817), *John Keats*, pp. 260-61.

possible range of reference that the literary text makes to the vast extra-textual universe. From a Christian point of view we may say that this type of effort is a way of seeking both to respect the ultimate unity of truth and, as important, a way to love our neighbors as ourselves. We speak of "seeking," "effort" and "endeavor" not least because such a challenging task is not possible for any individual critic; thus, those committed to using reason and evidence to establish literary interpretation must form scholarly communities of dialogue and debate. This too becomes a means of extending love to our neighbors.

THEOLOGICAL AESTHETICS

Is personal belief then an impertinence in literary criticism? Is there no place for a belief-centered critical approach, whether the foundations of the belief are Marxism, feminism, Christianity or any other worldview? On the contrary, critical realism must insist that real human persons—perhaps especially, serious scholars—are not capable of resting content with a strictly formal interpretation of the meaning of a literary work. Beyond our natural desire to know and understand in an intellectual sense, we have also the impulse to ask questions of value: we want to understand not only what something means but whether, why or why not, the object in question is valuable in the first place. Authors, critics and audiences, as well as literary texts themselves, frequently address what literature "is for," its causes, intentions and ultimate purposes. The absolute *need* for the human spirit to evaluate, to judge value rather than simply process information, largely accounts for the demise of the purely formal analysis of New Criticism, and the rise of explicitly ideological or political forms of literary criticism. Yet almost all major historical critics also made evaluative comments, for knowing well how something works often leads to knowing why it might be good. Aristotle's theory of *catharsis*, for example, offers an explanation of the purpose or broader good of watching tragedy, as one experiences pity for human suffering and fear that similar events could happen again.[27] Sometimes such claims are very specific and particular to the content

---

[27]Aristotle *Poetics*, p. 63.

of individual works, but inevitably evaluative criticism is guided by broader philosophical beliefs, whether epistemological, metaphysical, ethical or aesthetic, and then the critic's dominant worldview becomes of crucial importance. Certainly, major Christian writers such as Dante, Sidney and T. S. Eliot have reflected on the value of literature, and their work along with the judgments of many lesser-known critics can provide examples of responsible Christian literary evaluation. Initially, however, it will be helpful to outline our general approach to Christian literary criticism—theological aesthetics—as it is shaped by the linked imperatives of theistic and critical realism.

On the general order of interpretation and evaluation, and the need for both to operate responsibly if literary criticism is to remain a healthy academic discipline, a few preliminary points may be made. There can be no question that an effort at developed, mature interpretation is a prerequisite to responsible evaluation. Attempting to evaluate anything about which one has little understanding is obviously not likely to be a very productive exercise. It follows that self-serving interpretations that tell us more about the critic than the work of literature will produce unconvincing literary evaluations. In an important sense the now familiar claim of logical positivism, that there can be "no ought from is," had things backward; actually, there can be no ought, no ethics, *except* from what is metaphysically real. Accordingly, any evaluative comment in literary criticism ought to be preceded by clearly argued evidence for the interpretative judgment in the literary text itself. It is crucial, as E. D. Hirsch has cogently argued, to distinguish the fundamentally different intention of interpretation (the attempt to describe accurately the plausible range of meaning expressed by a literary text) from that of evaluation (the attempt to explore the broader value or significance of a text).[28] Nevertheless, concern about the simple fact-value distinction must not lead one to ignore how foundational metaphysical beliefs or ethical values can affect the selection of facts that guide an interpreter's work. It is obvious, for example, that a Nietzschean, nihilistic metaphysic frequently influences postmodern interpretations of literature.

---

[28]E. D. Hirsch, *The Aims of Interpretation* (Chicago: University of Chicago Press, 1976).

Christian interpreters are subject to a similar group bias, and, accordingly, may initially be more capable of accurately interpreting clearly Christian texts than texts foreign to their own beliefs. Still, it is possible to learn foreign beliefs, customs and practices; it is an aspect of loving our neighbor. Through the exercise of research and logical argument within scholarly communities, our biases can be corrected and literary criticism can produce progressively more accurate interpretations of the infinitely complex literary works written by great authors.

Once a fairly developed interpretation, accountable to the facts, form and language, has been achieved, however, the form of Christian literary evaluation we practice will differ quite radically from other kinds of literary criticism. In our view aesthetic evaluation merely begins with noticing the many pleasures evoked by intratextual artistic structures; the subtle coherence of plot, depth and complexity of character, the visual splendor of dramatic costumes or even the rhythm of complex rhyme schemes in poems such as Tennyson's "Lady of Shalott" (1842) all give pleasure that can and should be included in Christian literary evaluation. Yet theological aesthetics cannot stop at pleasure. In Christian understanding, an appreciation of beauty is much more than a matter of intellectual hedonism; rather, as David Hart has brilliantly explained, beauty is intrinsically linked, inseparably interdependent, with the intellectual truth and moral beauty existent within the life and presence of the Christian God.[29] Though revealed as distinct persons—Father, Son, and Holy Spirit—the three share one divine substance, one real life, one reality that, in St. Paul's words, will in eternity be "all in all" (1 Cor 15:28). This is the basis of the medieval conception of the five transcendentals (truth, love, goodness, beauty, being): the one life of God is expressed as an interdependent, united whole in which truth, goodness and beauty mutually reveal each other, and indeed cannot be understood apart from each other. In the highly developed theological aesthetics of Hans Urs von Balthasar, this one divine life of God is summarized by its most common biblical name: the *glory* of the Lord.[30]

---

[29]David Bentley Hart, *The Beauty of the Infinite: The Aesthetics of Christian Truth* (Grand Rapids: Eerdmans, 2003).

[30]Both the Greek word *doxa* in the Septuagint Old Testament and the Hebrew word for glory

Humans experience this glory through gifts of God's grace that allow self-transcendence, the transcending of temporal affections to rest in the eternally transcendent life of God. Yet self-transcendence is not an exclusive experience but rather a common one that occurs whenever the eye of faith is open to seeing reality, whether in life or within the *mimesis* of literary art. Balthasar, in a short resumé of his life's work, summarizes his extremely learned aesthetics with a simple example from everyday life, showing how the love of neighbor commanded by our Lord leads to the perception, within families, of transcendent reality:

> Now man exists only in dialogue with his neighbor. The infant is brought to consciousness of himself only by love, by the smile of his mother. In that encounter the horizon of unlimited being opens itself for him, revealing four things to him: (1) that he is one in love with the mother, even in being other than his mother, therefore all being is one; (2) that that love is good, therefore all being is good; (3) that that love is true, therefore all being is true; and (4) that that love evokes joy, therefore all being is beautiful.[31]

In God's glory, as Hopkins puts it, "Christ plays in ten thousand places."[32] Literary art is one of the more valuable of God's gifts of grace, for the complexity and variety of its *mimesis* has frequently allowed faithful Christian writers vividly to describe a moving experience of divine transcendence, seeing the whole world as "charged with the grandeur of God," its beauty shining out "like shook foil."[33] While the very substance and redemptive reality of Christ's work of re-creation is offered historically in time, recorded in Scripture and mediated anew within the Christian church's preaching and sacraments, John Paul II was surely correct, in his "Letter to Artists," that "art remains a kind of bridge to religious experience," that with the "help of artists the knowl-

---

it translates, *kavod,* are linked to beauty and sometimes translated as such. It is this reflected quality to which the psalmist invites us when he urges that we "worship the LORD in the beauty of holiness" (Ps 29:2; 96:9).

[31]Hans Urs von Balthasar, "A Résumé of My Thought," trans. Kelly Hamilton, *Communio* 15 (winter 1988): 468-73.

[32]Gerard Manley Hopkins, "As Kingfishers Catch Fire" (1877), in *Gerard Manley Hopkins: The Oxford Authors,* ed. Catherine Phillips (Oxford: Oxford University Press, 1986), p. 129.

[33]Hopkins, "God's Grandeur" (1877), in *Gerard Manley Hopkins: The Oxford Authors,* ed. Catherine Phillips (Oxford: Oxford University Press, 1986), p. 128.

edge of God can be better revealed."[34] The core of Christian theological aesthetics is the religious experience of reestablished communion with God, mediated in this case by aesthetic structures which create, facilitate or sometimes even require a triune meeting between the work of literary art, the spiritually awakened human person, and the divine life of God revealed by faith and reason.

The true. While many readers experience this communion in a silent, contemplative joy of personal, meditative reading, theological aesthetics can be practiced as literary criticism in at least three distinct ways. First, as *the apprehension of truth:* when an accurate interpretation of a work of literature demonstrates that the text in question offers, as many do, true portrayals of both physical and metaphysical reality, that text is mediating truth to the Christian mind. There are works of sacred art that present even the most profound theological truths, but again it is part of the versatility of literature that its words and artistic structures can convey a wide variety of transcendent intellectual truth. Nor does this occur only, or even primarily, through extratextual reference; in fact, often intratextual meaning in great literature deals with important truths of human experience. The sad frequency in human life of error, as well as deliberate falsehood, the lie, means that misprision must also be expected to play its part in realistic literary *mimesis*, but we must not forget that a lie can only be recognized as such to the degree that the truth becomes known. Christian literature frequently points toward the full truth by revealing the limitations of half-truths or lies, though when a literary text does not make this progression explicit it remains possible for the evaluating Christian critic to complete the connection and still find significant intellectual value within the text. In an entirely different category, of course, are literary texts which attempt to present fully developed lies, rhetoric specifically designed to deceive; in that case, the Christian critic has no choice but to argue that the *mimesis* offered by the text represents misleading error. Again, such a judgment often has less to do with the historical or empirically verifiable depiction in a text than with its broadly intentioned portrayal of

---

[34]John Paul II, "Letter to Artists" (Vatican City: Vatican Press, 1999).

truth; a fantasy novel, for example, may use fictional creatures to foster either a false portrait of the human person or a view more consistent with creational reality.

The good. A similar dialectic occurs in the second major area of Christian theological aesthetics, *the perception of good and evil* that is possible only because of Christ's atonement for the human Fall. Even while our sinful natures undergo the continuing process of sanctification, the incarnation, crucifixion and resurrection of Christ offers full redemption from the fall out of communion with God that accompanied disobedient experience of good and evil; therefore, through Christ's teaching and example, and continued guidance by the Holy Spirit, transcendent moral as well as intellectual knowledge of our fallen condition and the possibility of our restoration by grace is possible. Often concerned with ethical dilemmas and motives, literature may present situations that require clear ethical perception and a developed interpretative argument to describe the good accurately. Once that is achieved it is possible that the moral reality revealed in the text can reflect, illuminate and lead us to moral truths intended as part of the great store of moral wisdom that is fully revealed by Christ, truths that the Holy Spirit is still teaching by myriad ways and means. Given the philosophical confusion and lack of faith characteristic of the modern world, it is unsurprising that transcendent moral criticism of this kind is not on the theoretical map of much contemporary literary theory. It is part of the work of Christian intellectuals to put it back.

Real evil and grotesque distortions of desire are part of actual reality, and it can be no part of critical realism to ignore the ubiquitous evidence. Simplistic arguments against moralistic criticism or a fear that Christian emphasis on the good will lead to a blind ignorance of evil largely result from a failure to perceive St. Augustine's teaching that evil is an *absence* of good, a shadow of reality, a half-truth. This true doctrine recasts the old aesthetic problem of how Christians ought to view evil in artistic works. First it must be stated that recognizing evil and naming it as such is a crucial Christian virtue, and on this basic level it is difficult to censor any portrayal of evil. Indeed, revealing evil to be partial, temporal and ultimately self-destructive is a central element of every Christian's echoed rebuke of Satan—"Get thee behind me" (Mt 16:23); we should expect, thus, portrayals of evil to be part of Christian literary mimesis. A very different situation is posed by literary works based on philosophies "beyond good and evil," which claim that there is no such thing as evil, or which attempt to delude or deceive by portraying evil as good.[35] Such literary works are potentially dangerous, and Christian critics should not hesitate to critique and expose an amoral or anti-Christian ethos of this kind. Such work is a valuable form of Christian literary criticism.[36]

The beautiful. Finally, a broadly intellectual and moral understanding of literature's value leads toward a third major form of Christian literary evaluation, *the perception that the intellectual truth and moral wisdom of a literary text also offers an uncommon beauty*—not a beauty that is merely temporal, materialistic or hedonistic, but rather a joyful glimpse of eternal reality. This is the joy that surprised C. S. Lewis, which even before his conversion he perceived in myth as a bittersweet experience of what in German is called *Sehnsucht*, a longing for eternity while still trapped within our world of pain and suffering.[37] This is also the joy that Tolkien sees as the central emotional effect of the ultimate and true fairy story, God's story, the gospel of Jesus Christ.[38] Within Tolkien's own epic of redemptive struggle against evil, the destruction of the false lord Sauron and his ring leads even so humble an intellect as Samwise Gamgee to perceive eternal aesthetic beauty, falling on his ears "like the echo of all the joys he had ever known":

> "How do I feel?" he cried. "Well, I don't know how to say it. I feel, I feel"—he waved his arms in the air—"I feel like spring after winter, and

---

[35]As, commonly, in philosophies derived from Friedrich Nietzsche, *Beyond Good and Evil*, trans. Marianne Cowan (Chicago: Gateway, 1955).

[36]Here too some of the best work is coming from critics who are not Christian: George Steiner's *In Bluebeard's Castle: Some Notes Towards the Redefinition of Culture* (New Haven, Conn.: Yale University Press, 1971), and, more recently, Andrew Delbanco's *The Death of Satan: How Americans Have Lost the Sense of Evil* (New York: Farrar, Straus & Giroux, 1996), offer models for how a more honest literary and cultural criticism might proceed.

[37]C. S. Lewis, *Surprised by Joy: The Shape of My Early Life* (1955; reprint, New York: Harcourt Brace, 1997), p. 7.

[38]J. R. R. Tolkien, "On Fairy-Stories," in *Tree and Leaf* (1964; reprint, London: HarperCollins, 1988), pp. 64-66.

sun on the leaves; and like trumpets and harps and all the songs I have
ever heard!"[39]

In his own half-wise way Sam Gamgee is practicing a form of Balthasar's theological aesthetics, perceiving the glory of the one true Lord
of all rings, of any natural or aesthetic objects whose beauty is ultimately intended to lead us toward him. Neither visually discernable nor
empirically provable, joy in the glimpse of eternal glory is possible in
both created nature and transcendent art, for both point us toward seeing the full truth of the communion with God in which we are ultimately intended to live. So far from being dull or static, literary art that
facilitates such communion is a place of struggle, change and conversion that Christian literary criticism is privileged to witness, describe
and celebrate.

The sheer variety and depth of Christian literary art opens fields of
critical exploration that are at once extensive and rich. What then can
be accomplished within the pages of this book? We will focus our discussion primarily on significant Christian writers but certainly also
consider many writers who are not Christian or who may be denomi-
nated as Christian only in a loose cultural sense of the adjective. We
find it necessary, moreover, to take account of some writers who are
explicitly anti-Christian. Necessarily, we must be selective in our
choices, illustrating as best we can fundamental issues and the evolution of literary consciousness rather than giving adequate accounts of
all the writers whose work is worthy. Our goal, as we have said, is simply to provide a brief traveler's guide to essential landmarks that no
Christian student of literature should fail to encounter and seek to understand. Each of the following chapters offers a historical introduction
to the authors, texts, intellectual ideas, moral issues and even some political institutions that shape Christian literary art within different historical periods. Our ordering parallels in some respects the anthologized historical curriculum familiar to many, yet it will be evident that
we are not here attempting to provide a normative literary history.

---

[39]J. R. R. Tolkien, *The Return of the King* (1955; reprint, London: HarperCollins, 1999), p.
274.

Rather, we are reflecting our conviction that it will be particularly useful for Christian students to encounter English literature as a self-correcting, midrashic conversation, to borrow a phrase from Wilson N. Brissett, who views individual literary works "as essentially commentary upon a tradition."[40] Aspects of artistic method and religious belief crucial to particular authors will also be noted as a means of distinguishing the aesthetic form of these artists' major works—the "refracted light" of subcreators, as Tolkien put it, "through whom is splintered from a single White to many hues, and endlessly combined in living shapes that move from mind to mind."[41]

We begin, accordingly, by turning to the first datum of a Christian philosophy of literature, its ontological source.

SUGGESTIONS FOR FURTHER READING

Auerbach, Eric. *Mimesis: The Representation of Reality in Western Literature.* Translated by W. R. Trask. Princeton, N.J.: Princeton University Press, 1953.

Balthasar, Hans Urs von. *The Glory of the Lord: A Theological Aesthetics.* 7 volumes. Edited by Joseph Fessio and John Riches. Translated by Andrew Louth, Francis McDonagh, Brian McNeil et al. San Francisco: Ignatius, 1982-1989.

Barratt, David, Roger Pooler and Leland Ryken. *The Discerning Reader: Christian Perspectives on Literature and Theology.* Grand Rapids: Baker, 1995.

Begbie, Jeremy. *Voicing Creation's Praise: Towards a Theology of the Arts.* Edinburgh: T & T Clark, 1991.

Borgman, Erik, Bart Philipsen, and Lea Verstricht, eds. *Literary Canons and Religious Identity.* Aldershot, U.K.: Ashgate, 2004.

Boyle, Nicholas. *Sacred and Secular Scriptures: A Catholic Approach to Literature.* Notre Dame, Ind.: University of Notre Dame Press, 2005.

Brooks, Cleanth. *Community, Religion, and Literature.* Columbia: University of Missouri Press, 1995.

Countryman, Louis William. *The Poetic Imagination: An Anglican Tradition.* Maryknoll, N.Y.: Orbis, 2002.

---

[40]Wilson N. Brissett, "Subjectivity, Revolution, Invention," *Christianity and Literature* 58, no. 2 (2009): 219.

[41]J. R. R. Tolkien, "Mythopoeia" (1931), in *Tree and Leaf: Including Mythopoeia* (New York: HarperCollins, 1988), pp. 97-101.

Daiches, David. *God and the Poets*. Oxford: Oxford University Press, 1984.

Delbanco, Andrew. *The Death of Satan: How Americans Have Lost the Sense of Evil*. New York: Farrar, Straus & Giroux, 1996.

Donoghue, Denis. *Adam's Curse: Reflections on Religion and Literature*. Notre Dame, Ind.: University of Notre Dame Press, 2001.

Eliot, T. S. "Religion and Literature." In *Essays, Ancient and Modern*. New York: Harcourt, Brace, 1936.

Edwards, Michael. *Towards a Christian Poetics*. Grand Rapids: Eerdmans, 1984.

Ferretter, Luke. *Towards a Christian Literary Theory*. London: Macmillan, 2003.

Fiddes, Paul. *Freedom and Limit: A Dialogue Between Literature and Christian Doctrine*. Basingstoke, U.K.: Macmillan, 1991.

Forde, Nigel. *The Lantern and the Looking Glass: Literature and Christian Belief*. London: SPCK, 1997.

Gallagher, Susan V., and Roger Lundin. *Literature Through the Eyes of Faith*. San Francisco: HarperCollins, 1989.

Gallagher, Susan VanZanten, and Mark Walhout, ed. *The Civic Muse: Literature and the Renewal of the Public Square*. London: Macmillan, 2000.

Girard, René. *I See Satan Fall Like Lightning*. Paris, 1999. Translated by James G. Williams. Maryknoll, N.Y.: Orbis, 2005.

Hass, Andrew, David Jasper, and Elizabeth Jay, eds. *The Oxford Handbook of English Literature and Theology*. Oxford: Oxford University Press, 2007.

Hart, David Bentley. *The Beauty of the Infinite: The Aesthetics of Christian Truth*. Grand Rapids: Eerdmans, 2004.

Jacobs, Alan. *A Theology of Reading: The Hermeneutics of Love*. Boulder, Colo.: Westview, 2001.

Jasper, David. *The Study of Literature and Religion*. Minneapolis: Fortress, 1989.

Jeffrey, David Lyle. *People of the Book: Christian Identity and Literary Culture*. Grand Rapids: Eerdmans, 1996.

Lundin, Roger. *The Culture of Interpretation: Christian Faith and the Postmodern World*. Grand Rapids: Eerdmans, 1993.

Lynch, William. *Christ and Apollo: The Dimensions of Literary Imagination*. 1960. Reprint, Wilmington, Del.: ISI, 2004.

Mariani, Paul. *God and the Imagination: On Poets, Poetry, and the Ineffable*. Athens: University of Georgia Press, 2002.

Markos, Louis. *From Achilles to Christ: Why Christians Should Read the Pagan Classics*. Downers Grove, Ill.: InterVarsity Press, 2007.

Middleton, Darren J. N. *Theology After Reading: Christian Imagination and the Power of Fiction*. Waco, Tex.: Baylor University Press, 2008.

Murphy, Francesca Aran. *Christ the Form of Beauty: A Study in Theology and Literature*. Edinburgh: T & T Clark, 1995.

Nichols, Bridget. *Literature in Christian Perspective: Becoming Faithful Readers*. London: Darton, Longman, and Todd. 2000.

Scott, Nathan, Jr., ed. *The New Orpheus: Essays Towards a Christian Poetic*. New York: Sheed & Ward, 1964.

Sherry, Patrick. *Spirit and Beauty: An Introduction to Theological Aesthetics*. Oxford: Clarendon, 1992.

Steiner, George. *Grammars of Creation*. Yale: Yale University Press, 2001.

———. *Real Presences*. London: Faber & Faber, 1991.

Thiessen, Gesa Elsbeth. *Theological Aesthetics: A Reader*. Grand Rapids: Eerdmans, 2005.

Veith, Gene Edward, Jr. *Reading Between the Lines: A Christian Guide to Literature*. Wheaton, Ill.: Crossway, 1990.

Walhout, Clarence, and Leland Ryken, eds. *Contemporary Literary Theory: A Christian Appraisal*. Grand Rapids: Eerdmans, 1991.

Wright, T. R. *Theology and Literature*. Oxford: Blackwell, 1988.

Zimmerman, Jens. *Recovering Theological Hermeneutics: An Incarnational-Trinitarian Theory of Interpretation*. Grand Rapids: Baker, 2004.

Our Literary Bible

The Bible has had a literary influence upon English literature
not because it has been considered as literature, but because it has
been considered as the report of the Word of God.

T. S. Eliot

Seeing, as we do, mostly through the lenses of our own presumptively secular, postmodern culture, we may find it counterintuitive that the history of literary criticism in English owes more to the study of the Bible than to any other source. Oddly enough, one reason we may fail to reckon with this fact is because the general influence of biblical literature and its study has been so thoroughly absorbed in the reading practices of the well-educated English reader that the traces are almost invisible. Thus, more often than not, it has been critics and theorists grown indifferent or even hostile to biblical religion yet well educated in its interpretative methods, who have most sharply perceived the persistent yet unconscious absorption of biblically derived practices and readerly expectations. Some such secular critics have regarded persistence of biblical coloration as an irritating residue of religiosity they wish to excise from contemporary literary study. Yet ironically the work of notable late twentieth-century theorists who might be expected to think this way (Harold Bloom, Jacques Derrida, Jonathan Culler, Northrop Frye, Stanley Fish and Frank Kermode, among others) owes much of its considerable explanatory power in each case to the author's recognition of

biblical literary devices and particular historic strategies of biblical interpretation, both Jewish and Christian. These factors open up a natural
and distinctive way for Christian students to engage an integration of
faith and learning in the study of English literature, namely, a primary
engagement with the Bible as a foundational literary text with massive
influence on literature in the English-speaking world.

This opportunity is not merely transient, a feature of our contemporary situation; it connects to a venerable history of critical theory and
includes a full debate between persons of biblical faith on the one hand
and opponents of biblical faith on the other. Already in the nineteenth
century, to the mind of a reader alienated from religion such as Karl
Marx, the cultural lineaments of Christian hermeneutic theory and
practice were visible and problematic. Though he was speaking primarily of Germany, not England, and of social and political institutions
rather than canonical literary texts, what Marx observed in 1844 applies to the subsequent rise of vernacular literary criticism in general:
"Criticism of religion," Marx asserts, "is the premise of all criticism."[1]
Though he was clearly an important adversary of religion, biblical religion in particular, Marx's point was in fact drawn from the mainstream
of traditional biblical hermeneutics itself. Thus, to appreciate the pertinence of his remark, to grasp the accumulated weight of the supposition
he then identified is already to acquire a better sense of the historic
relationship between biblical study and literary criticism.

Much has been written on this subject, and only a brief exemplifica-
tion is needed here to point the reader toward the extremely interesting
resources available.[2] Notably, from the beginning of our specifically
Christian literary history writers borrowed from well-known pagan literary sources to facilitate biblical study. In his foundational early Christian treatise on method for reading the sacred page, St. Augustine in-

---

[1]Karl Marx, *Early Writings*, trans. Rodney Livingstone and Gregory Benton (New York: Vin-
tage Books, 1973), p. 63.
[2]See further Henning Graf Reventlow, *The Authority of the Bible and the Rise of the Modern World*
(London: SCM, 1984); Stephen Prickett, *Words and the Word: Language, Poetics and Biblical
Interpretation* (Cambridge: Cambridge University Press, 1986); David Lyle Jeffrey, "Biblical
Scholarship and the Rise of Literary Criticism," in *Cambridge History of Literary Criticism*, ed.
Rafey Habib, vol. 6 (Cambridge: Cambridge University Press, 2011).

sisted (decisively for Western tradition) that background literary texts
and literary training for a mature understanding of Holy Scriptures
were to be found in useful measure among the secular scriptures of
Greece and Rome. The idea of literary criticism as fundamentally a
species of cultural criticism, commonplace since Marx, in fact gets
much of its early momentum from the persistent influence of Augustine's method of reading the Bible. In his day the biblical text and ways
of reading it approved by the Church were believed by both friend and
foe to have subverted the religious and political value structures of Roman culture.[3] Thus, though Augustine's *De Doctrina Christiana* recom-
mends the reading of specific classical texts (e.g., by Virgil, Homer and
Plato), hallmark works among what he thought of as the "Egyptian
gold" of classical literature, it is evident to his contemporaries on all
sides that he assumes or adopts pre-Christian literature into a canon in
which the Bible finally orders literary understanding of all texts, even
as the Bible's ultimate ethical values come to qualify or redefine their
own aesthetic norms.[4] These colonizing assumptions persist well into
the nineteenth century, where resistance to the long-standing habit are
famously evident in Matthew Arnold's *Literature and Dogma* (1873),
which adduces Augustine if only to counteract his influence.

THE BIBLE AND THE RISE OF ENGLISH LITERARY CRITICISM

English literary study is a comparatively young discipline. Matthew
Arnold was appointed professor of poetry at Oxford in 1857, becoming
the first to hold that chair to practice primarily with respect to English
rather than Greek and Latin literature. Before that, one could study
classical literature, Oriental literature or biblical theology, but literature in the English vernacular was deemed an insufficiently mature
intellectual discipline to be included in the curriculum. Yet in European universities generally, from their beginnings in the thirteenth
century until early in the nineteenth century, the relationship of the

---

[3]Augustine's massive and foundational *The City of God* was written in large part as a response
to this charge. See the discussion by Peter Brown in *Augustine of Hippo: A Biography* (Berkeley:
University of California Press, 2000), pp. 312-29.
[4]Augustine, *On Christian Doctrine*, trans. D. W. Robertson Jr. (Upper Saddle River, N.J.: Library of the Liberal Arts, 2006).

entire arts syllabus (and even the study of law) to theology, at the heart of the curriculum, had been organic and more or less taken for granted. Even in the pursuit of classical languages and Greek and Roman literatures, while what we might take to be the normative object of study was self-evidently as advertised, there was at least tacit intellectual referral back to a foundation in biblical studies. This is clear in much more than matters of common method or overlapping linguistic training. Since the time of the monastic *studium*, with more or less predictable consequences, the ultimate object of *all* of the humanities disciplines had been the elaboration of humane learning as a kind of *ancilla* to the queen of the sciences. Thus, for example, when in the twelfth century the French humanist and educational theorist Hugh of St. Victor said, "we should study . . . so that the Gospel of Christ echoes in our hearts," or when in the thirteenth century St. Bonaventure wrote up his treatise on the relationships of the intellectual disciplines to an overall plan of Christian education, calling it *The Retracing of the Arts to Theology*, or when in the fourteenth century the Italian humanist and poet Petrarch referred to theology as "poetry about God," they were each articulating a traditional view of the relationship of Scripture to the disciplines of humanistic and even scientific inquiry in which biblical study provided the benchmark for method and the point at which the other disciplines came to a unity of truth.[5] Much in this traditional perspective remained normative for centuries, even as over time the conscious strength of it weakened. Isaac Newton, in the *Scholium Generale* appended to his *Philosophiae naturalis principia mathematica* (1713), connected his mechanics and his views of absolute time and space to a conception of God that these presuppose, and his cosmogony and theories of number are reiterated rather matter-of-factly in his commentaries on the biblical books of Daniel and Revelation.[6] In not dissimilar fashion, though it is seldom noticed now, the inter-

---

[5]For a general overview of this medieval Christian approach to Scripture and learning, see David Lyle Jeffrey, *People of the Book: Christian Identity and Literary Culture* (Grand Rapids: Eerdmans, 1996), chaps. 5-6.

[6]F. E. Manuel, *Isaac Newton, Historian* (Cambridge, Mass.: Harvard University Press, 1963), and, by the same author, *The Religion of Isaac Newton* (Oxford: Oxford University Press, 1974), are reliable accounts.

pretation of the Bible played a formative role in the philosophical thinking of Hobbes, Locke and Spinoza, as well as in the literary theory of John Dennis, for example, *The Grounds of Criticism in Poetry* (1704), William Wordsworth's *Prelude* (1805, 1850) and, of course, Coleridge's *Biographia Literaria* (1817), *Confessions of an Inquiring Spirit* and *The Statesman's Manual*.[7] But by the beginning of the nineteenth century, for a complex of reasons rehearsed by Henning Graf Reventlow and Hans Frei, among others, the status of the Bible as a kind of epistemological benchmark in legal, political, philosophical and literary thinking was coming to an end, along with confidence in its divine inspiration and inerrancy.[8] In Matthew Arnold's *Literature and Dogma* (1873) the traditional link between biblical and other forms of literary criticism is broken: it is quite precisely the intellectual authority of the Bible that Arnold wishes not merely to call into question, but now, especially at the religious level, finally to demolish.

THE BIBLE AS LITERATURE

Ironically perhaps, the attention recently given by literary theorists and critics to the residual and, as they often suspect, subversive influence of the Bible and biblical criticism, especially on such diverse schools as the New Critics, historical criticism and classical Marxism, has resulted in an unexpected return to literary criticism of the Bible itself among critics whose work had previously been primarily in English or some other modern literature.[9] A remarkable body of worthwhile study has resulted, the insight and tenor of which is typically marked by rejection of much of the modern critical method in formal biblical scholarship as still practiced by scholars in that discipline. In a fashion which would have surprised Arnold, who thought that Germanic biblical scholarship had forever undermined notions of literary unity in specific biblical books, many recent critics (e.g., Robert Alter, Meir Sternberg, Harold Fisch, David Damrosch, Frank Kermode) have found the textual

---

[7]Anthony Harding, *Coleridge and the Inspired Word* (Kingston, Ont.: McGill-Queens, 1985). See also Stephen Prickett, *Romanticism and Religion: The Tradition of Coleridge and Wordsworth in the Victorian Church* (Cambridge: Cambridge University Press, 1976).
[8]Prickett, *Words and the Word*, pp. 37-94.
[9]See "Suggestions for Further Reading" at the end of this chapter.

criticism that arose following Johann Gottfried Herder, Ludwig Feuerbach and Friedrich Schleiermacher, along with such nineteenth-century text-critical devices as the documentary hypothesis (JEPD) associated with Karl Heinrich Graf and Julius Wellhausen in particular, to be of marginal value for any serious *literary* appreciation of the Bible.[10] Rather, in works such as Alter's *The Art of Biblical Narrative* and *The Art of Biblical Poetry* the primary texts are examined with the refined skills of historical and philological criticism, essentially the methods approved by early Christian exegetes such as Augustine. The results have been remarkably invigorating for both biblical and literary study, and, along with the earlier work of structuralists such as Northrop Frye in his *The Great Code*, and of formalists such as Frank Kermode in his *The Genesis of Secrecy*, this secular criticism has helped bring formal study of the Bible as literature back into the traditional humanities curriculum (not so much the religious studies curriculum) around the world. While the pages that follow do not owe to these scholars' methods directly, they bear a genuine indebtedness to their contributions.

We are not, of course, suggesting that these contemporary critics provide sufficient insight for students of literature in a Christian context. We are sympathetic with the views of T. S. Eliot and C. S. Lewis, each of whom counseled that to study the Bible as just another literary volume and not as the Word of God is to miss entirely the self-evident character of the text.[11] It is probably the case that most of the "Bible as Literature" scholars thus far mentioned would position themselves outside of any religious tradition; many explicitly deny belief in the religious authority of the Bible taken as Holy Scripture. This posture, an epistemological limitation when considered from the viewpoint of many

---

[10]According to this theory, the mosaic of books as we have them represent an amalgamation of four separate textual traditions, designated for their supposed dominance of concern or language as Jahwist, Elohist, Priestly and Deuteronomist.

[11]Eliot wrote that "the Bible has had a *literary* influence upon English literature *not* because it has been considered as literature, but because it has been considered as the report of the Word of God" (T. S. Eliot, "Religion and Literature," in *Selected Prose*, ed. John Hayward [New York: Penguin, 1953], pp. 32-33). C. S. Lewis, "The Literary Impact of the Authorized Version," *They Asked for a Paper* (London: Geoffrey Bless, 1962), pp. 26-50, esp. 48-49, takes essentially the same view. For a review of the emerging "Bible as Literature" school see David Lyle Jeffrey, "The Bible as Literature in the 1980s: A Guide for the Perplexed," *University of Toronto Quarterly* 59, no. 4 (1990): 569-80.

of our most prominent poets, dramatists and other writers for whom the Bible is the Book of books, is, on our own view as well, likely to prevent understanding even of their *literary* accomplishment at critical junctures. Accordingly, our considered intent in this chapter is circumscribed: we want to try to reflect the understanding of prominent confessional authors down through literary history for whom the Bible has been spiritually authoritative, and therefore to refer pertinently to a theological understanding of the Bible shared by them and still available to us.

LITERARY FEATURES OF THE BIBLE

To acquire an appreciative understanding of the Bible as a literary foundation, we may begin quite simply in a reflection on the most obvious of literary features in terms of which the text of the Bible as we have it invites us to read it. In the pages that follow we suggest to thoughtful students that they refresh themselves on the biblical passages which serve as examples as we take up the following elements of biblical narrative and poetics: (1) binary construction, (2) archetypal narrative, (3) grand narrative, (4) covenant history, (5) the relationship between history and allegory, (6) confessional autobiography, (7) etiological or eponymous narration, (8) poetic language and biblical wisdom, (9) parables, (10) internal skepticism concerning the limits of literary language. We need additionally to consider, as we go along, typology, ironic reversal, the relationship of divine providence and irony, and, finally, the view projected by all of the Bible that time and history are finite. There is, of course, much more to reflect on, but for our introductory purposes this much must suffice.

1. Binary construction. A typical complaint of deconstructionists about literature of the Bible and texts in biblical tradition is that they are characteristically binary, positing either-or choices and characterizations.[12] The charge is clearly warranted, and on multiple accounts. At the very outset of the biblical narrative Adam and Eve are faced with a choice to either obey or disobey. The reader is then obliged to see

---

[12]See John M. Ellis, *Against Deconstruction* (Princeton, N.J.: Princeton University Press, 1989), for a considered criticism.

in the story of Cain and Abel that stark choices appear in everything from how one expresses gratitude to God to how one deals with disapproval. Even as the waters of the deep are separated from the dry land (Gen 1:9) and day from night (Gen 1:14), so also male is distinguished from female (Gen 1:27), morning from evening (Gen 1:5) and, ultimately, life from death: "I have set before you life and death, blessing and cursing," says Moses in Deuteronomy, "therefore choose life, that both thou and thy seed may live" (Deut 30:19).

For some modern critics of the biblical worldview such a basic binary construction of reality is too rigid, suggesting a species of the black-white fallacy. Surely, they suggest, it would be more realistic to show that there are shades, positions between these stark alternatives (e.g., casual torpor, sexual ambiguity, any state unwilled or indeterminate between life and death). A dramatic exemplar of this resistance to binaries is the play *Fin de Partie (Endgame)* (1957) by Samuel Beckett, in which no character is able to form a complete action or make a decision, and all live in a context where one is unable to discern between day and night, past and present, or ultimately even between life and death.

Anyone who reads the story of Abraham (Gen 12–25) will be struck by the way binary oppositions characterize that narrative at every turn: Lot goes down to the cities of the plain, Abraham takes to the hills; paired characters such as Hagar and Sarah or Ishmael and Isaac represent oppositions that will permeate the entire history of the Jewish people as well as, at least in the Jewish view, that of their neighbors. Likewise in Deuteronomy the formulas for blessings and curses on the covenant people make explicit that, as in the story of creation and Fall, the world the characters live in operates as a kind of moral ecology; obedience and faithfulness to the Lord will result in fruitfulness and health for both the people and the land (Deut 7:12-15; 11:13-15; 28:1-14), whereas disobedience and alienation of the affections from God will result in barrenness and disease for both the people and the land (Deut 11:16-17; 28:15-68). At the very least we can see from these passages that, on the biblical view, human moral choices have critical consequences both for those who choose, and for everything and everyone around them. Obedience to the Creator is critical to enjoyment of his creation, and spiritual holiness turns out to be inextricably related to wholeness or health in the natural and social order.

2. *Archetypal narrative*. One of the insights available to those who do close textual analysis of Genesis is the discovery that the forms of writing in what appears to us now as one literary entity prove to be composite, that we have in this book several distinct genres. Because the original Hebrew text is written without helpful spacing between words, let alone breaks in the narrative, and even without the vowels within words indicated anywhere until manuscripts of the European Middle Ages, these genre forms were not immediately apparent even to experienced readers of the Greek and Latin translations. This remains true elsewhere in the Bible even for obvious poetry, such as the Psalms, Song of Songs and parts of Isaiah. We might expect to see short lines set off with meter and rhyme perhaps, but because Hebrew poetry does not use rhyme and is marked by quite different forms of internal music and word play, translation into Greek, Latin, and modern vernaculars such as English has typically represented as continuous prose texts, or portions of text, that are in fact more proximate to various species or genres of poetry.[13] In Genesis 1:1–2:3 the actual form of the composition is a type of hymn or anthem in praise of the creation; it functions in Genesis much like the opening theme in a musical canon (such as Pachelbel's "Canon in D," a concerto allegro, or a fugue, such as J. S. Bach's "Prelude and Fugue in A Minor"): exposition of the original theme recurs in related keys as well as reiteration of the tonic, even though the musical episodes may appear individually as solo sections. Such a passage establishes a tone of celebratory anticipation for what follows.

This diversity in forms of expression also helps to account for the somewhat more elaborate "second version" of the creation story (Gen 2:4–3:24). The reader may well wonder why modern chapter divisions do not now accord neatly with this shift in genre. Here it is helpful to know that the chapter and verse divisions we are accustomed to were not present in the original texts of the Old Testament (or of the New Testa-

---

[13]Indispensable here is Robert Alter's *The Art of Biblical Poetry* (New York: Basic Books, 1985).

ment either). These were demarcations for convenience of scholastic study, introduced in the thirteenth century by Archbishop of Canterbury Stephen Langton, among others. Because these demarcations were inserted into Latin translations in which nuances of Hebrew in particular had been obscured, the modern divisions, however conventional, can now seem in any number of instances rather oddly misplaced.

The term *history* in some modern English translations of Genesis 2:4 is helpful in directing us toward the first shift of literary form in beginning the second version of the creation story. Actually, this new narrative does not really repeat the first account so much as take up the theme of the *introitus* in a different and, to our imaginations, more human way of understanding, suggesting how the far distant beginnings of our kind fit in relation to the creation as a whole. But the word *history* (e.g., NKJV) or, as in some translations "account" (NIV), needs a bit of explaining. In Hebrew the word is literally *generations* (as in the KJV—Heb. *toledot*); what we have here may be understood as "genealogical narrative," and in that rather specific sense, originary history. (In Genesis 2:4 the genealogical history is of "the heavens and of the earth"; the latter term, used also in Genesis 1:1, is actually a Sumerian borrowing, a rhetorical phrasing called *merismus,* which means something like "the cosmos.") *Toledot*—whether rendered "These are the generations" or "This is the history"—is a different introductory phrase than found in Genesis 1:1, *bereshit* which, since it lacks the definite article, might better be translated as a story-telling term: "by way of beginning," or "to begin with."[14] What these philological considerations would seem to imply for the first part of Genesis is less an indication of absolute temporal beginning than the basic fact of God's creative activity as the proper starting point for our understanding of all that follows, a point which Augustine seems to have intuited in his remark, "Not *in* time but *with* time God shaped the world."[15] When we come to the story of Abraham at Genesis 11:27, the term *toledot*, "these are the gen-

---

[14]See R. K. Harrison, *International Standard Bible Encyclopedia*, rev. ed. (Grand Rapids: Eerdmans, 1979), 2:438.

[15]Augustine *The City of God* 11.6 (emphasis added). A convenient modern edition is that prepared for the Cambridge Texts in the History of Political Thought series, ed. R. W. Dyson (Cambridge: Cambridge University Press, 1998).

erations," occurs again, this time introducing the narratives of Abraham, Isaac and Jacob, which are presented consecutively as a family history in much richer, place-specific detail than we have in the preceding chapters.

As Erich Auerbach has famously observed, "though the human beings in the biblical stories have greater depths of time, fate, and consciousness than do the human beings in Homer," in terms of language, when we compare biblical discourse with the ornate epic diction of Homer, even the most open of biblical narrative is spare, even minimalist.[16] This very minimalism has been enormously fruitful, however; much subsequent literary creativity in the biblical tradition has been occasioned by a desire to fill in the gaps. Ironically then, for imaginative responses to ancient literature over the ensuing centuries, less has proven to be more; biblical narrative has been far more foundational than classical story in the growth of Western literary tradition, not least because it has left more scope for creative representation.

It is possible to refine our sense of the central stories in Genesis and their literary form still further. For example, the first appearance of the word *book* in the Bible, in Genesis 5:1, "this is the book of the generations of Adam," has a word for "book" in Hebrew *(sepher)* which may in this context mean "clay tablet." But for the purposes of our literary introduction it will suffice to appreciate that the narratives from Genesis 2:4 of Adam and Eve, Cain and Abel, Noah and the Flood, as well as of the Tower of Babel, are literarily parallel in genre neither to the patriarchal history which comes after Genesis 11:27 nor to the creation hymn, which acts as an *introitus* to Genesis. For the sake of grasping the significance of this difference, we can think profitably of the early stories as archetypal narratives, stories that give us profound insight into the general human condition, not merely into the particular family associated with Abraham.[17]

Each of these foundational narratives establishes major themes of the wider biblical anthology, albeit in cryptic fashion. Adam (literally

---

[16]Erich Auerbach, *Mimesis: The Representation of Reality in Western Literature*, trans. Willard Trask (1956; reprint, Princeton, N.J.: Princeton University Press, 1968), p. 12.

[17]Cf. the tribes and nations listed in Gen 11.

"a man") is created from the "dust of the ground," the dirt at his feet (Heb. *adamah*). Adam's "humanity" is thus said to be in Hebrew, as in Latin, composed not only of the breath of God, but of the "humus," the soil which he will come in time to work (Gen 3:19, 23). He is *Adam/adamah*—of the earth, earthy. His wife, lifted organically from his own corporeal being and thus "flesh of his flesh," is called in the first account simply *isha*, "female." But after their transgression and at the brink of their expulsion from the unblemished Garden in which they had been placed, she is named by Adam "Eve" (Gen 3:20), which means "life," because, as the narrator puts it, she was to be the mother of all living. How ironic that just at the moment when our first parents have been condemned to experience suffering and death, Adam names his wife "Life." The gesture might seem to be charged with hope despite their recent experience of expulsion, or perhaps of desire overshadowed with a deep sense of loss, for all subsequent "Eves" will not only give life but also die, and in their turn their spouses and children will likewise pass away. Our very need for history, for "genealogical narrative," is predicated on this reality. To put it another way, this archetypal story explains our need for another kind of story.

It is in our human nature that we like to name things. By naming them we bring other created realities into a more intimate relationship with ourselves. The story of Adam as a kind of primal biologist joyously naming the animals, experiencing thus the freedom to which his Creator invites him (Gen 2:19-20), and the story of his poignant naming of his wife Eve both have a deep explanatory power. They tell us something about our inner nature, even our nature as participants, albeit imperfectly, made in the "image of God." By our creative use of the imagination we recollect our first purpose; by our creativity and procreation we experience our intended potential both as a deep yearning or desire and also as joyous exuberance in giving birth to something new. Artistic impulse is basic to both aspects of "naming" as reflected in the Genesis narrative; it may be that the artist's desire to make poems and stories arises out of pretty much the same impulse as the desire to bear children.[18]

---

[18]For a thoughtful study of the relationship between language and desire see George Steiner's *After Babel: Aspects of Language and Translation* (New York: Oxford University Press, 1975).

And so with the other early stories in Genesis from 2:4 through chapter 11. The story of Cain and Abel connects with us because at a deep psychological level we recognize in ourselves the potential for violence arising from envy, for the way in which sibling rivalry bespeaks as clearly as anything in our experience the defective character of our affections. In fact, defective violations of the creative spirit can grow to such a pitch that love becomes degraded to raw lust, while envy and individual rivalries, issuing from what the anthropological critic René Girard has called "mimetic desire," metastasize into anarchic violence.[19] The moral contagion described archetypally in Genesis 6 has in the fallen world become so pervasive that creation itself is contaminated, and divine judgment falls upon it in the form of a massive purgation, the flood. Though God in mercy redeems a remnant (another major theme in the Bible), and although he provides a new beginning, the human bent toward degrading every kind of creational good will recur again and again; indeed, the world can only persist because God repeatedly redeems a remnant, seed for a new creation. A universal propensity for sinful corruption of the good, and the evident human incapacity to stem the tide of its ravages, is again and again both the occasion and the subject of biblical stories. A particular recitative on these themes in psychological and philosophical language more proximate to us occurs in Paul's letter to the Romans, where he says,

> For the wrath of God is revealed from heaven against all ungodliness and unrighteousness of men, who hold the truth in unrighteousness;
>
> Because that which may be known of God is manifest in them; for God hath shewed it unto them.
>
> For the invisible things of him from the creation of the world are clearly seen, being understood by the things that are made, *even* his eternal power and Godhead; so that they are without excuse:
>
> Because that, when they knew God, they glorified him not as God, neither were thankful; but became vain in their imaginations, and their foolish heart was darkened.

---

[19]René Girard, *I See Satan Fall Like Lightning*, trans. James G. Williams (Maryknoll, N.Y.: Orbis, 2001).

Professing themselves to be wise, they became fools,

And changed the glory of the uncorruptible God into an image made like to corruptible man, and to birds, and four-footed beasts, and creeping things.

Wherefore God also gave them up to uncleanness, through the lusts of their own hearts, to dishonor their own bodies between themselves:

Who changed the truth of God into a lie, and worshipped and served the creature more than the Creator, who is blessed for ever. Amen. (Rom 1:18-25)

Thus, the normative spiritual condition of humankind, described here in language that calls to mind the creaking ark of Noah, with its cramped, weary and bellowing cargo tossing on the flood, is seen to be what Paul elsewhere describes as the whole creation groaning and laboring "with birth pangs" (Rom 8:22 NKJV), yearning for redemption and release, when, figuratively, the doors of the ark are opened and its inhabitants spring, wide-eyed, out into the light of a brand new world. When these Genesis narratives are read in the light of the New Testament their archetypal character becomes particularly evident.

So, finally, one comes to the disturbing story of the Tower of Babel. Here powerful men build a city and a tower whose top is to reach "into the heavens": the tower symbolizes an aspiration to achieve divine grandeur by the exercise of human power. "Let us make us a name" (Gen 11:4) is, perhaps, as much as to say, "let us become self-made men, owing gratitude to none," or "let us redefine human identity in our own terms." The consequence of God's displeasure with such ungrateful hubris is a massive confusion of the builders' terms, even their possibility of communicating with one another. Babel (Babylonian, "gate of God") becomes itself redefined (the name in Hebrew means "gate of confusion") under the supervening divine judgment. Thus, the Tower of Babel, whether in ancient or modern perspective, is archetypally symbolic of social fragmentation like unto that in the Fall itself, namely a loss of communion, community and even, finally, of communication. This view is echoed at various levels in writings from the sermons of Gregory the Great to modern novels such as *Le Fosse de Babel* by Raymond Abellio or the linguistic theory of George Steiner in *After Babel: Studies in*

Language and Translation.[20] But the depth of human confusion to which Babel stands as an archetypal witness cannot fully be measured until we recollect it in the light of the New Testament narrative, which is both commentary and correction. This is, of course, the story of Pentecost (Acts 2), with the descent of the Holy Spirit upon the apostles and Mary, that one who (in a moment also archetypal) said "Be it unto me according to thy word" (Lk 1:38). Pentecost is thus the birthday of the church, in which communion, community and communication, through obedience and love, can begin to be restored.

3. Grand narrative. The presence of several different types of writing in the Bible should not blind us to its dominant and remarkable overarching literary framework. Considered holistically the Bible tells a grand narrative of human redemption. In periods of developed biblical literacy, such as among the fathers of the church, the writers of the high Middle Ages, or the Protestant Reformers and some of their successors through to the nineteenth century, the great story lines of the Bible were relished as powerful literature in their own right. Extensive series of sermons on the Pentateuch or on the books of the kings of Israel are among the greatest interpretative commentary in Christian tradition, extending from Augustine, Ambrose, Jerome, Gregory and Bede through to the benchmark commentaries of Luther, Melanchthon, Calvin, Beza and Cornelius Lapide, globally reflecting on the entirety of sacred Scripture as a grand history of human salvation (Lat. *Humana historia salvationis*). This is true for both Catholics and Protestants—indeed, all traditional Christians. In a text like Augustine's *Confessions* we see that in an autobiographical reconstruction of his own life, his preconversion experience (bks. 1-9) is structured in such a way as to draw upon the pattern of Genesis 1–3, to which he turns in a close theological analysis (bks. 12-13). Something much like this happens for the whole biblical grand narrative in the structure of the eighteenth-century novel *Tom Jones* by Henry Fielding. The idea that the Bible provides a template for all of human history is reflected in the way in which, well into the twentieth century, printers inserted blank pages

---

[20]See Raymond Abellio, *La Fosse de Babel* (Paris: Gallimard, 1962).

for personal family histories of Bible owners, often between the closing words of Malachi in the Old Testament and the genealogy of Jesus in the opening of Matthew's Gospel. Both spiritually and imaginatively, individual family histories were seen as somehow connected to the great history of all the families of the Bible.[21]

By the nineteenth century, just before the time of Matthew Arnold, this strong sense of the Bible as composing, out of many stories, a larger or universal narrative, had been largely abandoned.[22] First, many seminary professors and other biblical critics, initially in Germany, then in England and America, narrowed their own focus to technical problems of textual transmission; still others shifted from biblical study to concerns of a more psychological nature, in particular to practical problems of pastoral care. In evangelical churches, where ostensibly the Bible still held its place as supreme authority, there was a tendency to package verses or segments as proof texts for doctrine, and gradually to ignore large sections of the biblical canon, especially of the Hebrew Scriptures, or Old Testament. More recently, as successive waves of new, colloquial and culturally specific translations and paraphrases have begun to appear (Bibles for teenage girls, green-letter Bibles for the environmentally conscious, gender-neutral Bibles and so forth, many at best ephemeral and at worst a crass commercial venture ultimately disrespectful of the text), *actual knowledge* of biblical narrative among the target readership has been rapidly disappearing, even among many in those churches which would have once described themselves as "biblical." The loss to active memory of biblical narrative in Christian churches on all sides, however, has been a fact of signal importance for both the teacher and the student of literature. Whereas Bible reading in the family and the public proclamation and interpretation of Scripture were once the foundation of literary education in Western culture, so that authors could depend on knowledge of the Bible as furniture al-

---

[21]Sometimes writers are able to make use of the association in fruitful fashion; for a brief study of some examples, see David Lyle Jeffrey, "Biblical Hermeneutic and Literary History in Modern Canadian Fiction," *Mosaic* 11, no. 3 (1978): 87-106.

[22]This history is closely documented in Hans Frei, *The Eclipse of Biblical Narrative: A Study in Eighteenth and Nineteenth Century Hermeneutics* (New Haven, Conn.: Yale University Press, 1974).

ready in the minds of their readers, this is now no longer the case; the minds of most readers, even Christian readers, are furnished (often badly) with other stuff.

When Jean-François Lyotard famously remarked (in 1979) on the disappearance of any overarching metanarrative in postmodern Western culture, his remarks were occasioned not only by the then obvious eclipse of biblical narrative, but the more recent and, for many postmoderns, more painful demise of the grand utopian narrative of Marxism, soon enough to be made politically cataclysmic in the fall of the old Soviet Union.[23] It seems that no replacement narrative of redemption has emerged in the developed West: fleeting images and diverting entertainments—hardly more than palliative distractions—have typically occupied the place either Christian or Marxist categories of future hope once held.

From a purely literary point of view, a loss of cultural memory is as disastrous as a loss of future hope and tends to go along with it. It means that, effectively, there is nothing much in many readers' minds for a great author to build upon, apart from a variety of ephemeral, diverting, typically ambiguous images. And if the images dominant in our imaginations are disconnected, or worse, mutually contradictory, it can seem that we live in a world that has lost its story. Nevertheless, even in such fragmented times, when an exceptional storyteller with a rich store of cultural memory comes along and creates a parallel story of human redemption, an instance of fictional grand narrative with inevitable obligations to the ideas, structure and ultimate truths of the biblical grand narrative, the work can meet a profound register of felt need in readers and authors alike. The extraordinary popularity of Tolkien's *The Lord of the Rings* is perhaps the greatest illustration of this principle in twentieth-century literature.

That said, for a Christian student of literature and literary history, there can be no substitute for a recovery of the undergirding biblical grand narrative itself. Obviously, true recovery would mean reading

---

[23]An address given at Quebec City to the assembled presidents and chancellors of Canadian public universities, "La Condition Postmoderne," later published in translation by the University of Minnesota Press as *The Postmodern Condition* (1984).

and studying pretty much the whole of the Bible, becoming acquainted with the entirety of this grand symphony from beginning to end, much as is suggested by the 2008 public reading, consecutively without pause, of the entire Bible in Rome.[24] There is inherently something more than merely literary, of course, about such a concerted effort.

For one thing, strictly speaking, the Bible is not a book in the ordinary sense of the term at all, but a large anthology of books. These books were written over a millennium or more by both Jewish and Gentile authors in three languages—Hebrew, Aramaic and Greek. The name given to this anthology, the Bible, derives from the Greek word *byblos* (inner bark of papyrus), in the plural *biblia* (sometimes confused because of identity in form with the genitive singular), which came to be the normative name for this collection of books. Jerome, as he was translating, called it *biblioteca divina*, "the divine library." A long-standing perception of overarching unity—regarding this whole library as if it were a single book—arises from the way the biblical books build upon each other as they engage an unfolding sense of an ultimate authorial presence, working in and through the manifold histories and poems, shaping them toward a fullness of meaning that casts a light of understanding back over the collection as a whole. Echo, reiteration and resonance lend to all of the Bible's diverse textual components a kind of retrospective coherence predicated on our sense, as readers, that the various narrative promises of more to come and understanding in "the fulness of the time" (Gal 4:4; Eph 1:10) have led up to a point at which the reader can not only discern a master plan somehow present all along in the Bible, but see this design as reflecting that governance and sovereignty of history itself, which the theologians call providence.

What all of this really comes to, in literary terms, is a sense emerging ineluctably from the text of the whole Bible, despite all of the misdirec-

---

[24]As this book was being written, Pope Benedict XVI was meeting in Rome with bishops from around the world to consider what might be done to restore knowledge of the Bible. Beginning with the pope himself reading the opening words of Genesis, there followed a continuous public reading of the entire Bible over a period of six days in which not only clerics but prominent laypersons from Jewish as well as Christian traditions participated. This seems a remarkable, albeit symbolic, development.

tion and contingent behavior the individual stories contain, of an overarching authorial hand in the composition and preservation of the text
as we have it. Even literary critics outside the faith sometimes have an
inescapable sense of this unity, and regard it as a remarkable literary
phenomenon.[25] Such a sense of a "presence" projected from the text and
alive in the community of its careful readers down through history is
sometimes referred to by Christian theologians as evidence of the work
of the Holy Spirit. What is meant in such a phrase is a conviction not
only that the Spirit of God was at work in directing the writers of the
Bible but also that his Spirit remains present, alive in the church, its
community of faithful interpreters, those readers who are in the way of
deep meaning because they have allowed the grand narrative of salvation history to be the encompassing matrix for their own personal stories as well. It is not only literary unity, then, but also continuity of
faithful identity that matters. When Christians of a previous generation sang "Tell me the old, old story, . . . that I have loved so long," this
was the sense of enclosure and meaning that they cherished and from
which arose their trust in a providential hand of guidance in their own
lives. Put in another way, it anchored their expectation of meaning in
history, even their own personal history, and to sing of it or to call it to
mind was a source of comfort.[26]

   4. Covenant and continuity. How might an appreciation of biblical
grand narrative, as familiar to our grandparents as to the great authors
of our literary history, be recovered by us today? Well, some of us think,
perhaps unsurprisingly, by reading the Bible, book by book, beginning
with Genesis and persevering to the end. This is also an ideal preparation for a Christian study of literature. Whether it happens formally in
classes in the liberal arts curriculum or informally, perhaps as a summer
reading project, this effort can be enriched if one is alert to certain narrative signposts that will help mark out a readerly map.

   One of the most important of these signposts is the idea of covenant

---

[25]Northrop Frye has commented on this effect of the compendium in his *The Great Code: The Bible and Literature* (Toronto: Academic Press, 1982).

[26]A recent novel that captures this sense very well is Marilynne Robinson's Pulitzer Prize–winning *Gilead* (New York: Farrar, Straus & Giroux, 2004).

(Heb. *berith*). From early on in the book of Genesis, covenants between God and principal characters in the various stories are both a major subject of the Bible and also a means of linking these individual narratives into one continuous whole. In fact, there may be no single narrative device more important in all of the Bible. A covenant is essentially a kind of binding agreement, a pact whereby parties commit to an ongoing relationship and shared history. The first of these is a commitment made by God to Noah and his family after the flood, and it takes the form of a renewal of the blessing given to Adam and Eve before the Fall (Gen 9:1-17; cf. Gen 1:28). This is called a *berith*, but in fact the commitments to future blessing are all made on God's side. The covenant with Abram recorded in Genesis 12 is different, consequent on Abram's obedience to God's call to leave his city and become a pilgrim, trusting in God to provide for him and his family future blessings (Gen 12:1-3). This covenant is renewed as Abram journeys, stage by stage (e.g., Gen 13:15; 15:18-20); even after Abram has doubted God's promise of a son and heir by natural means, and so accepted Sarah's substitution of her handmaiden Hagar, it is renewed once more (Gen 17:1-8). (God makes a covenant also with the Egyptian bondservant Hagar concerning her son Ishmael's progeny [Gen 16:10-12].) When, in prospect of Isaac's birth, God renews his covenant with Abram he renames him Abraham (Gen 17:5). The name itself is future oriented; it means "father of many nations." This new covenant identity requires of Abraham a reciprocal and specific obligation, circumcision of each male in the lineage, as a "sign of the covenant" that is valid not only for Abraham but for his descendents after him. The subsequent miraculous birth of Isaac and all that follows in the history of the patriarchs—Jacob, Joseph and onward—is both marked out and projected forward by the covenant. It is as though each reiteration marks a new chapter, each generation's experience saying that though individuals may complete their story and die, the end is not yet. The reader must press forward to the next story.

The idea that each of the biblical narratives contains in some fashion the seed of a story to follow is nicely pointed up by a merely human covenant between Abraham and his servant. It occurs a few years after the terrible test of Abraham's obedience and Isaac's trust on the mountain of Moriah, where God provided in the very nick of time a substitutionary sacrifice (Gen 22). Sarah has died, Abraham is old, and he wants Isaac to be able to marry. So he makes a covenant with his "oldest servant" to find Isaac a wife among his own kinsmen. This oath is sealed humanly by the gesture of the servant placing his hand "under the thigh" of Abraham while he pledges his fealty. This gesture we know from other ancient Near-Eastern depictions to have been, in fact, a placing of the hand under the testicles, so that figuratively the covenant agreement becomes binding on not only the individuals who make it but their descendants after them (Gen 24:1-3, 9). (The Latin word which we sometimes use for "covenant" is *testament*, and in both legal and literary contexts it still carries this binding intergenerational character, associated with the root word *testes*, as in someone's "last will and testament.") But in all of these examples the point is to indicate that there is more to follow.

It will be apparent to the reader of the larger biblical narrative that there is always a deeply inscribed sense that, at the end of any given life or story we read about in the overall narrative of the Bible, we are to understand that "the end is not yet." Even though there may be at the end of many of these stories a kind of settledness in respect of meaning and significance for the circumstances of some of the characters, nevertheless the reader will also sense a certain yearning for a sense of closure or completeness that no individual story, even a story like Abraham's, can entirely provide. In this way it can be fairly said that biblical narrative, even from the very beginning, looks toward an end far off on another horizon. Its sense of time is as of a quantum, gradually filling up toward a completeness not entirely foreseen but nonetheless already brimming with meaning and prompting the anticipation of more meaning to come. Qoheleth, the Teacher in Ecclesiastes, writes: "He has made everything beautiful in its time. He has also set eternity in the hearts of men; yet they cannot fathom what God has done from beginning to end" (Eccles 3:11 NIV). Our desire for meaning is aroused by meaning, even by all things beautiful, yet in our appreciation of beauty we feel an infinite, often inarticulate longing for an experience of ultimate closure we cannot yet grasp. It is a sign, perhaps, of our fallen mortality as much as of our immortal destiny. "Men perish," said the pre-Socratic Greek philosopher Alcaemon, "because they cannot join the beginning with the end." But in an evocative and reiterated saying of Jesus in the last book of the Christian Bible we get a sense of where such a longed for conjoining or closure must come from: "I am Alpha and Omega, the beginning and the ending, saith the Lord, which is, and which was, and which is to come, the Almighty" (Rev 1:8; cf. 21:6; 22:13). What God has done from beginning to end he will one day make clear to those who have eyes to see and ears to hear, when that one described as "the author and finisher of our faith . . . is set down at the right hand of the throne of God" (Heb 12:2). From that place and culminating point he will read the entire book, all that is "written within and on the backside" (Rev 5:1-10). All of time and history are here figured under the symbol of a book. In poetic figure, this is the essence of a grand narrative vision: history *sub specie aeternitas*—or history as transcendent poetry.

5. History and allegory: **Semper in figura loquens.** "When the fulness of time was come," Paul writes retrospectively, "God sent forth his Son, made of a woman, made under the law, To redeem them that were under the law" (Gal 4:4-5). That is, God's eventual disclosure of his grand narrative purpose is in Jesus. It is because of Jesus' sacrifice that not only Jews but also Gentiles can find a place in the grand narrative, for "if ye be Christ's, then are ye Abraham's seed, and heirs according to the promise" (Gal 3:29). Paul briefly retells the story of Abraham, Hagar, Sarah, Ishmael and Isaac as an allegory, so as to distinguish between "two covenants; the one from the mount Sinai, which gendereth to bondage, which is [Hagar]" and the other which is symbolized in Sarah and Isaac, here identified as "Jerusalem which is above," which is free (Gal 4:22-31). By treating the Genesis account from the life of Abraham as an *allegoria* (Gal 4:24) Paul is not in any sense discounting the value of the Abrahamic family history as real history. Rather, he is depending on his readers' deep appreciation for this ancient story to draw a distinction between two much larger covenants, the covenants of law and grace (or, we might say, of the Old Testament and New Testament.) But this way of understanding the dramatic reversal of expectations occasioned by Paul's exegesis is absolutely dependent on understanding of the Genesis story and the covenants that link them together. Paul then suggests that in Christ the meaning of salvation history has been fulfilled in such a way that the new covenant inaugurates a liberty (foreseen in Isaac), while the old covenant has become a kind of servitude (foreshadowed in Ishmael). This reversal was shocking to Jewish readers and yet illuminating in a way that no reader deprived of the Genesis narrative could discern. Its implications for Paul's immediate hearers was that rather than look backward, hoping for a return to the literal, historical Jerusalem, they should look forward and above for the heavenly Jerusalem to come. This too is history *sub specie aeternitas*.

It is in this larger future orientation of biblical grand narrative that we begin to appreciate how it is that the Bible is always giving us representative stories of deliverance, liberation from bondage, which—whether from Pharaoh in Egypt or the Babylonian captivity—foreshadow other reversals in which the fallen are raised, the underdog eventually wins, and ultimately death is defeated in the resurrection of Christ, the definitive liberation. Even in a single verse at the outset of the Ten Commandments, God identifies himself as the author of such liberation: "I am the LORD thy God, which have brought thee . . . out of the house of bondage" (Ex 20:2). From this point forward the biblical connection between law and liberty, obedience and freedom, so paradoxical to the secular mind, becomes more and more presuppositional to each succeeding narrative, until the otherwise contradictory invitation to "freely obey" becomes possible to the imagination.

We also come to a point as readers where we see how the entire historical grand narrative can constitute for its readers a kind of parable, which is precisely how the poet in Psalm 78 denominates his recollection of the biblical grand narrative to that point. From such a reader's point of view we begin to appreciate how trusting in the divine Author, from generation to generation (Heb. *dor le dor*; cf. Ps 145:4, from whence comes the reiterated rabbinic phrase) has required a kind of "willing suspension of disbelief" far more complete than anything latter day poets such as Coleridge had in mind. What makes the exemplars of the grand narrative celebrated by the author of the epistle to the Hebrews so commendable is that there was never any guarantee of a payoff in their lifetime. Indeed, as the text says, "these all died in faith, not having received the promises, but having seen them afar off, and were persuaded of them, and embraced them, and confessed that they were strangers and pilgrims on the earth" (Heb 11:13). Augustine, in his great work on meaning in history, *The City of God*, cites this passage in his preface as a way of saying that the meaning of faithfulness for all who read about the Old Testament saints in the light of Christ is that we should understand our own subsequent role in the universal history as a part in the ongoing pilgrimage of salvation history. Our spiritual forebears chose to journey out, to face the future. They could have turned back, the writer says, but since "now they desire a better country, that is, a heavenly: wherefore God is not ashamed to be called their God: for he hath prepared for them a city" (Heb 11:14-16).

This is far from hero worship or even a veneration of ancestors; it is a call to responsibility. The story of the Old Testament faithful cannot be completed without us, the author says—that is, without our part in the grand story. "Wherefore," he writes,

> seeing we also are compassed about with so great a cloud of witnesses,
> let us lay aside every weight, and the sin which doth so easily beset us,
> and let us run with patience the race that is set before us,
>> Looking unto Jesus, the author and finisher of our faith. (Heb 12:1-2).

The individual reader who responds to this invitation is not expected to run solo. The stirring call is to join in a relay, to participate in the greater story. The explicit linkage of personal with communal destiny is a literary reminder that, unlike typical Greek or Roman grand narratives (e.g., the epics of Homer and Virgil), the biblical grand narrative is less about any one human protagonist at any one time than about a lineage across time, a communion of saints who cannot be complete or in any sense heroic until the Author finishes the story that is his after all. He is the true protagonist of the grand narrative. Faithful readers join his story, and their forebears' story, which joyously now, by God's grace and through their own willing suspension of disbelief, is to become their story also.

6. Confessional autobiography. This conjoining of stories is the very essence of a distinctive biblical genre. One prototype in the Old Testament is the confession of the Babylonian tyrant Nebuchadnezzar, in the fourth chapter of the book of Daniel. The dominant emperor of the world in his time is represented as describing, in his own distinctive voice and language (though invisible in our English Bibles, the Aramaic is not translated into Hebrew), how in his imperious arrogance he had resisted any god other than himself. He tells how he failed to learn from the stunning signs and wonders accompanying the faithfulness of Daniel and his three friends. He failed to take seriously enough the remarkable dream interpretation of Daniel, and so suffered a nightmare come true. Broken by insanity and exile from human society, for seven years he crawled about on all fours like a beast of the field, eating grass. No human dignity was left to him until he remembered, raised his eyes (i.e., to God), whereby his reason returned and he was restored to his kingdom.

The form of Nebuchadnezzar's confession is about as public as it could be: the entire chapter is presented as an imperial proclamation "unto all peoples, nations, and languages, that dwell in all the earth," and it declares "the signs and wonders that the high God hath wrought toward me" (Dan 4:1-2), an accounting not only of the dream of forewarning which had come to him and Daniel's interpretation of it, but also the devastating precision with which it foretold his fate. Worse, as he reveals, the interpretation of Daniel also suggested an escape clause: if Nebuchadnezzar should repent and, as Daniel puts it to him, "break off thy sins by righteousness, and thine iniquities by shewing mercy to the poor," his fate might have even then been averted (Dan 4:27). But Nebuchadnezzar now admits the compounding of his shame: he did not amend his life, and so the full weight of the divine judgment fell on him. After seven long years, "his hairs were grown like eagles' feathers, and his nails like birds' claws" (Dan 4:33), he at last acknowledges One whose "dominion is an everlasting dominion, and his kingdom is from generation to generation" (Dan 4:34). He concludes by confessing (he who once claimed for himself the status of a deity) his new allegiance to One higher than himself, praising and extolling "the King of heaven, all whose works are truth, and his ways judgment" (Dan 4:37).

This is a very dramatic insertion into an already dramatic text, and much remains to be discovered about it. What we can say is that it is the first known instance of a first-person account confessing gross miscreance and describing a process of repentance and conversion to a new order of life and allegiance. That is, it is the farthest thing possible from self-serving imperial propaganda by a Gentile tyrant (as in Dan 2). As such, it offers an unusually intimate witness to transformative personal *events* in such a way as to reveal an account of fundamental character transformation as the primary literary purpose of the narrative. What such a narrative gives us—that no other type of narration quite does—is a deeper insight into character, psychological development and personal growth. It also confirms, in a way that no historical narrative with substantially static characters can, that in the process of telling a personal story, and of hearing it told, both authors and audience can be engaged in ways that make them more intimate to each other. This is the advantage which seems to have accrued to Augustine's much fuller and itself originary *Confessions* (an indispensable foundational book for understanding Christian tradition), and it has spawned important literary imitators of lesser candor and antithetical purpose, such as Jean-Jacques Rousseau's mockery of Augustine in his own *Confessions* (1782) and James Joyce's *Portrait of the Artist as a Young Man* (1916), a narrative not of conversion *to* faith but of a disconversion *out of* the Catholic faith in which both protagonist and author were raised.

7. Etiological narrative. People often speak of a song, movie or novel in this way: lovers will say, "That's our song they're playing," or one person will say to another she is just getting to know, "That's my movie; what's yours?" When we say such things we do not mean this in any legal or propriety sense, of course—no one imagines such a remark as a claim of authorship. Rather, we are expressing a deep sense of the way a given story (or song) connects to our personal identity. We can understand in general how Christians for centuries have felt this way about the Bible, or even certain parts of it; the prevalence among Jews and Christians of biblical names—and the names of saints—owes to similar impulses and is one manifestation of a deeply internalized form of biblical influence and identity.

We do not read long in the book of Genesis before we find a narrative that, in a strong prototypical way, both explains the identity of a primary character and confers a covenantal future on successors who will bear his name. The character is Jacob. In the narrative of his birth (Gen 25:22-26) we learn that even in the womb he and his twin brother "struggled" or, as the Hebrew word *('bq)* suggests, "wrestled" to see who would emerge first and thus be able to claim the rights accorded to firstborn children. In her pregnant discomfort their mother Rebekah asks the Lord what is going on, and learns that the twins she carries are to father two distinct peoples, one stronger than the other, and that "the elder shall serve the younger" (Gen 25:23). Sure enough, as the first son, Esau, red and "hairy all over," emerges, Jacob, the smooth one, is grasping Esau by the heel (Heb. *'qb*). This factors into his name: *Ja-qb* (rel. to the verb "one who follows closely" [cf. Ps 49:5]). Esau grew to be a "cunning hunter" and favored by his father; Jacob was by comparison a momma's boy (Gen 25:28). Yet, as if to confound the natural sensibilities of modern readers as well as the culture in which this happens, it is the momma's boy who—by still greater cunning, tricking his brother into trading his right of primogeniture (birthright) for a lentil stew on a day when Esau came home ravenously hungry from hunting—proves to be the bearer of the covenant.

God renews the covenant with Isaac on account of his father Abraham's faithfulness (Gen 26:2-5), but then, through another morally questionable, even more treacherous act involving the conniving assistance of Rebekah, Jacob deceives his blind father. He wants the aged patriarch to believe he is passing on the covenant blessing to Esau, as would be expected, so Jacob presents himself guilefully under some goat hides (to mimic his "hairy" brother) and thus obtains the blessing (Gen 27:1-40). Jacob succeeds in his improbable ruse. Esau seeks revenge, Jacob has to flee, and his long exile with his mother's kinsman Laban is a consequence.

God appears to Jacob in a dream as he sleeps en route and confers on him and his descendents the covenant earlier given to Abraham and Isaac (Gen 28). This is evidently not on account of any special merit on Jacob's part; the trickster is hardly (at this or perhaps any other point) an admirable character. Appropriately enough, Jacob himself soon suffers the deception he inflicts on others. He desires a wife but is tricked into taking two; he and his shifty father-in-law Laban richly deserve each other. After years of further trickery on both sides Jacob has nevertheless so impoverished and enraged Laban that he has to flee for his life with his wives, children and flocks. Along the way there is yet another encounter with God that simultaneously defines Jacob in terms of his past deviousness and projects upon him and his posterity a future identity and, indeed, a new name.

Here the text is at some pains to show how it happens. In his flight from Laban, Jacob is told by God to return to the territory of his estranged brother Esau and sue for peace. Many years have passed, and Jacob hopes that the memory of his fraud will have faded. Yet at the border of this territory, marked by the river Jabbok, he learns that Esau is coming to meet him with four hundred men, and his nerve fails. He sends the women and children across the river in two parties, hoping that at least one company will escape what he imagines to be the murderous wrath of his brother (Gen 32:4-8). He prays for God's protection and reminds God of the covenant of which he has been, however deviously, the recipient (Gen 32:9-12). He then sends a series of presents of flocks to meet Esau, with a message that Jacob himself follows closely behind (Gen 32:18-20). Yet in the end he quails and stays alone overnight by himself on the banks of the Jabbok (Gen 32:22-32).

During the night he is confronted with an unforeseen presence, and "wrestles with a man" until dawn. When the mysterious wrestler finds himself not having yet prevailed, he strikes Jacob a blow in "the hollow of his thigh," a blow below the belt as we might now say. The justice of this move, given Jacob's own unfair tactics on so many occasions, seems rather fitting. But at this juncture the reader of this story in

Hebrew will start to notice some ironic wordplay; as we look closely it heightens further our sense of just deserts. For Jacob to wrestle *('bq)* by a small river whose name, Jabbok, means "wrestling" or "twisting" recalls for the alert reader Jacob's wrestling with Esau in the womb (indeed, reverse puns are a feature of literary Hebrew, so that *'bq* inverts *'qb*, "heel"). When his mysterious adversary asks to be let go, Jacob astonishingly says, "I will not let thee go, except thou bless me" (v. 26). This chutzpah is resisted with a question: "What is thy name?" Jacob is suddenly, grudgingly, forced to admit his identity, pronouncing his name effectively as a confession: he is that heel-grasping, deceitful, conniving Jacob, a crooked man who has walked many a crooked mile. "Thy name shall be called no more Jacob," replies the angelic being, "but Israel."

Jacob now wishes to know his adversary's name in return but is firmly rebuffed (v. 29). Nonetheless he does receive the blessing. So Jacob, now Israel ("a prince . . . with power with God and with men" [v. 28]; also, perhaps, "God perseveres") names the place of his dark theophany Peniel ("face of God") for, as he says, "I have seen God face to face [*panim el-panim*], and my life is preserved" (v. 30). Persistence of his old name along with the new name in subsequent biblical references is a reminder of this dramatic event, as is his now permanent limp. Jacob's grasping, conniving nature will not be entirely forgotten, even though "Yisra'el" is a lasting sign of God's own covenant persistence. When later the psalmist wishes to signify the holiness appropriate to worshiping the Lord in his temple, he writes of all those qualities most evidently *not* found in the historical Jacob, namely, "clean hands, and a pure heart; [one] who hath not lifted up his soul unto vanity, nor sworn deceitfully" (Ps 24:4). A better man, the poet adds, "shall receive the blessing from the LORD," and "this is the generation of them that seek him, that seek thy face, O Jacob!" (Ps 24:5-6). The insertion of "Jacob" in this context is unexpected and arresting, suggesting ironically the need of one truer than Jacob, one made possible only by Yisra'el, through God's perseverance, and who can thus answer to the call to worship the Lord in holiness.

One other instance must conclude our reflection on the importance of understanding the role of Hebrew names for a sound literary understanding of the Bible.[27] The book of Exodus, so called in Latin and subsequently in English, refers to the liberation of Israel from bondage, a large part of its subject matter. But it is called in Hebrew *Shemoth*, or "Names," from its first words, "These are the names." Of these names the most famous is Moses. The text recounts that a baby boy, to be cast under Pharaoh's order into the river to die along with other Hebrew male children, is placed by his mother in a little *arca*, or box, and set to float in the reeds of the Nile. Before he can become yet one more tasty hors d'oeuvre for a crocodile, Pharaoh's daughter spies the floating crèche, has it drawn out of the water and takes pity on the baby (Ex 2:2-9). She adopts him and names him Moses, saying by way of explanation, "because I drew him out of the water" (Ex 2:10). The Hebrew verb to draw out, *mashah*, is here made to be indicative not only of the means of his deliverance but of Moses' future role, which will be to draw his people out of Egypt altogether. And yet there is another register to Moses' name, and this association portends how in the Bible really important understanding is often conveyed by assonance, or similarities in sound: if *mashah* is already a poetically suggestive verb, this resonance is enhanced by its similarity to the noun *mashal*, which means "poetic or figurative speech." This becomes fruitful wordplay both in rabbinic discourse and in Hebrew poetry of the medieval period.

8. Poetic language and biblical wisdom. So far we have been exploring types of biblical narratives, trying to come to a better understanding of how they work as genre and also to grasp how their context in an overarching grand narrative makes of them links or chapters in a larger story. Now it is time to consider more closely the language of the Bible, both in regard to its deployment of figurative speech and poetry, and also in the light of discussions within the Bible of the role and limits of language—any language—in relation to our apprehension of truth.

Moses makes a good point of departure for this shift in our focus, and not because the five books usually ascribed to him are more poetic than other books of the Bible (the opposite is true). Indeed, when the

---

[27]Augustine, in bk. 4 of his *On Christian Doctrine*, stresses the importance of this point even for those who do not know Hebrew as a language.

accounts of the law from Sinai and its reiteration in Deuteronomy (the "second law," or *mishneh* Torah) are thus concluded, in their discursive and even propositional fashion leaving us with apodictic imperatives and an extensive body of civil and ceremonial law, the Bible has only begun to unfold to us its full depiction of God's divine holiness essential to the grand narrative of human redemption, and the implications of covenant relationship with the Creator. More history will follow, certainly, but there will also be a rich collection of poetry and wisdom literature for which history may be the background but not the immediate subject, and in which the literary form of the texts we read makes possible a considerable extension of our understanding and a fresh engagement of our imagination concerning both human nature and the character of God.

In Hebrew, *mashal* is a term that covers a wide range of both figurative and aphoristic discourse. Yet it is not, as we saw in the example of Psalm 78, inappropriate to characterize a recapitulation and reflection on history itself as *mashal,* an exemplum or watchword for moral understanding. A parable, an epigram, a wisdom aphorism from Proverbs, an enigma or mystery, even a simple metaphor may be described as a *mashal.* In short, we may say that wherever biblical language is indirect rather than direct, ironic rather than indicative or imperative, one of the kinds of figurative language we associate with *mashal* is likely to appear.[28] Such language is typically more poetic or literary than prosaically descriptive or proscriptively analytic. Readers familiar with the New Testament may think here of some of the cryptic, often riddling sayings of Jesus that employ metaphor to convey mystery, such as in his conversation with Nicodemus in John 3:

> Nicodemus saith unto him, How can a man be born when he is old? Can he enter the second time into his mother's womb, and be born?
>
> Jesus answered, Verily, verily, I say unto thee, Except a man be born of water and of the Spirit, he cannot enter into the kingdom of God.
>
> That which is born of the flesh is flesh; and that which is born of the Spirit is spirit.

---

[28]See Jeffrey, *People of the Book,* pp. 360-65.

> Marvel not that I said unto thee, Ye must be born again.
>
> The wind bloweth where it listeth, and thou hearest the sound thereof, but canst not tell whence it cometh, and whither it goeth: so is every one that is born of the Spirit.
>
> Nicodemus answered and said unto him, How can these things be?
>
> Jesus answered and said unto him, Art thou a master of Israel, and knowest not these things? (Jn 3:4-10)

One of the things atheists and fundamentalists have in common is a tendency to fall down on metaphor. Jesus is disappointed at the way Nicodemus, for all his genuine theological learning, is, like many earnest religious people, deaf to the deeper truth of that which he professes to believe. Such truth, the teaching of Jesus suggests, if it is to be grasped at all, must be held in language that is openly figurative rather than legalistically or narrowly proscriptive. To push out the boundaries of literalistic or legalistic imagination in Nicodemus, the Greek text reveals to us that Jesus is using the same word *(pneuma)* for both "wind" and "spirit," a close reflection of the word *ruah* in Hebrew (perhaps the language Nicodemus and Jesus were conversing in), which permits the same double sense.

Or we might think of the way Jesus' Sermon on the Mount becomes a commentary on the law given to Moses on Mount Sinai, indicating that the way Jesus will fulfill it (Mt 5:17) involves no merely reductive or even performative reading of the Torah as legal discourse. Rather, Jesus offers an unsettling intensification of its meaning and apparent original intent. This Jesus accomplishes by wisdom aphorisms (e.g., Mt 5:13; 6:19-21), metaphor (e.g., Mt 7:1-20) and parable (Mt 7:24-27), as well as by riddling sayings that require extensive reflection even to begin to puzzle them out. The Beatitudes (Mt 5:1-12) are a case in point. This figurative, literary character of Jesus' teaching "astonished" his hearers, and yet in such a way as immediately identified it as authoritative, more convincing than the teaching of the scribes (the professional interpreters of the time). There is a lesson here.

The best-known example of figurative biblical discourse is probably parable, a simple story. In the "seminar" on parables conducted by Jesus with his disciples, he makes it clear to them that apparent bottom-line clarity, as with the declaration of a set of principles or precepts, is not necessarily productive of change in a hardened religious heart. He tells his stories, Jesus says in Matthew 13, to force people to deal with their own case-hardened refusal to hear what the Scriptures elsewhere plainly say, simply because they are confident that they understand more than enough already (Mt 13:10-17). To unpack the Greek term which gives rise to our English word, a parable is a story "to set alongside" another way of making a point, as perhaps in an argument or exhortation. In this way a parable, though fictive, can constitute an interpretation of something evidently propositional or historical. In the case of the parable told by the prophet Nathan to the adulterous murderer King David (2 Sam 12), David's impulsive interpretation and rush to judgment regarding the story of the purloined lamb constitutes much more than a literary interpretation. His response reveals that Nathan's parable has been diagnostic of the heart of its hearer; the story has interpreted the interpreter, exposing his own recent, sordid personal history. More extended stories can work in the same ironic fashion. Israel in its sagas of disobedience or obedience can thus be said to be a *mashal* to the nations (Deut 28:37; 1 Kings 9:7; Ps 44:14). In the case of Job, who describes his own experience as a "parable" or "byword" (*mashal:* Job 17:6; 30:9), his attempt at self-defense within the book that bears his name is likewise described by the narrator as a "parable" (*mashal:* Job 27:1; 29:1).

For the reader, the primary issue is not whether the story of Job is historical as distinct from fiction but rather whether recollection of the meaning or interpretation of such a story serves as a way of understanding what elsewhere in Scripture, as Augustine puts it (*On Christian Doctrine* 2.6.8), is stated more plainly. In this way, as we saw in Galatians 4:22-31, Paul retells the story of Abraham, Hagar, Sarah, Ishmael and Isaac, saying that these things "are an allegory" (Gal 4:24), but then goes on to reinterpret the Genesis story in such fashion as to comment on the "two covenants," one of bondage to the law and the other of freedom in grace. The apostle's point for his immediate audience in Galatia is that the meaning of the text in their own time is to be derived from retrospectively reading a well-known historical event as a *mashal* by which is conveyed, for those with ears to hear, the deeper, inner meaning of that now ancient history for their own present and future redemption. This recalls the figurative use of past narrative by Jesus with reference to himself, such as when he says "as Moses lifted up the serpent in the wilderness, even so must the Son of man be lifted up" (Jn 3:14) or in his recollection of the story of Jonah as a "sign" to an "evil and adulterous generation" (Mt 12:38-41; Lk 11:29-32); in both cases multiple aspects of the earlier narrative may be engaged in reflection on what Jesus is saying. When Old Testament narratives are remembered in New Testament narrative in these ways or are used as if the narrative or event prefigured something in the life of Christ, then literary devices such as typology are often invoked to describe the character of the allusion. Indeed, this too can be a helpful (if not the only) way to understand what is happening literarily. Whether read typologically or with an eye to the way in which not only pattern of event but also metaphor and other forms of poetic speech in the Old Testament are enlarged, intensified or given a heightened significance in the New, we can appreciate how all of the Bible, Old and New Testaments together, may thus be experienced by a knowledgeable reader as one continuous narrative, flowing toward and finding closure and terminus in Christ.

Boris Pasternak, the Russian poet who is best known in the West for his novel *Doctor Zhivago* (1954), has a poem, "Garden of Gethsemane," in which this sense of narrative fulfillment, as if in one great work of art, is memorably captured. In the poem, Christ is represented as correcting Peter's attempted resistance of Judas and his followers—and thus of a purpose in the divine grand narrative—with a sword. The speech of Jesus concludes the poem in this way:

> But now the book of life has reached a page
> Which is more precious than are all their holies.
> That which was written now must be fulfilled.
> Fulfilled be it, then. Amen.

> Seest thou, the passing of the ages is like a parable
> And in its passing it may burst to flame.
> In the name, then, of the awesome majesty
> I shall, in voluntary torments, descend into my grave.

> I shall descend into my grave. And on the third day rise again.

And, even as rafts flow down a river,
So shall the centuries drift, trailing like a caravan,
Coming for judgment, out of the dark, to me.[29]

Here is a biblical view of the meaning of history captured in metaphor. It comprehends the events of that most perfect Passover as if they were to human history what the experience of closure is to a great work of art. Pasternak's "Gethsemane" poem is accordingly not merely *about* the Bible or a poetic commentary on one passage; it is fundamentally biblical in its deeper theological understanding of history *sub specie aeternitas*—of history itself as the poetry of one who is the Author of all.

9. Parables of Jesus. It is not the function or purpose of all parts of the Bible to explain—or explain away—all of life's ambiguities. With novelist Iris Murdoch we must note that even in the manner of our seeking what is good, "there are times to stress, not the comprehensibility of the world, but its incomprehensibility." It is precisely in the context of the complexity that eludes our understanding, Murdoch writes, that we are invited to "consider the importance of parables and stories as moral guides."[30] This is a point that the biblically literate reader will grasp more firmly than most.

The parables of Jesus are the primary biblical texts by which we come to understand that when Jesus addresses questions of a deep nature, he prefers to give not a philosophical or theological dictum, but rather a story. An example from Matthew's Gospel conveniently summarizes the way in which *mashal*, or figurative discourse, teases out self-understanding in the reader in a way that more systematic informational teaching may not. The context is that the chief priests and elders have been questioning Jesus' authority to teach and heal in their jurisdiction (Mt 21:23-27). Jesus' reply to their inability to reason that his miracles are in themselves indicative that his authority is of a higher order comes in his story about two sons, one who talks about doing the will of his

---

[29]Boris Pasternak, "Garden of Gethsemane," trans. Bernard Guilbert Guerney, appended to the translation of *Doctor Zhivago* by Max Hayward and Manya Harari (New York: Pantheon, 1958), pp. 557-59.
[30]Iris Murdoch, in *Existentialists and Mystics: Writings on Philosophy and Literature*, ed. Peter Conradi (New York: Penguin Books, 1997), p. 90.

father and the other who at first resists but, unlike his brother, actually performs the necessary work. Then, to complete his point, namely, that the religious leaders are like the son who talks but does not perform, Jesus says:

> Hear another parable: There was a certain householder, which planted a vineyard, and hedged it round about, and digged a winepress in it, and built a tower, and let it out to husbandmen, and went into a far country:
>
> And when the time of the fruit drew near, he sent his servants to the husbandmen, that they might receive the fruits of it.
>
> And the husbandmen took his servants, and beat one, and killed another, and stoned another.
>
> Again, he sent other servants more than the first: and they did unto them likewise.
>
> But last of all he sent unto them his son, saying, They will reverence my son.
>
> But when the husbandmen saw the son, they said among themselves, This is the heir; come, let us kill him, and let us seize on his inheritance.
>
> And they caught him, and cast him out of the vineyard, and slew him.
>
> When the lord therefore of the vineyard cometh, what will he do unto those husbandmen? (Mt 21:33-40)

To Jesus' question the religious leaders give an immediate, indignant, self-righteous response: "He will miserably destroy those wicked men, and will let out his vineyard unto other husbandmen, which shall render him the fruits in their seasons" (Mt 21:41).

This parable works precisely in the fashion of Nathan's to King David; the guilty parties, who argumentatively have either resisted obedience to the law or, as here, the exposition of Jesus, all the while maintaining their self-righteousness, end up by angrily judging themselves out of their own mouths. That is, the function of such a literary device is to interpret the heart of the one who thinks he has mastered the art of interpretation (cf. Heb 4:12). It is not so much that the learned elders interpret the *mashal* of Jesus but rather that his *mashal*, his fiction, interprets them. The story also lays down the fundamental principles of providential irony whereby we learn that even when men mean evil by their actions, as in the story of Joseph and his brothers, God in his over-

riding providential purpose may have all along been intending an unforeseen greater good to which the apparent evil has been less a contradiction than, mysteriously, a means. So Paul in Romans: "All things
work together for good to them that love God, to them who are the
called according to his purpose" (Rom 8:28). The many ironic reversals
in biblical literature, from the story of Joseph or the surprising rise of
the youngest son, David, to be king, to "the stone that the builders rejected" becoming the "chief corner stone" or the last being first and the
first last, to the resurrection of Jesus itself show how irony is at the
heart of biblical story. Irony inherently involves indirect discourse;
philologically it is, as the fathers of the church used to say, "saying one
thing to mean another." But irony of plot is a characteristic feature of
biblical literature too and is profoundly implicated in plot resolution
throughout the Bible.[31]

For many people, an intuitive insight afforded by literature, perhaps
by a wise proverb, an analogy, metaphor or parable, is a more likely
means of our coming to transformative understanding than information acquired propositionally or even by dint of a well-ordered argument. The American poet Dana Gioia, in a lecture given at Baylor
University in 2008, observed that when he was a child his mother frequently quoted rather endearing, sometimes thought-provoking little
poems to him in the course of her daily activity around the house; he
came to understand that in sharing such poetry she was allowing him
to know part of her personhood that otherwise might have remained
inaccessible. We might quite properly think of the poetry in the Bible,
and especially perhaps the poetic language favored by Jesus in his parables, aphorisms and "dark sayings," as just such a means by which the
divine Author of Scripture discloses to us intimate insights into his
character, insights that might not be obtainable by us in any other way.
To put this more formally: poetry has its place in the search for truth,
and it is not a second-order place. The Bible demonstrates that art and
the creative imagination can get at some aspects of truth more effectively than systematic analysis in admirably logical prose. Parables are

---

[31]See here Anthony Esolen, *Ironies of Faith: The Laughter at the Heart of Christian Literature*
(Wilmington, Del.: Intercollegiate Institute Press, 2007).

in fact Jesus' own favorite means of teaching higher truth; *mashalim* of many other kinds go with them to make up the heart and soul of his teaching.

10. Biblical skepticism concerning the limits of literary language. All this is not to say that literary language is without its own limits where our desire to understand ultimate truth is concerned. For example, in Psalm 19 the poet shows how, though creation is a kind of language that tells forth the glory of God, and that even pagan poetry has its value, the law of the Lord in Torah more perfectly reveals his glory. Yet even here, where the specific historical event and legal precision of divine law is concerned, no one verbal formula suffices to capture its rich significance (Ps 19:7-10). Biblical literature suggests that our personal understanding is necessarily limited by our own subjectivity (Ps 19:12) and expressive capacity. Clearly, this poem suggests, we need as we read or write to pray with the psalmist for humility (Ps 19:13) lest our attempts at capturing divine truth in words lead us into presumptuous, hubristic denial of the very truth we seek to serve. We are always, if we are honest, in need of God's turning our own poorly ordered intentions, even in prayer, to his good purpose (Ps 19:14).[32]

Limited or not, it is evident that in many situations language is indispensable. Language, moreover, has been sanctified by God's use of it in the Bible historically in a wide range of truth-telling ways, hallowed sacramentally when his eternal Logos became flesh in Jesus; the Christian reader will appreciate that it has been given new life and re-creative power by virtue of Jesus' literary truth telling. For those with ears to hear and eyes to see there really is something more than the mere letter (2 Cor 3:6) by which we appropriate meaning.

Imaginative registers of language can in fact bridge the gap between imperfect hearing and transformative understanding of the sort that causes us to exclaim, on an occasion of having our perspective liberated by a metaphor, a paradox, a poem or a parable: "O! Now I see." For at some point we are all blind, even the most apparently intelligent of us, and even when surrounded by abundant evidence and many a noble at-

---

[32]For a detailed explication of Psalm 19 see Jeffrey, *People of the Book*, chap. 1.

tempt to explain to us the truth. Yet a careful apprenticeship to the study of literature may teach us that if we allow ourselves to ponder in our hearts those things we think we understand, and indeed those beyond our understanding, good will come of it. Here one last example must suffice to illustrate. Richard Wilbur has a poem in which he expresses his wonder at the pattern flying, sweeping and whirling about in unison of a flock of migrating birds in their autumn gathering. What he says indicates both the inevitable inadequacy of language, even the poet's language, to capture a deeply intuited but inarticulate meaning in such "An Event" (1956). Yet here is how he concludes his poem:

> They tower up, shatter, and madden space
> With their divergences, are each alone
> Swallowed from sight, and leave me in this place
> Shaping these images to make them stay:
> Meanwhile, in some formation of their own,
> They fly me still, and steal my thoughts away.
>
> Delighted with myself and with the birds,
> I set them down and give them leave to be.
> It is by words and the defeat of words,
> Down sudden vistas of the vain attempt,
> That for a flying moment one may see
> By what cross-purposes the world is dreamt. (13-24)[33]

Most readers have experiences that produce a similar, even if fleeting, "eureka" moment. In a way we had not consciously anticipated, a perceptual or cognitive breakthrough of some sort occurs. There are other experiences that, like Wilbur's insight in this poem, give us only a glimpse of what we yearn for, some sort of inkling. But such a glimpse as comes here, with its ironically understated reminder of the hard cost ("cross-purposes") of God's loving sacrifice, allows us to see somewhat into the antinomies and unsolved mysteries in the world, and peaceably to "set them down and give them leave to be." One day we shall perhaps see more, namely, how in his redemptive purposes in human history

---

[33]Richard Wilbur, "An Event," *Things of This World*, in *Collected Poems: 1943-2004* (Orlando: Harcourt, 2004), p. 347.

things "come together," how evil comports with good, which is to say, how "all things work together for good" (Rom 8:28). For now, we are glad for every glimpse. Understanding the limitation as well as the unique gift of the literary imagination is a good way to train ourselves to read the Bible "with eyes to see." Then when we come to the immense riches of later literature, we will by this preparation be much readier to appreciate them as well, for, as the seventeenth-century poet Herbert puts it so well in his "The Holy Scriptures I":

> This is the thankful glasse,
> that mends the lookers eyes: this is the well
> that washes what it shows. (8-10)[34]

Something very like Herbert's sense of the Bible's transforming power, experienced by countless readers in various but remarkably consistent ways, has not only inspired much of our subsequent literature but shaped the whole intellectual culture we call "Christian literary tradition." To that treasury, at least in its English expression, now we turn.

Suggestions for Further Reading

Alter, Robert. *The Art of Biblical Narrative.* New York: Basic Books, 1981.

———. *The Art of Biblical Poetry.* New York: Basic Books, 1985.

Alter, Robert, and Frank Kermode, eds. *The Literary Guide to the Bible.* Cambridge, Mass.: Harvard University Press, 1987.

Atwan, Robert, and Laurance Wieder. *Chapters into Verse: Poetry in English Inspired by the Bible.* 2 volumes. Oxford: Oxford University Press, 1993.

Atwan, Robert, et al. *Divine Inspiration: The Life of Jesus in World Poetry.* Oxford: Oxford University Press, 1998.

Bartholomew, Craig, and Michael Goheen. *The Drama of Scripture: Finding Our Place in the Biblical Story.* Grand Rapids: Baker, 2004.

Buechner, Frederick. *Telling the Truth: The Gospel as Tragedy, Comedy, and Fairy Tale.* New York: HarperSanFrancisco, 1985.

Curzon, David, ed. *The Gospels in Our Image: An Anthology of Twentieth-Century Poetry Based on Biblical Texts.* New York: Harcourt, 1995.

---

[34]George Herbert, "The Holy Scriptures I," *The Works of George Herbert,* ed. F. E. Hutchinson (1941; reprint, Oxford: Clarendon, 1972), p. 58.

———. *Modern Poems on the Bible: An Anthology*. New York: Jewish Publication Society, 1993.

Daniel, David. *The Bible in English*. New Haven, Conn.: Yale University Press, 2003.

Davie, Donald. *New Oxford Book of Christian Verse*. Oxford: Oxford University Press, 1988.

Fisch, Harold. *Poetry With a Purpose: Biblical Poetics and Interpretation*. Bloomington: Indiana University Press, 1988.

Fishbane, Michael. *The Garments of Torah: Essays in Biblical Hermeneutics*. Bloomington: Indiana University Press, 1989.

Frye, Northrop. *The Great Code: The Bible and Literature*. Toronto: Academic Press, 1981.

Gabel, John, Charles B. Wheeler, and Anthony D. York. *The Bible as Literature*. 4th edition. New York: Oxford University Press, 2000.

Harding, Anthony. *Coleridge and the Inspired Word*. Kingston, Ont.: McGill-Queens, 1985.

Hartman, Geoffrey H., and Sanford Budick, eds. *Midrash and Literature*. New Haven, Conn.: Yale University Press, 1986.

Jasper, David, and Stephen Prickett, eds. *The Bible and Literature: A Reader*. Oxford: Blackwell, 1999.

Jeffrey, David Lyle, ed. *A Dictionary of Biblical Tradition in English Literature*. Grand Rapids: Eerdmans, 1992.

Levering, Matthew. *Participatory Biblical Exegesis: A Theology of Biblical Interpretation*. Notre Dame, Ind.: University of Notre Dame, 2008.

Norton, David. *A History of the Bible as Literature*. 2 volumes. New York: Cambridge University Press, 1993.

Prickett, Stephen, ed. *Reading the Text: Biblical Criticism and Literary Theory*. Oxford: Blackwell, 1991.

———. *Words and the Word: Language, Poetics and Biblical Interpretation*. Cambridge: Cambridge University Press, 1988.

Schwartz, Regina, ed. *The Book and the Text: The Bible and Literary Theory*. Oxford: Blackwell, 1990.

PART TWO

LITERARY INTERPRETATION

Tradition, Liturgy and
the Medieval Imagination

But we should not think that we ought not to learn literature
because Mercury is said to be its inventor. . . .
Rather, every good and true Christian should understand
that wherever he finds truth, it is his Lord's.

Augustine

The history of literature, like the history of ideas of which it is a part, readily reflects significant changes in cultural self-understanding and aspiration. But the deepest questions and, perhaps especially for Christians, the fundamental tensions remain remarkably consistent within our tradition. In the teaching of Jesus we find two of these: in response to the dilemma posed by the Pharisees concerning allegiance, whether primarily it ought to be to God or to the state, Jesus says, "Render . . . unto Caesar the things which are Caesar's, and unto God the things that are God's" (Mt 22:21). Elsewhere, he parses a question about the place of affluence in the lives of the faithful, saying, "No servant can serve two masters. . . . Ye cannot serve God and mammon" (Lk 16:13), in the context indicating that these competing powers have each their legitimate claim, but that successful resolution of the tension depends on distinguishing rightly between intrinsic good (what belongs to God) and material necessities (e.g., political or physical obligations, money) as mere instrumental goods. The resolutions suggested by Jesus do not banish the lesser good but order it to its proper and ultimately warranted end.

Over the centuries it has seemed evident to thoughtful Christians that in the intellectual life also these perennial tensions must be resolved in such a way as to preserve the appropriate goods in their proper place. In Christian tradition since the beginning this has had cultural ramifications. Take for example the formulation of it cited in the first chapter of this volume: "What has Athens to do with Jerusalem?"[1] Tertullian's famous question has often been quoted as a way of characterizing the early Christians as somewhat philistine, suspicious of pagan art and learning. There is a similar passage in St. Jerome's letter to Estochium (*Epistulae* 22.29-30), and every student of later antiquity is familiar with it; it relates the troubled dream of this great fourth-century scholar in which "the Judge of all" accuses him of being not a Christian but a Ciceronian—conveying thus a remembered guilt which Jerome, in this instance for pedagogical purposes, confesses in his eloquent letter. Near the headwaters of Anglo-Saxon literature we hear the theme again, adapted now by Alcuin, likewise a formidable scholar, admonishing with authority the monks of Lindisfarne: *Quid Hineldus cum Christo?*—"What has Ingeld to do with Christ?" (*Epistulae* 169). Though the alien attraction that concerns Alcuin is Anglo-Saxon pagan epic whereas for Tertullian and Jerome it is the literary legacy of Greece and pre-Christian Rome, the point is evidently the same. *Caveat lector!* "Let the reader beware," all three seem to say: a grave risk of theological adultery attends upon dalliance with pagan authors. It is as if they wish to reiterate the apostle Paul in saying that the true philosopher of Christ will keep himself pure and unspotted from the world, and certainly "teach no other doctrine" (1 Tim 1:3-4).

Such reminders may seem an unpromising beginning for our topic. Typical modern citations of these famous injunctions continue to im-

---

[1]Tertullian *De praescriptione haereticorum* 18; cf. Tertullian *De spectaculis* 4, 26, 30, in *Ante-Nicene Fathers* 3 (Grand Rapids: Eerdmans, 1954). The argument in the first section of this chapter was first essayed in popular form in *Touchstone* (October 2007), to whose editor, David Miller, I am grateful for that opportunity. These pages both draw on that article and develop it.

plicate much of Christianity in a dour abstemiousness where the liberal arts or belle letters are concerned. They seem to indicate a desire to cordon off humane learning from what are taken to be the more pertinent spiritual preoccupations of monastic or ascetic Christianity. The wall of separation thus constructed can seem almost as steep as the rhetorical barrier erected between faith and rational discourse by advocates of liberal learning since the Enlightenment, whose august latter-day guardians of purity, facing from opposite ramparts, include such venerables as Edward Gibbon, David Hume and, in his 1809 decision to separate the study of theology from the other humanities disciplines at Berlin, Wilhelm von Humboldt.[2] Nor should we dismiss such tactical moves (perhaps on either side) as entirely misinformed concerning biblical counsel in the matter. The ancient voices were echoing St. Paul in his still more extreme warning to the Corinthian Greeks about both syncretism and idolatry: "What concord hath Christ with Belial?" (2 Cor 6:11-15). Subsequent separationists—pietists and secularists alike—have had more than a semblance of warrant for their uneasiness with the prospect of compromise.

But let us add to these rhetorical questions yet another: have such selective proof-texts, however motivated, accurately appreciated the actual character and method of the biblical influence on humane education in Western intellectual history? Here we are on much less firm ground. In this book we argue the contrary and further suggest several reasons why we may be grateful that the rich tradition of literature in the West has in fact remained at the most fundamental level of its priorities more integratively biblical than secular or classical, despite a contemporary academic bias toward representing it otherwise.

CHRISTIANS AND THE PRESERVATION OF CLASSICAL LITERATURE

In intellectual history ironies and contradictions are the norm. To take not the least example: what we know of many classical Roman as well

---

[2]See the discussion by Stephen Prickett, *Origins of Narrative: The Romantic Appropriation of the Bible* (Cambridge: Cambridge University Press, 1996), pp. xiv; 180ff.; and his *Words and the Word: Language, Poetics and Biblical Interpretation* (Cambridge: Cambridge University Press, 1986), pp. 196-97.

as pre-Christian Nordic authors owes to Christians, perhaps especially to monastic communities of Christians.[3] To be sure, there were convoluted attempts by some among the monastic librarians to justify holding on to texts that were not only pagan in the religious sense but, as in the case of Ovid or Catullus, wondrously lewd, even pornographic: the incongruity has led to not a little learned humor. But there is more to it. To take but one example, the allegorizations of Ovid's *Metamorphoses* by Petrus Berchorius *(Ovidius Moralizatus)* and the vernacular *Ovide Moralisé* represent a tenuous but prodigious medieval effort to baptize works of art that could not, in their native garb (or sometimes lack of it), have been licitly embraced.[4] None other than Jerome defended his own notably generous citation of pagan authors by an ingenious appeal to worthy precedent, namely, the practice of biblical authors themselves. In a kind of early Christian "defense of poetry" to the Roman orator Magnus (*Epistulae* 70), he established a pattern of argument and of intellectual/textual practice that helps to explain how it will be biblical and not Roman authors who eventually provide the apologia for humane learning generally, as well as a platform for method and pedagogical application.

Having asserted, on the authority of Josephus, that the Hebrew Scriptures themselves make learned and thoughtful use of Middle-Eastern and Hellenic pagan literature, Jerome next identified particular borrowings in the Pentateuch, the prophets and the wisdom books; modern scholarship has confirmed many of his ascriptions in considerable detail.[5] He notes in particular that in the New Testament Paul quotes from Greek poets such as Epimenides (Tit 1:12), Menander (1 Cor 15:33) and Aratus (Acts 17:28). This, he says, far from representing an impurity of purpose (or syncretism) on the part of the apostle

---

[3]See here Domenico Comparetti, *Vergil in the Middle Ages*, trans. E. F. M. Benecke (Princeton, N.J.: Princeton University Press, 1996); Winthrop Wetherbee, *Platonism and Poetry in the Twelfth Century* (Princeton, N.J.: Princeton University Press, 1972).

[4]Robert Edwards, *The Flight from Desire: Augustine and Ovid to Chaucer* (London: Palgrave Macmillan, 2006); Jeremy Dimmick, "Ovid in the Middle Ages," *The Cambridge Companion to Ovid*, ed. Phillip Hardie (Cambridge: Cambridge University Press, 2002).

[5]See, for example, F. F. Bruce, *New Testament History* (New York: Doubleday, 1972), pp. 45-46, 311-13; also Robert M. Grant, *Historical Introduction to the New Testament* (New York: Harper & Row, 1963), p. 211.

merely establishes an order of appropriation such that Paul can make skillful, fitting, often ironic use of alien instruments, much as when David uses Goliath's own sword to hack off the fallen giant's head. Drawing on another biblical narrative, tellingly for our subject, Jerome cites the Deuteronomic laws permitting marriage, after purification, of a captive woman (Deut 21:10-13), then asks rhetorically:

> What wonder . . . if I also, admiring the fairness of her from the grace of her eloquence, desire to make that secular wisdom which is my captive and my handmaid a rightful matron of the true Israel?[6]

Whatever we now may think of Jerome's nuptial analogy (in a postmodern context it sounds not only odd but offensive), it is clear enough in Jerome's argument that the wall of partition between pagan and biblical culture has proven much more permeable by the fourth century than might have seemed possible on the basis of the famous second-century quotation from Tertullian. Marriage is decidedly contrary to any abstemious Montanism, even metaphorically speaking. Indeed, when Jerome goes on to cite a large bibliography of Jewish and Christian writers, including fathers of the church, bishops and apologists, all of whom, he notes, have made deft use of Plato, Aristotle, Cicero, Virgil and Quintillian to extend the reach and defend the claims of the gospel, he has already begun to indicate the extraordinary explanatory power of his marriage narrative for our understanding of the growth of Christian philosophy and humane learning in the West. In his great four-volume study *Medieval Exegesis*, Henri de Lubac has shown that this argument becomes a medieval commonplace; allegorical practices in textual interpretation draw on both biblical and classical precedent, through which not only biblical authors but also Roman poets such as Virgil and Ovid are found by their Christian readers to have written truth.[7] This in turn allows the pagan authors to become credible authorities, even in Christian theological discourse. In this regard Je-

[6]Jerome *Epistulae* 70.2.
[7]Henri de Lubac, *Exégèse médiévale, les quatres sens de l'écriture*, 4 vols. (Paris: Aubier, 1959); Eng. trans.: *Medieval Exegesis: The Four Senses of Scripture*, vol. 1, trans. Mark Sebanc (Grand Rapids: Eerdmans, 1998), and vols. 2-4, trans. E. M. Macierowski (Grand Rapids: Eerdmans, 2000, 2009, forthcoming).

rome's argument echoes that of Origen or of Clement of Alexandria from the mid-second century. But it is clear that the pagan writers have not set the agenda. Clement was a master of Greek literature, yet celebrated the Hebrew Scriptures as "wisdom in all its splendor," distinctive and superior to the Hellenic library.[8] Indeed, as Robert Wilken argues, "in Clement's writings the Bible emerges for the first time as the foundation of a Christian culture."[9] Jerome is thus building confidently on an already established tradition for which the Scriptures have become, implicitly when not explicitly, the primary basis. Intellectually, as time goes on, marriage proves unsurprisingly more fruitful than abstaining from embrace; progeny abound and in their turn become fruitful. To continue with Jerome's metaphor, however, the language this progeny speaks is no longer Greek but a vernacular version of what the reader's preface to the 1611 King James Bible calls "the language of Canaan" and southerners in the United States have sometimes called "the language of Zion." Even as metaphor, such expressions indicate a cultural fact of decisive importance.

We would argue, then, that the subsequent development of the humanities disciplines in the West cannot be fully understood apart from an appreciation of scriptural husbandry and, if we may use the term somewhat flexibly, a kind of ecclesiastical mothering which, together, have birthed and nurtured Western intellectual life down to the present age. That is, we want to support and extend the thesis of Robert Wilken that any notion that there was a "hellenization of Christianity" should by now be regarded as having outlived its usefulness—indeed, "that a more apt expression would be the Christianization of Hellenism, though that expression does not capture either the originality of Christian thought nor the debt owed to Jewish ways of thinking and to the Jewish Bible."[10] But how, we may ask, through the centuries-old diaspora of the Jewish peoples whose ancestors wrote the texts, and despite their minimal demographic presence throughout Western Eu-

---

[8]Clement of Alexandria *Exhortation* 1.2.2-3; *Stromateis* 6.11.95-6.

[9]Robert Wilken, *The Spirit of Early Christian Thought* (New Haven, Conn.: Yale University Press, 2003), p. 56.

[10]Ibid., p. xvi. Wilken is here correcting the attempt at de-Judification of the Bible by Adolf von Harnack.

rope in particular, did this occur? The subject is massive and complex; here we can provide only a few cryptic observations.

It is essential to note, at least, the decisive role of St. Paul. As apostle to the Gentiles, he proclaimed the teaching of Jesus and the apostles in an overwhelmingly Hellenistic context. While at times he would accommodate his message to his audience, as in the Areopagus speech in Athens or in the rhetorical shape of his letters to the churches, in his views of the nature of God, the role and place of human potential as reflective of God's image in God's world, he remained fundamentally Jewish. This shaped the ways he discussed not only the resurrection of the body, but also his views of the relation of body and spirit and the nature of human sexuality, for example, far more profoundly than did any norms of Hellenistic culture. That these Jewish views had an inner logic that proved cogent and compelling for centuries of readers of St. Paul is now evident. Though relatively few converts after the first generations would have been conscious of the degree of it, Mediterranean, European and North African Christians learned to think in a Jewish way about fundamental theological, social and moral matters, and the influence soon showed up in their own writings, as it continues to do in ours.

St. Augustine and Christian Reading

Nor can we trace adequately the shaping of Western intellectual culture in the humane disciplines without considering the North African bishop Augustine, in particular through his enormously influential treatise *On Christian Doctrine*.[11] After the Bible itself no other work has been so important in the development of a Christian philosophy of literature. It may be, in fact, that the prominence of Augustine's text in the Western history both of hermeneutics and educational theory has helped to shape the way the Bible itself has come to be institutionalized in Western culture—even when invisibly. To be sure, what Augustine set out to accomplish in this book was probably much less: what he

---

[11]Augustine *On Christian Doctrine*, trans. D. W. Robertson Jr. (New York: Library of Liberal Arts, 1958); book and paragraph numbers are standard and followed in this edition throughout. For useful commentary see Edward B. English, *Reading and Wisdom: The De Doctrina of Augustine in the Middle Ages* (Notre Dame, Ind.: University of Notre Dame Press, 1995).

seems to encourage as well as in some measure to provide for is really just a broadly based guide to reading the Bible, sufficient, he hoped, to undergird an intelligent appreciation of Jewish texts in a Gentile culture. He was writing, after all, for provincial North African seminarians. But in his adequation of the goals of Ciceronian education to a biblical order of reasoning about language and truth, his work became a touchstone for more than a millennium of later humanistic authors. The list of those indebted to it is long, but certainly includes Cassiodorus, in his *The Principles of Divine and Sacred Literature* (c. 550); Hugh of St. Victor, *Didascalicon* (a case for studying the liberal arts—c. 1125); Bonaventure, *Retracing the Arts to Theology* (c. 1255); John Wyclif, *On the Truth of Sacred Scripture* (1378).[12] It extends also to the writings of Erasmus, Petrarch, Salutatti, Milton, John Henry (Cardinal) Newman, and C. S. Lewis, to name just a few. Even this abbreviated list should focus anew our appreciation of an enormous contribution that derives, essentially, from Augustine's magisterial attempt to develop a sound literary method for reading the Bible.

The pedagogical stratagems of Augustine (not only in *On Christian Doctrine* but in all of his huge corpus) regarding the disciplines required for an intelligent reading of Scripture became in some ways more influential than his specific exegesis, helping the Bible eventually to transcend theology and become not only the historical foundation for humane learning in the West but also the procedural and methodological basis of nearly all scholarship in the humanities. Textual criticism, philological analysis, poetics, language theory, narrative epistemology, historiography, anthropology, positive law and natural law are all among the immediate beneficiaries; the list is, of course, considerably longer.

With regard to the goals of education Augustine does not, at one level, seem to differ much from Cicero: eloquence and wisdom are the enduring *desiderata*. But Augustine is emphatic that eloquence is instrumental, not an intrinsic good. Why is this important? Well, because divine wisdom is essentially the burden of Scripture's content, and superior wisdom in the life of the reader is its purpose. Acquisition

---

[12]There are also translated sections of this text in the preface to the Wycliffite Bible (1396).

of this wisdom, in turn, provides a more reliable platform for a distinctive and superior grace in utterance. Thus, the former teacher of rhetoric writes, "one speaks more or less wisely to the extent that he has become more or less proficient in [the Holy Scriptures]" (4.5.8). Wisdom, rather than Ciceronian eloquence in itself, is the justification of all higher learning. Biblical language constitutes a special order of eloquence, "fitting for those of higher authority" (4.6.9). This conviction also has had incalculable influence on Christian thinking about reading, rhetoric and education generally.

Yet the instrumentality of language nevertheless requires careful and particular reflection. In Augustine's analysis of things and signs there emerges a biblically grounded basis for semiotic and linguistic ponderings that continue to echo through Saussure and beyond (1.2.2; all of 2). His polemic against "that miserable servitude of the spirit in the habit of mistaking signs for things" (3.6.9), opposing idolatry of the sign, echoes still in the swirling wake of twentieth-century deconstructionism; his adage that "it is a mark of good and distinguished minds to love the truth within words and not the words themselves" (4.11.26) reminds us of the perennial humanistic and biblical wisdom that it is all too possible to "multiplieth words without knowledge" (Job 35:16) and to "darkeneth counsel by words" (Job 38:2). Other texts were for him likewise a means, accordingly, and not an end; in the pursuit of wisdom, "we love those things by which we are carried along for the sake of that toward which we are carried" (1.35.39). The Augustinian motif of the educational journey, deeply obligated to the Exodus as well as Abrahamic narratives, is charged with implications for the practice of the intellectual and moral virtues. Ours is to be "a road of the affections" (1.17.16); we learn the good by doing the good (1.9.10). Not everything we use instrumentally is to be loved (1.23.22), but since the end of our pursuit is knowledge of that Being whose reflected image we call "human" (1.22.20), knowledge of the human is essential to our own participation in that Being. These formulations are echoed explicitly and influentially by Anselm of Canterbury toward the end of the eleventh century (*Monologion* 46) and suggested as a conceptual propaedeutic for all coherent intellectual reflection.

Implicitly, on this account, participation in the *imago Dei* makes of the study of the humanities something almost sacramental, at least as long as there is acknowledgement that much we recognize as the highest human good is not simply a product of our own acculturation—or as we might say, our social construction. Another way to say this is that the Christian tradition assumes that intelligence can distinguish between invention and discovery of something already given. Recognition of the magnitude and authority of our exemplar, Augustine wants to say, is essential, not least because it allows the mind formed by the Scriptures to become capable of a true cosmopolitanism. For example:

> If those who are called philosophers, especially the Platonists, have said things which are indeed true and are well accommodated to our faith, they should not be feared; rather, what they have said should be taken from them as from unjust possessors and converted to our use. Just as the Egyptians had not only idols and grave burdens which the people of Israel detested and avoided, so also they had vases and ornaments of gold and silver and clothing which the Israelites took with them secretly when they fled, as if to put them to a better use. . . . In the same way all the teachings of the pagans contain not only simulated and superstitious imaginings and grave burdens of unnecessary labor, which each one of us leaving the society of pagans under the leadership of Christ ought to abominate and avoid, but also liberal disciplines more suited to the uses of truth, and some most useful precepts concerning morals. (2.40.60)

That is, truth is truth wherever it comes from, and as such the Christian should know that, whatever its source, if it is truth then "it is his Lord's" (2.18.28). We can also expect there to be a harmony between the books of nature and Scripture, rightly placed and understood (2.39.59). Obscurity and figurative discourse in relation to the "big questions" are not necessarily a failure of language or a means of gnostic exclusion, but even in Scripture itself can be an artfully deliberate means of *inducare, educare*, leading to the truth (2.6.7-8). The appropriate method of learned investigation is thus hermeneutically ordered—patient unfolding of the layers of meaning hidden in the text, separating "fruit" from "chaff." This is the prototype of what would be called a millennium and a half later, by professional readers long secularized, "explication de texte."

THE MONASTIC *STUDIUM*

Many European cities have histories of cultural and civic development that begin either with a Roman garrison or a Benedictine monastery. The Roman garrisons have all disappeared; most were gone by the mid-fifth century. But the Benedictine monasteries persisted; even after Viking marauders annihilated some of the monks, others would return to take their place, briskly resuming their work of horticulture, medicine, translation and the building of libraries. This is because, in addition to poverty, chastity and obedience, the Benedictines took a vow to practice *stabilitas*, sticking with it. It is to their assiduous efforts at translation and paraphrase of the Bible that numerous European languages owe their first exhibition in written form; subsequent to biblical paraphrase and specifically Christian poetry, a literacy was created that allowed for the textual preservation of native poetry and written chronicle.[13] The very earliest recorded Anglo-Saxon poet was a common stable hand, Caedmon, who by a miraculous gifting recounted in the *Ecclesiastical History of England* (731) by the Venerable Bede, first produced a poem in praise of the creation, then some poetic biblical paraphrases, perhaps including *Genesis A* and *Genesis B* (influential on Milton). The cultural histories of Whitby, Wearmouth and Jarrow, as well as Bede's biographical vignettes of Caedmon, Abbess Hilda, and King Alfred the Great all make evident how efforts at missionary translation in monastic centers led directly to the growth of native as well as classical learning. The monasteries were centers not only for the study of Scripture and theological commentary but also for the growth of experimental science and medicine. Because monastic libraries were the repository of Greek and Latin texts—preserved (sometimes at the cost of life) from the ravages of war—they were enduring hubs of classical learning as well: if it were not so, Alcuin would hardly have needed to ask his version of Tertullian's rhetorical question.

---

[13]David Knowles, *Saints and Scholars* (Cambridge: Cambridge University Press, 1962), pp. 6-8.

But here is the point too often missed: classical learning, indeed all types of learning in the monasteries, was organized around a *studium* whose central preoccupation was the Bible. It was the study of the Bible—principally but not exclusively in Jerome's translation into Latin— far more than the study of Cicero and the classical authors generally that spread Latin literacy *and* produced also a textual tradition in several European vernaculars. Moreover, we can say confidently not only that the Bible in such a fashion was foundational for general humane learning in European culture but also that without it much of Roman secular learning and many of the ancient texts themselves would not have survived to be a part of our culture at all.[14]

LITURGY AND POETRY

It is important to note, however, that the Christian Scriptures were being made continuously present to the imaginative life of medieval culture not through private reading (the privilege of only a comparative few, mostly in monastic communities) but universally through worship, in the scheduled lectionary readings from the Old Testament, Psalms, New Testament Epistles and Gospels for each day of the year. In the long centuries before the advent of the printing press, Bibles were extremely costly to produce. (This situation pertained also in biblical times; the only time we see Jesus with the Scriptures in his hand is when he rises to read the text of Isaiah in the Nazareth synagogue from a hand-copied scroll [Lk 4:17].)

Collectively, the readings of the medieval church were orchestrated to guide the community of believers through the Christian year, beginning from Advent and culminating in the summer and autumn seasons after the feasts of Pentecost, Corpus Christi and Trinity Sunday, with further selections following on the great themes of the annual worship cycle. The overall theme of these readings was the *historia humanae salvationis*, the history of human redemption. Typically then, even those living in monastic communities did not read all of the Bible cover to

---

[14]A solid case for the place of classical literature in the curricula of Christian colleges has been made by Louis Markos, *From Achilles to Christ: Why Christians Should Read the Pagan Classics* (Downers Grove, Ill.: InterVarsity Press, 2007).

cover; rather, they *heard* a very substantial part of the Scriptures read aloud in a theologically symphonic, comparative fashion in the context of the daily office and regular eucharistic celebration. Several important consequences arise from this fact, among them that the Scriptures were deeply instituted in the collective oral-aural memory of communities as a shared heritage and common story, and also that the rhetorical-oratorical and literary character of the text was appreciated and learned by heart through a combination of public reading and meditative recollection, including the ancillary practice of praying the Scripture, *lectio divina*. This effectively made of large portions of the Scriptures, for many, an internalized imaginative reality to a degree seldom achieved by Christians today. Perhaps most importantly, however, this was a shared reality, tied naturally to the order of everyday community life. Christians came thus to associate the particular stories and counsel of Scripture with an annual cycle corresponding to the passing seasons of the agricultural year as well as with renewal and reconciliation in their life shared in Christ.[15] As in pagan times there had been stories for various seasons of the agricultural year, so now there were stories from the Bible coordinated to the liturgical year.

Readers sensitive to this liturgical context will appreciate that there is a wonderful appropriateness in the fact that the advent of English literature is deeply colored by the liturgical season of Advent. The inherent analogies are far richer than can be explored fully here, but the attentive reader of Anglo-Saxon poetry (even in translation) will immediately notice that one of the themes of this northern literature is the binary opposition of darkness and light, just as is the case in many of the Advent worship readings. Another echo is an elegiac recognition of the frailty and transience of human life (in Old English, a recurrent expression is *lif is laene*, "life is fleeting," as in the lyric poem "Ruin"). In many Anglo-Saxon lyrics a deep yearning for enduring peace is set against the dark realities of violence and terror, which are often in these poems explicitly connected with a legacy of the Fall. In *Beowulf*, the marauding Grendel is an age-old exile from human community, said to

---

[15]Thus, for example, the Ember Days, fasts that marked off the four seasons (Lat. *quattuor temporum*).

be "*Caines cynne,*" of the lineage of Cain, and the bright light and warm comforts of Hrothgar's hall are threatened by an evil *sheadu* representative of the dark and fallen wilderness beyond.[16] "The Wanderer" and "The Seafarer" capture hauntingly experiences of exile (OE *ut-lagu,* lit. "outside the law") and a longing for homecoming to the *hlaf-weard* (loaf-guardian, the origin of ME *lauerd* and then our contracted modern English word *lord*). The Anglo-Saxon speaker in these poems is not a happy wanderer, but one who keenly seeks a return to the Lord, and his reconciling embrace.[17] At another register we might say that these poems typically express a deep desire for closure, for a turn to meaning that might transform the chaos of fallen experience into a new day of grace and peace.

The beautiful Benedictine *Advent Lyrics of the Exeter Book* (late eighth century) offer a concise capturing of this theme and mood. These poems paraphrase the seven Latin "O" antiphons for the final octave of Advent until the Christmas Eve vigil (all drawn from messianic passages in Isaiah to characterize the anticipated Christ: "O Sapientia," "O Adonai," "O Radix Jesse," "O Clavis David," "O Oriens," "O Rex Gentium," "O Emmanuel"). The Advent Lyric based on the fifth of these liturgical antiphons, for December 21—the winter solstice and thus the longest night of the year—begins "*Eala Earendel,*" "O Dayspring," and celebrates the advent of a new dawning in the East, a light coming into the world in the form of God's promised son/sun (the pun in OE is ubiquitous). That this date was still for many the most momentous of the pagan year, characterized by dark ritual observances of barrow-wights in dank underground chambers awaiting the thin sliver of light to signal a sordid sacrifice, makes the "*Earendel*" antiphon trenchant with the tension between two contrasting imaginations of meaning in the moment. One perspective, inexorably cyclical, sees nothing beyond the annual round; the other sees through the cycle into another order of time, a far brighter light, shining unto a new and perfect day to come. The poet's prayer, doubtless for liturgical use in the worship for

---

[16]*Beowulf,* trans. Seamus Heaney (New York: Norton, 2000), 1.107.
[17]"The Wanderer" and "The Seafarer," in *Seven Old English Poems,* ed. John C. Pope (New York: Norton, 1981), pp. 28-38.

this night, constitutes both a joyous confession and a petition:

> that you send us the bright sun, and come yourself
> that you may illumine those who long before,
> covered with darkness and obscurity here,
> have been sitting in unbroken night, enshrouded in sin;
> we had to endure the dark shadow of death.
> Now in hope, we believe in the salvation
> brought to mankind by the Word of God.[18]

The meaning of Advent (as distinct from winter solstice) thus resides in a joyous hope. It will help us better to appreciate the lyric if we imagine it in its context and setting, as though we were members of the choir at a service of vespers, in a partly candle-lit abbey chapel such as that at Lindisfarne or Whitby, where the music was Gregorian plain chant. This antiphon (the term indicates singing of the alliterative half lines alternatively by monks on both sides of the choir) makes for those who hear as well as those who sing an uncompromisingly realistic acknowledgment, namely, that the worst of the long dark pagan night may well persist as a cold mirk in our own unholy souls. It expresses candidly the acuteness of our need for what we cannot ourselves, or by any of the dire old sacrifices, provide. And yet, for all that, this poem looks forward in confident, grateful hope to the only thing that could ever overcome the shadow of such darkness—the coming of the Son. It turns out that the rhetorical question ought perhaps to have been, "What has Christ to do with Ingeld?"—to which the answer is something like "Christ, to Ingeld, is the bringer of true light."

But the definitive answer may be that given in the greatest of all Anglo-Saxon poems, "The Dream of the Rood."[19] In this lyric, part of which was inscribed on a eighth-century stone cross at Ruthwell, Christ is presented as warrior hero to outdo every Ingeld, a champion who is willing to do battle with death itself and unflinchingly sacrifice his own life to gain a far greater victory—"by obedience unto death, even

---

[18]*The Advent Lyrics of the Exeter Book*, ed. and trans. Jackson J. Campbell (Princeton, N.J.: Princeton University Press, 1959), p. 54.

[19]Bruce Dickins and Alan S. C. Ross, *The Dream of the Rood* (New York: Appleton-Century-Crofts, 1966).

the death of the cross." For the poet the cross has power for his culture
both in its literal and symbolic dimensions:

> I saw the Cross
> Swiftly, varying vesture and hue,
> Now wet and stained with the Blood outwelling,
> Now beautifully jeweled with gold and gems.

What Christ brings to Ingeld, in short, is a higher, more noble vision of the heroic ideal than even the "best of men" in pagan culture
had yet achieved. In this sense, at least, we may say that Christ both
redeems and transfigures Ingeld, lending to that noble pagan gold a
luster that outshines mere mortality. In the words of a Franciscan poet
of the early fourteenth century—which might almost have been written as a commentary:

> Gold & al þis werdis wyn
> Is nouth but Christis rode.

> [Gold and all the joy of words—*or* all the wine in the world
>   *(the polyvalent phrase means both)*—
> is worthless, but for the cross of Christ.]

DRAMA AS (RE)PRESENTATION

After the Anglo-Saxon peoples lost the Battle of Hastings, their language and culture was largely suppressed. During the three centuries of
Anglo-Norman French dominance (1066-1360), little English poetry
was preserved, and apart from a flourishing of Anglo-Norman devotional lyrics, most vernacular literature in French resembled continen-
tal fabliaux and romance.[20] But by the fourteenth century a loose paraphrase of portions of the Bible, especially those narratives central to the
liturgical cycle of the Christian year, began to reach a wide popular
audience outside of the worship context in the form of vernacular
drama, the pageant plays of the Corpus Christi Cycle. (Biblical narrative also yields up individual plays like *The Conversion of St. Paul* and
Mary Magdalene, probably performed originally on or near the respec-

---

[20]David Lyle Jeffrey and Brian Levy, *The Anglo-Norman Lyric: An Anthology*, rev. ed. (Toronto:
Pontifical Institute of Medieval Studies, 2006).

tive feast days of these figures, June 29 and July 22.)[21] The form of the play cycles, such as those associated with Chester, York, Wakefield and the one now known as the N-Town Cycle, was a sequence of dramatized biblical stories beginning with the creation and extending through to "Domes-daeg" or the Last Judgment.[22] These presentations, each of them short, could together take all day—or even, as in the forty-eight play cycle at York, two or three days—to perform. They were performed outdoors, at the season of the year almost precisely opposite to the winter solstice, namely, the long days near midsummer's eve, June 21, and it is clear that the intended audience was not the French-speaking court but the English peasantry and town and trade culture. The feast of Corpus Christi itself falls on the Thursday after Trinity Sunday (post-Easter, a moveable feast occasionally falling in July), and in the Middle Ages it marked a culminating point in the liturgical year as well as the beginning of the "somer sesoun." The readings and hymns associated with the Corpus Christi Mass form a kind of recapitulation of the *historia humanae salvationis;* moreover, as the name suggests, Corpus Christi celebrates the eucharistic participation of the body of Christ (his church) in the redemptive offering of the Body of Christ (represented by the Host) in the Mass.

Re-presentation is, accordingly, both message and medium, theme and method in these dramatic cycles. As few people could understand the Latin of the readings in church, the biblical stories were kept present to the imagination of the community not only through painting, sculpture and stained glass, but through vivid dramatization in the preaching of the mendicant friars and perhaps most powerfully of all in this annual repetition of vernacular biblical plays. A very large local

---

[21]These plays are to be found conveniently in David Bevington, ed., *Medieval Drama* (Boston: Houghton Mifflin, 1975), pp. 664-753; for a study, see *Medieval Drama*, Stratford-Upon-Avon Studies 16, ed. Neville Denny (London: Edward Arnold, 1973), pp. 69-90. Modern English spelling texts include *English Mystery Plays: A Selection*, ed. Peter Happe (1975; reprint, Harmondsworth, U.K.: Penguin, 1985), and *York Mystery Plays: A Selection in Modern Spelling*, ed. Richard Beadle and Pamela M. King (1984; reprint, Oxford: Oxford University Press, 1999).

[22]Among the many studies of the medieval cycle drama, V. A. Kolve, *The Play Called Corpus Christi* (Stanford, Calif.: Stanford University Press, 1966), and O. B. Hardison Jr., *Christian Rite and Christian Drama in the Middle Ages* (Baltimore: Johns Hopkins University Press, 1965) are particularly valuable.

cast of amateurs was everywhere involved; typically each individual play in a cycle was sponsored and acted by members of a particular trade or guild (readers of Chaucer may remember that Absalon the clerk in the Miller's Tale "pleyeth Herodes upon a scaffold hye" [1.3384]). In this way the present life of the local community and the past history of biblical people came to seem part of one seamless story. This is entirely consistent with the medieval conception of meaning in history. In the light of an overarching, unifying sense of participation in one grand narrative of which God is the ultimate Author, differences of time and place seem insignificant to the playwrights. The shepherds of Wakefield look and speak as those in Judea might if they had spoken Middle English. In these plays Jesus *is* born in Bethlehem, but so is he born among villagers in the dales of Yorkshire; he *is* present in the Eucharist in any N-Town; the "house of bread" (Heb. *Beth-lehem*) in which he comes to be *hlaf-weard*, as Lord both guest and Host, is representatively to be found in Beverly or Lincoln or Chester in the here and now; his real presence requires of the Christian only that to the symbols of that presence his faith be awake. After all, the Savior's name is Emmanuel, "God with us."

This context helps us to see how "Christmas in July" in these plays, with their imagery of darkness turned to light, was less jarring, more natural associatively than it is likely to be for many of our contemporaries. The plays are filled with earthy humor, but also high purpose. In the famous *Second Shepherd's Play* of the anonymous Wakefield Master, the shepherds are at first shown not in harmonious piety but in realistic struggle with the persistence of sin and disordered affections.[23] That some of their language is rather vigorously vernacular is not, in the medieval context, the primary evidence of this spiritual realism. This particular play also acknowledges the problem of disharmony among the shepherds themselves, competitiveness in their pastoral care, even as they are constantly having to ward off Mak, a scurrilous sheep stealer who is no shepherd of any kind. In fact, before the angels can sing their glad tidings, Mak dupes the distracted shepherds, disguises a

---

[23]*The Second Shepherd's Pageant (Wakefield)*, in *Medieval Drama*, ed. David Bevington (Boston: Houghton Mifflin, 1975), pp. 383-408.

stolen sheep with swaddling cloths as if it is a new bairn in the cradle of his shrewish wife, and so sets up the contrast of a false son born of sin with the true Son and holy Lamb of God who takes away the sin of the world. The discovery and unmasking of Mak's foul artifice by the shepherds, especially once they combine active charity with working in harmony, is in itself a reminder of the perennial distinction to be made between true and false shepherds, even as it foils an antichrist with the true Messiah, who then may be proclaimed and beautifully, harmoniously worshiped in "Bethlehem."

The "Mak-subplot," as sometimes it is called, functions as a species of ironic commentary on the main biblical plot; it is a kind of burlesque by which the truth of the incarnation may be all the more clearly highlighted by a foil of darkness and fraud. This pastoral emphasis in the retelling of the story from Luke's Gospel points to the collective well-being and harmony of those who faithfully serve the flock as opposed to those who don't, contextualizing the Christmas shepherds as if they were characters in the parables of Jesus. Thus, on a humble stage in the rude vernacular of rural folk, the Word has effectually become flesh in a way that touches on the shared experience of flock and shepherds. As the subsequent plays involving Jesus' life and ministry make ever more clear, the "true Shepherd of the sheep," whose example set the standard for every kind of faithful stewardship, of clergy and laity alike, has "dwelt among us, . . . full of grace and truth" (Jn 1:14). *The Second Shepherd's Play* thus initiates a commentary on the gospel more broadly, and in spirit as well as method is akin to the kind of Bible commentary practiced by Ambrose, Augustine, Gregory and the Venerable Bede. Such a way of reading and commenting is less like an academic interpretation, and far more like active participation in a search for the Author. Realized understanding is in this sense a product of discovery, and it tends to produce "a poem of love."

PILGRIM NARRATIVE

Sometimes medieval literary references to the Christian year are initially muted so as to add pleasure and an accumulated weight of meaning to their subsequent discovery in a later context. One often-over-

looked example is in Dante's *Divine Comedy* (c. 1310-1320), where we
learn in canto 21, line 112 of the *Inferno* (and there only by inference)
that the pilgrim's journey begins on Good Friday, ending in *Paradiso* on
Easter Sunday. Another notable instance is in Chaucer's late fourteenth-
century *Canterbury Tales* where, though it is clear enough in the opening lines that the pilgrims set forth in springtime, according to the
zodiac evidently after the end of March, we learn only in the prologue
to the Man of Law's Tale on the "second day" that the pilgrims have
left the inn in London's suburban Southwerk on April 17 precisely. This
knowledge adds much to our sense of the journey: "Bifil that in that
seson on a day," says the narrator; inescapably the trek is a penitential
pilgrimage of the sort frequently undertaken in Lent, and the specific
date links Chaucer's pilgrim company to the itinerary of the whole
church.[24] That this particular pilgrim journey sets out from a very
worldly city and that the pilgrims' destination is the primary English
spiritual city of Canterbury are features suggestive in themselves that
the fictional journey is somehow symbolic of a larger reality. For one
thing, the principal site of veneration at Canterbury, we are reminded,
is the tomb of St. Thomas à Beckett, who was murdered at the altar for
defending the independence of the church from the state. T. S. Eliot's
play on the subject, *Murder in the Cathedral* (1935), tells the story powerfully. The struggle portrayed is recurrent; in their own fashion Shakespeare's *Henry VIII* (1593), William Roper's *Life of Sir Thomas More*
(1626) and Robert Bolt's *A Man for all Seasons* (1960) all bear witness to
this theme of deep tension between the city of this world and the city
of God that has, since well before the time of Augustine, been a major
theme of Christian literature. Rendering unto Caesar what is Caesar's
and to God what is God's is a more difficult task than it might seem; it
remains a perennial challenge to Christian discernment.

In order to appreciate *The Canterbury Tales* it may help us to recognize that Chaucer's readers were actually hearers in a thoroughly po-

---

[24]See Chauncey Wood, "The April Date as a Structural Device in the Canterbury Tales," *Mod-
ern Language Quarterly* 25 (1964): 259-71. A sound basic edition is Geoffrey Chaucer, *The
Canterbury Tales*, in *The Riverside Chaucer*, ed. Larry D. Benson, 3rd ed. (Boston: Houghton
Mifflin, 1987), pp. 23-328.

liticized public setting (his work was read aloud in the court). As the audience listened to Chaucer read his tales, doubtless after a day of court business and an elegant dinner, they could hardly help but sense a certain audacity in his implication that among the kinds of misbehavior requiring repentance in his day was abuse of the prerogatives of both civic and ecclesiastical authority. Some of his audience might easily have become uncomfortable, and for varying reasons. Though of necessity a medieval poet was required to get at his courtly audience indirectly through their functionaries, Chaucer's Friar, Summoner, Monk, Prioress and Pardoner are all openly presented as servants of two masters; their hypocritical practice bears witness that mammon is the actual God among too many of the clergy. Civic authorities such as the Miller, Reeve, Man of Law and Squire, each in his own way, are shown to be little better as examples of a right ordering of the affections, almost never distinguishing between intrinsic and merely instrumental goods. Each of these characters is, as a consequence, a socially disruptive figure.

But not, we should note, irredeemable. The penitential themes associated with Lent presuppose that the life of Christian community is a self-correcting journey, and it will be helpful to readers of *The Canterbury Tales* to know that Chaucer's pervasive themes of right intention (entente), of gaining a balanced and sound interpretation of the texts (or stories) one chooses to tell, and of the necessity of "good entente" to successful judgment take their place within this epistemological and theological context.[25] Many of Chaucer's fictive narrators illustrate the principle that if our intentions in any act of re-presentation or interpretation include deception, evasion or self-justification, then folly, self-deception, misunderstanding of narratives as well as of other persons, and ultimately personal sorrow will be the result. This is certainly no less true where the text of Scripture itself is concerned: the Wife of Bath (who, like the woman by the well in John 4, has had five husbands and seeks a sixth) cites the Bible and church fathers more than anyone except the faithful Parson, but she misquotes, quotes out of context and

---

[25]Jeffrey, *People of the Book*, pp. 191-202.

misinterprets in a fashion both hilarious and spiritually perilous. In her willfulness she is a falsifier, a perverter of truth. In her "entente" to defend her own promiscuity and advocate the whorish abuse of marriage as an institution, she represents, however comically, the Babylon of this world from which the Christian pilgrim is urged to flee. Flamboyant in her spurs and scarlet leotards, her voluminous saddleback instruction is hyperbolic and antiphrastic. Yet there is an overtone of poignancy as well: sadly, the Wife of Bath turns out to be a victim of her own willfulness even as, in symbolic terms, she plays the role of spiritual siren, as potentially dangerous as the Whore of Babylon.

Characters in medieval poetry tend to be pretty much "ideas dressed up like people," as John Fleming puts it; there is little attempt by most writers to provide psychological realism in our sense.[26] Though in Chaucer a great deal of verisimilitude is used in characterization and especially voice, the attuned reader will notice readily how much of what passes for description is in fact verbal iconography and symbol, and that much of what seems at first merely homely talk turns out to be citation of Scripture, the fathers of the church or Latin authors of the sort from which Augustine had recommended the mining of "Egyptian gold" (*On Christian Doctrine* 2.40.60). It is highly doubtful that Chaucer had many actual contemporaries in mind as direct models for his pilgrims. The kind of truth the pilgrims point to is less local or material than universal and spiritual; their place in Chaucer's fiction is instrumental to a richer view of reality and higher truth and good. Chaucer's worldview entails a theology of history analogous to that in Augustine or the medieval cycle plays: he points to our need for a "better county" (cf. Heb 11:13-16), and thus our need for redirection, turning away from our old life of disordered affections to a new life and better itinerary. It is no accident that as the troupe nears Canterbury and the possibility of restored communion at Easter, the last tale is his Parson's sermon on repentance, artfully anticipated in the prologue to the Parson's Tale. Chaucer has his good shepherd figure make explicit an anal-

---

[26]John V. Fleming, *The Roman de la Rose: A Study in Allegory and Iconography* (Princeton, N.J.: Princeton University Press, 1969); see also on this general point Rosemond Tuve, *Allegorical Imagery* (Princeton, N.J.: Princeton University Press, 1966).

ogy heretofore only implicit, namely, that all along the poet has been thinking "of that pilgrimage that highte Jerusalem celestial." The stories told by his pilgrim narrators are not merely a means of passing the time but of assessing life choices in the prospect of ultimate destiny.

Such a view of the "sentence" or meaning in history does not require that, as individuals, we sew up all the loose ends ourselves (Chaucer is not Dante, much less James Joyce). Completion and closure can only come, Chaucer suggests in his final farewell to the reader, when we submit all we have imagined to the grand narrative purpose of "oure Auctor," seeking his forgiveness, the "grace of verray [true] penitence" and above all the saving "grace of hym that is kyng of kynges and preest over all preestes, that boghte us with the precious blood of his herte" (1.1081-90). As this prayerful liturgical language (derived ultimately from Hebrews) suggests, it will only be in what the Parson calls the "blissful regne" (1.1079) of the City of God (cf. Heb 11:13-16) that all tensions experienced in our long pilgrimage will be forever resolved, and not by us. To fail to understand Chaucer on this point would be to misunderstand utterly the focus of his fierce social criticism. He is not in our sense calling for a political revolution but for examination of conscience and repentance on the part of all, not for social reformation alone but for the Christian sacrament of reconciliation, and thus for corrective self-knowledge and personal obedience to Christ on the part of all who would be faithful members of his body. Any attempt to read *The Canterbury Tales* that fails to account for its deliberative, artful, prophetic conclusion will deny to the larger work both its architectonic and moral unity, which is as much to say, its imaginative residence within the Christian grand narrative from which it draws so much of its literary beauty and power.

TALES OF RESURRECTION AND THE WORLD TO COME

Easter themes in medieval literature, while not always suggesting a performance context in the season itself, are a significant feature of the hopefulness and good cheer that so much medieval poetry projects. This is a feature that can hardly be too much emphasized. It is remarkable that in a world in which grim, epidemic death was such a pervasive reality (the Black Death swept away more than half of the population during Chaucer's boyhood and there were significant recurrences of plague several times before the end of the century), depictions of such death and even illness scarcely feature in the work of Chaucer and his contemporaries. Poetry that offers comfort in the face of death's inevitability, such as Chaucer's *Book of the Duchess* (c. 1368), or that celebrates the resurrection and the life to come, such as *Saint Erkenwald* (c. 1386),[27] is a notable feature of this literature, however, and it is appropriate that we should conclude our introduction to medieval English literature with some mention of it.[28] In poems such as these the sacramental life of Christians is shown to be the transformative agent that had been missing in even the best of pre-Christian culture.

In the brief but hauntingly beautiful late thirteenth-century Breton lai called *Sir Orfeo*, we are offered a powerful contrast between a classical tale (from Ovid) and the redemptive Easter story. In Ovid the tale of Orpheus and Eurydice strikes the old, familiar theme that death cannot be cheated or even somehow assuaged by the grace of art. Yet in *Sir Orfeo* there steals upon the reader a tacit metamorphoses in which— just as that familiar dark conclusion is about to occur, when Orpheus, unable to resist his backward glance, sorrowfully witnesses the second death of his bride—an astonishing, unanticipated escape from death's dark dominion occurs. It happens in only two lines: Eurydice is freed from Pluto's power. As the poem concludes—with the reward of a faithful steward and revelation of the true, triumphant king—the reader recognizes that a stunning reversal has come about, so to speak, in the twinkling of an eye. Because of Christ, a powerful old story has been retold precisely so that it might be transformed: death is overcome, the bride is restored and the world rejoices in an epithalamium that every worthy harper now can sound.[29]

---

[27] *Saint Erkenwald*, in *The Complete Works of the Pearl Poet*, trans. Casey Finch, ed. Malcolm Andrew, Ronald Waldron and Clifford Peterson (Berkeley: University of California Press, 1993), pp. 323-39.

[28] The sacramental character and efficacy of baptism is a major theme in this poem. Although the Middle English is challenging to render in contemporary prose, a reasonable translation has been made by Brian Stone in *The Owl and the Nightingale, Cleanness and St. Erkenwald* (Harmondsworth, U.K.: Penguin, 1971).

[29] *Sir Orfeo*, trans. J. R. R. Tolkien (Boston: Houghton-Mifflin, 1978), this short work can be

It may be that *Pearl* (late fourteenth century) is of all English poems of this type the best known.[30] It is also arguably the most beautiful poem of the entire period. Dream vision is a genre frequently used when poets wish to speak of eternal rather than merely temporal realities (one might think here of Dante's great poem, but also of the Revelation of St. John, which concludes the New Testament and provides much imagery for *Pearl*). The *Pearl* poet describes himself as having been in a state of spiritual sloth and melancholy (we might today call it depression) that, in retrospect, he knows turning to Christ completely would have cured. The occasion for this dejection is said to be loss of his matchless pearl—he describes himself as a jeweler—which gem is later identified with an innocent maiden. The maiden, apparently a child, then appears in the poem, much as does Beatrice to Dante, to teach him about the heavenly kingdom where she dwells.

This work is an elaborate allegory, and at one level the "oriens" (dayspring) pearl can reasonably be associated with the "pearl of great price" in the kingdom parable of Matthew 13:45-46, for medieval exegetes an image of the resurrected Christ. Morally, the pearl signals the blessedness of a state of spiritual innocence; hence the identification of the pearl as a maiden. At the anagogical level, as the poem's conclusion makes clear, the matchless pearl, without spot or blemish, is to be identified with the redeemed bride of Christ in the world to come.

The speaker in the poem recounts that his revelatory vision of the pearl came to him while he was morose and idle in the "hye seson," in August. Even as the harvest was coming in, he fell asleep in a "herber," a little garden within a garden—in Christian poetry a location typically suggestive of Edenic loss as well as of unfulfilled love longing. There may well be subtle overtones of the Christian year here also, for the

---

read successfully by most students in the original Middle English. See A. J. Bliss, ed., *Sir Orfeo* (Oxford: Clarendon, 1966). For an expanded explication of this poem see David Lyle Jeffrey, *Houses of the Interpreter: Reading Scripture, Reading Culture* (Waco, Tex.: Baylor University Press, 2003), 155-72.

[30]*Pearl*, in *Complete Works of the Pearl Poet*, pp. 42-101. A modern English translation without the facing medieval text is *Pearl* in *Sir Gawain and the Green Knight, Pearl, and Sir Orfeo*, trans. J. R. R. Tolkien (London: George Allen & Unwin, 1975), pp. 89-122.

season after Whitsunday (or Pentecost) is in the readings of the medieval church the time for practical instruction in the Christian life (many parables of Jesus and practical epistles), and the "hye seson" may invoke not only the harvest of souls but also a major feast of that month, the Transfiguration (August 6), a high Mass in the ancient Sarum breviary then in use, that begins with reference to the light of revelation and chants in its introit Psalm 84, "How amiable are thy tabernacles, O Lord of hosts! My soul longeth [and] fainteth for the courts of the LORD" (Ps 84:1-3). Indeed, beauty is a major theme throughout this particular liturgy, with Christ himself addressed as "beautiful above the sons of men" in the "unspotted mirror and image of his goodness" (Gradual). The eucharistic preface comes from Matthew, "Tell the vision to no man, until the Son of man be risen again from the dead" (Mt 17:9), here to be understood also as "after the Easter season."

Aesthetically, if there is any English analogue to Dante's *Divine Comedy*, *Pearl* is the best candidate. While unlike in Dante's vision in *Paradiso* the dreamer in the English poem cannot cross the celestial river into heaven and return to mortal life (hence much more is withheld in this vision than revealed); the magnificent Gothic design of this poem certainly rivals that found in the great Italian work. In beautifully crafted alliterative lines of four stresses each, the poet has produced a work of 1212 lines, one hundred and one twelve-line stanzas (ababababab/bcbc). These are grouped into twenty fits of five stanzas each, except for the fifteenth fit, which has six stanzas. The rhymes are so arranged that they are knotted together, stanza to stanza and fit to fit, with the final word of each becoming the first of the next stanza, each of such terms being thematic keys. The structural achievement is itself astonishing, as mathematically rich as the architecture of a Gothic cathedral. Amplifying the symbolic richness, as in the Apocalypse, or Revelation of St. John, the celestial Jerusalem is described as having cubed dimensions of the ratio 12 x 12 x 12, with twelve gates and 144,000 "innocents" as the symbolic number of those who sing forever the praises of the Lamb. The pearl maiden is one of this number.[31] This

---

[31]For excellent brief essays on the poem see D. W. Robertson, *Essays in Medieval Culture* (Princeton, N.J.: Princeton University Press, 1980), pp. 209-17.

kind of medieval obsession with number and with architectonic unity and symbolic congruence can now estrange modern readers. The Christian literary critic, however, will recognize that these features convey for the medieval author and his audience deep truths, and will ponder the meaning of such worshipful high craftsmanship in relation to other aspects of such poetry.

Thus, even as the subject of *Pearl* is spiritual perfection (the possibility, through confession of sin and the transformation of imperfections by divine grace, of entrance into the perfect state of the redeemed), so too its form is literary perfection. Or almost. Clearly capable of it, the poet has nonetheless added an extra stanza, turning his poem, as a work of art, away from a closed circle, away even from the illusion of perfected closure, perhaps because it would involve pretence to offer in art what grace alone can provide. The extra stanza still implies a *ymbren*, a circuit, a return to beginnings in the diurnal round which must be our sufficient consolation as long as this mortal life shall last. In the poem's closing section the dreamer, overcome with desire to be where his treasure is, steps into the river that separates them and is immediately awakened out of his dream. He finds himself in the little inner garden in which he has first fallen asleep. But he now realizes that he is not yet ready for full union with his heart's desire, and that he has at hand a means of splendid interim consolation and anticipation—the Mass, Holy Communion, where he may share with his Lord a real and present blessing provided by his love "in the form of bread and wine," until he is himself ready to be among the "precious pearls" to please the King. Healed of his sin through grace following the confession that is the poem, he and his readers with him can with joyful hearts be restored to the community of the church, the beauty of Communion, and the adoration of the Lamb.

This keen aspiration and hope for closure animates much of medieval literature, and is a powerful presence even when one might overlook it, as in the *Pearl* poet's beautiful Arthurian romance, *Sir Gawain and the Green Knight*. It also is structured on the liturgical year, with misunderstanding, temptation, sin and repentance as the occasion of desire that human achievement by itself cannot fulfill.[32]

The remaining two alliterative poems in the *Pearl* manuscript have received much less attention generally, but deserve more from Christian students of medieval literature. *Cleannesse* (or Purity) is concerned to show how without personal holiness it is impossible to please God. Using the parable of the man without a wedding garment (Mt 22) to build a biblical case for its thesis, the poem reiterates the story of the flood and of Sodom and Gomorrah from Genesis as well as of Belshazzar's feast from Daniel 5 to draw a sharp contrast between the sacred and the profane. Closing with a prayer for God's grace to cover a multitude of unspecified sins, the poet attempts to create in his readers a strong sense of desire to respond to the divine command, "Be ye holy even as I am holy." The last of the quartet of poems by the *Pearl* author is *Patience*, which is largely a treatment of the story of Jonah as a parable of warning to clerics who resist obedience to their calling.

Pearl, Cleannesse and *Patience* are in each case skillfully composed poems of deep and orthodox Christian teaching drawn in large measure from the Bible as in the lections for the liturgy it might be encountered worshipfully. One result is that each of these three poems represents one voice in a dialogue with Holy Scripture, and makes best sense in that light, almost as if each was a homiletic commentary. This fact has suggested to some a clerical author, yet as with many medieval works, the poems are unsigned and remain unattributed. Perhaps we might wisely conclude that they speak, in effect, with the collective voice of the church; in so doing they help to reveal just how deeply Scripture and liturgy had, by this period, penetrated the poetic imagination of English poets.

SUGGESTIONS FOR FURTHER READING

Besserman, Lawrence L. *Chaucer's Biblical Poetics*. Norman: University of Oklahoma Press, 1998.

---

[32]Gawain's return from his mission as a wounded hero occurs on New Year's Day, when medieval Christians celebrated the circumcision of Christ (Lk 2:21), a suggestive date given the poem's themes. See, for example, R. A. Shoaf, *The Poem as Green Girdle: Commercium in Sir Gawain and the Green Knight* (Gainesville: University Press of Florida, 1984), chap. 2. A good edition of the poem is *Sir Gawain and the Green Knight*, in *Complete Works of the Pearl Poet*, pp. 209-321.

————. *The Legend of Job in the Middle Ages.* Cambridge, Mass.: Harvard University Press, 1979.

Hollander, Robert. "Typology and Secular Literature: Some Medieval Problems and Examples." In *Literary Uses of Typology from the Late Middle Ages to the Present.* Edited by Earl Miner. Princeton, N.J.: Princeton University Press, 1977.

Huppé, Bernard F. *Doctrine and Poetry: Augustine's Influence on Old English Poetry.* Binghamton: SUNY Press, 1959.

Jeffrey, David Lyle, ed. *Chaucer and Scriptural Tradition.* Ottawa: University of Ottawa Press, 1984.

Lewis, C. S. *The Discarded Image: An Introduction to Medieval and Renaissance Literature.* Cambridge: Cambridge University Press, 1964.

Maritain, Jacques. *Art and Scholasticism.* London: Sheed & Ward, 1930.

Miller, Robert P. *Chaucer: Sources and Backgrounds.* New York: Oxford University Press, 1977.

Nolan, Barbara. *The Gothic Visionary Perspective.* Princeton, N.J.: Princeton University Press, 1977.

Robertson, D. W., Jr. *A Preface to Chaucer: Studies in Medieval Perspectives.* Princeton, N.J.: Princeton University Press, 1962.

Wilken, Robert Louis. *The Spirit of Early Christian Thought: Seeking the Face of God.* New Haven, Conn.: Yale University Press, 2003.

Wilson, James H. *Christian Theology and Old English Poetry.* The Hague: Mouton, 1974.

FAITH AND FICTION IN
RENAISSANCE LITERATURE

Is there in truth no beauty?

GEORGE HERBERT

Renaissance English literature includes so many brilliant writers that it has always attracted serious and capable students. Despite the linguistic and cultural changes that have occurred since that time and the denominational divisions that began in this period and to some extent still define Western Christianity, informed Christian readers can hardly fail to encounter Renaissance authors who are, *inter alia*, eloquent exponents of orthodox theological wisdom. From Sir Philip Sidney, who writes a careful apologetic for the place of poetry in a Reformation worldview, to John Milton, who writes perhaps the most elaborate of poetic apologetics for the authority of biblical theology itself, Renaissance writers in England are at the heart of the formative relationship of literature to religion in English-speaking culture. While the Reformation, in both its Protestant forms and Catholic response, was undoubtedly a time of religious renewal, it also introduced such radical change and diverse configurations for interpretation of the biblical heritage that great controversies ensued. On all sides, to a degree not equaled in any other period, the poets are witnesses of an energetic Christian culture such as makes possible a largely positive philological and expositional approach to their texts; this in turn enables students to see the poets themselves as integrating faith and understanding.

Awareness of the conditions peculiar to Renaissance culture must begin with the invention of the printing press by Gutenberg in 1450. This created a much larger literate audience than had ever existed in Europe. The transition from an oral to a written popular culture made it materially possible for people to read the Bible as well as a much wider range of classical literature in their own vernacular tongue. Accordingly, these are the two "reborn" (or rediscovered) foundational sources most frequently cited to define literary innovations of the period. Wider access to biblical and classical foundations allowed Renaissance authors to offer more developed and often more nuanced literary allusions than their medieval counterparts. (Dante is among the exceptions, but he is already a transitional poet.) Indeed, modern comprehension of such rich intertextuality requires deliberate acquaintance with the linguistic, historical, political, educational and theological contexts peculiar to the Renaissance period. While it is well known that, phonetically speaking, the fourteenth-century vowel shift created what we call modern English, extensive philological work is needed to recover many once common medieval words, especially in the realm of ethics and aesthetics, that have now fallen out of use, and to determine for other words contemporary meanings often quite different from those that, as moderns, we assume. Far from being an incidental matter the presence of even one such lost or misunderstood word can render a whole sentence almost unintelligible. This unsettling fact makes the creation of footnotes in scholarly editions a critical necessity. Even so, such notes are not always accurate; nor is their application sufficiently consistent. A great literature's capacity still to convey its intertextual and extratextual richness requires that readers as well as critics consult a broad range of cultural resources, almost as might an anthropologist. That is, the task is to come to understand as much as possible the classical, biblical, medieval and contemporary background of Renaissance literature, *as it was understood by Renaissance authors.*

Political culture is a crucial element in this sort of anthropological recovery. Intertextual references were often made within an environment in which art was, to borrow Shakespeare's phrase, frequently "tongue-tied by authority."[1] Within most Renaissance monarchies, which grew in strength as medieval feudalism declined, political and religious censorship was common, though not consistently enforced. For this reason contemporary interpretation must often remain tentative. If these difficulties are not daunting enough, scholars committed to studying the period's primary texts also require paleographic skills and the patience to decipher notoriously inconsistent Renaissance orthography, as well as some ability to cope with Latin and Greek, which even the grammar school-educated writer of the time possessed in abundance. All of these factors together can seem to erect a truly formidable barrier to the understanding of Renaissance English literature, and in one form or another they have to many seemed to justify the reduction or excision of Renaissance texts from the normative English curriculum.

Christian students, however, bring to the task a distinctive point of view and incentive. One of the elements of our interest should be an appreciation of the systems of basic education that created such a high degree of Christian literacy. It helps us both to situate and to understand more sympathetically our texts if we know that the grammar schools, which provided primary education to all of the great Renaissance writers, were founded on the Christian humanism of Erasmus, Thomas More and John Colet, and always maintained an overtly Christian approach to classical culture. It was very common, indeed expected, to baptize the classical gods by assigning them Christian symbolic significance, as in the medieval moralized versions of Ovid. Yet these Christian humanists rejected the dialectical logic of medieval scholasticism in favor of narrative, paradox, irony and "copia" made possible through literary language; thus Cicero, for example, ranked for them (far less ambivalently than for St. Jerome) among the noblest speakers of the secular world. Further, Christian humanists stressed the classical trivium of rhetoric, grammar and logic. Renaissance writ-

[1]William Shakespeare, "Sonnet 66," *William Shakespeare: The Complete Works*, ed. Stanley Wells and Gary Taylor (Oxford: Clarendon, 1988), p. 759. Unless otherwise noted, all subsequent Shakespeare references are to this edition.

ers would use, in prose and poetry, a vast number of tropes (or figurative language) and schemes (or aesthetic arrangements) distinguished
by classical rhetoricians and by English writers such as Henry Peacham
and George Puttenham, as well as the many strategies for argument (a
term that dramatists and poets also apply to literary plots) available to
the orators and courtiers also educated in the persuasive arts, in order
both "to teach and to delight."

The more hybrid Renaissance Christian appropriation of classical
philosophy is also instructive. "St. Socrates" becomes a type of Christian integrity, Plato a model poet, and a neo-Platonism drawn primarily from Plotinus or Italian Renaissance thinkers like Pico Della
Miranda posits an ideal world that for some Renaissance poets becomes
a valid means to describe God's eternal glory. Many of Aristotle's literary concepts also become well known, as does at least the broad outline
of philosophies like Stoicism, Epicureanism and even Pythagorean reincarnation—though often as much an object of learned jest as of admiration. Finally, there are more obscure areas of knowledge, whether
subjects like numerology, allegory and typology, or the new transition
away from Ptolemaic cosmology, with all of its symbolic, moral and
religious connotations, and the rise of post-Copernican science and
technology exemplified by Galileo's telescope.

The restriction of public schools to males, so that usually only aristocratic, homeschooled females became literate, meant that few women
became major Renaissance writers. Contrary to the now famous argument of Virginia Woolf's *A Room of One's Own* (1929), there are, however, important exceptions. These include Anne Lock, the poet friend
of John Knox, and Sir Philip Sidney's sister, Mary Sidney Herbert,
with whom he composed the long prose romance *Arcadia* (1593), and
who wrote many of the translations of the Psalms attached as an ap-
pendix to the long prose work. Later the Sidneys' niece, Lady Mary
Wroth, would publish a painfully honest account of the female experience of courtship in her own sonnet sequence, "Pamphilia to Am-
philanthus" (1621). Those concerned to counteract the simplistic, mi-
sogynist blaming of Eve for the fall should also read Aemilia Lanyer's
"Eve's Apology in Defense of Women" (1611), which asks male readers

to confront some of their own biases in reading Genesis. Even in male-authored works, moreover, there are large numbers of memorably wise and eloquent female characters. Milton's Eve, in both her prefallen and postfallen perspectives, despite Milton's own problematic relationship to women, has much to teach us. Many of Shakespeare's heroines, further, display a linguistic wit and practical wisdom that may descend in part from various "strong women" models in biblical literature or from the high Catholic view of Mary. That women's roles were performed in Renaissance times only by boys and men seems not to have detracted much from either their imaginative conception or dramatic efficacy. Renaissance theater, which replaced the traveling medieval biblical mysteries and morality plays banned as blasphemous by the authorities of the English Reformation, became a place for imaginative exploration, ethical analysis and comic playfulness that successfully evaded political and religious censorship.

The topic much less jested about in this period than in the high Middle Ages, of course, is "correct" religion. The religious wars that followed the Protestant Reformation and the Catholic Council of Trent (sometimes termed the *Counter Reformation*) often made subscription to certain doctrines a matter of life and death, though here again England's unique history is crucial to our subject. The clearly immoral and self-serving nature of Henry VIII's initial break with Rome ensured an England sharply divided, for at least the next 150 years, between Anglicans loyal to a church that state law required everyone to attend, Catholic recusants who practiced their faith secretly (except during the brief reign of Henry's daughter, Mary [1553-1558]), and a range of Puritan believers who favored more radical reformation such as eventually led to the civil war and execution of Charles I in 1649—an act publicly justified by the poet John Milton. Success in the civil war allowed Cromwell's Commonwealth to flourish until his death in 1657 and the restoration of Charles II in 1660. Such facts are common knowledge, but what much literary scholarship has shown in the past thirty years is how difficult it can be to gauge authorial intentions or audience response within this divided religious culture, even when church affiliation is clear, which it frequently is not. The theological investigation of

Renaissance literature is nevertheless one of the most active areas of English studies today, and a prominent part of a more general turn to religion in current literary criticism.

SPEAKING PICTURES OF FAITH: SIXTEENTH-CENTURY PROTESTANT POETICS

Sir Philip Sidney may be the least well-known of our writers, notwithstanding the fame he achieved during his brief thirty-two-year life as the prototypical Renaissance man—soldier, courtier, poet—whose death in battle prompted one of the largest public funerals in English history. His stature derives mainly not from creative writing but from criticism, specifically his "Defence of Poesy."[2] Certainly we can also admire the extraordinary rhetorical style and ethical sophistication of his long prose romance, *Arcadia* (1590). His *Astrophel and Stella* (1591), moreover, is one of the most skillfully drawn psychological portraits of the melancholy inherent in the Petrarchan sonnet sequence, in which an infatuated male lover engages in seemingly endless pursuit of a scornful female love always beyond his reach. Sidney's "Defence," however, is must reading not only because of its vivid, imaginative prose and uniquely Renaissance-era mingling of classical and Christian theological aesthetics but also simply because of the many compelling answers that Sidney provides to that recurring and never fully answerable existential question: Why should poetry matter to a Christian culture? Or, as Sidney puts it, can we make the case that poetry "deserveth not to be scourged out of the Church of God"?[3] The commonplace (but not Miltonic!) Puritan and Platonic view of poetry as a form of deception, or lying, was the immediate cultural adversary against which Sidney's arguments were aimed, but a much wider sense of classical and Christian thought pervades the work and amply rewards the effort it takes to follow Sidney's arguments.

Beginning by noting that poetry is the earliest kind of writing in many cultures, Sidney finds in the Judeo-Christian tradition special

---

[2]"The Defence of Poesy" (1595), *Sir Philip Sidney: The Oxford Authors*, ed. Katherine Duncan-Jones (Oxford: Oxford University Press, 1989), pp. 212-50.
[3]Ibid., p. 215.

justification for according it high value. David's psalms, for example, are "divine poem[s]," which allow one to "see God coming in His majesty," "heavenly poesy" in which David "showeth himself a passionate lover of that unspeakable and everlasting beauty to be seen by the eyes of the mind, only cleared by faith." If this language seems a bit hyperbolic, Sidney asks that one "look a little deeper into it," and "give right honour to the Heavenly Maker of that maker," "maker" being a synonym for poet in many languages.[4] Focusing on Genesis, Sidney thus sees poetry as evidence of God "having made man to his own likeness," for in the "divine breath" that poets breathe again, there is a twofold argument for the reality of both Adam's fall and the second Adam's incarnation: through the latter, "our first erected wit maketh us know what perfection is," yet the continuing effects of the former mean that "our infected will keepeth us from reaching unto it."[5] Neither idealizing human creativity nor demeaning its divine origins, Sidney instead calls for a bold but intelligent application of the unique resources that poetry offers the Christian church.

In analyzing those resources, Sidney also draws on classical sources, especially Aristotle and Horace. First, Sidney defines "poesy" as "an art of imitation, for so Aristotle termeth it in his word *Mimesis*, that is to say, a representing, counterfeiting, or figuring forth—to speak metaphorically, a speaking picture; with this end, to teach and delight." Sidney then explains, in a distinction missed by many, that poetic mimesis can be of three kinds. First, there are those poets "that did imitate the inconceivable excellencies of God," such as King David. The second group explore a huge range of possible poetic matter: "either moral . . . or natural . . . or astronomical . . . or historical"; Sidney is not completely certain whether all such work qualifies as poetry because its focus is often "the proposed subject" rather than "the course of his own invention."[6] To grasp the third form of mimesis, and Sidney's subsequent explanation of it, one must also have in mind Aristotle's analysis of mimesis, in which he argues that the poet imitates things "that were

---

[4]Ibid., pp. 215-17.
[5]Ibid., p. 217.
[6]Ibid., pp. 217-18.

in the past, or are now, or that people say and think to be or those things that ought to be."[7] Not disputing the possibility of poets accurately presenting the reality of any particular subject, Sidney means to stress that it is not unethical for poets to employ fictions to present ideals or possibilities; poets can consciously choose, in other words, not to focus on "what is, hath been, or shall be," but rather attempt "the divine consideration of what may be, and should be."[8]

Indeed, the dual realities of the two Adams would suggest that this third kind of mimesis, which one might call the poetics of conversion, might be the more important task of the Christian poet. For if our wills are infected but our wits erected, so that we are living unworthy lives but aware of an ideal to which we must aspire, then practical change requires some imaginative vision of transformative possibility: "what may be, and should be." These arguments provide the context for the oft-misquoted line, later in the "Defense," when Sidney writes that the poet "nothing affirms, and therefore never lieth."[9] Far from being a manifesto of antirealistic, anti-ethical, "art for art's sake" approach to mimesis, as many have taken this one line to be, Sidney's point here is much more obvious, namely, that many of the fictions created by poets were never intended to be taken as true in a historical sense; anyone who reads Aesop's beast fables and "thinks that Aesop writ it for actually true," Sidney quips, "were well worthy to have his name chronicled among the beasts he writeth of." Similarly, Sidney asks rhetorically, "What child is there that, coming to a play, and seeing *Thebes* written in great letters upon an old door, doth believe that it is Thebes?"[10] Humans are capable of "entertaining the offered fallacy" (2.2.189) as Shakespeare puts it in *The Comedy of Errors*, without jumping to the conclusion that everything a poet presents is also false. Instead of strictly "laboring to tell you what is, or is not," the Christian poet instead aims more directly, Sidney asserts, at an ethical poetry that shows

---

[7]Aristotle, *Poetics*, trans. Leon Golden, in *The Critical Tradition: Classical Texts and Contemporary Trends*, ed. David H. Richter (Boston: Bedford St. Martin's, 2007), p. 79.
[8]Sidney, "Defence," p. 218.
[9]Ibid., p. 235.
[10]Ibid.

"what should or should not be."[11] Clearly, an amoral interpretation that "the poet never affirmeth" cannot explain the many other places where Sidney stresses the moral value of poets who "imitate both to delight and teach; and delight, to move men to take that goodness in hand, which without delight they would fly as from a stranger; and teach, to make them know that goodness whereunto they are moved."[12] It is the Fall that makes us flee goodness, but the delightful tales of poets draw us back to the goodness of original and still eternal realities. The poet offers "words set in delightful proportion" and "a tale which holdeth children from play, and old men from the chimney corner." Thus, "pretending no more," truly the poet "doth intend the winning of the mind from wickedness to virtue."[13]

Sidney further clarifies the ethical value of poetry via comparison with philosophy and history, two subjects already highly valued by his Puritan contemporaries. These two subjects, he writes, "would win the goal, the one by precept, the other by example. But both, not having both, do both halt." In other words, the philosopher's thought is too "abstract and general" to be applied by most people, whereas the historian "is so tied, not to what should be but to what is . . . that his example draweth no necessary consequences, and [is] therefore a less fruitful doctrine." By contrast, "now doth the peerless poet perform both; for whatsoever the philosopher saith should be done, he giveth a perfect picture of it in some one by whom he presupposeth it was done; so as he coupleth the general notion with the particular example."[14] Here Sidney perhaps falls into hyperbole, for not all poets achieve this lofty goal; conversely, moral philosophers could provide particular examples, while philosophers of history could posit ethical or even providential patterns in history. Still, Sidney's aims for poetry are clear: he believes it can have the intellectual richness of both philosophy and history by including both ethical precept and practical example, and thus promote an active virtue "with the end of well doing and not of

---

[11]Ibid.
[12]Ibid., p. 218.
[13]Ibid., p. 227.
[14]Ibid., p. 221.

well knowing only." Yet the classical ideal is not Sidney's ultimate aim; rather, "this purifying of wit, this enriching of memory, enabling of judgement, and enlarging of conceit," all made possible through the "learning" common to poetry, has as its "final end" or intention "to lead and draw us to as high a perfection as our degenerate souls, made worse by their clayey lodgings, can be capable of."[15]

However much we may find such a statement tainted by a neo-Platonic preference for the soul over the body or an overly optimistic, over-reaching aim for fallen humanity to become more than it is capable of being, Sidney's bold vision for poetry should move Christian readers to thoughtful reflection. Like St. Paul, Sidney speaks candidly of the war between flesh and spirit, but he also cannot help but be aware of the immense creative gifts bestowed on us by our Creator, or of the supreme gifts given our intellects, or "wits," by the direct revelation and incarnation of God's own Son. This definitive self-disclosure of divine Being allows us to know what perfection is and what our souls should become. Whether or not Sidney overestimates the capacity of poetry to help enable that aim or underestimates the value of other areas of human learning, Christianity owes Sidney a debt for stating so clearly the educational potential of poetry, a potential which later Renaissance writers do much to realize.

It is doubtful that any poet so directly reflects Sidney's theory of poetry as his fellow Anglican and close contemporary Edmund Spenser. This is particularly evident in Spenser's masterpiece, *The Faerie Queene* (1596), but we can also see it in some of his more important minor works. First among these is the *Amoretti* (1595), or love letters, which stands out as one of the few Renaissance sonnet sequences that has a happy and sanctioned ending—the courtship ends in betrothal (engagement) and mature covenanted love. Many of these sonnets seem to have been written for Spenser's wife, Catherine Boyle; from a Christian point of view the mutual love they describe has its source in God, who alone, on a Christian view of marriage, is truly capable of uniting human souls. Central here is Sonnet 68, which begins as an Easter sonnet:

---

[15]Ibid., p. 219.

"Most glorious Lord of lyfe, that on this day / Didst make thy triumph over death and sin," then asks specifically that this triumph may apply to marriage, allowing that couples

> May live for ever in felicity.
> And that thy love we weighing worthily,
> May likewise love thee for the same againe . . .
> So let us love, dear love, lyke as we ought,
> Love is the lesson which the Lord us taught. (8-10, 13-14)[16]

Though hardly original or unusual, Spenser's application of the atonement to marriage (the analogy traces back to St. Paul) directs lovers to the one, eternal source of love in an eloquent, memorable way. He achieves this again in Sonnet 75, writing of a lover "who wrote her name upon the strand [beach] / but came the waves and washed it away" (1-2). Here poetry is a testament to a love that endures:

> My verse your virtues rare shall eternize,
> And in the hevens wryte your glorious name.
> Where whenas death shall all the world subdew,
> Our love shall live, and later life renew. (11-14)[17]

The hope expressed here provides a transcendent Christian context for both poetry and love. Spenser has a deep, clear sense that, as he puts it in Sonnet 79, "true beautie" must be "derived from that fayre Spirit, from whom al true / and perfect beauty did at first proceed" (11-12).[18]

C. S. Lewis, in addressing the neo-Platonist elements of Spenser's art, argued that "it is certainly possible to combine and interchange" Christianity and Platonism "for a considerable time without finding a contradiction."[19] Spenser perhaps pushes this union to its fullest point in his "Fowre Hymns" (1596) on "Love," "Beautie," "Heavenly Love" and "Heavenly Beautie."[20] As the titles suggest, the belief that love and

---

[16]Edmund Spenser, "Sonnet 68," *Amoretti*, in *The Poetical Works of Edmund Spenser*, ed. J. C. Smith and E. De Selincourt (Oxford: Oxford University Press, 1970), p. 573.

[17]Spenser, "Sonnet 75," *Amoretti*, p. 575.

[18]Spenser, "Sonnet 79," *Amoretti*, p. 575.

[19]C. S. Lewis, "Edmund Spenser," *Major British Writers I*, ed. G. B. Harrison (New York: Harcourt, Brace & World, 1959), p. 103.

[20]Edmund Spenser, *Fowre Hymns*, in *The Poetical Works of Edmund Spenser*, ed. J. C. Smith and E. De Selincourt (Oxford: Oxford University Press, 1970), pp. 585-99.

beauty link time and eternity is central, and to illustrate this point countless illustrations from Scripture and classical literature are employed, though as with most Renaissance writers the preeminence of Christian revelation is always maintained. "Leander . . . Aeneas . . . Achilles . . . Orpheus" (231-34) were all driven by passionate loves, but to know heavenly love is to learn to love Christ "with all thy hart, with all thy soule and mind," and "give thy self unto him full and free / that full and freely gave himself" to God (260-65). Similarly, "faire is that, where those Idees on hie, / Enraunged be, which Plato so admired" (82-83), yet "fairer than all the rest" is "that Highest farre beyond all telling," God himself (100-101). If ever Spenser does lose sight of such hierarchies, it is only in the humanly excusable moment of celebrating his marriage in another extraordinary poem, *Epithalamion* (1595).[21] As Lewis says, "in this buoyant poem Spenser has worked all the diverse associations of marriage, actual and poetic, pagan and Christian," and within the verse at least "are all harmonized."[22] Partly this is through a very natural appropriation of the Boethian concept of the "music of the spheres," the Ptolemaic cosmological notion that one hears music when perceiving God's loving hand in ultimate control of the universe; in repetitive though varying choruses each stanza in the poem celebrates mutual love, "how all the woods may answer and your echo ring" (36). Yet beyond the sensual "fayre love of lillyes and of roses," "of the birds lovelearned song," the song of "Orpheus . . . for his owne bride" (16), the gaze upon "her snowie necke lyke to a marble towre" (177; cf. Song 7:4), Spenser also sings of "the inward beauty of her lively spright" (186), and asks, "Sing ye sweet Angels, Alleluya sing" (240), for his ultimate hope is that they "may heavenly tabernacles there inherit," a place of eternal rest when "the woods no more us answer, nor our echo ring" (426). Far from leading to syncretism, Spenser's rich classical learning simply gives him further poetic images by which to contrast, and thus magnify, the eternal spiritual love that is Christian marriage.

To appreciate the comparable but far more complex levels of mean-

---

[21]Edmund Spenser, *Epithalamion*, in *The Poetical Works of Edmund Spenser*, ed. J. C. Smith and E. De Selincourt (Oxford: Oxford University Press, 1970), pp. 579-84.
[22]Lewis, "Edmund Spenser," p. 95.

ing in Spenser's *The Faerie Queene*, it is necessary to understand something of his conception of allegory.[23] The broad allegorical intention of the poem is bluntly outlined by Spenser in a letter to Sir Walter Raleigh included in the first edition of 1590, in which he states that various knights will progress toward particular virtues: Redcrosse Knight, "Holyness" (bk. 1); Sir Guyon, "Temperaunce" (bk. 2); Britomartis, "Chastity" (bk. 3).[24] The second edition (1596) includes Cambell and other knights, representing "Friendship" (bk. 4), Artegall, "Justice" (bk. 5), and Calidore, "Courtesie" (bk. 6). The fragmentary, aptly-named "Mutabalitie" cantos conclude a very long poem that would have been much longer still had not Spenser's life been cut short in 1599. Few contemporary students have likely lamented the curtailment of *The Faerie Queene*, for the effort to navigate what Spenser did complete requires some strong premodern habits. First, one is expected to desire not only to understand but also to live the virtues explored in each book. That is, without dismissing C. S. Lewis's useful observation that *The Faerie Queene* appeals to "a child's love of marvels and dread of bogies, a boy's thirst for adventures, a young man's passion for physical beauty" and that "the poem is a great palace, but the door into it is so low that you must stoop to go in," it is also important to recognize, with A. C. Hamilton, Spenser's debt and contribution to the tradition of Christian allegory.[25] Hamilton compares the allegorical content of Spenser's famous opening scene, with its "gentle knight pricking on the plain" with the opening scene of Dante's *Divine Comedy*.[26] In both cases, Hamilton suggests, one should focus first on the literal image given in the poem, recognizing both its "extrinsic meaning which relates the episode to our world," and its "intrinsic" meaning, "the inner coherence which binds all parts of the poem."[27] Once we learn to read this way, he says, we need not treat "the narration as a veil to be torn aside for the hidden meaning," but can instead follow "Sidney's art

---

[23]Edmund Spenser, *The Faerie Queene* (1596), ed. A. C. Hamilton (London: Longman, 2001).
[24]Edmund Spenser, "A Letter of the Author to Sir Walter Raleigh" (1590); ibid., pp. 714-18.
[25]Lewis, "Edmund Spenser," p. 97.
[26]A. C. Hamilton's *The Structure of Allegory in The Faerie Queene* (Oxford: Clarendon Press, 1961), pp. 30-43.
[27]Ibid., p. 34.

of reading poetry" as "an imaginative groundplot of a profitable invention."[28] The allegory of *The Faerie Queene* thus becomes not "a complicated puzzle concealing riddles" but rather "an unfolding drama revealing more and greater significance as it brings the reader to full understanding."[29] This approach can be applied to many scenes within the poem, but a good starting point for students is canto 9 of book 1, in which Redcrosse Knight encounters Despair, and journeys so far from holiness that he almost commits suicide.

By this point Redcrosse has struggled with Error, been deceived by Archimago and committed adultery with Duessa, whom he mistook for his true love Una; in sum, he seems even more spiritually vulnerable than Sir Terwin, the knight who, scorned by his lover, committed suicide and now lies dead inside Despair's cave. Though despair is a major Renaissance topic, often considered abstractly in relation to the "humour" of melancholy and more concretely identified by some theologians with the unforgivable "sin against the Holy Spirit" (as when Faustus tells himself, "despair, and die,"[30] or Richard III's victims haunt him with the same line[31]) we also see Despair here as clearly as any character in realistic fiction:

> His griesie lockes, long growen, and unbound,
> Disordered hung about his shoulders round,
> And hid his face; through which his hollow eyne
> Lookt deadly dull, and stared as astound. (1.9.310-14)

Despair's hideous appearance is forgotten, however, once he begins to speak some of the most rhetorically seductive speeches in Spenser. He first presents death as an especially attractive form of sleep, extolling the benefits to those who enter it quickly; such are also pleasing to God, he continues, for "the lenger life, I wote the greater sin" (379). Only the dead are sure to sin no more and thus avoid further eternal

---

[28]Ibid., p. 43.
[29]Ibid.
[30]Christopher Marlowe, *Doctor Faustus* (1592), ed. Russell A. Fraser and Norman Rabkin, *Drama of the English Renaissance I: The Tudor Period* (New York: Collier Macmillan, 1976), pp. 169-203.
[31]Shakespeare, *Richard III*, act 5, scene 3, in *Complete Works*, pp. 217-18.

punishments, Despair argues, and so death should be accepted as one's predestined end, for it is already written in God's "eternall booke of fate" (374). Despair rhetorically asks, "who then can strive with strong necessitie . . . or shunne the death ordained by destinie" (375), so, logically, if one's sin shows one to be among the damned, the sooner the end comes the more pleased God will be. Potently uniting an appeal to hedonism with a logic ruthless even for the most hardened advocate of double predestination, Despair reminds Redcrosse that "his sinful hire" faces a "day of wrath" from a "just" god who proclaims "let every sinner die" (408-19). Just as Faustus remembers the scriptural assertion that "the reward of sin is death" without its complementary promise,[32] here Redcrosse is persuaded by half truths, choosing his own spiritual and physical death: "At last resolved to work his final smart, / He lifted up his hand, that back again did start" (458-59). With a sudden, unexpected response that enacts the grace of God, Una arrives and reminds our knight of the one truth which all sinners must never forget:

> In heavenly mercies hast thou not a part?
> Why shouldst thou then despeire, that chosen art?
> Where justice grows, there grows eke greater grace. (472-74)

Whereas Despair's lies require many stanzas of polished rhetorical argument, the simple truth of Una speaks directly to Redcrosse's heart and immediately liberates him. "So up he rose, and thence amounted straight" (478), freed by the grace of God. Despair, meanwhile, could not die, "till he should die his last, that is eternally" (486).

Within this brief scene a conception of predestination as the foreordained damnation of God—which, rightly or wrongly, many attributed to Calvin's notion of double predestination—is roundly defeated by the certain truth that one is chosen for heavenly mercy; however much justice requires judgment, a greater grace offers forgiveness. This brief example shows how moving Spenser's allegory can be even to those who may not fully share the particulars of Spenser's Anglican and strongly anti-Catholic viewpoint. So committed an Anglican as C. S.

---

[32]"For the wages of sin is death; but the gift of God is eternal life through Jesus Christ our Lord" (Rom 6:23). See the discussion of *Faustus*, following.

Lewis, in fact, argues that Spenser's "historical allegory" should be of least importance to the modern student. On the central object of each knight's quest, Lewis claims that it is more important to see Spenser's "Gloriana" as the "divine glory or splendor which the Christian soul will not only see but share in Heaven" than as an allegory of Elizabeth I, although someone of Spenser's class would surely have hoped for the English royal court to truly reflect or at least be a shadow or trace of the divine court.[33] However quaint we may find such political notions today, the aesthetic achievement and spiritual wisdom of *The Fairie Queene* ensures that students can still be entertained and instructed by following Spenser's knights through the fair forest of Fairyland.

SACRED THEMES IN SECULAR THEATRE

The 1560s marked the end of the medieval mystery plays, the biblical narratives performed by working guilds in English towns for over three hundred years. They were replaced within a few decades by the public theater productions that thrived in London. Much of this material is not of particular Christian interest, but amid much drama appealing to lower tastes, Thomas Kyd's *The Spanish Tragedy* (1592) represents a serious ethical exploration of Romans 12:19 ("Avenge not yourselves, . . . for it is written, Vengeance is mine; I will repay, saith the Lord").[34] It portrays a conflict in which the only son of the dramatic hero has been cruelly murdered. Though often grotesque and melodramatic, Kyd's play memorably transcends the narrow conventions of the revenge tragedy genre.

Another deeply Christian play of the period is Christopher Marlowe's *The Tragical History of Doctor Faustus*. There is irony here: despite Marlowe's alleged atheism, *Faustus* remains one of the most theologically compelling accounts of human damnation ever written. The title character is a professor from Wittenberg, the German university famously associated with Luther (and from which both Hamlet and Horatio come, in Shakespeare's later play). As the play opens Faustus is in

---

[33]C. S. Lewis, "Edmund Spenser," p. 103.
[34]Thomas Kyd, *The Spanish Tragedy* (1592), ed. Andrew Cairncross (Lincoln: University of Nebraska Press, 1967), pp. 57-176.

his study, weighing vocational options and notoriously reciting scriptural passages only partially (of Romans 6:23 he recalls that "the wages of sin is death" but not that "the gift of God is eternal life"; similarly he cites 1 John 1:8-9, "If we say that we have no sin, we deceive ourselves," but fails to continue, as the verse does, "if we confess our sins, [God] is faithful and just to forgive us our sins, and to cleanse us from all unrighteousness"). Having dismissed all other professions as unworthy of his interest, Faustus settles on necromancy, or Satanic magic. The remainder of the play concerns Faustus's exploration of the meaning of damnation and the suspenseful question of whether or not he can still be saved after selling his soul to the devil. Lucifer's main emissary in this task is the demon Mephistopheles, but it is not Faustus's magic circle or learned incantations that summon him; "the shortest cut for conjuring," the demon explains, "is stoutly to abjure the Holy Trinity / And pray devoutly to the Prince of Hell" (1.4.55-56). When Faustus cynically mocks his own adventures, saying, "I think hell's a fable," Mephistopheles retorts, "Ay, think so, till experience change thy mind" (2.1.127-28). When Faustus in his derisive curiosity inquires as to the precise location of hell, Mephistopheles offers a poignant reply:

Why this is hell, nor am I out of it:
Think'st that I, that saw the face of God,
And tasted the eternal joys of heaven,
Am not tormented with ten thousand hells,
In being deprived of everlasting bliss?
O Faustus, leave these frivolous demands. (1.4.74-9)

Yet Mephistopheles further deludes Faustus, telling him that he can have a demon appear as Helen, the Greek beauty "who launched a thousand ships," but that he cannot have one true wife, since marriage, a sacrament, is a gift of God and hence a means of grace; likewise, Faustus can mock and play pranks on the pope of Rome, but not prevent him from making the sign of the cross. The hubristic professor can, in short, be granted only "frivolous demands." But can he ever repent? That is the central question of the play, and while Marlowe adopts the "good angel / bad angel" of medieval morality plays to portray the *psychomachia* within Faustus's soul, the more controversial Calvinist form of predestination also seems at issue: when Faustus exclaims at one point, "O Christ, my Savior, my Savior, / Help to save distressed Faustus' soul!" (2.2.91-92), only the unholy trinity of Lucifer, Beelzebub and Mephistopheles immediately appear to him. What exactly has caused Faustus to say, "My heart is hardened, I cannot repent" (2.2.18)? Is it his action or, as Calvinists claim of Romans 9:18, evidence that God has "mercy on whom he will have mercy, and whom he will he hardeneth"?

The play itself does not answer such hard questions, but few can ever forget the agony of Faustus's final speech: "See, see, where Christ's blood streams in the firmament! / One drop would save my soul, half a drop: oh my Christ!" (5.1.287-88). Even at this late hour, why will Christ not respond? However one answers this question, Marlowe's work unforgettably illustrates the painful consummation of a Christian tragedy, portrayed through the stage device of "hell mouth" into which Faustus descends with one final, desperate cry of repentance: "I'll burn my books!" But no answer comes, only the leering presence of his now constant companion: "Oh, Mephistopheles!" (5.1.331). Here then is a profoundly theological work written with an apprehension of the consequences of willed apostasy, yet penned by a writer who would seem to have been an atheist.

No writer's work squeezes less comfortably into our small book than the "infinite variety" to be found in the plays of William Shakespeare.[35] Yet given that our culture has canonized his plays "as humanistic scriptures," and given the mass of unsubstantiated conjecture about his personal biography, it is necessary to explain why "gentle Will" (a nickname used by his friends) should belong to the ranks of Christian writers of this period.[36] Curiously, a rather small number of factual records survive for this most famous of English authors. Some, however, are significant. Since baptism was required by law, we have a record of Shakespeare's baptism at Holy Trinity Anglican Church on April 26,

---

[35]Shakespeare *Antony and Cleopatra* 2.2.242, in *Complete Works*, p. 1011.
[36]Harry Levin, "General Introduction," *The Riverside Shakespeare*, ed. G. Blakemore Evans (Boston: Houghton Mifflin, 1974), pp. 1-25.

1564. A much more important record of his beliefs is given in a final will dated March 25, 1616, one month before his death, which begins: "to saye ffirst I Comend my Soule into the handes of god my Creator hoping & assuredlie believing through thonelie merittes of Iesus Christ my Savior to be made partaker of lyfe everlasting."[37] Taken together with the epitaph on Shakespeare's grave, imploring "Good Frend for Iesvs sake forbeare" to move his bones from the cemetery of the church where he had been baptized, these records would suggest that Shakespeare died with a living Christian faith.[38]

As for which church Shakespeare identified with, we have few of the clear public evidences of church allegiance associated with some other major authors of his day. Such issues are thus likely to remain a matter of speculation peripheral to persuasive interpretation. There is a substantial and growing body of evidence that suggests that Shakespeare's allegiances were more toward the Catholic than the Puritan side of the English church divide, but the same can be said for many Anglicans of his time.[39] Unless much clearer evidence is discovered, it seems best to interpret the theological elements of his plays within the broad Christian heritage still readily available to common people in Shakespeare's day. This includes the medieval Catholic traditions in which Shakespeare may have been raised, if the Jesuit will of his father was authentic, and the still emerging Anglican ecclesiastical observances to which state law required both Shakespeare and his audience to conform.[40] In general, an understanding of the whole Christian tradition seems necessary to convincing interpretation of the religious elements in Shake-

---

[37]See G. Blakemore Evans, "Shakespeare's Will," in G. Blakemore Evans, "Records, Documents, and Allusions," *Riverside Shakespeare*, pp. 1832-33.

[38]See G. Blakemore Evans, "Shakespeare's Epitaphs," in G. Blakemore Evans, "Records, Documents, and Allusions," *Riverside Shakespeare*, pp. 1832-33.

[39]*Twelfth Night*, for example, notably contrasts the transformations celebrated in the traditional Catholic and Anglican feast of the Epiphany with the self-love and identity based on power and wealth satirized in the pseudo-Puritan aspirations of Malvolio. Elsewhere, *Measure for Measure*'s judge Angelo has been seen as exemplifying Puritan self-righteousness and hypocrisy. For a recent treatment of Shakespeare's religious identity, see Dennis Taylor and David N. Beauregard, *Shakespeare and the Culture of Christianity in Early Modern England* (New York: Fordham University Press, 2003).

[40]See Samuel Schoenbaum, *William Shakespeare: A Compact Documentary Life* (Oxford: Oxford University Press, 1987).

speare's plays; the view that Shakespeare was an "average" Anglican or a "quiet" Catholic are alike historically plausible.[41]

There is no evidence of any kind that Shakespeare was an adulterer who abandoned his children to become a London "player," as portrayed in the Oscar-winning film, *Shakespeare in Love*. For all we know, the "mistress' eyes" may well have been those of Anne Hathaway,[42] especially since *mistress* was as common an Elizabethan term for "wife" as "master" was for husband.[43] Nor does the commonly cited part of Shakespeare's will, his leaving Anne the "second best bed," prove alienation; clearly he did retire to Stratford with her, legal provisions for widows ensured her just inheritance, and much of his final will provides for their two surviving daughters. Given Shakespeare's often bawdy humor and the obviously amorous start to his marriage, the "bed" may have been a final personal joke recalling where their children had been conceived before the move to the larger home at "New Place." Though the three Shakespeare children indicate the playwright's heterosexuality, that has not stopped some readers of the sonnets from positing Mr. W. H., to whom the sonnets are dedicated, as the playwright's "true," or perhaps bisexual love; however, the majority of the sonnets specifically addressed to the young man (and most have a more general audience), urge him to marry and have children, who alone "gainst Time's scythe can make defense."[44] By contrast, the sonnets that seem to evidence personal beliefs that are repeated time after time in the plays include Sonnet 116, the famous poem that defines love by alluding to the Anglican wedding vows—"Let me not to the marriage of true minds / admit impediments"—and then insisting that love is an unchanging vow that ultimately is "not Time's fool."[45] Another is Sonnet 129, which defines lust as "th'expense of spirit in a waste of shame" that often serves as a precursor to many other kinds of

---

[41]On the complexity of this issue, and the need for continued conversation on it, see the review of recent scholarship by John D. Cox, "Was Shakespeare a Christian, and If So, What Kind of Christian Was He?" *Christianity and Literature* 55, no. 4 (2006): 539-66.

[42]Shakespeare, "Sonnet 130," in *Complete Works*, p. 767.

[43]As, for example, when Ferdinand calls Miranda, "My mistress, dearest," and she understands him to mean, "My husband, then?" (*Tempest* 3.1.87-89).

[44]Shakespeare, "Sonnet 12," in *Complete Works*, p. 752.

[45]Shakespeare, "Sonnet 116," in *Complete Works*, p. 765.

violence.[46] There is no more reason to accept uncritically the "troubled rebel-artist" portrait of Shakespeare that currently finds favor in the North American academy than to fashion a devout, saintly Shakespeare whose religious commitments were as clear as Milton's. Yet even a brief summary of Shakespeare's plays, made in roughly chronological order but organized according to genre as found in the First Folio (history, comedy and tragedy), reveals a growing interest in many central Christian concepts.

The early Shakespeare canon includes obvious apprentice work in imitation of Roman writers, focusing on topical Elizabethan themes. His history plays, however, evidence Christian reflection on the meaning of kingship as informed by biblical precedent. Did the failure of the judges, under whose leadership "every man did that which was right in his own eyes" (Judg 21:25), cause God to decide that Israel needed a king? If so, why did God first have his faithful servant Samuel anoint Saul? Did Saul's own wickedness cause God to withdraw this anointing? If so, did the same withdrawal occur after the sin of David with Bathsheba and the murder of her husband Uriah (2 Sam 11:15), leading to the prophet Nathan's rebuke and the immediate death of David's firstborn son? Was the covenant with David also maintained, however, to be fulfilled in his generations' line years later by the service of Joseph the carpenter, stepfather to the King of kings? After Christ's birth and within the proclaimed reign of the kingdom now at hand, are Christians to accept the government of those anointed by church, state or democratic vote (1 Pet 2:11-16), or does the evil that some rulers perpetrate mean that they must be morally or even militarily opposed? Faced with the troubled and complex annals of English history, Shakespeare writes history plays that forthrightly describe the sins of men and monarchs while always remaining watchful for signs of God's providential will at work within human history to bring good out of evil.

Shakespeare's first tetralogy of English history plays is *Henry VI*, parts 1, 2 and 3, concluded by *Richard III*. This chronicle of the War of the Roses seems to accept the "Tudor myth," the notion that God willed

---

[46]Shakespeare, "Sonnet 129," in *Complete Works*, p. 767.

Henry VII to establish a Tudor house which would unite the York and Lancaster combatants and produce the united England carried forward by Henry VIII and Elizabeth I. Both sides of the war seem very corrupt, however, and the notion that a providential God, as predicted by the bitter prophetess Margaret of Anjou, is using the villainous Richard III to destroy evil and make way for good is difficult for any modern to accept. Still, in the final speech of Richmond, who has vanquished Richard III and is soon to be crowned Henry VII, God is the source of victory:

> All that divided York and Lancaster,
> United in their dire division,
> O now let Richmond and Elizabeth,
> The true succeeders of each royal house,
> By God's fair ordinance conjoin together. (5.6.27-31)

Whether or not the Tudor myth represents Shakespeare's own view or simply a theatrically popular dramatization of Tudor historiography, God's means and motives seem less transparent in the later plays.

The second tetralogy is set earlier in time, during the fourteenth-century reign of Richard II, a king deposed and then murdered in prison under suspicious circumstances. Famously, a performance of this play by Shakespeare's company in 1602 was prevented because authorities thought it was being used to promote the coronation of the Earl of Essex to replace the aging, heirless Elizabeth, but the theological politics of the play itself seem far more ambiguous. Richard himself says:

> Not all the water in the rough rude sea
> Can wash the balm from an anointed king;
> The breath of worldly men cannot depose
> The deputy elected by the Lord. (3.2.50-53)

And later in the play, after the Duke of York falsely claims that Richard "with willing soul" yields Bolingbroke the throne, Bishop Carlisle rebukes him by saying: "if you crown him, let me prophesy, / The blood of England shall manure the ground" (4.1.127-28), a very accurate prediction of the Wars of the Roses that came upon the next generation. Complicating matters, though, is another "prophet" (2.1.31),

John of Gaunt. Called upon early in the play to avenge the murder of his brother Gloucester, for which Richard may have been responsible, Gaunt at first seems to support divine right, saying that if Richard is guilty then "God's is the quarrel, for God's substitute, / His deputy anointed in His sight, / Hath caused his death, / the which if wrongfully / let heaven revenge" (1.2.37-40). But is Bolingbroke the means to this vengeance? Soon afterward Gaunt laments how "this blessed plot, this earth, this realm, this England" (2.1.50) is "now leas'd out," and he makes the metaphor explicit a few lines later by directly telling Richard: "Landlord of England art thou now, not king" (2.1.113). Since Richard was an incompetent king, bringing his nation near economic ruin, is it possible that God removes his anointing, despite the plea of his church's ministers? Or, rather than making this extraordinary theological claim, is Shakespeare illustrating a view that many in his time shared, that the ideal ruler must be not only a pelican (symbolically, a mediator of Christ's kingship) but also as sly as a fox in statecraft and strong as a lion in battle? Henry IV has only the second quality, and his grandson Henry VI will have only the first.

The final three plays of the second tetralogy focus on a prince who develops all three qualities, Henry IV's son Hal, especially the education he is given through the fat, jolly but also thieving and thoroughly dissolute Falstaff. While Falstaff eventually has to be banished (though Shakespeare brings him back, perhaps at Elizabeth I's request, in *The Merry Wives of Windsor*) Hal grows up to become Henry V, "the mirror of all Christian kings" (2.0.6), who symbolically and militarily reverses English history by reclaiming France, which the play's concluding Chorus calls "the world's best garden" (Epilogue 7). The Chorus also reminds us, however, how short-lived will be this reclamation of Eden, how quickly the reign of a king "in infant bands crown'd" quickly "made his England bleed" in wars that "oft our stage hath shown" (Epilogue 9-13).

"Political Shakespeare" thus gives few untempered plaudits to political power. This is also evident in Shakespeare's great Roman play, *Julius Caesar*, in which it is extremely difficult for the audience to identify either with the imperial authority of Caesar and Antony on one side or with the Republicanism of Brutus and Cassius on the other. *Macbeth,* a Scottish history play probably written to welcome James I to his throne, seems unambiguous about God's support for the overthrow and execution of a tyrant, but that word itself was so controversial in Shakespeare's time that it was expressly banned from the 1611 King James Version of the Bible, despite Mary Sidney Herbert's use of the word in translating Psalm 52 in the 1580s.[47] *Henry VIII* presents a surprisingly benign monarch, one more confused than convicted over the question of divorce, but over a century of scholarship on the play's likely dual authorship has not settled Shakespeare's role in it.[48]

While Shakespeare's histories explore the English past to grapple with complex political issues relevant to his time (and sometimes our own), his comedies and tragedies are usually set within a foreign, nominally Catholic country, with Italy being the most common choice. Clergy typically play key roles, such as administering the multiple marriage sacraments that conclude comedies, or the funeral rites essential to tragedy. Specifically Reformation doctrinal issues are rarely mentioned, but Christian culture forms an assumed background within which the plays' main plots develop; even when the setting is pre-Christian, anachronistic allusions often speak directly to contemporary Christian culture. We must remember that genre is not value free; to borrow Sidney's terms, on a basic level comedy is about what *should* happen if obstacles to love are to be overcome, while tragedy is about what *should not* happen in cases of conflict, though sometimes tragic consequences are truly unavoidable. *Romeo and Juliet,* for example, is about much more than a glorification of youthful passion or even, as more classically-minded critics often claim, the struggle between fate and free will.

Christian motifs pervade Shakespeare's late tragicomedies and romances, but many elements common to the comedies also have Christian roots. *The Merchant of Venice,* for example, develops the conflict of mercy and justice in formal biblical terms. St. Paul's statement that

---

[47]Mary (Sidney) Herbert, "Psalm 52" (c. 1595), in *The Psalms of Sir Philip Sidney and the Countess of Pembroke,* ed. J. C. A. Rathmell (New York: New York University Press, 1963), pp. 122-23.
[48]See Herschel Baker, "Henry VIII," in *Riverside Shakespeare,* pp. 1976-79.

God "hath chosen the foolish things of the world to confound the wise" (1 Cor 1:27; cf. 1 Cor 1:20), reflected in Erasmus's *Praise of Folly* (1511), combined with the historical Renaissance practice of appointing court jesters whose simple counsel countered the flattery of courtiers, lies behind Shakespeare's many memorable wise fools.[49] Thus, in *Much Ado About Nothing* (1598), Constable Dogberry, despite his malapropisms and evident silliness, uncovers the plot to slander Hero, prompting the villain Borachio to tell Prince Don Pedro: "what your wisdoms could not discover, these shallow fools have brought to light" (5.1.225-26). Likewise, the linguistically challenged character Bottom, in *A Midsummer Night's Dream* (1596), physically embodies the proposition that "man is but an ass" (4.1.204), but also has a dream that transposes St. Paul's vision of paradise (1 Cor 2:9); "the eye of man hath not heard, the ear of man hath not seen" (4.1.208-9). More intelligent, intellectual fools such as Feste in *Twelfth Night* or the fool in *King Lear* memorably achieve a union of linguistic wit and wisdom.[50] As in St. Paul and Erasmus, what is foolishness to the world can in the end prove the very wisdom of Christ.

Among Shakespeare's tragedies, *Hamlet* (1600) is the longest. Like so much Renaissance and Jacobean tragedy, it is focused on the subject of revenge. There are several hints of Shakespeare's Catholic sympathies in the play, and competing religious views may in part underlie some of the complexity of the protagonist's sense of obligation to avenge his murdered father. The ghost clearly claims to be from purgatory, confined until his "foul crimes" are "burnt and purged away" (1.5.12-13), and if he is indeed Hamlet's father, then the revenge against Claudius can appear as not only just but perhaps ethically necessary. That *if* is the great question of the play for, as Hamlet says, the ghost "may be the devil" who "abuses me to damn me" (2.2.601, 605). Scholars like Roland Frye can thus argue that within the genre of revenge tragedy, which stressed that vengeance is a divine rather than human prerogative (Rom 12:19), Hamlet (like Lu-

---

[49]Desiderius Erasmus, *Praise of Folly*, ed. A. H. T. Levi (Harmondsworth, U.K.: Penguin, 1994).
[50]See Enid Welsford, *The Fool: His Social and Literary History* (Gloucester, Mass.: Peter Smith, 1966).

ther and Faustus, from the great Protestant University of Wittenberg) could be damned for enacting revenge, dying with the blood of innocent Ophelia, especially, on his own hands.[51] Finally, Catholic or Protestant readers must decide whether Hamlet's slaying of Claudius is the apt conclusion of a just war or simply part of the multiple tragic consequences of what Claudius himself admits to be "the primal eldest curse . . . a brother's murder" (3.2.37-38).

A Christian theological structure can also be seen to undergird *Othello*, if one understands the general hermeneutic of ironic antonyms that runs throughout the play. The name of the play's murderous villain, Iago, is the Spanish form of James, Spain's patron saint, though an English audience trusts him as "honest" no more than it can regard the saintly heroine, "Desdemona," as "of the (female) devils"; nevertheless, this evil and good angel are engaged in a medieval-style *pyschomachia*, fighting for the soul of Othello. The Moor of Venice, an "outsider" perhaps linked to the Ottoman empire, has through his pre-play baptism and marriage become a Christian everyman, forced to choose between the love and sacramental grace embodied in his marriage to Desdemona, and the demonic deception woven by Iago. This theological drama is matched or even surpassed in *King Lear* (1605), which can be read as a struggle between "the gods" who "kill us for their sport" (4.1.38), as the blinded Gloucester describes them, and the "clearest gods" (4.5.73) embodied by the self-sacrificial love of his son Edgar and Lear's daughter Cordelia. No commentary seems more apt than John Keats's "On Sitting Down to Read *King Lear* Once Again."[52] Keats sees within Lear "our deep eternal theme," the "fierce dispute / Betwixt damnation and impassioned clay" (5-10).

The miracle of resurrection is absolutely central to the tragicomedies and romances that conclude Shakespeare's distinguished career, where it typically appears alongside the theme of testing a faithful (or converting an unfaithful) steward or lover, often via the exceptional endurance of an exemplary heroine. *Measure for Measure* (1604) provides the

---

[51]Roland M. Frye, *The Renaissance Hamlet* (Princeton, N.J.: Princeton University Press, 1984).
[52]John Keats, "On Sitting Down to Read *King Lear* Once Again" (1818), in *John Keats: Selected Poems and Letters*, ed. Douglas Bush (Boston: Houghton Mifflin, 1959), pp. 132-33.

basic pattern for such plays, as the Duke of Vienna leaves the apparently saintly Angelo in charge of enforcing long-forgotten law. Claudio, having impregnated his betrothed Juliet, is about to be executed, but his sister, the nun Isabella, pleads for her brother's life. Puritanical Angelo succumbs to a lustful attraction to Isabella, much as he had years earlier with a woman named Mariana, though he broke off their betrothal after her dowry was lost at sea. Isabella and Juliet join with the Duke to manipulate dramatic situations that ultimately illustrate the wisdom of the Sermon on the Mount to which the play's title refers: "With what judgment ye judge, ye shall be judged: and with what measure ye mete, it shall be measured to you again" (Mt 7:2). The faithful endurance of women is also central to *Pericles, Prince of Tyre* (1609), where the hero's wife Thaisa serves in the temple of chaste Diana and their daughter Marina converts lustful men until the long-suffering Pericles is reunited with both and hears "the music of the spheres," suggesting, in the Boethian language of Ptolemaic astronomy, that he now sees how divine providence has been at work in his life. *Cymbeline* (1609) also tests a wayward hero, Posthumus, who like Othello is duped by a villain, here named Iachimo, into believing that his beloved wife, Imogen, has been unfaithful. Shakespeare has the god Jupiter eventually teach Posthumus the truth in a dream vision: following the Acts of the Abuses in 1606 which censored direct references to Christianity, Shakespeare often uses classical gods to deliver clearly Christian messages.

For all the constraints of the political culture, no play presents Christian first principles in clearer or more compelling fashion than *The Winter's Tale* (1611). The play begins, significantly, with a willful misrepresentation, a false accusation of adultery made by King Leontes against his wife Hermione. From the time of Henry VIII on, the dangers of false accusations of adultery were all too obvious. As in almost all of Shakespeare's plays on the topic, the heroine is here proven innocent—this time by her friend Paulina, but not before her daughter Perdita is banished to another country and Hermione herself seems to die from grief. Sixteen years pass and the play moves from winter to spring, from tragedy to comedy. The transformation cannot be complete, however, until Leontes comes face to face with a brilliantly carved statue of his long-dead wife. Wanting to kiss her, much like Pygmalion, Leontes is halted in his tracks. Paulina commands him that, first, "it is required / you do awake your faith" (5.3.94-95).[53] By means far too complex to recount here, all reflecting recognition of the ironic character of divine Providence itself, Shakespeare's art then gives life to those who retain faith in "heaven's directing" (5.3.151).[54] Through the grace of art, truth prevails over falsehood. Indeed, so moving is this play's argument for the power of art that the burden of Shakespeare's final complete play, *The Tempest* (1611), seems almost to fall in an opposite, course-correcting direction, expressing the need for the living finally to relinquish art and come to accept another aspect of truth, namely, the inevitability of suffering and death. Allusions to "the great globe itself" (4.1.153) make plausible the oft-held claim that this is Shakespeare's farewell to the stage, though the philosopher/magus Prospero can only partially be seen as a dramatic artist. He is also a deposed ruler who now, twelve years later, has his enemies (including his brother) in his sights and justly wants to allow his daughter Miranda to reign in a beautiful new kingdom with the young Italian prince Ferdinand. For this "project" to bear fruit, however, Prospero must see that "the rarer action is / in virtue than in vengeance" (5.1.27-28), for only by forgiving his enemies can he "keep them [all] living" (2.1.304) and allow them to "rejoice beyond a common joy" (5.1.209-210). Finally, in the extremely intimate, personal epilogue spoken to the audience, Prospero (and, it has seemed to many, Shakespeare himself) must appeal to God, "Mercy itself," and seek forgiveness from sins in terms that recall both the words of the Lord's Prayer and the Catholic system of ecclesiastical forgiveness grounded in that text ("forgive us our debts, as we forgive our debtors") that had helped to divide Christian England: "As you from crimes would pardoned be, / Let your indulgence set me free" (Epilogue 18-20).

---

[53]On the nature of this "faith," see Gregory Maillet, "'Fidelity to the Word': Lonerganian Conversion Through Shakespeare's *The Winter's Tale* and Dante's *Purgatorio*," *Religion and the Arts* 10, no. 2 (2006): 219-43.

[54]This foundational theme is wonderfully explored over a broad range of literary works in Anthony Esolen's *Ironies of Faith: the Laughter at the Heart of Christian Literature* (Wilmington, Del.: ISI Books, 2007).

SEVENTEENTH-CENTURY CHRISTIAN POETRY: DONNE, HERBERT AND MILTON

Although various social realities conspired against seventeenth-century Christian drama, the same cannot be said of poetry. After the nearly complete public suppression of Catholicism that followed the Guy Fawkes gunpowder plot to blow up Parliament (1605), English social and religious culture diverged into two well-defined camps, each of which produced extraordinary poets. On the Anglican side the theological foundation was articulated in the theology of Richard Hooker and Thomas Cranmer, along with the spirituality of Nicholas Ferrar and the spiritual community at Little Gidding. Meanwhile, the irresistible social force of Puritanism encompassed many different groups, ranging from radically devout individualists like the Anabaptists to the Calvinist theocrats that eventually elected Cromwell and executed Charles I. Out of the public outlawing of Catholicism emerged John Donne.[55] Anglican spirituality was eloquently versed by George Herbert. Later, the poet John Milton not only publicly justified the execution of Charles I, but, after the defeat of the Commonwealth he had so ardently defended, composed arguably the theologically most developed Christian poetry ever written.

Donne (1572-1631). Partly because of the work of seventeenth-century biographer Izaak Walton, and partly because John Donne eventually grew up to become a well-known preacher and the dean of St. Paul's Cathedral in London, we know a good deal more about Donne's life than one would expect of a poet who published little in his lifetime and was not considered a major author until heralded by H. J. C. Grierson and T. S. Eliot in the early twentieth century.[56] Born into an aristocratic Catholic family, Donne forfeited some of the privileges associated with nobility; though an Oxford student, he could not take a degree, and evidently went through a period of youthful spiritual rebellion. While the exact date of writing for most of his poems is uncertain,

---

[55]John Donne, *John Donne: The Complete English Poems*, ed. C. A. Patrides (London: J. M. Dent, 1994). Unless noted, all references are to this edition. Many of Donne's poems circulated in manuscript but were not published until 1633 or in later posthumous editions.

[56]Izaak Walton, *The Life of Dr. Donne* (1640), *The Lives of John Donne and George Herbert* (New York: Collier, 1937), pp. 323-69.

during the 1590s a witty, amorous poetry in imitation of Ovid was his favored genre, as in the almost grotesque poem "The Flea." At times, a cynical tone pervades this verse, as in "The Indifferent," where a self-centered speaker rejects constancy and claims that "love's sweetest part" is "variety"; should any seek "to 'stablish dangerous constancy," Venus herself proclaims: "since you will be true / You shall be true to them who are false to you" (20, 25-26). By the late 1590s, however, Donne had joined the Church of England and become private secretary to Sir Thomas Egerton, later Lord Chancellor. During this time Donne fell into lasting love with Egerton's seventeen-year-old niece, Ann More, whom he secretly married in 1601. Her father, who objected strenuously to the marriage, had him thrown for a time into Fleet Prison. Walton, registering the impact of the scandal, called this marriage "the remarkable error of [Donne's] life," but it produced, in addition to many children, some of the most passionate love poetry ever written.[57]

The ultimate spiritual unity of these two lovers is the subject of "The Extasie," perhaps Donne's most complex poem. The title, and opening lines, refer to an almost mystical detachment of soul from body, which in conversation somehow pleads "Love, these mixt soules, doth mixe againe" (35), and as love "interanimates two souls" (42), the "soul into the soul may flow / though it to body first repair" (59-60). In language that hints at neo-Platonism, Donne expresses the metaphysical Christian truth about marriage, the fact that the God of love sacramentally unites two souls into perfect unity. Developing language to describe this reality is always a challenge; Donne becomes known for his imaginative "conceits," which in Renaissance terms are elaborate and often startling metaphors that help us see reality in new ways. "A Valediction: Forbidding Mourning" is a word of solace from Donne to his wife before he leaves on a trip. Here, a series of conceits demonstrates that though they will be physically separate, spiritually they remain united; in the final, most famous conceit, the lovers' two souls,

> If they be two, are two so
> As stiff twin compasses are two.

---

[57] Walton, *Life of Dr. Donne*, p. 351.

Thy soul the fixed foot, makes no show
To move, but doth, if th' other doe.
And though it in the center sit,
Yet when the other far doth roam,
It leans, and hearkens after it,
And grows erect, as that comes home. (25-32)

The sensual connotations of Donne's spirituality are often noted, but
the priorities of Donne's paradoxes are in fact reversed; our sexual experience of love is, for him, but a dim foreshadowing of the ultimate joy
one day to be experienced in full communion with God in heaven. "Holy
Sonnet 10," for example, expresses this hope by echoing 1 Corinthians
15, Paul's great chapter on the resurrection. Donne here mocks Death as
a pathetic creature, "slave to fate, chance, kings, and desperate men" (9),
confidently concluding with this paradoxical assurance: "One short
sleep, we wake eternally, / And death shall be no more; Death, thou
shall die" (13-14). In Donne's "Holy Sonnet 14," God is a passionate
lover seeking to invade and occupy his heart; rather than presenting
Christ simply knocking on the door of his soul, Donne needs more:
"Batter my heart, three-personed God. . . . Break, blow, burn, and make
me new" (1, 4). Such force is necessary, Donne explains, because "reason, your viceroy in me," is "betrothed unto [God's] enemy" (7, 10).
Donne does not name exactly whom this enemy is, but only a passionate
lover can free him: "Except you enthrall me," Donne concludes, "never
shall [I] be free, / Nor ever chaste, except you ravish me" (13-14). *Ravish*
here does not, as some editors claim, necessarily mean "rape," but as
today can also refer to the kind of passionate love implicit in the biblical
metaphor of Christ as the Bridegroom coming to marry the church (e.g.,
1 Thess 4:17). This is the conceit that begins the heartfelt "Sonnet 18":
"Show me, dear Christ, thy Spouse, so bright and clear." Yet rather than
coming to any clear decision between she who goes "richly painted," the
Roman Church, or she who "laments and mourns in Germany and here"
(3-4), the Reformation church, or between the visible, institutional
church and the invisible church of believers, Donne's search concludes
only with a plea that the "kind husband," who is Christ, allow his church
also to be she who "is embraced and open to most men" (14).

The ongoing sense of spiritual search, journey and struggle comes together most powerfully, perhaps, in "Good Friday, 1613, Riding Westward." Like many others, on this Easter Donne seems distracted from spiritual thoughts by "pleasure or business," which so often "our souls admit / for their first mover" (7-8). Donne explains the Christian desire to know God in neo-Platonic language: the "soul's form bends toward the east," and

> There I should see a Sun, by rising set,
> And by that setting endless day beget;
> But that Christ on this cross, did rise and fall,
> Sin had eternally benighted all. (10-14)

The universal relevance of Christ's atonement, its resolution of every personal spiritual struggle, is here known only as an abstract truth; Donne himself admits, of God's agony on the cross, "on these things I durst [darest] not look" (29). In one of the most extraordinary moments in any Christian poem, however, suddenly the recollection of Christ's sacrifice is transformed into a "present" moment; Donne's backward glance at the first Easter becomes suddenly a recognition in present tense: "thou look'st towards me, / O Saviour, as thou hang'st upon the tree" (35-36). In this moment of real spiritual conversion and change, Donne again appeals to God to truly transform him by whatever means necessary:

> O think me worth thine anger, punish me,
> Burn off my rusts, and my deformity,
> Restore thine image, so much, by thy grace,
> That thou may'st know me, and I'll turn my face. (39-42)

The final granting of these requests appears to be recorded by Donne in his final poems, "A Hymn to Christ," "Hymn to God My God in My Sickness" and "A Hymn to God the Father." In all three, what seems most striking is Donne's acceptance both of his own sinfulness, and a full understanding that God's grace is sufficient for his salvation. In the "Hymn to Christ," for example, the "historical" Jesus is not explicitly mentioned, but the poet is certain that as he enters old age and death, "in my winter now I go," there "none but thee, th' eternal root /

Of true Love I may know" (14-16). In the "Sickness" hymn, Donne again returns to 1 Corinthians 15 to explain a sinner's salvation:

> We think that Paradise and Calvary,
> Christ's cross, and Adam's tree, stood in one place;
> Look Lord, and find both Adams met in me;
> As the first Adam's sweat surrounds my face,
> May the last Adam's blood my soul embrace. (21-25)

It is in the final hymn, to "God the Father," that Donne speaks most personally, and wittily, perhaps recalling his youth and the wife who, God helping, transformed his life. According to Walton, Donne himself said that "the words of this hymn have restored to me the same thoughts of joy that possessed my soul in my sickness, when I composed it," thoughts of "an unexpressible tranquility of mind, and a willingness to leave the world."[58] Rather than senility or forgetfulness, these thoughts spring, as always, from Donne's vivid remembrance of his own sinfulness and sincere questioning of whether the living God can truly forgive both the original sin in which he was born and his own misdeeds: "Wilt thou forgive that sin where I begun / Which is my sin, though it were done before?"; "Wilt thou forgive me that sin, by which I have won / Others to sin?" (1-2, 7-8). Knowing Christ well enough to know the answer to these questions, Donne yet wittily puns on his name, and perhaps his wife's maiden name, by first giving his own human answer: "When thou hast done, thou hast not done, / For I have more" (5-6, 11-12). Only in the poem's final stanza does Donne reveal the sin that truly separates him from God, "a sin of fear" that physical death will be his end. The light of the Son's presence can alone calm this fear; knowing that "at my death thy son / shall shine as he shines now," when God "hast done," the ever ardent poet looks forward to reunion with his already canonized, eternally beloved wife, and is able finally to say, "I fear no more" (13-18).

Herbert (1593-1633). George Herbert is often linked with Donne, as the two were contemporaries, friends and fellow Anglican priests

---

[58]Walton, *Life of Dr. Donne*, pp. 352-53.

and poets whose biographies were written by Izaak Walton.[59] Both also later became classified as "metaphysical" poets whose reputations were disdained in the Enlightenment and only rehabilitated by the twentieth-century New Critics. Yet while apparent vocational and spiritual angst characterizes Donne's poetry, Herbert's work reflects a calmer spirit. He grew up in an aristocratic Anglican family and by 1620 had risen to the academically prestigious position of Chief Orator at Cambridge University. He remained there until 1628, during which time he was also a Member of Parliament, but he then left these careers to take up full-time ministry as an Anglican priest in the small rural parish of Bemerton in Wiltshire. By all accounts Herbert served the church ably from 1630 until his death in 1633, due to tuberculosis, and there was no public record of him writing poetry during this time. However, on his deathbed, Herbert bequeathed a single manuscript of poems, *The Temple*, to Nicholas Ferrar, the founder of the Anglican religious community at Little Gidding, later to be praised so eloquently in T. S. Eliot's *Four Quartets*. While the number of his poems is small, Herbert's rare combination of deep faith, academic learning, rhetorical skill and poetic creativity makes almost every poem within *The Temple* worthy of any Christian reader's time and prayer.

Many of these poems display strikingly creative aesthetic techniques in the service of central yet simple Christian truths. The poetic vocation is announced, indeed baptized, in "Jordan I," which begins with rhetorical questions: "Who says that fictions only and false hair / Become a verse? Is there in truth no beauty?" (1-2). Poetry, in the hands of a faithful writer, Herbert suggests, can and should be an instrument of truth. Accordingly, he concludes, do not "punish me with loss of rhyme, / Who plainly say, *My God, My King*" (14-15). Paradoxically it is Herbert's simple faith that gives rise to the wide variety of complex aesthetic structures he employs. Some of his forms are uniquely memorable, such as the shaped poems "The Altar" and "Easter Wings," in

---

[59]George Herbert, *The Temple* (1633), in *George Herbert and Henry Vaughn: The Oxford Authors*, ed. Louis L. Martz (Oxford: Oxford University Press, 1992). Unless noted, all Herbert references are to this edition. Izaak Walton, *The Life of Mr. George Herbert* (1640), *The Lives of John Donne and George Herbert* (New York: Collier, 1937), pp. 373-418.

which the shape of the lines images the poem's subject; even here, however, Herbert's arrangements are never merely decorative. Within the heart of the altar the word offered for sacrifice is "a heart alone" (5), while the pattern of each "Easter wing" is the lines' diminishing with Christ to become "most poor," "most thin," until finally we rise with Christ because we can "imp [our] wing on [his]" (5, 15, 19). "Prayer I" uses another apparently simple technique, metonymy, to explore a deceptively complex question: What is prayer? For Herbert, it is "the Church's banquet," to begin with a traditional image, but also "angels' age," "sinners' tower," "exalted manna" and "the land of spices" (1-14), plus twenty other metonymies that can only be summarized by this hopeful concluding phrase: "something understood" (14).

One of Herbert's most famous vocational poems, "The Collar" (whose title contains at least four puns), seems to describe a period of serious doubt or even rebellion in the life of a pastor; yet as he "raved and grew more fierce and wild," the speaker also "heard one calling, *Child!*—and he replied simply, faithfully, '*My Lord*'" (33-36). The italicized inner voice of God presented here appears in other poems as well, giving a powerful sense of an intimate friendship between the poet and his Lord, reflective of the relationship Christ wants with his disciples: "I call you not servants; for the servant knoweth not what his lord doeth: but I have called you friends" (Jn 15:15). Perhaps Herbert's most moving poem illustrating the true friendship of Christ is the concluding poem of *The Temple*, in which the servant-friend distinction is extended beyond the personal and applied to the more universal situation of a sinner feeling unworthy before the pure holiness of the living God who here, as in 1 John 4, has the simple name of Love.

> Love bade me welcome: yet my soul drew back,
> Guilty of dust and sin.
> But quick-eyed Love, observing me grow slack,
> From my first entrance in,
> Drew nearer to me, sweetly questioning,
> If I lacked anything. (1-6)

Using the sweet language common to medieval and Renaissance descriptions of prayer, Herbert's God initiates conversation and is seeking communion with humanity; the speaker represents the human sinner. Herbert the pastor knows that most encounters with the living God will produce fear rather than comfort, a painful awareness of the contrast between God's holiness and our sinfulness. Thus the speaker replies, and God rebukes:

> A guest, I answered, worthy to be here:
> Love said, You shall be he.
> I the unkind, ungrateful? Ah my dear,
> I cannot look on thee.
> Love took my hand, and smiling did reply,
> Who made the eyes but I? (7-12)

Radically aware of our insufficiency, we are likely to respond to Christ much as the Jews did to God in the Old Testament, averting our eyes for fear that if we look on the face of the living God we will die. Yet Herbert's God is revealing a new depth of love, and a reminder that this one and only living God made us in his own image. Acknowledging God as creator does not necessarily entail confessing him as redeemer, and the sinner, ashamed, responds: "Truth Lord, but I have marred them: let my shame / Go where it doth deserve" (13-14). Faced with the just self-condemnation of sin, Herbert's Love appeals boldly to the atonement of Christ:

> And know you not, says Love, who bore the blame?
> My dear, then I will serve.
> You must sit down, says Love, and taste my meat. (15-17)

Even after hearing of Christ's atonement, Herbert suggests, the sinner does not truly understand the nature of the relationship that God desires, and wants merely to remain a servant. Herbert's God will nevertheless require the human sinner to understand Love's true nature and to personally experience this love. "Taste my meat" is almost certainly a layered reference to the eucharistic celebration, to the nourishing substance of Christ himself, the bread of life, and to the great banquet in heaven, when Christ "shall gird himself, and make them to sit down to meat, and will come forth and serve them" (Lk 12:37). However one understands the resonance of this call, Herbert concludes *The Temple* with perhaps the simplest affirmation of faith in all of English poetry: "So I did sit and eat." Never has the reality of God as the fundamental need of our souls been more purely or profoundly expressed. In Herbert, poetry becomes prayer, a means of worship.[60]

Milton (1608-1674). In Milton, poetry takes the form of theological argument, specifically of the type called "apologetics." This task is by definition highly intellectual and philosophical in nature. The simplicity of Herbert's humble Anglican faith contrasts sharply with the extraordinary erudition of John Milton, whose poetry truly does pursue, as he puts it in the introduction to *Paradise Lost*, "things unattempted yet in prose or rhyme" (1.16).[61] His early poems such as "On the Morning of Christ's Nativity" and "Lycidas" (an elegy for his friend Edward King) are technically and linguistically accomplished, and political and religious tracts like *Areopagitica* (a tract against government censorship) or *On Christian Doctrine* (which includes an infamous questioning of traditional trinitarian doctrine) were written before the turbulent political events of the English Civil War. The poems of most interest to the Christian reader today are surely *Paradise Lost* and *Paradise Regained*, both written and published after the Restoration of the English monarchy, during a period of quiet exile in which the blind poet dictated his works aloud to his wife or daughters. While much conjecture is possible, there is no definitive proof that either of these two great poems is topical or political in any specific sense; instead both begin with fairly short scriptural passages that Milton brilliantly develops into narrative and dramatic poetry that explores a wide variety of foundational theological questions.

Indeed, the most common objection to *Paradise Lost* and *Paradise Regained* is their elaboration on very short biblical passages; does Milton perhaps distort Scripture or add material in a manner at best imaginative and at worst blasphemous? What authority can the reader grant

---

[60]See Terry G. Sherwood, *George Herbert's Prayerful Art* (Toronto: University of Toronto Press, 1989).

[61]John Milton, *Paradise Lost* (1674), *John Milton: The Major Works*, ed. Stephen Orgel and Jonathan Goldberg (Oxford: Oxford University Press, 2003), pp. 355-618. Unless noted, all subsequent Milton references are to this edition.

Milton as interpreter of Scripture, and what is the status of his poetry in relation to Scripture? While Milton can be admired for poetically fulfilling the broad baptismal promise made to every Christian, serving as a "prophet, priest and king," does Milton perhaps himself become a spiritual overreacher of the kind often satirized in Renaissance literature? These objections are much more serious for Christian readers than the easily refuted Romantic distortions of men like Shelley, who claim that Satan is Milton's true epic hero without noticing how often the poem itself, whether in Milton's narrative voice or through the perspective of God himself, clearly shows the logical fallacies, ethical errors and internal anguish of the fallen angel.[62] The purpose of *Paradise Lost* is to "justify the ways of God to men" (1.26), and its structural order is designed first to show us the fallen perspective of Satan (in whom we often recognize our own fallen natures) and then contrast it to the perspective of God the Father and his only Son. Rather than arrogantly claiming some unique access to Christ, Milton attributes his poetic insights to the always-present Muse who is the Holy Spirit, the underlying source of all true learning (1.16-24). If readers accept this perspective, then Milton's major poems can be viewed as intelligent biblical commentary, exploring basic questions likely to occur to any reader of Scripture and offering dramatic portraits of biblical figures that enliven both our imaginations and our intellects.

The most basic question suggested by the Genesis account of "paradise lost," of course, is this: who is the serpent slithering into the garden, and where did it come from? The existence of Satan and his fall from heaven is well attested in Scripture, especially by Christ himself in his rebuke of the fallen angel in the desert, but these are brief passages. Books 1 and 2 of *Paradise Lost* are more expansive and imagine Satan awakening in hell just after being expelled from heaven, pondering with many other fallen angels how yet they may take revenge against a God so much more powerful than they could ever be. Here, especially, Satan's never-say-die attitude and genius for political leadership draws inordinate praise from libertarian individualists. "The mind is its

---

[62]See Percy Bysshe Shelley, *A Defence of Poetry, The Critical Tradition: Classic Texts and Contemporary Trends*, ed. David H. Richter (Boston: Bedford St. Martin's, 2006), p. 357.

own place / and can make a heaven of hell or a hell of heaven" (1.254-55), Satan proclaims, an aphorism that, in at least its first half, is oft-quoted by subjective idealists everywhere. The Prince of Pride then offers this single sentence summation of his credo: "Better to reign in hell than serve in Heaven" (1.263). These confident assertions, however, beg key questions: does Satan ever really reign, even over hell? And, while granting that Satan attempted to make a hell of heaven, has his malicious will ever come close to making a heaven of hell? Considered logically, Satan's rhetoric can be rejected for the empty, nihilistic and power-hungry posturing that it is; instead, via what Milton calls, following a number of church fathers, "right reason" (9.352), readers can understand and accept the more complete, divine perspective offered in Book 3 of *Paradise Lost*.

Having witnessed the fallen angels' rebellion, and having foreknowledge of the human Fall soon to come, Book 3 shows God the Father and his "only begotten Son" (3.80), in whom "his father shone / substantially expressed" (3.138-39)—no hint of Arianism here—providing both a rational understanding of controversial theological questions such as free will and predestination, and a dramatically moving presentation of their plan of salvation. The Father makes the first, most essential point about the creation of both angels and humans: "I made him just and right, / Sufficient to have stood, though free to fall . . . / freely they stood who stood, and fell who fell" (3.99-102). Freedom, according to Milton's God, is an essential part of both angelic and human natures, part of a "high Decree / Unchangeable, Eternal," and the Fall cannot be ascribed to the notion that "predestination overruled / their will" (3.114-15), for God's "foreknowledge had not influence on their fault" (3.118). Nevertheless humanity, having been "deceived" by the angels, "shall find grace," and God will act in history to express "mercy and justice both," and thankfully "mercy first and last shall brightest shine" (3.131-34). In response to this eloquent speech by God the Father, "ambrosial fragrance filled / all heaven, and in the blessed spirits elect / Sense of new joy ineffable diffused" (3.135-37). Those privy to a heavenly perspective, in other words, fully comprehend the goodness of the Father, and it is in a spirit of freedom and joy that the

Son offers himself "life for life" on the cross, confident, nay certain, that "I shall rise victorious, and subdue / My vanquisher" (3.250-51). Properly understood, Book 3 should impart a similar sense of peace and confidence to the reader, even though it closes with the scene of Satan successfully deceiving the angel Uriel and entering Eden.

Books 4-7 function mainly to enhance our sense of the goodness of God's creation, and the "sufficient" goodness of both angels and humans in being fully prepared and able to resist the temptations of evil. Creation, and created human nature, is not perfect, in the sense of some static ideal, but it is abundant, flourishing and, while in communion with God, capable of allowing finite nature to be led into infinity. Satan looks on Eden with "envy and despair" (4.115) and obstinately declares his absolute perversion: "evil be thou my good" (4.110). By contrast, after Milton beautifully describes the abundance of creation and the creation of humanity, Adam and Eve join in mutual praise, thanking God for

> mutual love, the crown of all our bliss
> Ordained by thee; and this delicious place
> For us too large, where thy abundance wants
> Partakers, and uncropt falls to the ground.
> But thou hast promised from us two a race
> To fill the earth, who shall with us extol
> Thy goodness infinite. (4.728-734)

Sleep and lovemaking follow, the human parents untroubled by sin or Satan's presence, even though Milton does portray Satan whispering a tempting dream into Eve's ear before Gabriel's angels remove him from paradise. This extrabiblical scene stresses, as Milton believes Genesis does teach, that Eden is itself postlapsarian, in the sense that Adam and Eve are created after the fall of Satan's angels, and born into a danger from which the free movement of angels and men dictates they cannot be separated forever. Surely God's wisdom and goodness would not place them as helpless infants in front of an arch-criminal, but how did God prepare them to face this danger?

Sufficient goodness might simply have been infused by "prevenient grace" into Adam and Eve, but Milton instead stresses the gradual de-

velopment of humanity's "right reason" by having Books 5-8 portray an
angel named Raphael visit Adam and Eve and serve as their divine
teacher. Biblically, "Raphael" is an angel found only in apocryphal
books such as Tobit, and Milton may intentionally be choosing what he
regards as a fictional angel to stress the admittedly speculative character of these books. On the other hand, Milton's narrator states that in
calling Raphael the "eternal Father . . . fulfilled all justice" (5.246),
which suggests that a defense of God's goodness and justice truly did
require Adam and Eve to be spiritually prepared in some fashion. However one views Raphael, this spiritual fiction not only warns humanity
about Satan but teaches them the nature of their own freedom (5.520-
543) and illustrates the dangers of this freedom by recounting the wars
in heaven. On the other hand, Raphael also teaches the sufficiency of
the will to reject evil through the moving portrait of Abdiel, who
though surrounded by faithless followers of Satan remained "faithful
only he" (5.897), earning this praise from God:

> Servant of God, well done, well hast thou fought
> The better fight, who single hast maintained
>
> Against revolted multitudes the cause
> Of truth, in word mightier than they in arms. (6.29-32)

Truth is mightier in heaven and will also be so on earth, and in Book
7 Raphael goes on to stress that Earth too is worth defending. Functioning almost as a poetic commentary on the first two chapters of
Genesis, Raphael here seeks to give Adam and Eve, and by implication
future human readers, a full sense of wonder and awe at the beauty and
goodness of creation. Book 8, however, then stresses Adam and Eve's
place within this created order, arguing that humans by their nature
can have only limited knowledge of some matters outside their experience, for "heaven is for thee too high / to know what passes there"
(8.172-3). At the same time, Raphael's presence and teaching indicates
that God's revealed knowledge is sufficient for Adam and Eve "to stand
or fall / Free in thine own arbitrament it lies" (8.641).[63]

---

[63]See Phillip J. Donnelly, *Milton's Scriptural Reasoning: Narrative and Protestant Toleration*
(Cambridge: Cambridge University Press, 2009).

Book 9 of *Paradise Lost* carries us to Milton's central subject, the Fall, or what the poem's opening lines call "man's first disobedience"; immediately, however, this opening line raises the central question that must be asked of Genesis 2–3: what is "the fruit / Of that forbidden tree, whose mortal taste brought death into the world" (1.2-3)? In other words, what did God mean when he told Adam and Eve: "But of the tree of the knowledge of good and evil, thou shalt not eat of it: for in the day that thou eatest thereof thou shalt surely die" (Gen 2:17). What is the tree of the knowledge of good and evil, and what is its relationship to the tree of life also planted in the middle of the garden? Milton's initial description of Eden had already evoked this relationship, his narrator first reminding fallen readers that "so little knows / any, but God alone, to value right / the good before him" (4.201-3); if this is true of all, how completely mistaken is the fallen angel, Satan, who in his despair declares: "all good to me is lost / Evil be thou my good" (4.109-10)? Milton foreshadows the tragic irony by having Satan land in Eden "on the tree of life" (4.194), and then showing that "next to [the tree of] life / our death the tree of knowledge grew fat by, / Knowledge of good bought dear by knowing ill" (4.220-22).

Early in Book 9 Adam reminds Eve that the human capacity for right reason, even before the Fall, is incomplete and capable of error (as Milton often showed through Raphael), and could be "by some fair-appearing good surprised" (9.354) despite God's warning. Making the tree of knowledge appear entirely good is the central strategy of Milton's Satan, as he calls it a "sacred, wise, and wisdom-giving Plant, / Mother of science!" (9.679-80): he lauds its ability to make even a humble snake not only speak but also reason and ask apparently irrefutable rhetorical questions. Referring to God's mortal warning, Satan says that "whatever thing death be," Eve should be

Deterred not from achieving what might lead
To happier life, knowledge of good and evil;
Of good, how just? of evil, if what is evil
Be real, why not known, since easier shunned?
God therefore cannot hurt ye, and be just;
Not just, not God; not feared then, nor obeyed. (9.696-701)

The initial doubt about the nature of death here should be warning enough that Satan's own knowledge is not absolute; however, his logical claim that eating of the tree of knowledge, even in disobedience of God, will allow one to choose better between good and evil seems to overpower Eve's reason. In just these seven short lines, Satan rapidly deduces that a God who bans such wisdom cannot be God at all. Once this conclusion is reached, the attractiveness, indeed inevitability, of Satan's central biblical temptation can be understood: "God doth know that in the day ye eat thereof, then your eyes shall be opened, and ye shall be as gods, knowing good and evil" (Gen 3:5). Or, as Milton's Satan puts it, again using a rhetorical question: "what are gods, that man may not become as they, participating godlike food?" (9.716-17). Milton's Eve is persuaded, believing she will gain "knowledge of both good and evil," and with her "rash hand in an evil hour" she eats the forbidden fruit. Her initial "expectation high / of knowledge" and "god-head" meant that she "engorged without restraint," but ironically, like Satan, she "knew not eating death" (9.792).

Milton has been criticized for separating Eve from Adam in these scenes, and it can be argued that the biblical account shows the couple falling together, but the tragic split between the two does enhance the pathos of the horrible choice that now awaits Adam. He, like all creatures after the Fall, is now cut off from the tree of life intended by God; as Adam says here to Eve, "How can I live without thee . . . if death / consort with thee, death is to me as life," for "we are one / one flesh; to lose thee were to lose my self" (9.908, 953-9). In perhaps the most essential sense, the meaning of death is to be out of communion with God—no longer in the presence of the giver of life. Yet it must also mean that we cannot expect to continue learning the difference between good and evil without being in communion with the God who designed all things according to his purpose. After eating from the tree of knowledge himself, Adam makes this point succinctly:

> since our eyes
> Opened we find indeed, and find we know
> Both good and evil; good lost, and evil got;
> Bad fruit of knowledge, if this be to know. (9.1070-73)

Most painful of all is not merely the newly experienced knowledge of evil but the knowledge and persistent memory of the expansive present knowledge now lost. Echoing Marlowe's Mephistopheles and Satan himself, Milton's Adam asks his own rhetorical question:

> How shall I behold the face
> Henceforth of God or Angel, erst with joy
> And rapture so oft beheld? (9.1079-82)

Of course the Fall has many other consequences, from shame in nakedness to loss of joy in lovemaking and a persistent tendency for couples to engage in "mutual accusation" (9.1187) without ever "self-condemning" or admitting one's own flaws. Yet again the central question that arises from Genesis 3 is the Fall's relationship to the tree of life. In other words, why are Adam and Eve evicted from the garden and separated from this tree? Is it simply punishment for their transgression from "the threatener" (9.687), as Satan names God? Are not they punished enough? Milton's Adam and Eve's woe is so great, indeed, that Eve is afraid to bear children, telling Adam: "childless thou art, childless remain: so Death shall be deceived his glut" (10.989-90).

Milton's God sees the full justice of the Fall, telling the angels that humanity can now "boast / his knowledge of good lost, and evil got; / Happier . . . to have known / Good by itself, and evil not at all" (11.84-89). Of course, God himself had given humanity at least partial knowledge of evil through the warning about death. Yet, knowing Adam and Eve's "sorrow unfeign'd, and humiliation meek" (10.1104), Milton's loving Father God provides this final, crucial insight into the relationship of the two trees:

> I, at first, with two fair gifts
> Created him endowed; with happiness,
> And immortality: that fondly lost,
> This other served but to eternize woe;
> Till I provided death: so death becomes
> His final remedy. (11.57-62)

In other words, without communion with the One who alone can teach the difference between good and evil, happiness in this life is not possible; combined with immortality, such unhappiness would be endless, humanity remaining in eternal woe. Death, though, is a "remedy" because, as the Father goes on to explain, much grace is yet to be offered humanity, including a general "renovation of the just" (11. 65) made possible after the work of his Son. Milton's God, pace Blake, is a good God; he then sends Adam another angel, Michael, who in a vision reveals the Old Testament, teaching him through typology, "from shadowy types to truth; from flesh to spirit" (12.303) until finally showing him also the work of Christ, the founding of the church, and even the final judgment and New Jerusalem.[64] His hope for the future fully restored, Adam exclaims:

> O Goodness infinite, Goodness immense!
> That all this good of evil shall produce,
> And evil turn to good; more wonderful
> Than that which by creation first brought forth
> Light out of darkness! (12.469-73)

Rejoining Eve, who has received the same gift of hope interiorly, spiritually, in a dream, the two are led out of Eden into a world that Milton's final lines describe as an enormous gift, and a place where God's presence and action can still partially be known but must also be marked by the lonely sojourn that any separation from God entails:

> The World was all before them, where to choose
> Their place of rest, and Providence their guide:
> They, hand in hand, with wand'ring steps and slow,
> Through *Eden* took their solitary way. (12.646-49)

The extraordinarily comprehensive character of *Paradise Lost* obviously requires no sequel, so another question that any Christian student of Milton must consider is this: why did Milton then write *Paradise Regained* (1671)?[65] Furthermore, why is the main subject of this sequel not Christ's crucifixion, which Michael in Book 12 certainly

---

[64]See Dennis Richard Danielson, *Milton's Good God: A Study in Literary Theodicy* (Cambridge: Cambridge University Press, 1982).

[65]John Milton, *Paradise Regained*, in *John Milton*, pp. 355-618. Unless noted, all subsequent references are to this edition. See also Barbara Lewalski, *Milton's Brief Epic: The Genre, Meaning and Art of Paradise Regained* (Providence, R.I.: Brown University Press, 1966).

presents as the essential means by which humanity was saved and access to God regained, but instead focuses on Jesus' meeting with Satan in the desert during the forty-day fast that follows his baptism, according to Matthew 4 and Luke 4? Following mainly the account of Luke, Milton may simply have been attracted to the New Testament scene that most dramatically presents a direct confrontation between Satan and Jesus, given that both are so fully presented in *Paradise Lost* but do not actually meet face to face before this meeting in the desert. Certainly Milton brings his characteristic dramatic touches to the poem, adding to Scripture such notions as Satan taking on different disguises, accents and approaches to the three temptations presented by Luke. But the most important element of the poem, as in the lengthy scenes that *Paradise Lost* recreated from Genesis, is Milton's exploration of key theological questions suggested but not fully explained in the biblical account. Why does Satan choose particular temptations? What is the significance of each of Jesus' short replies? What symbolic or typological elements relate this New Testament event to the Old Testament? More broadly, what is the general importance of this obviously significant meeting in the life and ministry of the Savior, and in what sense was, as Milton's title implies, "paradise regained" during this encounter?

The opening lines of *Paradise Regained* suggest that Christ's forty-day fast in the desert is chosen because it is a clear example of how, by this "one man's firm obedience fully tried / Through all temptation" (1.4-5), in contrast to the disobedience of Adam and Eve, paradisal communion with God is to be regained. The obvious physical contrast between Eden and the desert reinforces the point that Christ's work is spiritual, dedicated to revealing that he is the saving Son of God, the primary means by which humanity becomes reunited to God. Milton's Satan here witnesses the baptism and hears "the testimony of heaven" concerning "who he is" (1.78)—"this is my Son beloved" (1.85)—but of the dove that descends can only casually remark, "whate'er it meant" (1.83). Unable to know the Holy Spirit, Satan does not really grasp the meaning of the incarnation, and so he will tempt Christ in the desert because "who this is we must learn, for man he seems / In all his linea-

ments, though in his face / The glimpses of his father's glory shine"
(1.91-93). How can human and divine be in one person, and how will
their unique combination affect Christ's ministry?

Milton's first temptation follows Luke precisely, and directly tests
Christ's divine power: "if thou be the Son of God, command / That out
of these hard stones be made thee bread" (1.342-43). The reply of Milton's Christ likewise follows Scripture exactly—"Man lives not by bread
only but each word / proceeding from the mouth of God" (1.349-50)—
but the dramatic dispute that follows clarifies the fuller meaning of
Christ's rebuke. Recalling Israel being fed manna in the desert, Moses
on Mount Sinai and Elijah in the desert as parallel examples, Jesus
makes clear his complete reliance on God for the sustenance of life.
Any "magic tricks" involving material bread are irrelevant to the spiritual truths revealed by God, which instantly allow him to see through
Satan's first disguise as "an aged man in rural weeds" and rebuke him
with the clarity of which Adam and Eve proved incapable: "lying is thy
sustenance, thy food" (1.428). The second temptation in Luke, the
power and glory of "all the kingdoms of the world" (Lk 4:5), is divided
by Milton into different elements—such as banquets of food, wealth,
fame and glory—and here Milton gives Christ fairly long responses
that draw from many other sections of his New Testament teachings.
The stark contrast between Satan's and Christ's worldview is clearly
delineated, and the "right reason" of Milton's Jesus is particularly developed here, in contrast again to Adam and Eve, to prove that God can
use reason, logic and argument in far superior ways, and for far superior
purposes, than Satan. Against the apparently obvious claim that "great
acts require great means of enterprise" (2.412) or wealth, Jesus "pa-
tiently replied" by showing that far more important to the kingdom of
God is "he who reigns within himself, and rules / passions, desires, and
fears" (2.465-6), for he is the King who can "guide nations in the way
of truth / by saving doctrine" (2.473). Even from a strictly logical perspective, this is the rationale for Christ's final reply here, which reminds us of the foundational importance of "the first of all commandments": "Thou shalt worship / The Lord thy God, and only him shalt
serve" (4.176-7).

The climactic contrast between paradise lost and regained, Satan's deception and Christ's true steadfastness, occurs during the third temptation when, as in Luke, Satan sets Christ high on a pinnacle of the temple and again tempts him by testing his identity. Poetically stressing a single word, a single test, Milton's Satan says: "There stand, if thou wilt stand . . . if not to stand, / cast thyself down; safely if Son of God" (4.551-5). Jesus replies, as in Luke, "Also it is written, / Tempt not the Lord thy God," before Milton provides the two-line climax of his entire poem, two lines that reveal the defeat of Satan, the reversal of the Fall and paradise regained: "he said and stood. / But Satan smitten with amazement fell" (4.560-62). Why was Jesus' simple quotation from Scripture so amazing? Faced with the ultimate danger of losing his life and weakened physically by the forty-day fast in the desert, Jesus' communion with and trust in his Father is yet so absolute that he can rely on him even while lodged precariously on the peak of the earthly temple, and rather than experiencing either a literal fall or the Fall into sin of Adam and Eve, Milton's angels, perhaps "in the power of the Spirit" (Lk 4:14), bear Jesus to an Edenic "flowery valley," setting him now "on a green bank" and spread before him "fruits fetched from the tree of life" (4.581-89). Poetically, typologically, Jesus did "vanquish by wisdom hellish wiles" (1.175). By the integrity of his personal reliance on the Father and rejection of Satan's pathetically limited version of knowledge, the second Adam personally regained paradise, reopening access to communion with the Godhead.

Milton's genius is so remarkable and his achievement so singular that it cannot likely be imitated or duplicated. Political events such as the Restoration and emigration of Puritans made it unlikely that there would continue to be so direct a relationship between English literature and Scripture, though certainly John Bunyan and many others continued to write theologically informed poetry, drama and fiction. Yet while writers after Milton chose to go in a different direction, his poetry stands as a fitting conclusion to the extraordinarily rich legacy of Renaissance literature. Though space here has limited us mainly to an introduction to the greatest of these writers—Sidney, Spenser, Marlowe, Shakespeare, Donne, Herbert and Milton—such an "infinite variety" of characters and situations is found within even these writers that a fuller account of the theological aesthetics of the period would be very elaborate fare indeed. While churches and denominations continue to ponder the general merits and flaws of the Reformation and Counter-Reformation debates that to some extent remain an important element of historic Christianity, the Christian literary critic and general reader alike can be grateful to God for the generative power these movements contributed to this, the golden age of English literary history. As Jonson said of Shakespeare, these writers "were not of an age, but for all time."[66]

SUGGESTIONS FOR FURTHER READING

Asquith, Clare. *Shadowplay: The Hidden Beliefs and Coded Politics of William Shakespeare*. New York: Public Affairs, 2005.

Baldwin, T. W. *William Shakspeare's Small Latine & Less Greeke*. 2 vols. Urbana: University of Illinois Press, 1944.

Batson, E. Beatrice. *Shakespeare and the Christian Tradition*. Lewiston, N.Y.: Edwin Mellen, 1994.

Battenhouse, Roy, ed. *Shakespeare's Christian Dimension: An Anthology of Commentary*. Bloomington: Indiana University Press, 1994.

Carey, John. *John Donne: Life, Mind, and Art*. London: Faber & Faber, 1981.

Cox, John. *Seeming Knowledge: Shakespeare and Skeptical Faith*. Waco, Tex.: Baylor University Press, 2007.

Danielson, Dennis. *Milton's Good God: A Study in Literary Theodicy*. Cambridge: Cambridge University Press, 1982.

Donnelly, Philip J. *Milton's Scriptural Reasoning: Narrative and Protestant Toleration*. Cambridge: Cambridge University Press, 2009.

Duffy, Eamon. *The Stripping of the Altars: Traditional Religion in England c. 1400-c. 1580*. New Haven, Conn.: Yale University Press, 1992; 2005.

Fish, Stanley. *How Milton Works*. Cambridge, Mass.: Belknap, 2001.

Hamilton, A. C. *The Spenser Encyclopedia*. Toronto: University of Toronto Press, 1997.

Hassel, R. Chris. *Shakespeare's Religious Language: A Dictionary*. New York and London: Continuum, 2005.

---

[66]Ben Jonson, "To the Memory of My Beloved, the Author, Mr. William Shakespeare" (1623), *Ben Jonson: The Complete Poems*, ed. George Parfitt (Harmondsworth, U.K.: Penguin, 1996), pp. 263-65.

Hill, John Spencer. *Infinity, Faith, and Time: Christian Humanism and Renaissance Literature.* Montreal: McGill-Queens University Press, 1997.

King, J. N. *English Reformation Literature: The Tudor Origins of the Protestant Tradition.* Princeton, N.J.: Princeton University Press, 1982.

Lake, Peter, and Michael Questier. *The Antichrist's Lewd Hat: Protestants, Papists and Players in Post-Reformation England.* New Haven, Conn.: Yale University Press, 2002.

Lewalski, Barbara K. *Milton's Brief Epic: The Genre, Meaning, and Art of "Paradise Regained."* Providence, R.I.: Brown University Press, 1966.

————. *Protestant Poetics and the Seventeenth-Century Religious Lyric.* Princeton, N.J.: Princeton University Press, 1979.

Lewis, C. S. *The Discarded Image: An Introduction to Medieval and Renaissance Literature.* Cambridge: Cambridge University Press, 1964.

————. *A Preface to Paradise Lost.* London: Oxford University Press, 1942.

Lieb, Michael. *Theological Milton.* Pittsburgh: Duquesne University Press, 2006.

Martz, Louis L. *The Poetry of Meditation: A Study in English Religious Literature of the Seventeenth Century.* New Haven, Conn.: Yale University Press, 1962.

Park, Youngwon. *Milton and Isaiah: A Journey Through the Drama of Salvation in "Paradise Lost."* New York: Peter Lang, 2000.

Patrides, C. A. *Milton and the Christian Tradition.* Oxford: Oxford University Press, 1966.

Rivers, Isobel. *Classical and Christian Ideas in English Renaissance Poetry.* London: Routledge, 1994.

Seznec, Jean. *The Survival of the Pagan Gods.* Translated by Barbara F. Sessions. 1940. Reprint, Princeton, N.J.: Princeton University Press, 1953.

Shell, Alison. *Catholicism, Controversy, and the English Literary Imagination: 1558-1660.* Cambridge: Cambridge University Press, 1999.

Strier, Richard. *Love Known: Theology and Experience in George Herbert's Poetry.* Chicago: University of Chicago Press, 1983.

Taylor, Dennis, and David Beauregard. *Shakespeare and the Culture of Christianity in Early Modern England.* New York: Fordham University Press, 2003.

Tuve, Rosemond. *A Reading of George Herbert.* London: Faber & Faber, 1952.

6

LITERATURE AND RELIGION
IN AN AGE OF SKEPTICISM

Unerring NATURE, still divinely bright,
One clear, unchang'd, and universal light,
Life, force, and beauty, must to all impart,
At once the source, and end, and test of Art.

ALEXANDER POPE

Our purpose in this volume, as announced from the outset, is not to outline a literary history: the historical organization that governs the arrangement of our chapters nonetheless serves an important purpose, namely, to reveal the lineaments of evolving theories of reading and right living as articulated by signal English authors. Reading their work in the light of the main worldview debates in which they engaged enables us to appreciate some of the ways that Christian practices of reading and responding to Scripture contribute as well as respond to ongoing, self-correcting (or evolving) literary and philosophical discourse in the English-speaking tradition. For literature of the period under review in this chapter, we think that one of the most fruitful approaches for faith-learning integration would be to study closely the way literary works begin to secularize and then, in a way which transcended previous understandings of genre and the role of literature, to enter into cultural and overtly political debates about everything from the nature of truth to acceptable ecclesial practice. After all, we too live in an age when literature and literary criticism have often been pressed into the service of a political agenda.

In the period extending roughly from the Restoration of the monarchy under Charles II (1660) to the beginning of the twentieth century, deep religious conflict between various denominations in Christian England and between all of them and emerging secularist resistance to religious claims to truth (and hence authority) dominates both political and sectarian religious writing to a degree that these spheres are often indistinguishable. The imaginative literature of this period likewise, while lacking much of the vigor and primary imaginative power of Renaissance literature, can richly repay the effort of contemporary students of political history as well as of the relationship between literature and theology. It is not insignificant for our own purposes that the cultural authority of imaginative literature itself was increasingly at stake in the religio-political fray.

The Puritans, having deposed King Charles I and beheaded him in 1649, ushered in a short-lived republican form of government in England that unfortunately proved incapable of restoring political order. In the absence of a compelling authority figure (Oliver Cromwell never achieved this status), their misbegotten attempt at imposing a Calvinist theocracy (repressing the theater by edict was but one of their cultural stringencies) and the Puritan penchant for independent-mindedness and fraternal contestation produced a track record of incompetent management of internal divisions. The fear of more general social chaos brought about a widespread clamor for restoration of the hereditary king. Charles II was brought back from exile in France, and though his undisguised profligacy, intrigues surrounding his many mistresses and his general disinterest in practice of virtues made him seem in many ways less suited than any other monarch since Henry VIII to be head of the "Established" Church, there was such widespread antipathy to the previous Puritan regime that many serious and thoughtful Christians came to prefer a semblance of unified political order—even under a wanton miscreant—to any Puritan version of theological rectitude.

But as frequently happens in such situations, religious and political

dissension was far from over. Now it was the Puritans' turn to be re-
pressed. Clergymen who would not swear an oath of loyalty to the new
order were deposed. Puritans in dissenting communities were forbidden to gather for worship, even in the small house groups now derided
as "conventicles," and many—as John Bunyan's case illustrates—were
sent to prison, ironically resulting in prison literature of unsurpassed
importance and ongoing influence, as most famously in the case of Bunyan's *Pilgrim's Progress* (1679; 1684). The repression was, however, far-
reaching and severe: religious dissenters were forbidden to enlist in the
military, hold government office or even attend university.[1] Conscien-
tious dissenters, moreover, were themselves increasingly divided into
various groups with wideningly divergent theological convictions, and
while many sought hidden ways to worship privately with their coreli-
gionists, they were, once discovered, persecuted relentlessly. Samuel
Pepys, content as he was with the new order and his own prosperity in
it, was among those whose conscience was troubled by the persecu-
tions—though not enough to protest. Observing "several poor creatures" being herded along by police "for being at a conventicle," he
writes in his diary: "They go like lambs, without any resistance. I would
to God they would either conform, or be more wise, and not be
catched!"[2] But "catched" they were, and eventually in such numbers
that the prisons could not contain them; in larger urban prisons disease
was rampant, and many died. Recusant Catholics, who had long been
so persecuted, were driven further underground.

It is not perhaps surprising that many among the Puritans compromised under the political pressure, but they compromised in different
ways. Some sought to remake their religious identity, others to eschew

---

[1]The Conventicle Act (1664) punished with fines, imprisonment and transportation to penal
colonies abroad those who met in unauthorized gatherings of more than five persons. When
pastors organized groups of five and traveled to serve them, the government instituted the
Five Mile Act (1665), which levied a fine of one year's salary and six months in jail for a cler-
gyman who came within five miles of any parish in which, before his expulsion, he once had
worked. For further background, see Isobel Rivers, *Reason, Grace and Sentiment: A Study of the
Language of Religion and Ethics in England*, 2 vols. (Cambridge: Cambridge University Press,
1991, 2000).
[2]August 7, 1664, entry in Samuel Pepys, *The Diary of Samuel Pepys* (1660-1669), ed. Richard Le
Gallienne (London: Modern Library, 2001).

formal religion altogether in favor of an identity grounded in general
social values and refinements of Reason (almost always capitalized in
the eighteenth century) as opposed to the dictates of revelation (less
and less often capitalized). Three representative figures help us to appreciate the rise to preeminence of reason as a kind of absolute.

John Locke (1632-1704), now regarded as the father of modern
analytic philosophy of mind, was a private physician to the First Earl
of Shaftesbury and, like him, a primary opponent of those who sought
to enable the Roman Catholic Duke of York to succeed Charles II to
the throne. Locke's interests were varied: his major publications include a powerful argument for religious liberty for all but avowed
atheists and Roman Catholics (*Letters Concerning Toleration* [1689-
1692]). He also published *The Reasonableness of Christianity as Delivered in the Scriptures* (1695), in which he maintains that reason must
govern the interpretation of Scripture, rather than either the accumulated weight of tradition or private "spiritual" insight. This approach
led to later works whose arguments rest on this presupposition, notably *A Paraphrase and Notes on the Epistles of St. Paul* (1705-1707) and *A
Discourse on Miracles* (1706).

But none of his writings was more important for literary reflection
than his *Essay Concerning Human Understanding* (1690), in which Locke
attacks Platonic "innate ideas" as well as the *sola scriptura* notion of
biblical authority that undergirded Puritan religious thought and practice. He expresses the conviction that the human mind is a *tabula rasa*,
a kind of blank slate upon which human ideas, mediated rationally,
constitute the only reliable basis of knowledge (2.1), and he attacks religious "enthusiasm" as a false authority, "which laying by Reason would
set up Revelation without it" (4.19). By "enthusiasm" Locke means notions "of a warmed or over-weening brain" leading not to authoritative
judgment but, more dangerously, to "an opinion of greater familiarity
with God," and in effect a rejection of the "labour of strict reasoning."
Religious thinking so warranted upon revelation he takes to be circu-
lar: "It is a Revelation because they firmly believe it, and they believe it
because it is a Revelation." This solipsistic ground of conviction, he
argues, can only lead to division, conflict and social unrest. Passion in

a conviction ("the strength of our Perswasions") is no guarantee of rectitude, but a dangerous delusion. Hence, "Reason must be our last Judge
and Guide in every Thing" (4.19). This portion of Locke's *Essay* is included in most anthologies of eighteenth-century literature because it
succinctly captures a dominant aversion of many mainstream writers of
the post-Puritan era.

For an Anglican divine such as the widely popular preacher John
Tillotson, archbishop of Canterbury, Locke's thinking also provided
amiable grist for the mill of broad churchmanship in the state-autho-
rized Anglican establishment. Tillotson, himself of Puritan stock, had
moved with the intellectual and political fashions; in his often-anthol-
ogized sermon on Micah 6:6-8 he represents Christianity as "natural
religion," reasonably articulating a morality of self-interest and drawing
its ethical standards in Baconian fashion from a broad social consensus
concerning normative virtue and vice. Tillotson evidently does not
think he needs "revelation" to make his argument convincing.

DRYDEN AND THE POLITICIZATION OF POETRY

Against such trend-setting voices we must nevertheless set another, curiously countercultural and yet most certainly equally prominent voice.
John Dryden (1631-1700), dramatist, poet and critic, had also come of
Puritan stock and, indeed, like Milton, held a post in Cromwell's Commonwealth government; he wrote a funeral oration, *Heroic Stanzas to
the Glorious Memory of Oliver* (1659), a publication which might have
been more than enough to shut him out of further public life had he not
also, rather prudently, written *Astrea Redux* (1660) to welcome the restoration of Charles II. Dryden was self-consciously a public orator on
the Roman model, and at this time saw himself as herald of a new Augustan age. He was appointed Poet Laureate in 1668, Historiographer
Royal in 1670 and by 1681 had become a master of political satire in
support of his royal patron in *Absalom and Achitophel*, a poem that employs biblical history to create a dubious allegory in support of the king's
policies and (however tenuously) his notorious philandering. What
could not yet have been well perceived, however, perhaps even by
Dryden himself, is the way his political versification was about to re-

configure the role of public poetry as public theology, thus establishing a precedent for many an English author in the decades to follow.

Dryden's poem of greatest interest in this regard is his *Religio Laici* (1682). Here he deals with another significant challenge to the authority of the Bible in the era, Father Richard Simon's *Histoire critique du Vieux Testament*, earlier that year published in English translation. Simon had set out to deny the authorship of Moses for most of the Pentateuch, and to show inconsistencies and inaccuracies throughout the Hebrew Scriptures. Although Simon's book was later to be censured by Rome, at the time of its publication it was seen as an argument against *sola scriptura* theology among the Reformed (Puritan) churches, and also against its residual place (Articles VI and VII) in the theology of the Established Church. Having, as he and his supporters thought, thoroughly undermined every effort to ground Christian authority principally in the Bible, Simon proclaimed the Roman Church as the only reliable authority in matters of faith. Dryden, already "inclined to skepticism in philosophy," was by this book confirmed in his Lockean rejection of "enthusiasm" and, at the same time, somewhat unsettled at evident residues of the same biblical foundationalism among many Anglican divines. He dedicated *Religio Laici; Or, A Layman's Faith*, to the translator of Simon's book.[3]

Dryden's criticism now was directed not only against the Puritans, "Non-conformists and Republicans . . . dubbing themselves the People of God," whose preachers "cannot dip into the Bible, but one Text or another will turn up for their purpose," but also against "the Fanaticks, or Schismatiks of the English Church" who, "since the Bible has been translated into our Tongue . . . have used it so, as if their business was not to be sav'd but to be damned by its Contents" (preface). Under Simon's influence Dryden had become profoundly doubtful of the rational capacity of untutored individuals to read, let alone translate, the Scriptures responsibly. In the body of *Religio Laici* he condenses Father Simon's argument to say that private or personalistic interpretation has created a kind of theological anarchy in which

---

[3]Fr. Richard Simon, *Histoire critique de Vieux Testament* (Paris, 1678), English trans., anonymous, *A Critical History of the Old Testament* (London, 1681).

The tender Page with horny Fists was gaul'd;
And he was gifted most that loudest baul'd. (404-5)

Where, then, ought one to locate religious authority? Here Dryden
still holds, though unsteadily, for "waving" each extreme (Catholicism
as well as Dissenter or Reformed views) and for trust in what he regards
as the essentialist tradition of the early church (425-40), ostensibly in
the interests of "Common quiet" (450). But he is just as skeptical about
"private Reason" (446) as he is about private interpretation. As he puts
it trenchantly in his preface:

> They who wou'd prove Religion by Reason, do but weaken the cause
> which they endeavour to support: 'tis to take away the Pillars from our
> Faith, and to prop it only with a twig.

Since "Reason is always striving, and always at a loss," then we need
to be skeptical about reason too and to entrust ourselves to faith in such
as God has chosen to reveal of himself in Scripture without asking for
more. There is, of course, a looming self-contradiction in Dryden's position at this point; his skeptical fideism was not yet fully anchored as
to authority because that question was still incompletely answered in
the terms he had set for it.

It must be said on Dryden's behalf that, as public orator of the state,
with the head of state since Henry VIII being also head of the Established Church, he was inevitably compromised by the conflation of
these two entities in English public discourse. He did not yet sense
them as two masters. Ironically, Thomas Hobbes's conception of the
need for "absolute obedience to a state church," as Louis Bredvold has
observed, "was not so very different from the submission to an infal-
lible church demanded by the Roman Catholics,"[4] only in England
secular power tended to have supremacy (one thinks of Lord Cado-
gan's tart rebuke to Olympic runner Eric Liddell in *Chariots of Fire*:
"Hear, hear. In my day it was King first and God after"). Dryden was
more than anxious to serve what he hoped was properly sovereign, and
no issue was more important to him than sovereign authority. The

---

[4]Louis I. Bredvold, *The Intellectual Milieu of John Dryden* (1956; reprint, Ann Arbor: University
of Michigan Press, 1962), p. 126.

trajectory of his own evolving thought was thus preparing him, in however curious a fashion, for the ascent to the throne of Catholic King James II in 1685.

James's regency was turbulent and short-lived; he was effectively deposed in 1688, and succeeded by William of Orange. But Dryden had in matters of religious authority made his own choice, and in his long poem *The Hind and the Panther* (1687) he both reiterates his rejection of the Reformation and follows the logic of his own earlier argument to what he there had sought without fully admitting it.

> Such an *Omniscient* Church we wish indeed;
> 'Twere worth *Both Testaments*, and cast in the Creed. (*Religio Laici*, 281-2)

The Hind and the Panther is confessional in both senses of the term; it includes a confession of personal sin as well as of national apostasy, and it was immediately recognized as a public confession of the poet's now Catholic faith. Dryden's thinking has now developed to a conviction that sinfulness is often an immediate if unselfconscious motive when people assume that "each may be his own Interpreter" (*Hind and Panther*, 463), and with respect to the broader claims to righteousness of Henry VIII, the chief begetter and first head of the Established Church in England, he admits that all one needs to do is look at the record to find a damning analogue:

> In Henry's change his charge as ill succeeds;
> To that long story little answer needs,
> Confront but *Henry's* words with *Henry's* deeds. (*Hind and Panther*, 320-22)

The poem's third and longest section urges Catholics and Anglicans to seek mutual forbearance and deeper common historical understanding. Even at this distance what will be clear to a careful student who reads both *Religio Laici* and *The Hind and the Panther* successively in the order they were composed is that Dryden's first effort at public theology is in almost all respects an unwitting prolegomenon to his second. England was not convinced by *The Hind and the Panther*, and few followed its author. But that poetry could become a powerful vehicle for public theology was now firmly established. Thus, through much of the century to follow, it was not only the usual pamphleteers, essayists and journalists who carried on in rancorous theological debate; poets and dramatists also entered vigorously into the fray.

SWIFT, POPE AND TORY SATIRE

Dryden, in his office as Poet Laureate, had become the first official Tory satirist, but hardly the only one. Daniel Defoe (1660-1731), his younger contemporary, was early on employed in the same enterprise. He enjoyed working as a kind of double agent; himself a Dissenter, he nonetheless wrote a satirical attack called *The Shortest Way with Dissenters* (1702), calling for repression of his own people so extreme that it occasioned political resistance on their behalf. When it was discovered that the author was actually himself a Dissenter, he was humiliated in the pillory and sent to prison. Best known for his novels, especially *Robinson Crusoe* (1719) and the scandalous *Moll Flanders* (1722), each a fictionalized version of Puritan spiritual autobiography of the sort made most famous by Bunyan's *Grace Abounding to the Chief of Sinners* (1666), Defoe turned his writing toward the end of his life, in the pay of the Whigs, to political satire and propaganda.

The best known of all satirists in the period is Jonathan Swift (1667-1745), an Anglican high-churchman and priest, born in Dublin, who spent his life in frustrated pursuit of offices higher than he ever got, both from the church and from the crown. Like Defoe he worked as a journalist for both Tories and Whigs; unlike Defoe he genuinely despised the Dissenters and Presbyterians, as well as Catholics. His early religious tracts, all satirical, give a sense of his preoccupations: *Sentiments of a Church of England Man*, *An Argument Against the Abolishing of Christianity in England*, *A Project for the Advancement of Religion* and *A Letter Concerning the Sacramental Test*—all in 1707 and 1708.

His most systematic dissection of religious factionalism is now seldom read, but *A Tale of a Tub* (1704), with its allegorical send-up of three representatives of Christian tradition, namely Martin (Luther), Peter (the pope) and Jack (for John Calvin), is a good guide to the strength and character of Anglican bias against Catholics and Dissenters alike. *Abolishing Christianity*, by contrast, follows Defoe in arguing satirically for what Swift actually opposes. He does not intend to argue, he says, "in Defence of *real* Christianity, such as used in Primitive Times . . . to have an influence upon Mens Belief and Actions," but rather postures as making "a Defence of *nominal* Christianity, the other having been for some time wholly laid aside by general Consent, as utterly inconsistent with our present Schemes of Wealth and Power."[5] His jest reveals a critical truth.

Alexander Pope (1688-1744), while raised as a homeschooled Catholic (his first poem, at the age of twelve, was a paraphrase of Thomas à Kempis's *Imitation of Christ*), came as a young man to be at first anti-clerical and finally deistic in his philosophy. In his *Essay on Criticism* (1711), written at the astonishing age of twenty-two, Pope combines naturalism with classical wisdom to create perhaps the best brief guide to aesthetic judgment in this period. He exemplified admirably the standard he praises:

> *True Wit* is *Nature* to Advantage drest,
> What oft was *Thought*, but ne'er so well *Exprest*,
> *Something*, whose Truth convinc'd at Sight we find,
> That gives us back the image of our Mind. (*Essay on Criticism*, 297-300)[6]

By "true wit" Pope means great literature; he holds with Horace that eloquence must serve sense, and that a good writer will "avoid *Extreams*" (384) in language, even as in religion. He disdains the Middle Ages, in which

> Much was *Believ'd*, but little *understood*,
> And to be *dull* was constru'd to be *good*. (689-90)

For Pope and many of his peers, Rome was civilization's pinnacle, and when it fell a true barbarism infected everything: "the Monks finish'd what the *Goths* begun." Only with Erasmus and the Renaissance, he thought, did culture begin to mend. But it is in *An Essay on Man* (1733-1734), a poem which was to the eighteenth century what

---

[5]*The Works of Jonathan Swift*, ed. Sir Walter Scott (Edinburgh: Constable and Co., 1824) 8:63-64.
[6]Cited here from John Butt, ed., *The Poems of Alexander Pope* (London: Methuen, 1965), based on the Twickenham text. Further citations of Pope are also from this edition.

Paradise Lost was to the seventeenth, that Pope most fully develops the enlightenment humanism for which he became the standard-bearer in literature. Like Milton's great poem, the *Essay on Man* is a theodicy, but one that makes reason rather than revelation its authority:

> Say first, of God above or Man below
> What can we reason, but from what we know?
> Of Man, what see we but his station here,
> From which to reason, or to which refer? (*Essay on Man*, 1.17-20)

Pope's thesis is that the world, with its evident calamities and imperfections, is as it should be; what appears to us as disorder is in fact a part of the larger mechanism. It is as though the deity, invisible and abstracted from the world that he made, is a clockmaker; having built his timepiece, he winds it, leaves it running, and never interferes with it again:

> All Nature is but Art, unknown to thee;
> All Chance, Direction, which thou canst not see;
> All Discord, Harmony, not understood;
> All partial Evil, universal Good:
> And, spite of Pride, in erring Reason's spite,
> One truth is clear, "Whatever IS, is RIGHT." (1.289-94)

Pope's conclusion, then, is that certain kinds of inquiry, especially metaphysical or theological speculation, are inherently unprofitable:

> Know then thyself, presume not God to scan;
> The proper study of Mankind is Man. (2.1-2)

Self-knowledge, he argues, will lead to a temperate balance between "two Principles in Human Nature," namely, "Self-love, to urge; and Reason, to restrain" (2.53-54). What orders the world is the Platonic great chain of being; man's end is happiness (4.1), a balance in which self-interest and the common good coincide to create the supreme good as a human condition:

> Self-love thus push'd to social, to divine,
> Gives thee to make thy neighbour's blessing thine.
> ... WHATEVER IS, IS RIGHT;

That REASON, PASSION, answer one great aim;
That true SELF-LOVE and SOCIAL are the same;
That VIRTUE only makes our Bliss below;
And all our KNOWLEDGE is, OURSELVES TO KNOW. (4.353-
54; 395-98)

The modern student wishing to understand what the Enlightenment stood for would be hard-pressed to find a more concise representative answer than the poetic manifesto of Alexander Pope. Pope's
views became widespread, both among deists and "broad-church" Anglicans, with significant consequences for traditional Christian teaching as well as statecraft.[7] In the apt words of A. S. Turberville, many of
the broad-church clergy were "expert controversialists, not inspiring
leaders and teachers; were often better witnesses of the 'reasonableness
of Christianity' than of its spiritual force."[8] Predictably, their parishioners grew to have a firm opinion that God, while a venerable conjecture,
had little or no personal immediacy. This chapter does not permit us to
go into these matters in close detail, but a brief passage on prayer by the
poet and essayist William Shenstone will serve as an index to one of the
implications:

> Prayer is not used to inform, for God is omniscient. Nor to move com-
> passion, for God is without passions. Not to shew our gratitude, for God
> knows our hearts. May not a man, that has true notions, be a pious man
> though he be silent?[9]

Gradually, in ways unanticipated in English history for a millennium, the silence spread.

POEMS, PRAYERS AND MEDITATIONS

But not to everyone. Samuel Johnson (1709-1784), poet, essayist, editor

---

[7]Basil Willey observes that "eighteenth-century optimism was not thus essentially a joyous or
hopeful creed, though it may well have suited the complacent and the shallow. It was in essence
an apologia for the status quo" (*The Eighteenth-Century Background: Studies on the Idea of Nature
in the Thought of the Period* [Boston: Beacon, 1961], p. 48).

[8]A. S. Turberville, *English Men and Manners in the Eighteenth Century* (New York: Oxford University Press, 1964), p. 288.

[9]William Shenstone, cited in Geoffrey Tillotson, Paul Fussell and Marshall Waingrow,
Eighteenth-Century English Literature (New York: Harcourt, 1969), p. 913.

of Shakespeare and maker of the *Dictionary* (1755), which established
his reputation as the foremost authority on the English language, was
one for whom not only common prayer in worship but also personal
prayer was anything but nugatory. Eminently well read in a wide range
of subjects, he was regarded among his countrymen as an apostle of
common sense, a legendary conversationalist and a formidable debater.
Most of these qualities are captured admirably in James Boswell's *Life
of Samuel Johnson* (1791), largely by way simply of recording Johnson's
conversations with an astonishing range of people. But Boswell misses
a dimension that modern editors and readers have subsequently found
fascinating, namely, Johnson's personal diary of prayers and meditations.[10] For though Johnson had been a convinced member of the Established Church since reading William Law's *Serious Call to a Devout
and Holy Life* (1729) while still a teenager at Oxford, and regularly used
the Book of Common Prayer and read the Bible thoughtfully, he was
plagued with guilt and a sense of his own failing to live up to the standard set by the Gospels. His personal prayers, as he records them, are
earnest and repentantly self-critical, pleading for God's mercy in language infused by the Book of Common Prayer (1662):

> Almighty God, heavenly Father, who desirest not the death of a sinner,
> look down with mercy upon me, depraved with vain imaginations and
> entangled with long habits of Sin. Grant me that grace without which I
> can neither will nor do what is acceptable to thee. (April 25, 1752)

Year by year, often in the Easter season, Johnson examines his memory and conscience and is repeatedly tormented by evident failings—
typically sloth and gluttonous excess—and the knowledge that, as he
puts it succinctly, "my appetites have prevailed over my reason" (April
21, 1764). His prayers show a persistent desire to "renew the great covenant with my Maker and my Judge" (March 30, 1777), to pledge himself to a more disciplined life, diligent Bible reading and resistance of
religious doubts, and to order his writings to the increase of what he
thinks of as "the promotion of Piety" (April 2, 1779). But he never for

---

[10]Samuel Johnson, *Diaries, Prayers and Annals*, ed. E. L. McAdam Jr., with Donald and Mary
Hyde (New Haven, Conn.: Yale University Press, 1958).

long escaped a deeply conflicted sense of his failure to live up to his avowed calling. In his case, reason was not sufficient to the peace of an ordered life, and he knew it all too well. With the old sage in his philosophical novel *Rasselas* (1759), Johnson recognized that though reason is necessary, it is inadequate to "that happiness which here I could not find" (chap. 45). Even his *Dictionary*, as Robert DeMaria Jr. has observed, "stands in opposition to the growing rationalism . . . in the theology of its day"; indeed, "the existence of God is not only the prime object of faith in the world of the *Dictionary*, it is also the foremost point of knowledge and, paradoxically, of ignorance."[11] That is to say, for Johnson even a troubled faith provided a way of knowing and yet also, simultaneously, a sobering awareness of the limits of human knowledge. Perhaps accordingly, he was much less interested than many among his contemporaries in politics.

In the closing years of the eighteenth century, as the social fabric of England frayed under the loss of America, plagues of alcoholism, crime and abject urban poverty at home, other poets began to reflect in their verse that the rule of reason and what passed for the consensus wisdom of the state were proving inadequate to the common good, let alone the achievement of personal tranquility. A kind of privatization of poetry was underway; a few examples will help us to see how much the sphere of literature had begun to move. Christopher Smart (1722-1771), probably a secret Catholic and certainly a charismatic in piety, turned to the Psalms for more immediate solace in the spiritual life. Smart's *A Song to David* praises the psalmist for a spiritual realism that takes its comfort from the faithfulness of God rather than the wisdom of men. In Smart, whose lyricism William Wordsworth and Robert Browning were to find the high watermark of eighteenth-century verse, we see a poet whose own mercurial swings of melancholy and jubilation found in the psalmist a companionable register of authentic relationship with the divine. Smart, who wrote his curious and exhilarating *Jubilate Agno* while he was confined in an asylum for such eccentricities as falling down on his knees to pray in public places, was certainly emotionally

---

[11]Robert DeMaria Jr., *Johnson's Dictionary and the Language of Learning* (Chapel Hill: University of North Carolina Press, 1986), pp. 25, 233.

fractured and no rationalist. Yet he had the secret admiration of Samuel Johnson, who visited him in Bedlam. Johnson, in a remark that reveals as much about himself as Smart, thought "he ought not to be shut up" and that "his infirmities were not noxious to society." Johnson adds, "He insisted on people praying with him; and I'd as lief pray with Kit Smart as any one else." Smart published a poetic *Translation of the Psalms of David* (1765) and a collection of *Hymns for the Amusement of Children* (1770), and though he died in debtors' prison, he died as he lived, to all appearances in good cheer, quietly confident in God's saving grace.

The great evangelical poet William Cowper (1731-1800) had similar struggles with mental health. Brought to faith through the intercession of his cousin, the Methodist Martin Madan, he was in and out of asylum and hospice care much of his life. Of his bouts with severe depression he wrote powerfully, as also of his conversion:

> I was a stricken deer that left the herd
> Long since; with many an arrow deep infixt
> My panting side was charged when I withdrew
> To seek a tranquil death in distant shades.
> There I was found by one who had himself
> Been hurt by th'archers. In his side he bore
> And in his hands and feet the cruel scars.
> With gentle force soliciting the darts
> He drew them forth, and heal'd and bade me live. (*The Task*, 3.108-16)[12]

Cowper, who was mentored and protected by the reformed slave-trader and Calvinist Anglican priest, John Newton (1725-1807), rejects in this same poem the general idea of his time that redemption comes from "human wisdom" or natural revelation. Divine revelation is not only necessary for Cowper, it is also indispensable solace when reason comes up against its limits:

> [H]e commands us in his word

---

[12]William Cowper, *The Poems of William Cowper*, ed. John Baird and Charles Ryskamp, 3 vols. (Oxford: Oxford University Press, 1980-1995), vol. 2. A more affordable edition for students is *William Cowper: Selected Poetry and Prose*, ed. David Lyle Jeffrey (Vancouver: Regent Publishing, 2007), pp. 88-89.

To seek him rather, where his mercy shines.
The mind indeed enlighten'd from above
Views him in all. Ascribes to the grand cause
The grand effect. Acknowledges with joy
His manner, and with rapture tastes his style. (*The Task*, 3.223-28)

Newton coauthored with Cowper *The Olney Hymns* (1779), containing Newton's "Amazing Grace," perhaps still one of the best-known hymns of the evangelical revival in that period. Yet Cowper's recurring depression and, with it, despair of his election, hounded him to his dying days. The grace of which Smart seemed so calmly possessed was for Cowper, as his last poem *The Castaway* suggests, elusive—even out of reach.[13]

There are here deeper theological and psychological reflections than this volume can explore.[14] But it would be unfair to conclude our reflections on poetry as public theology in the eighteenth century without mentioning one more remarkable poet, the Methodist Charles Wesley (1707-1788). Wesley wrote as many as 6,500 poems and hymns. Isaac Watts thought his poem "Wrestling Jacob" a masterpiece, but his hymns form the apex of his poetry of prayer and praise: hymns such as "Love Divine, All Loves Excelling," "Come, Thou Almighty King," "Jesus, Lover of My Soul," "And Can It Be That I Should Gain," "Come, Thou Long-Expected Jesus," "Christ the Lord Is Risen Today," and "Lo, He Comes with Clouds Descending" are still sung today by evangelicals, Presbyterians, Anglicans and more recently by Roman Catholics. Thus, though unrecognized as such by many, among the best-known poems of the eighteenth century in our time are actually the hymns of Charles Wesley. Most evidently, his is poetry in praise not of reason but of grace and revelation. Charles Wesley's conviction was that the power of living Christian faith depended on complete self-abandonment to the mysteries of faith, to Scripture and to prayer. He

---

[13]David Lyle Jeffrey, *English Spirituality in the Age of Wesley* (1987; reprint, Vancouver: Regent Publishing, 2008), pp. 453-57.

[14]In addition to the volume cited, highly recommended sources are Bruce Hindmarsh, *John Newton and the English Evangelical Tradition* (Grand Rapids: Eerdmans, 2001); and his *The Evangelical Conversion Narrative: Spiritual Autobiography in Early Modern England* (New York: Oxford University Press, 2008).

wrote two hymns on the real presence of Christ in the Eucharist, in
which he reveals himself to have had perhaps more in common with St.
Bernard of Clairvaux than with most of the Protestant poets and divines of his own era.[15]

DISSENTING FROM DISSENT

It might well be imagined that the political and social marginalization
of Dissenters and evangelicals by late in the eighteenth century meant
that their presence in literature had also grown negligible. This was not
the case. Where they persisted volubly, however—and William Blake,
Robert Burns and James Hogg are all examples to illustrate this—they
had become dissenters against the dissenting tradition in which they
were raised.

William Blake (1757-1827), for example, was born into a dissenting
shopkeeper's family in London, and was exclusively homeschooled. Always a visionary, he became early on a visual artist, illustrating other
poets (Milton, Dante) as well as his own work. Although his longer
poems remained virtually unknown in his own lifetime, in his eccentri-
cally independent, visionary appropriation of the Bible he was to create
a kind of romantic antitheology, in which, for example, Satan is the
true hero of Milton's *Paradise Lost* and Milton thus "of the Devil's party
without knowing it."[16] In a representative way Blake is an advocate for
individualistic interpretation of the Christian tradition unfettered by
subscription of any kind to the wisdom of that tradition. A thoroughly
anarchic reader, he was as happy to effect poetically *The Marriage of
Heaven and Hell* (1793) as to satirize natural religion (*There Is No Natural Religion* [1788]), and although he believed firmly in "revelation," he
took it to mean artistic inspiration and insight. In *A Memorable Fancy*
he avers that the prophets Ezekiel and Isaiah had dinner with him,
during which time they revealed that the "voice of God" for them was

---

[15]See John R. Tyson, *Charles Wesley: A Reader* (New York: Oxford University Press, 1989); also
Jeffrey, *English Spirituality in the Age of Wesley*, pp. 252, 265-66.
[16]In a note to his "The Voice of the Devil," Blake claims that Milton "wrote in fetters when he
wrote of angels and God, and at liberty when of Devils and Hell . . . because he was a true Poet
and of the Devil's party without knowing it" (William Blake, *The Marriage of Heaven and Hell*,
ed. Geoffrey Keynes [Oxford: Clarendon, 1966], p. 150).

really just "the voice of honest indignation" and that divine inspiration is, in fact, merely poetic genius. Blake saw himself as similarly called to be a voice for social justice and a prophet of the sublime. He rejected the eighteenth-century idea that poetry was an art acquired by study and imitation *(poeta fit)*, insisting rather that

> Knowledge of Ideal Beauty is Not to be Acquired.
> It is born with us. Innate ideas are in Every Man.
> Born with him, they are truly Himself.[17]

The inspired poet is thus the born poet *(poeta nascitur)*: "Taste and genius are Not Teachable."[18] His revolutionary idea that the poet was akin to the biblical prophet and that his authority was that of a special genius, was clearly an outgrowth of the Dissenters' independent Bible reader and strongly willed personal interpretation, but in Blake and the Romantic poets who followed him, this conception of the poet, a secular version of the religious "enthusiast" who so troubled Locke and Dryden, was to develop a more powerful antireligious, privatizing character.[19]

One aspect of this may be seen in Robert Burns (1759-1796), a poor farmer's son in the western lowlands of Scotland, and even more than Blake an autodidact. But his early prodigious reading and extraordinary intellect served him well: he was able to maintain the persona of an uncouth, untaught bard whilst shrewdly marketing poems both romantically nostalgic and wickedly satirical with respect to the Calvinism of the kirk in which he was raised. In "Holy Fair" and "Address to the Unco Guid, or the Rigidly Righteous," he hammers the posturing would-be sanctity of the leading Presbyterians. In "Holy Willie's Prayer: A Poem," unpublished until after his death, he sets the words of an elder in the kirk against the prayer of the Pharisee in Luke 18, but in fact his purpose is to denounce the Calvinist precept that some people are

---

[17]William Blake, *Annotations to Reynolds' Discourses on Art* (published 1907), 3. A convenient modern edition is Joshua Reynolds, *Discourses: Including "Annotations to Reynolds' Discourses,"* *by William Blake,* ed. Pat Rogers (New York: Penguin, 1992).
[18]Ibid.
[19]This idea is developed in Harold Bloom, *The Visionary Company: A Reading of English Romantic Poetry* (Ithaca, N.Y.: Cornell University Press, 1971).

elect and others eternally damned with no possibility of a will to change affecting the outcome. It is the height of Holy Willie's smug, self-congratulatory arrogance that he can say:

> O Thou that in the heavens does dwell
> Wha, as it pleases best thysel'
> Sends ane to heaven an' ten to Hell,
> A' for Thy glory,
> And no for onie guid or ill
> They've done before thee! (*Holy Willie's Prayer*, 1-6)

Burns rejects this sort of strict Calvinism as both a monstrous misrepresentation of God's justice and, inevitably, as an effective invitation to self-abandoned moral depravity. (It is of interest that he fathered nine illegitimate children with apparently wanton cheer.)

A darker rejection of strict Calvinism is to be met in James Hogg (1770-1835), the early Romantic poet who also wrote a chilling novel called *The Private Memoirs and Confessions of a Justified Sinner* (1824).[20] In it, the bastard son of a Calvinist minister, Mr. Wringham, makes a pact with the devil in some ways reminiscent of that in Christopher Marlowe's *Doctor Faustus* (1616). Convinced by the minister that one of the elect such as he believes himself to be experiences unchecked liberty, since "a justified person can do no wrong" (p. 13), Robert Colwan murders his morally upright brother and several other persons, invariably with the aid of his sophistical double, the Satan figure in the novel, a theologically and psychologically seductive shape-shifter who goes by the name of Gil-Martin. Gil-Martin is rhetorically skillful in persuading his victim to an antinomian extreme of the Calvinism in which Hogg himself was raised, in which, effectively, for one who has been baptized, repentance is unnecessary. Thus prodded, the protagonist Robert convinces himself that if he is of the elect, he is "a justified person, adopted among the number of God's children—my name written in the Lamb's book of life . . . no bypast transgression or any future act of my own, or of other men, could be instrumental in altering the de-

---

[20]References here are to James Hogg, *The Private Memoirs and Confessions of a Justified Sinner*, World's Classics, ed. John Carey (Oxford: Oxford University Press, 1981).

cree" (p. 115). On the other hand, he has already said,

> If my name is not written in the book of life from all eternity, it is vain
> for me to presume that either vows or prayers of mine, or those of all
> mankind combined, can ever procure it now. (p. 100)

According to this logic, moral discernment is as chimerical as repentance is pointless; the devilish Gil-Martin is able to play Robert's strict Calvinism upon him like a siren's harp. Robert's habitual prayers and Bible readings notwithstanding, he descends into the depths of evil, all the while believing himself to be "covered" by the grace of the elect. Meeting the old scholar printer, Mr. Watson, he says, "I could not but despise the man in my heart who laid such a stress upon morals, leaving grace out of the question" (p. 281), but in apprenticing himself to the printer, he persuades him to print up his diabolical journal as "a religious parable, such as the Pilgrim's Progress" (p. 281). Watson, on reading the journal, is horrified and refuses to print it. Only after the fictional author's death is the work published. This multilayered novel surely is a "religious parable," but for many years it was the darkest of its kind. By comparison, the cheerful profligacy of Burns and even the antitheology of Blake seems almost lighthearted, yet the serious student of Christian literature will not want to miss reading this novel, for in its theological criticism and psychological brilliance it presages (and far surpasses) such later Romantic tales as Herman Melville's *The Confidence Man: His Masquerade* (1857) and Robert Louis Stevenson's *The Strange Case of Dr. Jekyll and Mr. Hyde* (1886). Oscar Wilde's better-known *The Picture of Dorian Gray* (1890), an almost clinical amoral and a-theological account of devilish seduction and progress in depravity, likewise owes more than a little to Hogg.

Much additional literature of this period will be of great interest to Christian students. The rise of the novel is particularly worthy of note, especially the striking achievement of Samuel Richardson in transforming aspects of Puritan spiritual autobiography into ingenious epistolary novels such as *Pamela* (1741) and *Sir Charles Grandison* (1754), the brilliant and more humorous novels of Henry Fielding, especially *Joseph Andrews* (1742) and *Tom Jones: A Foundling* (1749), and the incomparable *Tristram Shandy* (1759) by Laurence Sterne. Our purposes in this chapter have necessarily restricted our selections; the material covered has been chosen in such a way as to reveal features of particular pertinence in the context of this book, namely, the politicization of literature as writers were pressed into party service early in the period, and then the subsequent breakdown of effective public voice in literature as party interest became more fragmented. This shift inevitably aided a turn to the private sphere in literary writing as the century developed. The Enlightenment, as historians have tended to call this period, made some grand experiments in philosophy and polity, but as a milieu for literary creativity it was not so fruitful as had been the previous era.

SUGGESTIONS FOR FURTHER READING

Boyle, Nicholas. *Sacred and Secular Scriptures: A Catholic Approach to Literature.* Notre Dame, Ind.: Notre Dame University Press, 2005.

Bredvold, Louis I. *The Intellectual Milieu of John Dryden: Studies in Some Aspects of Seventeenth-Century Thought.* Ann Arbor: University of Michigan Press, 1934; 1962.

Canuel, M. *Religion, Toleration, and British Writing: 1790-1830.* Cambridge: Cambridge University Press, 2002.

Frei, Hans W. *The Eclipse of Biblical Narrative: A Study in Eighteenth and Nineteenth Century Biblical Hermeneutics.* New Haven, Conn.: Yale University Press, 1974.

Greaves, Richard L. *Glimpses of Glory: John Bunyan and English Dissent.* Stanford, Calif.: Stanford University Press, 2001.

Hill, Christopher. *The English Bible and the Seventeenth-Century Revolution.* New York: Penguin, 1993.

Hopps, G., and J. Stabler, eds. *Romanticism and Religion from William Cowper to Wallace Stevens.* Aldershot, U.K.: Ashgate, 2006.

Israel, Jonathan I. *Radical Enlightenment: Philosophy and the Making of Modernity 1650-1750.* Oxford: Oxford University Press, 2003.

Jeffrey, David Lyle. *English Spirituality in the Age of Wesley.* 1987. Reprint, Vancouver: Regent Publishing, 2008.

Knight, Mark, and Thomas Woodman. *Biblical Religion and the Novel, 1700-2000.* Aldershot, U.K.: Ashgate, 2006.

Ritchie, D. E. *Reconstructing Literature in an Ideological Age: A Biblical Poetics and Literary Studies from Milton to Burke*. Grand Rapids: Eerdmans, 1996.

Rivers, Isobel. *Reason, Grace, and Sentiment: A Study of the Language of Religion and Ethics in England*. 2 vols. Cambridge: Cambridge University Press, 1991, 2000.

Tillotson, Geoffrey, Paul Russell Jr. and Marshall Waingrow, eds. *Eighteenth-Century English Literature*. New York: Harcourt Brace Jovanovich, 1969.

Ward, Bruce. *Redeeming the Enlightenment: Theological Reflections on the Liberal Virtues*. Grand Rapids: Eerdmans, 2010.

Young, Brian W. *Religion and Enlightenment in Eighteenth-Century England: Theological Debate from Locke to Burke*. Oxford: Clarendon, 1998.

PART THREE

CONTESTED AUTHORITY

7

AGNOSTICISM AND
THE QUEST FOR AUTHORITY

The Sea of Faith
Was once, too, at the full, and round earth's shore...
But now I only hear
Its melancholy, long, withdrawing roar.

MATTHEW ARNOLD

Romanticism in England shares some features with that of France and America, even with that of Germany. But the student will notice significant differences. Among these, there had been no comparable event to the revolutions that shaped French and American sensibilities (each in their own way), and the British appetite, whether for decadence or for iconoclasm, was more muted. Monarchy and social hierarchy were still factors in cultural consciousness, and literary tastes remained more formal and reflective of social decorum. Nor was there quite the German ideal of the *Übermensch*, as a German reader could find it first in Goethe, then in Wagner and Nietzsche. If anyone in the British literary scene after William Blake had a taste for such things, it would be Percy Bysshe Shelley (1792-1822). Shelley was avowedly antireligious and got himself expelled from Oxford for refusing to answer questions about his *The Necessity of Atheism* (1811). In truth he was an apostle of Voltaire, opposed to Christianity primarily because of its restrictive morality. His personal practice was consistent with his principles, his bohemian lifestyle as detrimental to the women he was involved with as his poetry was dismissive of all forms of conventional morality. *Queen Mab* (1813) sees Christianity as a prop for monarchs and a means of oppression of freedom generally, which for Shelley included freedom from legal restraints, including marriage, and freedom of speech. In his "Essay on the Devil" he declares himself to be cheerfully of the devil's party and proud of it. Percy and Mary Shelley famously read aloud to each other from the Bible as a form of evening entertainment, but with no religious motive in mind. Mary was a daughter of the progressive philosopher William Godwin and Mary Wollstonecraft, who penned the often persuasive *Vindication of the Rights of Women*, but sadly died at her daughter's birth. In her *Frankenstein: or, the Modern Prometheus* (1818) Mary Shelley writes prophetically of the dangers involved in science usurping God and creating creatures beyond human control or comprehension. It now seems ironic that this work, written following a rainy vacation with Percy in Switzerland (1806), in some respects raises questions about her husband's views. It appears that they had spent a good deal of time reading each other German ghost stories and decided upon each writing a horror tale of their own; his was never finished, and her *Frankenstein* was published only after his death.

Percy Shelley's sometime friend and fellow poet George Gordon Byron (1788-1824) had similar principles and led a riotous life not unlike the one he celebrates in his *Don Juan* (1819, 1820). Byron's biblically inspired poems *Cain* and *Heaven and Earth* (1821) challenge orthodox Christianity much as had Blake, aggressively asserting an Enlightenment view of the primacy of human reason and heroizing Satan as one who dares "look the Omnipotent tyrant in the face."[1] John Keats (1795-1821) was by far the best lyricist of these three short-lived poets, and in his brief yet far more tranquil life he produced poetry of compelling beauty. Keats, though not a Christian, was apparently less obsessively

---

[1]George Gordon Byron, *Cain* 1.1.138-9. See *The Dramatic Works of Lord Byron: Including* Manfred, Cain, Doge of Venice, Sardanapalus *and* The Two Foscari . . . (Whitefish, Mont.: Kessinger, 2008).

averse to normative Christian views. He nevertheless diverts his readers' attention to the attractions of classical and medieval imaginary worlds, engaging these matters with an aesthetic rather than a philosophical eye. "The Eve of St. Agnes," "La Belle Dame sans Merci," "Ode to a Nightingale" and "Ode on a Grecian Urn" are among the finest individual poems in this century; their reverence for classical beauty and their meticulous literary form are still inspiring, yet one can see in them a characteristic romantic shift in the content of key terms. This is subtly hinted at in Keats's revision of the medieval transcendentals, as when his "Ode on a Grecian Urn" famously concludes by saying that "Beauty is truth, truth beauty," before simplistically contradicting this traditional concept by adding "that is all / Ye know on earth, and all ye need to know." Aesthetic idealism here becomes, as Roger Lundin puts it, "a surrogate for a seemingly discredited system of Christian belief."[2] About classical literature Keats had more enthusiasm: "On First Looking into Chapman's Homer" celebrates the way that good translation can release the power of a great literary work of one culture and era to imaginative engagement by people in another time and place. But in Keats one might almost say that there is neither religion nor quarrel with religion, and this freedom from the fray has bequeathed to his enduring reputation an admirable aura of serenity much appreciated by his readers. In him we can sense English poetry seeking its enduring values in another source.[3] That source was to be for many "the religion of nature," as protean as universal, and first among its apostles in poetry was William Wordsworth (1770-1850).

In English literature after Blake, a consideration of the sea change effected by the two great national revolutions, those of France and America, may usefully begin with *Lyrical Ballads*.[4] This influential, slim volume was jointly published in 1798 by Wordsworth and Samuel Taylor Coleridge. Wordsworth added an explanatory critical pref-

---

[2]Roger Lundin, *Believing Again: Doubt and Faith in a Secular Age* (Grand Rapids: Eerdmans, 2009), p. 212.

[3]M. H. Abrams, *Natural Supernaturalism: Tradition and Revolution in Romantic Literature* (New York: W. W. Norton, 1973).

[4]William Wordsworth and Samuel Taylor Coleridge, *Lyrical Ballads*, ed. Michael Schmidt (New York: Penguin, 2007).

ace in 1800. This preface presents a number of the ideas now most associated with literary Romanticism. For Wordsworth, poetry is "the spontaneous overflow of powerful feelings" that "takes its origin from emotion recollected in tranquility," a process succinctly presented in his "I Wandered Lonely as a Cloud." A poet is "a man speaking to men," a term conveying here a fresh, more democratic consideration of humanity—children, the elderly, the insane, outcasts, criminals and all those marginalized by society and sparingly represented, to be sure, in neoclassical poetry. Yet surprisingly, this preface also cites Aristotle to claim that poetry's "object is truth, not individual and local, but general, and operative," though "carried alive into the heart by passion."

While *Lyrical Ballads* certainly celebrates physical beauty, it consistently stresses the moral and spiritual transformation made possible by contemplation of nature; at times the claims seem hyperbolic, as when "The Tables Turned" argues that "one impulse from a vernal wood" can teach more "of moral evil and of good / than all the sages can." Wordsworth's most cogent argument in this regard (if *argument* is indeed the term) is presented in "Tintern Abbey." This well-received poem focuses on the impressions made on Wordsworth's mind by the decayed monastery on the River Wye, a symbol of the depredations of both Henry VIII and Oliver Cromwell. This is a landscape of misted memory, charged with nostalgia, whose "beauteous forms" enter the poet's "purer mind" and not only allow "tranquil restoration" but also influence "the best portion of a good man's life, / His little, nameless, unremembered acts / Of kindness and love." Nature offers Wordsworth a substitute for both religious consolation and spiritual insight, for within it we become aware of our "living soul" and "with an eye made quiet by the power / Of harmony, and the deep power of joy, / We see into the life of things."

Whether or not this final claim is "but a vain belief," as Wordsworth himself immediately queries, has been a question for readers since his own time. How should such a belief find credible warrant? Wordsworth justifies his claims by reference to his own autobiography (a self-referential apologetic much more fully developed in *The Prelude*, not published until his death in 1850). This raises the issue at the heart of the Christian debate over Romanticism. For while "the heavens declare the glory of God; and the firmament sheweth his handywork" (Ps 19:1), Christians have also been concerned, as George Herbert puts it, about the danger of resting "in nature" and "not the God of nature."[5] Medieval poets had been far less ambiguous; Christian poets of the twentieth century would be clearer about the distinction as well. For example, Paul Claudel (1868-1955), writing of his own poetic principles, puts the relation characteristically for Christian tradition when he writes, "We know that the world is, in effect, a text, and that it speaks to us, humbly and joyfully, of its own emptiness, but also of the presence of someone else, namely its Creator."[6] In some respects these matters appear in a more Christian perspective in Coleridge's contributions to *Lyrical Ballads.* While focusing on supernatural tales rather than the realism of rural life, Coleridge's lifelong affection for pre-Enlightenment, "spiritual" old England subjects his potential pantheism to sharper correction from historic Christianity. For when his "The Eolian Harp" asks whether "animated nature" might be "one intellectual breeze / At once the Soul of each, and God of all?" his wife Sara, "meek daughter in the family of Christ," "holily dispraised / these shapings of the unregenerate mind," reminding him of the "awe" and "Faith" necessary when speaking of God. Much more reverent is "Frost at Midnight," a meditation spoken as Coleridge cradles the couple's infant son, Hartley, praying that his child shall be raised by "lakes and shores / and mountain crags" rather than urban London, for

> [S]o shalt thou see and hear
> The lovely shapes and sounds intelligible
> Of that eternal language, which thy God
> Utters, who from eternity doth teach
> Himself in all, and all things in himself.

Coleridge here draws fairly close to the central medieval Christian metaphor of God as Author of the book of nature.

---

[5]George Herbert, "The Pulley," line 15.
[6]Paul Claudel, *Positions et Propositions* (Paris: Gallimard, 1928), 1.206.

Wordsworth's principal goal seems to have been a "philosophic" poetry expressing a unified view of "Nature, Man, and Society": what he achieved is a good deal less. There is little of society in his poetry, even as an abstraction, and almost no representation of strong character or personality in others. He is admired today for his technical excellence and for his capacity to arouse pathos by means of descriptive landscapes and sentimental vignettes, psychological snapshots that he famously described as the product of "emotions recollected in tranquility" (preface to *The Lyrical Ballads*). Yet it may be that he is the best representative of a shift in worldview that during the nineteenth century would reach across the Atlantic. The problem, as we shall see in both English and American contexts, was in finding a source of authority comparable in utility to the biblical conception of a creator God. A major concern Wordsworth shared with some earlier poets and philosophers was to find nontraditional (perhaps especially nondoctrinal) sources of emotional and spiritual authority for literature; this led him to pursue and attempt to define a natural property of nature reflected in reflexive human perception that paralleled in some way the emotional experience once associated with Christian worship. The closest approximation to spiritual, even mystical, experience, was thought by Wordsworth to be something called the "aesthetic sublime." Edmund Burke's characterization of the sublime had already established itself:

> Whatever is in any sort terrible . . . or operates in a manner analogous to terror, is a source of the sublime, that is, productive of the strongest emotions of which the mind is capable of feeling.[7]

One can see this conception of the sublime at work in texts as various as the gothic novels of Samuel Monk and Edward Young's poem "Night Thoughts," as well as in Wordsworth's own predilection for vistas with a precipice or the ruin of an abbey destroyed in the dissolution of the monasteries. Emotions aroused by sudden vertigo or

---

[7]Edmund Burke, *A Philosophical Enquiry into the Origin of Our Ideas on the Sublime and the Beautiful* (London, 1757). A good modern edition is that edited by Adam Phillips for the Oxford World's Classics series (reissued 2009).

feelings of "Vacuity, Darkness, Solitude, and Silence" (Burke's list) came for many more than Wordsworth to be substitutes for religious experience. But this made the perceiving, emotional self the reference for the experience, rather than anything objectively external. Thus, the "Wordsworthian egotistical sublime," as Keats called Wordsworth's poetic, was seen by his young contemporary as little more than a literary preoccupation with himself and his own sentiment, to which external objects of all kinds were merely props: on Keats's reading, "Tintern Abbey" is overwhelmingly about the poet's own mental state; the turn away from the objective reality to subjective impression makes the ultimate spiritual authority the self of the poet. Although more understated than Whitman's "Song of Myself" (1855, 1860), which effects a certain charm by its sheer audacity, Wordsworth's poetry has ceased to be public in any sense that might have been understood by Dryden.

It will be evident (cf. Rom 1:18-23) that a transfer of authority from God to the self has the concomitant effect of diminishing the authority of reason. This aspect of Wordsworth's rejection of the Augustan Age, usually muted, is explicit in his attempt at tragedy, *The Borderers* (written in 1796-1797, but not published until 1842). The play is not stageworthy, but its plot strikes themes we have met before. A sinister bandit named Oswald commits dark crimes but is remorseless because he is convinced all human emotion is weakness unworthy of a man. As he persists in his ways he becomes poisonously amoral. *The Borderers* makes it clear that any effort to live by the light of reason is ultimately doomed to failure, since attempting to repress feelings inevitably backfires. There are also strong connections here to Wordsworth's "Ode on Intimations of Immortality" (1802) and "The Excursion" (1814), in the notion that a proper balance in the human psyche is better effected in a perceived harmony with nature than in any other way. Much in the latter poem ironically recalls in this respect part of Pope's *Essay on Man*; personal harmony depends on acceptance of one's place in the natural harmony, the great chain of being.

Wordsworth had become a member of the Established Church about 1810, yet his *Ecclesiastical Sonnets* (1822), 132 in number, reveal a strik-

ingly dispassionate religious sensibility.[8] Of the collection's three parts
the first is effectively a recapitulated history of religion in England from
the Druids to the Renaissance papacy; the second goes from the English
Puritans to Archbishop Laud; the third from the "Restoration to the
Present Times," though many of the poems are actually meditations on
some of the offices in the Book of Common Prayer. The poems are
perfunctory, their tone enervated, even dyspeptic; in comparison with
John Donne's nineteen "Holy Sonnets" there is an almost complete lack
of personal spiritual feeling. In the end, despite some memorably lovely
passages in poems such as "Tintern Abbey" and his reflections on the
creative process in *The Prelude*, there has been surprisingly little in
Wordsworth to hold the imagination of contemporary students. Artisti-
cally, he has much to commend him; but even here it is no longer common, as once it was, to hear his name as part of a supreme triumvirate
(with Shakespeare and Milton) in the English literary canon.

Samuel Taylor Coleridge (1772-1834), Wordsworth's sometime
friend and hiking companion, is, for all his opium addiction and intermittent incoherence and opacity, more interesting in our context. For
one thing, Coleridge is more passionate, and his lyricism hits higher if
irregular notes in poems such as "Kubla Khan," an opium vision, "Frost
at Midnight," "This Lime-Tree Bower My Prison" and "Desertion: An
Ode" (1802). His familiarity with physical pain and spiritual suffering
is memorably portrayed in his most famous poem, "The Rime of the
Ancient Mariner," which uses archaic diction, simple rhymes, and both
visible and invisible spiritual creatures to portray the distress of a sailor
whose "soul hath been / Alone on a wide, wide sea / So lonely 'twas,
that God himself / Scarce seemed there to be" (597-600). In this tale
psychological pain came after the Mariner slew an albatross, a seemingly trivial act that Coleridge nevertheless presents as a metaphor of
irrational violence enacted upon an innocent creature, an evil act whose
consequences cannot be atoned for by the Mariner himself, and which

---

[8]For a thoughtful analysis of Wordsworth's religious debts to Methodism, see Richard Brantley,
Wordsworth's "Natural Methodism" (New Haven, Conn.: Yale University Press, 1975), and by
the same author, *Locke, Wesley, and the Method of English Romanticism* (Gainesville: University
Presses of Florida, 1984).

led indirectly to the further death of his fellow sailors. References to the Christian problem of atonement occur throughout the poem, as "instead of the cross, the Albatross" on the Mariner's "neck was hung," though it troubles some Christian readers that the sin here is not explicitly redeemed by Christ's crucifixion. Rather, it is the Mariner's natural theology, implicitly linked to the medieval transcendentals, that prompts his remorse; the once ugly "water snakes" (273) near the ship now reveal "beauty," and as "a spring of love" comes from his heart, the Mariner has "blessed them unaware" and again can pray.[9] His hearer is led to believe that a long process of penance has preceded his ability to pronounce the poem's central, famous moral:

> He prayeth best, who loveth best
> All things great and small;
> For the dear God who loveth us,
> He made and loveth all.

Coleridge himself found this moral sentiment didactic, but never revised it. Both he and Wordsworth (who both eventually become practicing members of the Anglican Church) may be distinguished from the more openly rebellious, second-generation Romantic poets by occasional expressions of a characteristically vague and diffused piety.

There is a bit more to Coleridge than Wordsworth in this regard. Though his turn from poetry to neo-Platonizing philosophy produced what can now seem an excess of muddy pseudo-Germanic prose, as he describes his movement from Unitarianism toward more orthodox trinitarian Christianity (a reverse movement to that in Emerson and other contemporary American writers), especially in such works as *Christianity: The One True Philosophy* (1814), *The Statesman's Manual* (1816), *Aids to Reflection* (1825), *Church and State* (1830) and the posthumous *Confessions of an Inquiring Spirit* (1840), he articulates a vision that was to be profoundly influential for a generation of rising Christian socialists, including Charles Kingsley.[10] There is nothing quite like

---

[9]On the nature of this aesthetic conversion, see Gregory Maillet, "'A poem should not mean / but be': Lonergan and Literary Aesthetics," *Method: Journal of Lonergan Studies* 21 (2004): 57-91.

[10]See Owen Barfield, *What Coleridge Thought* (Middletown, Conn.: Wesleyan University Press,

this particular development in American literature of the same period. It is, however, an important characteristic of the relationship between Christian thought in its more radical form and the social matrix in England. Coleridge's later work had a direct influence on Matthew Arnold and John Henry Newman as well as F. D. Maurice. What one may regret, given the intellect of Coleridge, is a greatness that might have been, hints of which we only see now in flashes of intermittent brilliance. For the student of Christianity in literature there nevertheless remains in his prose writings, perhaps especially the last of these, worthy matter for reflection on the general theological trajectory of his time.[11]

THE AMERICAN RENAISSANCE

Despite the intervening ocean and pilgrim intentions to pursue an independent course, during the seventeenth century "British America," as it was then known, was not exempt from the struggles between a dominant Calvinistic theology and church government on the one hand and a resistant Enlightenment deism on the other. Universities such as Harvard and Princeton began as expressions of the intellectual interests of Congregationalists (moderate Calvinists) and many of the founding fathers later in the eighteenth century owed as much to this branch of Christianity as did their Puritan counterparts in England. Yet the high levels of personal devotion necessary to maintain effective Congregationalism were not uniformly to be found. Moreover, as the founding generations passed, something of the fervor passed away with them on a general scale. A poem such as Timothy Dwight's "Conquest of Canaan" (1785) still, in the manner of Cotton Mather's *Magnalia Christi Americana* (1702), represents America as designed by God to be a second, flawless Eden, the place of Christ's coming millennial reign, but his rhetoric seems more self-consciously political than Mather's. Dwight, eighth president of Yale, is here acting as a public orator in the

1971); Robert J. Barth, *Coleridge and Christian Doctrine* (Cambridge, Mass.: Harvard University Press, 1969); Anthony Harding, *Coleridge and the Inspired Word* (Montreal: McGill-Queens University Press, 1985).
[11]David Lyle Jeffrey, *People of the Book: Christian Identity and Literary Culture* (Grand Rapids: Eerdmans, 1996), pp. 300-308.

Ciceronian vein, rousing patriotism by powerful mythographic analogy. Mather was a theologian (and a learned one at that) and seems to have believed his prophetic scenario quite literally.

The latter years of the eighteenth century and the first half of the nineteenth century afforded a mixed legacy to these high prophetic imaginations—not in respect of material success but in terms of preserving credibly a vision of America as, in effect, a divine manifestation or, eschatologically, the concluding chapter to the Bible itself, ushering in the millennium.[12] It should be of central interest to Christian students of American literature that the successors of Mather and Dwight were less and less inclined to persevere as Calvinists, and more and more disposed to attack the kind of Christian vision their predecessors had articulated in ways made possible, ironically, by their own childhood catechism.

Melville's *Moby Dick* (1851), an epic novel that draws heavily on biblical allusions for its mythographic power, nevertheless sees the conflict between human pridefulness and the sovereignty of God expressed in the quest to kill "Leviathan" as socially destructive, and casts into deepest doubt both Melville's own childhood Calvinism and the political messianism inscribed in its political vision. In *White-Jacket; or, The World in a Man-of-War* (1850), Melville had already made explicit his skepticism about both Christianity and its chauvinistic political appropriation to the national sense of "manifest destiny," and he deepened his attack in *The Confidence-Man* (1857).[13]

Nathaniel Hawthorne is more subtle, but his resistance to the Calvinism he was raised in is famously (as well as ambiguously) manifest in his best-known novel, *The Scarlet Letter* (1850). Here Hawthorne uses the Bible against the Puritans, so to speak, in a fashion reminiscent of Shakespeare's *Measure for Measure* (c. 1603), focusing not on personal and ethical miscreance but, in the vein of Melville, on public and political perversion of the Christian ideal.[14] We should also pay attention

---

[12]See Giles Gunn, ed., *The Bible in American Arts and Letters* (Philadelphia: Fortress, 1983; also Edmund S. Morgan, *Visible Saints: The History of a Puritan Idea* (Ithaca, N.Y.: Cornell University Press, 1963).

[13]See the discussion by Jeffrey in *People of the Book*, pp. 323-25.

[14]Ibid., pp. 325-26 and notes.

to Hawthorne's short fiction, in which his tendency to draw on Christian literature of the Renaissance as well as Scripture to problematize the religious culture of his time is often productive of what amounts to a refined literary as well as cultural criticism. For our purposes we may call to witness his story "The Celestial Railroad" from *Mosses from an Old Manse* (1854).[15] The plot of this tale is made analogous to, and a commentary on, Bunyan's *Pilgrim's Progress* as it might be considered in the light of a more skeptical, even agnostic age. The idea is that in an age of progress one needs no longer to travel laboriously by foot on a pilgrimage from the City of Destruction to the Celestial City, but may do so with much less trial and hardship on a railroad that "by the public spirit of some of the inhabitants . . . has recently been established." The point of the railroad is to make the journey easier and, as Hawthorne's superbly detached narrator puts it, "to gratify a liberal curiosity" (p. 168). The narrator travels, as on a touristical whim, in the company of a certain Mr. Smooth-it-Away, "who, though he had never actually visited the Celestial City, yet seemed as well acquainted with its laws, customs, policy and statistics as with those of the City of Destruction, of which he was a native townsman" and not incidentally "a director of the railroad corporation and one of its largest stockholders" (p. 168). Mr. Smooth-it-Away is evidently a stand-in for the Unitarian theologians who had so commonly descended from the moderate Calvinists of an earlier generation; in a sinister touch the train's conductor is Apollyon. This story is a brilliant satire, not so much against Bunyan's text as against the diminished Christianity of America from which, in effect, the Christianity known to Bunyan is now to be distinguished. Hawthorne makes his ironical deconstruction explicit right from the outset, saying:

> The reader of John Bunyan will be glad to know that Christian's old friend Evangelist, who was accustomed to supply each pilgrim with a mystic roll, now presides at the ticket-office. Some malicious persons, it is true, deny the identity of this reputable character with the Evangelist of

---

[15]The edition cited here is Nathaniel Hawthorne, *Mosses from an Old Manse*, American Authors in Prose and Poetry, 12 vols. (New York: P. F. Collier, 1925), 5:168-86.

old times, and even pretend to bring competent evidence of an imposture. Without involving myself in a dispute, I shall merely observe that, so far as my experience goes, the square pieces of pasteboard now delivered to passengers are much more convenient and useful along the road than the antique roll of parchment. Whether they will be as readily received at the gate of the Celestial City I decline to give an opinion. (pp. 169-70)

In Hawthorne's revision of Bunyan, the ominous figures of "Pope" and "Pagan" have been replaced by "The Great Transcendentalist." He is of German origin and speaks like it, "in so strange a phraseology that we know not what he meant, nor whether to be encouraged or af-frighted" (p. 178). For his part, Mr. Smooth-it-Away thinks anything but Christian orthodoxy is liberating; he is possessed of a keen admiration for Vanity Fair. The narrator, however, finds it disconcerting that neither he nor any of the other reverend divines there (Mr. Shallow-Deep, Mr. Stumble-at-Truth, Mr. This-Today, Mr. That-to-Morrow, Mr. Bewilderment, Mr. Clog-the-Spirit and Dr. Wind-of-Doctrine), for all their "wonderful improvements in ethics, religion and literature," are much concerned with actually getting to the Celestial City. It is no accident that in Hawthorne's tale, just as the train was "rushing by the place where Christian's burdens fell from his shoulders at the sight of the cross" (p. 173), the passengers are given palliative anodynes in the form of a gaggle of clerics from the evidently decadent Calvinist "town of Shun-Repentance," who in a fashion probably intended to evoke Ralph Waldo Emerson, began to "descant upon the inestimable advantages resulting from the safety of our baggage" (p. 173).

Hawthorne is surely one of the most gifted of all American satirists. Yet unlike Melville, whose anti-Christianity and vigorous "Quarrel with God" is unmistakable, it is not so easy to count him among those who seek to undermine Christianity altogether. In another splendid satire from the same volume, "Earth's Holocaust," his parable is about a burning of all the books that constitute literary culture, "the weight of dead men's thought" (p. 308) as the organizer of the conflagration puts it, but the similarly detached narrator notes that the works of writers such as Milton and Shakespeare "endure longer than almost any other material of the pile." He also spies "among the wallowing flames a copy of the Holy Scriptures, the pages of which, instead of being blackened into tinder, only assumed a more dazzling whiteness as the finger-marks of human imperfection were purified away" (p. 365). One wonders if, widely read in Christian texts as he was, Hawthorne might have come across the Puritan Richard Baxter's criticism of the subjective interpretation of Scripture, with which he roundly concurred. Baxter had seen the potential for a spiritually counterproductive anti-intellectualism to arise from the insistence that a Christian needed for guidance only the Bible and his own personal interpretation of it: "He that will have no books but his creed and his Bible," Baxter warns, "may follow that sectary, who, when he had burnt all his other books as human inventions, at last burnt the Bible, when he grew learned enough to understand that the translation of that was human too."[16] In any case, Baxter's remark seems an apt epigraph; Hawthorne is surely among the fiercest critics of the institutional Christianity of his time, but not of Scripture itself. At the very least the respect for Scripture he shows in several places makes him a "doubtful case." Hawthorne may perhaps best be thought of as a respectful agnostic, one who saw more clearly than many of the most impassioned culture warriors of his era what was at stake in the evolving worldview of American Protestant Christianity. As a species of both theological and literary criticism, his "The Celestial Railroad" provides not only an interesting retrospect on Bunyan's *Pilgrim's Progress* but also a fascinating prospective preparation for reading C. S. Lewis's *The Great Divorce* (1945).

Overall, however, American literature in this period tends to make its departure from Christian presuppositions more explicit than do writers in Britain. Thus, while his work is steeped in biblical allusions, a poet such as Walt Whitman, in *Leaves of Grass* (1855, expanded in 1856 and 1860) and especially "Song of Myself," makes triumphantly egoist what might in a British author such as Wordsworth or even Shelley be more muted, or disguised by allusions to nature, classical poetry or perhaps the detritus of medieval Christianity as recalled by ruins. As a consequence the student sees in the "American Renaissance" less a hearkening back to

---

[16]Richard Baxter, *The Practical Works of the Late Reverend and Pious Mr. Richard Baxter*, 4 vols. (London: n.p., 1707), 2:xiii-xiv.

the English Renaissance or even an attunement to the Romanticism of the Lake District than a pressing forward to modernity.

This is particularly evident in the essays of Ralph Waldo Emerson (1841). Emerson, he liked to point out, was also descended from old Puritan stock, and he certainly knew its texts. But he also knew and admired the work of Rousseau, Montaigne and Goethe; his Romanticism was not nostalgic but was concerned with the emergence of a modern man as triumphant individual, much in their vein. His famous essay "On Self-Reliance" is tacitly a post-Christian text, a protomodernist manifesto in prose, book-ending Whitman's "Song of Myself" in such a way as effectively to legitimize self-justification as the author's primary subject. Critics such as Roger Lundin have done an excellent job of making the American writers of this period accessible to our understanding in terms of worldview. Lundin in particular, writing of the complex poetry of Emily Dickinson, has shown just how useful the reflexive agnosticism so prevalent among literary authors of this period can be as a corrective to shallow Christian reflection in our own time.[17] Agnostics—as distinct from enthusiastic atheists and underinformed Christians alike—open the window to productive consideration of many a central tenet of faith itself, not merely of the intersections of religion and literature.

VICTORIANS AND EDWARDIANS

The Victorian period is rich in literary triumphs, and standard literary histories and anthologies typically treat the period well. What may perhaps be added, at least from a Christian perspective, is some suggestion as to both the representation of evolving theological debate at that time and also an encouragement to the student to look for deeply religious purpose in poetry and fiction where one might not perhaps at first expect to find it.[18]

---

[17]See Roger Lundin, *From Nature to Experience: The American Search for Cultural Authority* (Lanham, Md.: Rowman & Littlefield, 2005); also his *Emily Dickinson and the Art of Belief* (Grand Rapids: Eerdmans, 2004).

[18]Among recent books Lauren M. E. Goodlad, *Victorian Literature and the Victorian State: Character and Governance in a Liberal Society* (Baltimore: Johns Hopkins University Press, 2003), takes a new historicist approach. Most useful for our subject are Stephen Prickett, *Words and*

This was the great age of the English novel. Following on the achievement of Sir Walter Scott (1771-1832), who in his Waverly novels roman-
ticized both Scottish and medieval history (though in *Old Mortality*
[1816] he took a somber look at the religious persecution of the Cove-
nanters), Jane Austen, especially in *Pride and Prejudice* (1813), by her
extraordinary talent also helped develop a strong popular market for the
genre. Part of Austen's success then—still reflected in the popularity of
cinematic versions of her novels in our own time—owes to the skill with
which she negotiates the neoclassical and Romantic divide to create enduring fictional characters; these characters often explore the application of traditional Christian virtues in an aristocratic social setting.

Charles Dickens (1812-1870) and George Eliot (1819-1880) stand
out for different reasons. Dickens, though in personality often as his
brilliant *Bleak House* (1853) seems, was indisputably one of the best
novelists of character ever to take up the pen. His themes combine romance with a concern for social justice (especially in *Hard Times* [1854]).
His uncanny ability to write as though seeing the world through the
eyes of a precocious child in novels such as *David Copperfield* (1849-
1850) and his mastery of suspense and patient revelation of character in
the subtly allegorical *Our Mutual Friend* (1865) amply reveal an enormous talent. His characters include not only stock figures of the upper
classes but creatures in abject poverty, and he notably treats the latter
with great sympathy.

If Dickens tended on the whole to avoid the doctrinal substance of
Christian theology (his *Christmas Carol* may be considered an excep-
tion),[19] George Eliot (the *nom de plume* of Marian Evans) took the subject very seriously, though in a critical spirit. While she had been a
schoolgirl convert to evangelicalism, she was later influenced by distinctly alternative views, including those of her long-time amorous partner, G. H. Lewes. Her early work includes a translation of David
Strauss's *Life of Jesus* (1846) and Ludwig Feuerbach's *Essence of Christian-*

---

the Word: Language, Poetics and Biblical Interpretation (Cambridge: Cambridge University
Press, 1988), and his *Romanticism and Religion: The Tradition of Coleridge and Wordsworth in
the Victorian Church* (1976; reprint, Cambridge: Cambridge University Press, 2008).
[19]See Janet Larson, *Dickens and the Broken Scripture* (1985; reprint, Athens: University of Georgia Press, 2008).

ity (1854), both of which view the Bible as historically unreliable and, in Feuerbach's case, argue that religious belief fulfills an imaginative need but is essentially palliative. Eliot's fiction, which came to supersede that of Dickens in critical esteem, includes three novellas in one volume, *Scenes from a Clerical Life* (1857), which present evangelical clergymen and parishioners sympathetically. Her magnum opus is *Middlemarch* (1872). Eliot's essentially post-Christian moral philosophy is expounded in *Daniel Deronda* (1876), but her earlier conviction that personal integrity resides in freedom of the will, and that moral choice defines human character, is more artfully displayed in *Adam Bede* (1857).

There are other worthy writers, though we cannot detain ourselves with them here: Elizabeth Gaskell (1810-1865), the brilliant bluestocking essayist, Hannah More (1745-1833) and Charlotte Yonge (1823-1901) all have something of the evangelical sensibility George Eliot left behind, though none stands up to her in literary talent. Nor do Charlotte or Emily Brontë, though their novels continue to attract interest, and in Charlotte's case make intelligent use of biblical allusion. By century's end the novel had eclipsed poetry as the dominant genre, and in crowning a trend begun more than a century earlier its readership had become predominantly female. From the point of view of the book market alone, this was a fact of enormous importance. There were, of course—and still are—other and deeper implications for literary study which continued to develop in the twentieth century.[20] One of these is reflected in the fact that the comparatively minor novelists discussed in this last paragraph now receive professional attention on a scale denied to them in their own lifetime. Their general readership, however, is relatively small. An eccentric and still interesting Scots writer, George MacDonald (1824-1905), known to his own time as a minor poet, essayist and preacher as well as novelist, has on account of the influence of his writing on C. S. Lewis and the persistent popularity of his children's fiction (e.g., *At the Back of the North Wind* [1871] and *The Princess and the Goblin* [1872]) reemerged to considerable popularity. His mythopoeic novels *Phantastes* (1858) and especially *Lilith* (1895) exhibit

---

[20]One of the most significant developments in the professional study of literature may be that a strong majority of all graduate students in the discipline are now women.

a soteriological universalism sharply at odds with the normative doctrine of the Scottish Kirk in which he was a minister, but these works offer interesting and otherwise substantially traditional expressions of the theological imagination of orthodox Christianity. They are each characterized by an ebullient sense of religious hope.

PROGRESS AND AMBIGUITY

The phenomenologist Paul Ricoeur, in an essay titled "Christianity and History," argues that there are "three stages" in the recurrent flux of history, "three ways of understanding and recovering meaning, and three levels of interpretation: the abstract level of progress, the existential level of ambiguity, and the mysterious level of hope."[21] As a Christian himself, Ricoeur argues for meaning in history comparable to that suggested by the grand narrative of the Bible. He frames this, however, by referring to Pascal's *Fragment d'un traite du vide*, in which Pascal asserts that "the whole succession of mankind ought to be considered as one and the same man who continues to exist and learn."[22] This way of looking at the vast array of literary texts suggested to the reader in this chapter can be helpful, for the Enlightenment was above all self-conceived as an age of progress, subtended by reason. But with the nineteenth century there came many a doubt—doubts to add to those of later eighteenth-century writers as diverse as Cowper and Johnson—that the "rational life" was still possible or even a life worth aspiring to; with Romantic poets such as Blake, Shelley and Byron there was even suspicion about whether rationality was compatible with vital creativity.[23] By the time George Eliot was translating Strauss and Feuerbach, the foundations of biblical authority in revelation had likewise, for many, been thoroughly shaken.[24] Thus unsettled, despite relative prosperity and the expansion of empire, literature begins noticeably to turn

---

[21]Paul Ricoeur, *History and Truth*, trans. Charles A. Kelbley (Evanston, Ill.: Northwestern University Press, 1965), p. 82.

[22]Ibid., p. 83.

[23]Prickett, *Romanticism and Religion*.

[24]David Lyle Jeffrey, "Biblical Scholarship and Literary Criticism," *Cambridge History of Literary Criticism*, ed. Rafey Habib, vol. 6 (Cambridge: Cambridge University Press, 2010); Prickett, *Words and the Word*.

in on itself, and authors begin to justify such inwardness as a form of sincerity, as if sincerity in itself might provide a kind of authority.

One sees this unsteadiness readily in the most eminent poets, Tennyson, Clough and Arnold. Alfred Lord Tennyson (1809-1892) succeeded Wordsworth as Poet Laureate in 1850, the year of his *In Memoriam*. He was almost as active as Dryden in writing poems on affairs of state, but in his long dramatic monologue "Maud" (1853) his irresolution and uncertainty about meaning in history—personal as well as national—is really the subject. His Arthurian medievalism in poems such as "Beowulf" (1879) and especially *Idylls of the King* (1859) reveals a nostalgic desire to create meaning in a history he feared might not be really there; like the "Ulysses" of his famous dramatic monologue, he is not content that the grand narrative of history in which he has so prominently participated has the possibility of projecting a convincing sense of closure for his own time, and he is fundamentally disquieted. As Louis Markos has shown, Tennyson was skeptical about the Victorian myth of progress, and in his *Idylls of the King* he especially shows himself to be a principled critic of the emergent philosophical materialism of his time.[25]

Arthur Hugh Clough (1819-1861) showed great early promise, but an inability to choose among influences and his eventual loss of Christian faith because of the German biblical criticism embraced also by George Eliot added to his indecisiveness: in his "Easter Day" he rejects the evidence for the resurrection but goes on to make of the story a kind of faintly affirming metaphor. This was a time characterized by calls for religion based less on doctrine than on the need of the state and society for ethical guidelines, what Thomas Carlyle (1795-1881) and Matthew Arnold's father, the headmaster of Rugby School, thought most important, namely, a sense of duty, especially "duty to England." This call to patriotic duty was an attempt to stabilize the ethical ambiguity introduced by uncertainty about the authority of biblical revelation, and perhaps even of reason, by putting in its place an authoritative state. This program had its adherents, but among the younger genera-

---

[25]Louis Markos, *Pressing Forward: Alfred, Lord Tennyson and the Victorian Age* (Naples, Fla.: Sapientia Press, 2007).

tion of writers it found few confident proponents.

Matthew Arnold (1822-1888) thought it better to trust in the enlightened self in the manner suggested by Goethe; in this sense his early collected *Poems* (1853, 1855) are a natural companion to Ralph Waldo Emerson's "Self-Reliance" essay (1841). But where society is concerned, he is much less confident than was Emerson. Thinking about social realities makes him, as in "Dover Beach" (1851), increasingly despondent and melancholy. The spiritual void in Victorian life, of which he writes, seems to have been less of a burden to him, however, after he was elected professor of poetry at Oxford and became the first of that succession to lecture exclusively in English. He also became, through works such as *Essays in Criticism* (1865), *Literature and Dogma* (1873) and *Culture and Anarchy* (1869), effectively the father of English literary studies as a university discipline (before that one studied Latin or Greek classics).[26] In this role he stressed that the social cohesion and ethical standard once provided by religion ought now to be seen as better provided by high culture; criticism of literature becomes on this view above all cultural criticism, and, even as Shelley once fancied that poets were unacknowledged "legislators of the world," Arnold now asserts that role for the literary critic. Poetry, authoritatively taught, must subsume the role of failed religion in pointing the way to human perfection, both the "best self" and a "national right reason."

This objective required Arnold to engage to some degree in biblical and theological criticism, in which he was influenced by Schleiermacher and the neo-Hegelians, especially in his *St. Paul and Protestantism* (1870) and *God and the Bible* (1875).[27] Here he reveals that his desire, like that of Ernst Renan, is to keep the spirit of Christianity without the annoying particulars of its creeds; he wishes that the Bible would be preserved not for religious but for high literary reasons. Much of his quasi-theological work was so amateurish as to bring upon him the vituperative criticism of both liberal biblical scholars and traditional Christians in equal measure, though the justice of this double rebuke has not prevented a cohort of Arnoldian successors from conceiving of

---

[26]Jeffrey, *People of the Book*, pp. 308-15.
[27]Ibid., pp. 311-15.

the role of literary criticism as a discipline in much his way.[28] Christian students of literature need to be aware that something of Arnold's presupposition still characterizes a wide range of literary schools and theoretical approaches; this category mistake, tacit or explicit, is something a thoughtful Christian student will want to eschew.

Robert Browning (1812-1889), best known and beloved for superb dramatic monologues like "My Last Duchess," "Soliloquy in a Spanish Cloister," "Fra Lippo Lippi" and "The Bishop Orders his Tomb at St. Praxed's" (all 1840s), is a poet who moved away from his mother's evangelical faith, like others, under the influence of German biblical criticism. By 1850 he was writing poems such as "Christmas Eve" and "Easter Day," in which faith and reason now seem to him incompatible. He came to think that human faith ought not to be placed either in nature or in reason, but in love. Although he was uncertain about the authority of biblical texts, he felt that he could trust his intuitions to confirm that God is love. This enabled Brown to persist in the Victorian ideal of progress in a way different but parallel to that by which Arnold's "national right reason" had enabled him.

Elizabeth Barrett Browning (1806-1861), Robert's wife, exhibits something of the same order of residual confidence in the spiritual capital of a declining Christianity to motivate social justice for women and children in "The Cry of the Children" (1843) and *Aurora Leigh* (1857). Elizabeth was raised in a devout evangelical home and published her first mature poetry in a volume called "The Seraphim and Other Poems" (1838), though some of her greatest work comes after she began her famous romance with Robert Browning. The best known of the love poems written to Robert, "How do I love thee? Let me count the ways" (*Sonnets from the Portuguese*, p. xliii) subtly alludes to Ephesians 3:17-19, though in such a way as to divert the love of God and her "lost saints" toward the man who would be her husband. Though the Brownings eloped to Italy and lived happily there until Elizabeth's

---

[28]A notable twentieth-century example is Northrop Frye, in his *The Educated Imagination* (1957; reprint, Bloomington: Indiana University Press, 1998); *The Secular Scripture* (Cambridge, Mass.: Harvard University Press, 1978); and *The Great Code: The Bible and Literature* (New York: Harcourt Brace Jovanovich, 1982).

death in 1861, they did not in much else follow in the footsteps of the Romantics. *Aurora Leigh* is a long poem about the growth of a female writer, and its narrative drama portrays a realistic, serious artist who will not subvert her art for economic or political purposes, but rather sees it as a means of keeping open the possibility of acquiring a vision particular and universal.

All such aspirations notwithstanding, in Arnold's metaphor, "the sea of faith," once "at the full," had fallen to a low ebb, and few prominent writers heard more than its "melancholy, long withdrawing roar." The figure here is not original to Arnold. Lucretius had written with dispassionate irony in his *On the Nature of Things* (2.1-13) that "it is a pleasure to stand upon the shore, and to see the ships tossed upon the sea . . . but no pleasure is comparable to standing upon the vantage ground of Truth, and to see the errors, and wanderings, and mists and tempests in the vale below." Francis Bacon had quoted it with less overt irony in his problematic essay "On Truth."[29] Neither reason nor revelation any longer offered any solution to the sense of cultural and religious ambiguity into which England had so clearly fallen and which, in the writings of Hawthorne and Melville, among others, had become evident also in America. As Ricoeur's paradigm suggests, such a state of ambiguity is inherently unstable. It is likely to deteriorate into some sort of crisis, personal or national, which must be resolved either by a confident choice for hope or by assent to melancholic drift and despair. Despair, the stance of many writers, takes many forms: morbidity, anaesthetization and escapism are among the forms typically reflected in literature. The popular writers of the late nineteenth century, such as William Morris, were writing, in the vein of Tennyson, neo-medieval fantasies such as Morris's "Well at the World's End" (1894), a fanciful prose romance that was to be the introduction, even for C. S. Lewis, to an idealized medievalism, emptied of its Christian substance. The Pre-Raphaelite poets and painters, Dante Gabriel Rossetti (1828-1882) perhaps foremost among them, invented an aesthetic pseudo-Catholicism, which included a creedless and impenitent idealization of love as

---

[29]Francis Bacon, *Francis Bacon: A Selection of his Works*, trans. Sydney Warhaft (London: Collier, 1982), p. 48.

"free love." Rossetti's sister Christina, buffeted by the excesses of her brother's circle, clung to the High Anglican convictions of her mother and in her religious poetry, some of which is beautiful (e.g., "In the Bleak Mid-winter"), shows the influence of the Tractarians. One of the foremost of the Tractarians, John Keble (1792-1866), wrote a volume of sacred verse, *On the Christian Year* (1827), immensely popular as devotional reading in its own time but little read today. Francis Thompson (1859-1907), sometime seminarian and homeless drug addict, was taken in by minor Catholic poets Wilfred and Alice Meynell, and enabled to write his memorable poems "The Hound of Heaven" and "The Kingdom of God." All these poets are now deemed marginal, even for Christian readers. But hidden from the world in his own time there was a poet more luminous than them all, and, in retrospect, he has taken the highest place.

Gerard Manley Hopkins (1844-1899) was already a brilliant student and gifted poet at Oxford where, under the influence of John Henry (later Cardinal) Newman (1801-1890), he converted to Catholicism. On account of this conversion he was prevented from taking up a teaching fellowship at the university, and he suffered complete rejection from his family. When he entered the Jesuit order he burned many of his poems, but sent some to Robert Bridges, his classmate, for safekeeping. These poems, along with others recovered by Bridges after Hopkins's death, were published only in 1918. This is no place to attempt an elucidation of the most original, dynamic and Christian poetry of the entire post-Restoration period; it must suffice here to say that far beyond the commonly anthologized verses such as "God's Grandeur," "Pied Beauty," "Hurrahing in Harvest" and "To the Windhover," Hopkins's small body of poetry will more amply repay the efforts of close reading, both for poetics and for spiritual richness, than almost any other lyric poetry in the English language.[30] His work has the unusual distinction of theological probity and profundity; here are no cheap evasions of either the vacuity of a dying culture or the personal dark night of the

---

[30]See Walter J. Ong, *Hopkins, the Self, and God* (Toronto: University of Toronto Press, 1986); Paul Mariano, *Gerard Manley Hopkins* (New York: Penguin, 2008); and the novel by Ron Hansen, *Exiles* (New York: Farrar, Straus & Giroux, 2009).

soul; he faces both with a hard-earned yet gracious candor. But in his sacramental understanding of the grace of God in creation and re-creation alike, he has no peer. Hopkins holds to a Christian rather than romantic perspective: for him, "nature is never spent. . . . / Because the Holy Ghost over the bent / World broods with warm breast and with ah! Bright wings" ("God's Grandeur"). His brilliant and original lyri-cism—as seen to advantage in his poetic understanding of the self which can only find its own meaning and hope in the mystery of Christ so powerfully articulated in "As Kingfishers Catch Fire"—shows him to be a poet who both seizes hope from the gullet of despair and pro-claims that hope to all who seek it for generations to come. Hopkins is not "of his culture" but is to it a sign of joyous contradiction such as makes him a Christian poet for all seasons. In their fullness Hopkins's poems are exemplars of the thesis in Newman's *The Grammar of Assent* (1870), namely, that we achieve a convincing sense of abiding authority in the universe not through the deductive powers of our own reason, or logic, but through flashes of intuitive perception by which we see, even if only momentarily, into the heart of created reality and find there a glimpse of the glory of God.

EPILOGUE: DECADENCE

For much of the literary and artistic scene, however, the full sea of faith was receding faster than even Arnold had imagined. There are many examples of that form of resignation to despair that earns the term decadent in late Victorian and Edwardian literature. A. E. Housman, Aubrey Beardsley, Algernon Charles Swinburne ("the apostle of de-spair," as he was called by critics) and even that genuinely worthy nov-elist Thomas Hardy (1840-1928) all offer expressions of it in their work. Hardy's anti-Christian tone is often bitter, even sinister: in *Tess of the d'Urbervilles* (1891) and *Jude the Obscure* (1895) he became a prophet of defiant despair; his protagonists are often victims of a blind determin-ism as inexorable as the gruesome *moira* of Sophocles.

For those writers for whom despair took the form of a retreat into aestheticism, Walter Pater (1839-1894) was likewise a prophet: material beauty had become for him a substitute for spiritual transcendence and was to replace it as ultimate cultural authority. With the aid of John Ruskin (1819-1900), a genuinely talented art historian, aesthetic beauty, even in the trappings of religious ritual, became a substitute for the doctrinal content of faith. But the most celebrated and still the most engaging of Pater's disciples was Oscar Wilde (1856-1900), with whom the neo-Epicureanism of the "decadent" writers reached its literary apogee. Wilde was a student of Ruskin at Oxford, but a more faithful disciple of Pater. He made of his own public persona a walking statement of decadent disregard for truth, logic and moral accountability. In his essays "The Decay of Lying" and "The Critic as Artist" (taking Arnold at his word and then some) he presages the world of postmodern literary theory in its love of scandal and self-fashioning opportunism. In both efforts he was a kind of genius; his cleverness and disorienting paradox has in retrospect become a kind of paradigm for one of the most entertaining—yet ultimately destructive—aspects of contemporary practice in literary theory. But the Christian student should grant him the utmost attention, and not simply on account of these qualities. *The Picture of Dorian Gray* (1890) is Wilde's attempt to assert the amorality of art. He claims in his preface that "there is no such thing as a moral or an immoral book. Books are well written, or badly written. That is all." But despite that, in this reincarnation of the *pactum diaboli* theme from Marlowe's *The Tragical History of Doctor Faustus* and Hogg's *Confessions of a Justified Sinner*, Wilde creates a psychological study of the process of decline through decadence to utter depravity that more than mirrors Hogg and Marlowe for its sheer persuasiveness and imaginative power. In *Dorian Gray*, in which Dorian is in fact "poisoned by a book" and then shaped like a wax sculpture toward self-destruction by the devilish artifice of his Wilde-like aesthetic mentor, there is insight of a sort that the St. Paul of Romans 1 might well approve as chilling spiritual realism.[31] Wilde here exemplifies his ostensible literary theory, a notion of reverse *mimesis* in which "Life imitates art far more than Art imitates Life." Indeed, he will go so far as to

---

[31]Dominic Manganiello, "The Voice(s) of Conscience: Wilde's Dialogue with Newman in *The Picture of Dorian Gray*," in *The Picture of Dorian Gray*, Ignatius Critical Editions, ed. Joseph Pearce (San Francisco: Ignatius, 2008).

claim that "Nature, no less than Life, is an imitation of Art. . . . She is our creation" ("The Decay of Lying"). Here, in an antithesis of what we have called critical (and theistic) realism, Wilde verges on a prophecy to which the twentieth century as well as our own has born ample, if troubling, fulfillment.

SUGGESTIONS FOR FURTHER READING

Armstrong, C. I. "The Absolute Implied: Coleridge on Wordsworth and the Bible." *Literature and Theology* 14, no. 4 (2000): 363-72.

Arseneau, Mary. *Recovering Christina Rossetti: Female Community and Incarnational Poetics*. Basingstoke, U.K.: Palgrave, 2004.

Baltazar, L. "The Critique of Anglican Biblical Scholarship in George Eliot's *Middlemarch*." *Literature and Theology* 15, no. 1 (2001): 40-60.

Boyle, Nicholas. *Sacred and Secular Scriptures: A Catholic Approach to Literature.* Notre Dame, Ind.: Notre Dame University Press, 2005.

Brantley, Richard E. *Locke, Wesley, and the Method of English Romanticism.* Gainesville: University Presses of Florida, 1984.

Canuel, Mark. *Religion, Toleration, and British Writing: 1790-1830.* Cambridge: Cambridge University Press, 2002.

Colon, Susan. *The Professional Ideal in the Victorian Novel: The Works of Disraeli, Trollope, Gaskell and Eliot.* Basingstoke, U.K.: Palgrave Macmillan, 2007.

Cunningham, Valentine. "Dickens and Christianity." In *A Companion to Charles Dickens.* Edited by David Paroissien, pp. 255-76. London: Blackwell, 2008.

Delbanco, Andrew. *Melville: His World and Work.* New York: Knopf, 2005.

Eberwein, Jane Donahue. "Emily Dickinson and the Calvinist Sacramental Tradition." In *Emily Dickinson: A Collection of Critical Essays.* Edited by Judith Farr, pp. 89-104. Upper Saddle River, N.J.: Prentice Hall, 1996.

Emsley, Sarah. *Jane Austen's Philosophy of the Virtues.* New York: Palgrave Macmillan, 2005.

Ferris, Ina. *The Achievement of Literary Authority: Gender, History, and the Waverley Novels.* Ithaca, N.Y.: Cornell University Press, 1991.

Gunn, Giles B. *The Interpretation of Otherness: Literature, Religion, and the American Imagination.* London: Oxford University Press, 1979.

Hapgood, L. "'The Reconceiving of Christianity': Secularisation, Realism, and the Religious Novel: 1888-1900." *Literature and Theology* 10, no. 4 (1996): 329-50.

Harding, Anthony. *Coleridge and the Inspired Word.* Kingston, Ont.: McGill-Queens, 1985.

Hempton, David. *Evangelical Disenchantment: Nine Portraits of Faith and Doubt.* New Haven, Conn.: Yale University Press, 2008.

Hopps, G., and J. Stabler, eds. *Romanticism and Religion from William Cowper to Wallace Stevens.* Aldershot, U.K.: Ashgate, 2006.

Jay, Elizabeth, ed. *The Evangelical and Oxford Movements.* Cambridge: Cambridge University Press, 1983.

Jeffrey, David Lyle. "Biblical Scholarship and the Rise of Literary Criticism in the Nineteenth Century." In *The Cambridge History of Literary Criticism,* ed. Rafey Habib, vol. 6. Cambridge: Cambridge University Press, 2011.

Kazin, Alfred. *God and the American Writer.* New York: Alfred A. Knopf, 1997.

Knight, Mark, and Emma Mason. *Nineteenth-Century Religion and Literature: An Introduction.* Oxford: Oxford University Press, 2006.

Knight, Mark, and Thomas Woodman. *Biblical Religion and the Novel, 1700-2000.* Aldershot, U.K.: Ashgate, 2006.

Landow, George P. *Victorian Types, Victorian Shadows: Biblical Typology in Victorian Literature, Art and Thought.* Boston: Routledge & Kegan Paul, 1980.

Larsen, Timothy. *Crisis of Doubt: Honest Faith in Nineteenth-Century England.* Oxford: Oxford University Press, 2006.

Larson, Janet L. *Dickens and the Broken Scripture.* Athens: University of Georgia Press, 1985.

Leithart, Peter J. *Miniatures and Morals: The Christian Novels of Jane Austen.* Moscow, Idaho: Canon Press, 2004.

Lundin, Roger. *Believing Again: Doubt and Faith in a Secular Age.* Grand Rapids: Eerdmans, 2009.

———. *From Nature to Experience: The American Search for Cultural Authority.* Lanham, Md.: Rowman & Littlefield, 2007.

———. *There Before Us: Literature, Religion and Culture from Emerson to Wendell Berry.* Grand Rapids: Eerdmans, 2007.

Markos, Louis. *Pressing Forward: Alfred, Lord Tennyson and the Victorian Age.* Naples, Fla.: Sapientia Press, 2007.

Masson, Scott. *Romanticism, Hermeneutics, and the Crisis of the Human Sciences.* Aldershot, U.K.: Ashgate, 2004.

Morris, David B. *The Religious Sublime: Christian Poetry and Critical Tradition in Eighteenth-Century England.* Lexington: University of Kentucky Press, 1972.

Netland, John T. "A Modest Apologia for Romanticism." *Christian Schol-*

ars Review 25, no. 3 (1996): 297-317.

Oberhaus, Dorothy Huff. "Tender Pioneer: Emily Dickinson's Poems on the Life of Christ." In *Emily Dickinson: A Collection of Critical Essays*. Edited by Judith Farr, pp. 105-18. Upper Saddle River, N.J.: Prentice Hall, 1996.

Perkin, J. Russell. *Theology and the Victorian Novel: Reclaiming the Victorian Novel from Presumed Secularity*. Montreal: McGill University Press, 2009.

Prickett, Stephen. *Origins of Narrative: The Romantic Appropriation of the Bible*. Cambridge: Cambridge University Press, 1996.

———. *Romanticism and Religion: The Tradition of Coleridge and Wordsworth in the Victorian Church*. Cambridge: Cambridge University Press, 1976.

Scheinburg, Cynthia. "Victorian Poetry and Religious Diversity." In *The Cambridge Companion to Victorian Poetry*, pp. 159-79. Cambridge: Cambridge University Press, 2000.

Vogel, Jane. *Allegory in Dickens*. Birmingham: University of Alabama Press, 1977.

Watson, J. R. "Romantic Poetry and the Wholly Spirit." In *The Discerning Reader: Christian Perspectives on Literature and Theory*. Edited by David Barratt, Roger Pooley, and Leland Ryken, pp. 195-217. Grand Rapids: Baker, 1995.

Wheeler, M. *Death and the Future Life in Victorian Literature and Theology*. Cambridge: Cambridge University Press, 1990.

———. *The Old Enemies: Catholic and Protestant in Nineteenth-Century Culture*. Cambridge: Cambridge University Press, 2006.

White, D. E. *Early Romanticism and Religious Dissent*. Cambridge: Cambridge University Press, 2006.

Whitla, William. *The Central Truth: The Incarnation in Robert Browning's Poetry*. Toronto: University of Toronto Press, 1963.

Willey, Basil. *More Nineteenth-Century Studies: A Group of Honest Doubters*. New York: Harper & Row, 1966.

———. *Nineteenth-Century Studies: Coleridge to Matthew Arnold*. New York: Harper & Row, 1966.

Wilson, A. N. *God's Funeral: A Biography of Faith and Doubt in Victorian England*. New York: Ballantine, 2000.

Wolff, Robert Lee. *Gains and Losses: Novels of Faith and Doubt in Victorian England*. London: John Murray, 1977.

8

Modernism, Postmodernism
and Christian Literature

*It is a dark century. . . . To look into this darkness
and see there the victory of Christ is to see the essence of hope.*

Dottrina (now Pope Benedict XVI)
in Michael O'Brien's *Father Elijah*

As Christian students arrive finally at the literature of the twentieth
and twenty-first centuries, they may sense that they have stumbled into
a cultural world untethered from its Christian past, and feel a certain
nostalgia for the faithful authors of earlier periods. This is an under-
standable reaction; ours has been for some time and is likely to continue
to be a post-Christian age. Yet *modernism* and *postmodernism* are terms
that Christian students of contemporary literature must learn to understand and ultimately transcend if they are to pursue the discipline. As
artificial rather than historical markers of literary periods, these words
have multiple meanings and certainly signify distinctive aesthetic
trends. Far more significant, however, is the atheistic metaphysic typically inherent in both modernism and postmodernism. In accessible
psychological terms, we can appreciate that modernism is characterized
by the triumph of individualism and the quest for personal identity.
The self-actualization theory of Abraham Maslow is an elaborated
modern affirmation for what was still viewed as a character defect by
Keats when he described the self-preoccupation of Wordsworth's po-

etry as an assertion of the "egotistical sublime." The emergence of the self as subject, as Charles Taylor has shown in his *Sources of the Self* is, in effect, the primary trajectory of Western thought since the Enlightenment and more particularly since Romanticism.[1] One of the ways that postmodernism may be distinguished from modernism is by the further elaboration of group identity politics and advocacies. These advocacies, at their best, can more intentionally serve to articulate the purposes of social justice for marginalized groups. Frequently, however, postmodern intensifications of the modernist trajectory produce a view that the self is the only authentic literary subject. For postmodernism at its worst the self is all there is. Christian approaches to postmodern literature will necessarily vary according to the place such literature occupies on this spectrum.

Modernists typically critique both Enlightenment rationalism and Victorian propriety. They tend to favor radically avant-garde aesthetic techniques that scorn popular appeal, preferring instead a coterie culture ostensibly committed to art for art's sake. Postmodernists carry such a critique of culture still further. Discontented with what they tend to regard as the tepidity of much modernism, these writers employ techniques like irony, pastiche and playful black humor to create a self-consciously aesthetic metafiction and, much more radically, to question the very capacity of words to communicate stable meanings, let alone reality or truth of any kind. From a metaphysical viewpoint, however, it makes little difference whether the modernist accepts atheism as the inevitable conclusion of scientific materialism, or the postmodernist, following Nietzsche, accepts nihilism with a laugh and a shrug: for theists, for Christian readers, the denial of God in both movements is in itself far more significant than their different approaches.

Nevertheless, there are at least three important reasons for Christians to study twentieth- and twenty-first-century literature in the light of their increasingly distinctive worldview. First, a good way to grasp the importance of faith and the value it contributes is to imagine life lived without God, especially in the concrete and graphic way typically

---

[1]Charles Taylor, *Sources of the Self: The Making of the Modern Identity* (Cambridge, Mass.: Harvard University Press, 1992).

afforded by imaginative literature. Compassion requires listening attentively to lonely, lost souls convinced of the death of God; the absolute emptiness in the nihilism of some of the most talented modernist writers provides its own self-critique; sometimes, in fact, the spiritual void they represent can seem clearly God-shaped. Second, the consequences of nihilism, both personal and social, have been powerfully challenged by some notable twentieth-century writers, especially novelists; Christian writers have sometimes directly participated in this critique from the prospect afforded by a Christian worldview, offering to what Taylor has called the "malaise of modernity" a prophetic biblical response. Finally, and encouragingly, students of contemporary literature will also discover devoutly Christian writers whose distinctive voices are "signs of contradiction" to the prevailing literary ethos, expressing the eternal truths of Christian faith in ways that speak powerfully to contemporary readers of no particular religious persuasion.

EX NIHILO: NIHILISM AND CHRISTIANITY IN MODERNIST FICTION, POETRY AND DRAMA

Jacques Maritain has pertinently observed of this period that those writers

> who have rejected faith in Transcendence, and entered into the spiritual experience of the void, are bound—as men—to turn toward a substitute for what they have rejected: a new god of their own, or a system of revolt against and hatred for the celestial Intruder.[2]

The potential for early twentieth-century fiction to offer Christian students valuable insight into the real nature and effect of nihilism can readily be seen in the work of novelists such as James Joyce and Virginia Woolf. Joyce's lapsed Catholicism is obvious in early work such as the "The Dead" (1914), in which the failed lover Gabriel remains alienated to the end in a cold, heartless universe in which the snow falls "like the descent of their last end, upon all the living and the dead." In Joyce's semi-autobiographical *A Portrait of the Artist as a Young Man* (1916), young Stephen Dedalus studies Thomist aesthetics, but apparently

---

[2]Jacques Maritain, *Creative Intuition in Art and Poetry* (New York: Pantheon, 1953), p. 181.

comprehends no element of Catholic doctrine except references to the sufferings of hell. Indebted to confessional autobiography such as Rousseau's *Confessions* and ultimately to the *Confessions* of Augustine in its form, this is a novel about dis-conversion, a principled exit from Christian faith prompted by what Jean Daniélou has in another context called "the Satanic refusal to adore."[3] In Joyce's most famous novel, *Ulysses* (1922), the single-day walk around Dublin of a lapsed Jew, Leopold Bloom, is systematically compared to the wanderings of the ancient Homeric hero. T. S. Eliot initially thought the "continuous parallel" being drawn was meant to give "a shape and a significance to the immense panorama of futility and anarchy which is contemporary history."[4] Others, much less sure about what Joyce "meant," have joined a long and colorful debate about the method in his madness, including his deconstructive semiotic and rhetorical innovations.[5] The novel's self-conscious modernism is perhaps best exemplified in the contrast between Penelope, whose faithfulness in the ancient epic confirms the value of Ulysses's sacrifice, and the adulterous Molly Bloom, who continues to deceive the deluded Leopold. Finally, in *Finnegan's Wake* (1939), Joyce exhibits a postmodernist's obsession with the unstable possibilities of linguistic meaning. The novel is an experimental demonstration of the arbitrary relations of signifier and signified that Derrida was to celebrate in his famous lecture "Structure, Sign, and Play" in 1966, but which few readers could comprehend long enough to concelebrate in any sustained manner.[6] The evolution visible in the literary career of James Joyce presages in this way the more general development from modernism to postmodernism.

Virginia Woolf employs many of Joyce's literary techniques, such as stream of consciousness and the subjective representation of experience, to offer a more sensitive and compassionate aesthetic, but ultimately her

---

[3]Jean Daniélou, *Scandal of Truth* (Baltimore: Helicon, 1962), p. 50.

[4]T. S. Eliot, "'Ulysses,' Order, and Myth," *The Dial*, November 1923, reprinted in *Selected Prose of T. S. Eliot* (London: Faber & Faber, 1975).

[5]Perhaps the most remarkable of these conversations is recorded in Samuel Beckett et al. (including William Carlos Williams), *Our Exagmination Round His Factification for Incamination of Work in Progress* (Paris: Shakespeare, 1929).

[6]The lecture "Structure, Sign, and Play," delivered at Johns Hopkins University, was published in *Writing and Difference*, trans. Alan Bass (London: Routledge, 1978).

atheism is comparably bleak in outlook. The extreme difficulty of knowing or preserving a real, lasting relationship with others is depicted, for example, in Woolf's portrayal of the Ramsay family in *To the Lighthouse* (1927).[7] Except for the novel's middle section, in which a more traditional omniscient third-person narrator recounts a decade's passage within which Britain goes through World War I and Mrs. Ramsay dies, readers gain only brief, fleeting impressions of Mr. Ramsay, his son James and daughter Camilla. Framed by an interrupted plan to deliver supplies to the lighthouse workers off the Isle of Skye, the novel concludes with Cam's vision of her father "all a blur." She and James hear him quoting lines from William Cowper's desolate poem "The Castaway" as they make their way across the water: "But I beneath a rougher sea / Was whelmed in deeper gulfs than he" (pp. 256-57), and imagine him repeating, from the same poem: "we perished, each alone." Cowper's poem affords an interior commentary on the novel, as Woolf herself confirms in her diaries.[8] When, arriving at their destination, Mr. Ramsay orders his children to "Bring those parcels . . . for the Lighthouse men," James hears it "as if he were saying, 'There is no God'" (pp. 190-91). In the novel's final two pages the painter Lily Briscoe observes that Mr. Ramsay "has landed" at the lighthouse and so "it is finished," but the *consumatum est* is ambiguous, referring perhaps to Lily's painting or Woolf's novel as much as to any redemptive action achieved by Mr. Ramsay. The final paragraph explicitly adopts a position of confused despair, in fact, as Lily realizes that her painting will simply be "hung in the attics" and "destroyed." "What did that matter?" she asks (p. 191). Hers is a question that hangs over much contemporary fiction.

Nihilistic skepticism figures strongly in the novels of American writers such as F. Scott Fitzgerald, whose *The Great Gatsby* (1925) chronicles a sad cycle of adultery, suicide and murder amid the supposedly lighthearted atmosphere of the Roaring Twenties. Similarly, Ernest Hem-

---

[7]Virginia Woolf, *To the Lighthouse* (London: Granada, 1981).
[8]"The centre is father's character, sitting in a boat, reciting We Perished, Each Alone" (Diary, May 14, 1925), in *The Diary of Virginia Woolf: Volume Three 1925-1930,* ed. Anne Oliver Belle (New York: Harcourt Brace, 1981), p. 19

ingway's failed romances and alcoholic antiheroes usually end up in something like the atmosphere of his ironically titled short story "A Clean, Well-Lighted Place" (1926), in which young waiters counsel suicide and old waiters practice a parodic liturgical form of nihilism; mockingly they pray, "our nada who art in nada, nada be thy name," or "Hail nothing, full of nothing, nothing is with thee."[9] Yet how many of his readers know that Hemingway grew up in an evangelical home and, as a twelve-year-old boy, preached a sermon on "Saul on the Road to Damascus" for a missionary convention in Chicago? Obviously, a rejection of Christianity so complete as his is of itself an occasion for reflection.

A very different attitude to religion can be found in the novels of William Faulkner. Though Faulkner gives little evidence of religious piety in his personal life, New Critics such as Cleanth Brooks could find in Faulkner's "emphasis upon discipline, sacrifice, and redemption," attitudes famously summarized in his Nobel Prize acceptance speech of 1949, an aesthetic that could "be understood only by reference to Christian premises."[10] Perhaps the best single example of Faulkner's response to modernist nihilism is *The Sound and the Fury* (1929), which alludes to and is fully developed around the imagery of Macbeth's despairing, dying proclamation that life itself "is a tale / told by an idiot, full of sound and fury, / signifying nothing" (5.5.25-27).[11]

Like Joyce and Woolf, Faulkner focuses on a dysfunctional modern family, the Compsons, and readers of this novel similarly struggle to find within various characters' stream of consciousness any coherent moral principle by which to explain or judge the family's troubles. This is equally true of Benjy, the mentally challenged thirty-three-year-old "idiot" who first tells the tale, and Quentin, the guilt-stricken Harvard student who eventually commits suicide after being estranged from his sister Caddy, perhaps due to incest (though the reader cannot be sure).

---

[9]Ernest Hemingway, "A Clean, Well-Lighted Place," in *Literature: An Introduction to Fiction, Poetry, Drama, and Writing*, ed. X. J. Kennedy and Dana Gioia (New York: Pearson Longman, 2007), p. 150.

[10]Cleanth Brooks, "Faulkner's Vision of Good and Evil," in *Religious Perspectives in Faulkner's Fiction: Yoknapatawpha and Beyond*, ed. J. Robert Barth (South Bend, Ind.: University of Notre Dame Press, 1972), p. 57.

[11]William Faulkner, *The Sound and the Fury* (1929; reprint, New York: Vintage, 1954).

Most incomprehensible of all is the extremely intelligent but ultimately meaningless and amoral scheming of Jason Compson, the older brother fighting to preserve the decaying Compson estate. Yet rather than leaving readers as hopeless as the Compsons themselves, Faulkner instead concludes the novel with a detailed, third-person, partially omniscient portrayal of the quietly noble Christian life of the Compson's black servant, Dilsey. It is surely not coincidental that this fourth section of the novel occurs on April 8, 1928, an Easter Sunday: whereas Jason ignores the significance of Good Friday on April 6, and Benjy is entirely ignorant of anything happening on April 7, Holy Saturday, the Easter service that Dilsey attends on Sunday features a preacher who portrays the redeemed Christian life as vividly as the Jesuit homilist in Joyce's *Portrait* depicts the sorrows of hell. "I got the recollection and the blood of the Lamb!" he proclaims, and then, in a moment of mystical transformation, "nothing" is exchanged for an emphatic "Yes":

> And the congregation seemed to watch with its own eyes while the voice consumed him, until he was *nothing* and they were *nothing* and there was not even a voice but instead their hearts were speaking to one another in chanting measures beyond the need for words, so that when he came to rest against the reading desk, his monkey face lifted and his whole attitude that of a serene, tortured crucifix that transcended its shabbiness and insignificance and made it of no moment, a long moaning expulsion of breath rose from them, and a woman's single soprano: "Yes, Jesus!"[12]

Dilsey's perspective, which offers compassion for all of the Compsons' suffering, seems to transcend authorial intention and become the implied standard by which the family is not so much to be judged as loved and forgiven. As a southern writer, Faulkner is clearly interested in religion to a degree that exceeds his personal practice of it; in the American South, one might say, without such an interest and attunement it would be nearly impossible to write well about the culture.

This remains true where the novels of a later writer, influenced by Faulkner, among others, is concerned; Toni Morrison, herself born of

---

[12]Ibid., pp. 367-68, emphasis added.

emigrant southerners in Ohio, offers an important perspective on the
African American experience of perpetual dislocation. Especially in
Song of Solomon (1977) and *Beloved* (1987), she writes of a syncretistic
African American world of passion, fear, hope and despair in which
elements of Christian and Black Muslim religious worldviews inter-
mingle in fascinating ways. Morrison began her career with a master's
thesis at Cornell on the theme of suicide in the writings of Faulkner
and Virginia Woolf. Her fiction is postmodern in a fashion comparable
to the free-forming religious innovations of her characters. Little in
this world is stable, and some of it is magical. Through her lyrical prose
and angular characterizations there breathes a remarkable sense of the
fragility of meaning itself, and a persuasive apprehension that in the
end the forces of darkness are all too likely to shape our destiny. These
are among the factors in her fiction that earned her the Nobel Prize for
literature in 1993.

A similar syncretistic religious ethos, though in this case with elements from Catholic and Hindu as well as Islamic traditions, swirls in
a colorful yet volatile mix in the novels of Salman Rushdie. This Indian
writer, one of the most eminent novelists of his generation, is best
known for *Satanic Verses* (1988). Publication of this novel led to a *fatwa*
against him by the Ayatollah Khomeini, the Supreme Leader of Iran,
obligating Muslims to assassinate Rushdie for his blasphemy of the
prophet Mohammed. *Satanic Verses*, read in the light of the issues of
religious representation and religious tolerance, is worthy of some notice. It is not, however, either as finely written or so broadly useful an
example of postcolonial literature as his earlier historical novel—an in-
triguing blend of history and mythographic fabulation—*Midnight's
Children* (1981). Many works of postcolonial literature from the former
British Empire are important reading for students of literature in a
Christian context particularly, not least because some of the best of
them, such as Chinua Achebe's *Things Fall Apart* (1958), inspired by
Yeats's "Second Coming," and *Arrow of God* (1986), show Christianity
in the harsh but realistic light of its appropriation, consciously or oth-
erwise, by Anglo-imperialism both cultural and political. Here too
Christianity meets other religious worldviews, and in Achebe's power-

ful narratives both secular materialism and native, animist religious practices act as a foil to Christian practice as it might more authentically be construed, namely, in the light of Christ.

It is necessary to take a step backward to early in the century for perspective on some of these larger trends that shaped the twentieth century in so complex a fashion. In Britain the varied response of religious faith to the nihilism inherent in modernism can be demonstrated in the writing of perhaps the two most influential of all early twentieth-century modernist poets, W. B. Yeats and T. S. Eliot. Yeats's "The Second Coming" follows Nietzsche in prophesying the political consequences of the death of God. With religion and morality confused, for Yeats a "blood-dimmed tide is loosed," but "the best lack all conviction / while the worst / are full of passionate intensity" (5-8). Either attitude may be pressed unwittingly into tacit service of "a rough beast" which in shape ("lion body and the head of a man") and temperament ("a gaze blank and pitiless as the sun") embodies the spirit of antichrist (14-15). Like other modernists Yeats constructs his own mythology in *A Vision*, but the aesthetic ideal he advances is found in the center of medieval Eastern Christendom, Byzantium (modern Istanbul), around the sixth century A.D., when in a unique way "religious, aesthetic, and practical life were one."[13] In "Sailing to Byzantium" (1926) Yeats laments the secular humanism that leaves humans but "a tattered coat upon a stick," unless "soul clap its hand and sing" of "sages standing in God's holy fire" (10-11, 17), who can become "the singing masters of my soul" (20); the sages gather Yeats "into the artifice of eternity" (24) and sing forever "of what is past, or passing, or to come" (32). "Byzantium" (1930) offers an eternal present-tense portrait of such bardic art, which Yeats insists is "more miracle than bird or handiwork," and here the dominant beast becomes a traditional Christian symbol of providence: "astraddle on the dolphin's mire and blood," sit "Spirit after Spirit" (33-34), symbolically rescued from the dying material world and transported to eternity. Art's capacity to transcend mundane existence and human suffering is celebrated also in late poems such as "Lapis Lazuli" and

---

[13]W. B. Yeats, *A Vision* (1925; reprint, London: Macmillan, 1962), p. 279.

perhaps most fully in "Under Ben Bulben" (1938). Referring to a mountain over the graveyard where Yeats intends to be buried, and containing his gravestone's actual epitaph, the poem contains "the gist" (12) of his spiritual aesthetic. In its fourth and clearest section, this aesthetic is opposed to fashionably atheistic modernism and instead places Yeats himself within the ranks of traditional religious artists:

> Poet and sculptor do the work
> Nor let the modish painter shirk
> What his great forefathers did,
> Bring the soul of man to God,
> Make him fill the cradles right. (37-41)

The conversion of art, from describing the birth of nihilism to restoring the always present creativity of the divine, can be seen more dramatically in the life and poetry of T. S. Eliot. Early in his career Eliot followed Browning in using the dramatic monologue ironically to reveal character. The frustrated speaker in "The Love Song of J. Alfred Prufrock" (1915) ruefully (and ironically) acknowledges that "I am not Prince Hamlet," that he is entirely unable to communicate or sustain any significant action; utterly isolated, Prufrock symbolizes modern people, whose souls are more crab than human, "scuttling across the floors of silent seas." The poem concludes by suggesting that if real "human voices" were to "wake us" from fantasies of mermaids singing, "we drown." In "The Wasteland" (1921), Eliot connects Prufrock's muffled voice, in deliberately incoherent modernist fashion, with many other voices of sexual sterility and spiritual despair. This famous poem's tone is indicated clearly in its epigraph, quoted from the *Satyricon* of Petronius, in which the Sibyl at Cumae is asked what she wants, and she replies, "I want to die." In deliberate contrast to Chaucer's *Canterbury Tales*, Eliot's poem proper famously begins by claiming that "April is the cruelest month," for humans do not know the source of life; citing Ecclesiastes, Eliot preaches that the "Son of Man" can "know only a heap of broken images" (22), only "fear in a handful of dust" (30). Though filled with complex literary allusions that could image hope, new life and even transcendent meaning,

Eliot's point is that the modern reader is a "hypocrite lecteur" similar to the modernist writer; indeed, Eliot calls him "mon semblable, mon frère" (76). The poem's nameless narrator asks, "Do you know nothing? Do you see nothing? Do you remember nothing?" to which someone replies: "I remember / those are pearls that were his eyes" (120-25). Ariel from Shakespeare's *The Tempest* is being quoted here, in the song he sings when young Ferdinand laments his father, shipwrecked and apparently drowned. Yet how many moderns recall or even, perhaps, comprehend what Ariel sings next: "Nothing of him that doth fade / But doth suffer a sea change / Into something rich and strange" (1.2.401-403)? Eliot's point, as so often in "The Wasteland," is that modern readers see death without the hope of resurrection that sustained earlier generations.

Yet within "The Wasteland" itself, Eliot hints at the possibility of spiritual renewal. The poem's third section, "The Fire Sermon," alludes to the Buddha's rejection of physical desires, albeit through satirizing modern seduction, and concludes with the speaker amid the flames, speaking the words of the chastened St. Augustine: "O Lord Thou pluckest me out." The poem's final section, "What the Thunder Said," turns to a third religious tradition, Hinduism, for further religious wisdom: "Datta. Dayadhvam. Damyata" ("Give, sympathize, control"). These precepts for compassion and self-discipline offer some hope for spiritual renewal, although few readers, and certainly not Eliot himself, could sufficiently grasp what he calls the "fragments I have shored up against my ruin" in order to make the leap from the Hindu precepts to the poem's shockingly hopeful final lines, "Shantih shantih shantih," the Hindu concept which Eliot's note compares to "the peace . . . which passeth all understanding" in Philippians 4:7. Eliot himself experienced a mental breakdown after writing "The Wasteland" and eventually was divorced from his wife, Vivienne Haigh-Wood, who was also mentally ill. In the midst of this traumatic period, however, Eliot also began seriously to study Christianity, as reflected in his *Ariel Poems*, which include meditations on Christ's birth in "Journey of the Magi" and "A Song for Simeon," and further appreciation of the spirit of Shakespearean romance in "Marina." In 1927 Eliot announced his conversion to the Anglican Church through his Lenten poem, "Ash Wednesday." Such poems served as preparation for the work Eliot came to regard as his masterpiece, *Four Quartets* (1944).

Opening this series of four distinct but connected poems are two epigraphs from the ancient Greek philosopher Heraclitus, whose thoughts on the *logos* were given particular Christian significance by the opening of John's Gospel. The first translates as a warning to individualism, stating that "Although the *logos* is common to all, most people live as though they have a wisdom of their own," while the second provides a link more specifically to the incarnate "Word and Wisdom of God" who became the "way, truth, and life" of all: "the Way up is the way down."[14] Though deeply Christian, *Four Quartets* does not offer systematic theology but rather a series of concrete settings and symbols that first tend to immerse one in the material suffering of time before finally teaching the reader to trust in and be transformed by the eternal, transcendent love of God. Each of the four quartets—"Burnt Norton," "East Coker," "The Dry Salvages" and "Little Gidding"—portrays transcendence in a similar but distinct manner. Each is named after a particular location or setting, linked fairly clearly to the four classical substances of earth, air, water and fire, and each uses free verse while maintaining a fairly regular pattern of five similar sections. Within this structure, a nameless narrator presents many concrete and allusive symbols along with paradoxical philosophical and theological concepts that explore one central question: can human suffering experienced in time yet be redeemed eternally by God?

The title of the fourth, most famous quartet, "Little Gidding," refers to the Anglican worship community founded by the saintly Nicholas Ferrar in 1625. It is this place to which, restored after being destroyed in the Puritan revolution, Eliot comes, in 1941, to "kneel where prayer has been valid," to join together with all the saints gathered in unity by the "pentecostal fire" of Acts 2. Yet how, as an Anglican, should Eliot regard the English Civil War? And how, as a poet, can he learn from past geniuses of Christian poetry who seem to oppose him in both

---

[14]T. S. Eliot, *Four Quartets* (1944), *The Complete Poems & Plays of T. S. Eliot* (London: Faber & Faber, 2004), p. 171.

secular and ecclesiastical polity, such as the great Puritan John Milton? Finally, how can Eliot turn either to the task of "Little Gidding" or ecumenical Christian dialogue while England is being bombarded by the Nazis in 1941? A purgatory-like meeting with the "compound-ghost" of Dante and Yeats stresses the need for Eliot's own humility and repentance. Then follows a meditation on the distinction between three spiritual attitudes—attachment, detachment and indifference—that leads the speaker in this poem to the insight that love must include the ability, with a certain detachment, but never indifference, to accept that God's providence allows other selves, even enemies, "to become renewed, transfigured, in another pattern" (165). Our prayer requires "the purification of the motive / in the ground of our beseeching," for rather than seeking to be preserved from suffering or from our enemies, we must ask the Holy Spirit to purify and prepare us for eternal life with God. In the stark symbolism of section IV, our only option "lies in the choice of pyre or pyre—to be redeemed from [the world's] fire by fire" ("for our God is a consuming fire," according to Heb 12:29).

More peacefully, Eliot returns to the wisdom of the medieval mystic Julian of Norwich, who, while admitting that "sin is behovely" (or inevitable), nevertheless promises that "All shall be well" through "the drawing of this Love and the voice of this Calling," the call of God that draws us again into the eternal communion of eternal life. In the extraordinary conclusion of "Little Gidding," Eliot extends this call to individual readers, symbolically inviting them to return again to Eden, or the New Jerusalem, or to the vision of heaven metaphorically and beautifully portrayed in Dante's *Paradiso*, in which the fire of God's love has consumed all sin and transfigured human love into another pattern, the aesthetically perfect pattern of an undying rose. Within the true beauty of these justly famous concluding lines, one can even imagine the symbolism of modernism itself having been redeemed: for Eliot, Christian courage means that "We shall not cease from exploration" until we arrive at our Edenic homeland, "And know the place for the first time." This implies a goal of innocence, such as of "children in the apple-tree," "Not known, because not looked for." Eliot's call is for a complex modern world to be experienced in a "condition of complete simplicity / (Costing not less than everything)," a gift made possible by the life of humanity's Redeemer and enacted as the uncompromised commitment required to truly acknowledge him as Lord. Only then, says Eliot in words drawn from the fourteenth-century mystic Julian of Norwich, shall "all be well," and only then, in an image drawn from the *Paradiso* of Dante, will all of the operations of the Holy Spirit down through the transtemporal life of the church, be as "tongues of flame . . . infolded" into a knot in which all loose threads, all of the heaps of broken images find their predestined unity, "and the fire and the rose are one" (239-59).[15]

While Eliot's poetry provides an extraordinary example of modernism's engagement by a thoughtful Christian perspective, more problematic terrain is found in another genre, drama, to which Eliot devoted himself after finishing *Four Quartets*. For the most part twentieth-century drama seems caught between two aesthetic extremes, the popular but spiritually vacuous comedies and tragedies of modern life found in plays by British or American playwrights such as Noel Coward or Arthur Miller, or the absurdist dramas of explicit nihilism written more commonly by European writers such as Samuel Beckett, Eugène Ionesco or Bertold Brecht. Beckett's *Waiting for Godot* (1954) is an especially worthwhile example of the latter, honestly expressing the modern or postmodern feeling that there is "nothing to be done" (p. 7) about the pervasive suffering or paralyzing uncertainty of modern life; it poses existential intellectual and spiritual challenges to contemporary Christianity.[16] "Did you ever read the Bible," Vladimir asks his one friend, Estragon, before puzzling over why, "of the four Evangelists," "only one speaks of a thief being saved" from the cross beside Christ (p. 9). Why believe only one of four accounts, he suggests, but moreover, why believe humanity can be saved by any God, or Godot, at all? While Vladimir admits "we are not saints," he also asserts that "we have kept our appointment" with the mysterious, always

---

[15]On the further theological implications of these images, see Gregory Maillet, "'At the still point' where 'there is only the dance': Logos, Lonergan, and T. S. Eliot's *Four Quartets.*" *Lonergan Workshop* 20 (2008): 271-294.

[16]Samuel Beckett, *Waiting for Godot* (New York: Grove, 1974).

absent Godot; Estragon believes that this is also true of "billions" of other people (p. 52). For them, prayer seems nothing more than "a vague supplication," and even mutual friendship itself seems as unstable and irrational; "in an instant," Vladimir predicts, summing up the play's expected conclusion after a plot in which nothing happens, "all will vanish and we'll be alone once more, in the midst of nothingness" (p. 52). In the existential reality created by the countless dramas of suffering so commonly found in the twentieth century, where is God?

Although T. S. Eliot's plays typically show moderns redeemed after a tragicomic spiritual struggle, the contexts necessary to explicate clear Christian beliefs are rarely sustained. These beliefs are most fully portrayed in his historical play on the twelfth-century martyrdom of Archbishop Thomas Beckett in 1170, *Murder in the Cathedral* (1935).[17] Here Eliot brilliantly dramatized the worldly temptations faced by any man, and especially a prince of the church, in order to depict what it means to "make perfect [our] will" by fully, completely accepting the will of God for our lives. While the murderous knights justify their actions in terms typical of those seeking an extreme separation of church and state, and even attempt to deride the martyr as a "Suicide while of Unsound Mind" (p. 279), Beckett's "Christian Sermon" demonstrates the true meaning of Christian martyrdom:

> The true martyr is he who has become the instrument of God, who has lost his will in the will of God, and who no longer desires anything for himself, not even the glory of being a martyr. So thus on earth the Church mourns and rejoices at once, in a fashion the world cannot understand; so in Heaven the Saints are most high, having made themselves most low, and are seen, not as we see them, but in the light of the Godhead from which they draw their being.[18]

Thanks to such clarity of transcending vision, the play's concluding Chorus can affirm, after witnessing Beckett's brutal and apparently nihilistic death, that God's "glory is declared even in that which denies

---

[17]T. S. Eliot, *Murder in the Cathedral*, in *The Complete Poems & Plays of T. S. Eliot* (London: Faber & Faber, 2004), pp. 237-82.
[18]Ibid., p. 261.

Thee; the darkness declares the glory of light" (p. 282). Echoing Tertullian's ancient promise that "the blood of the martyrs is the seed of the Church," Eliot's Chorus knows that from the blood of "such ground springs that which forever renews the earth / though it is forever denied" (p. 282). This, for Eliot, was a crucial encouragement to modern Christian hope. As the twentieth century progressed into a world in which rational action became ever more difficult, Christian institutions ever more marginalized by both public statecraft and popular culture, and the denial of God ever more deafening, more and more children of God died apparently pointless and violent deaths. Though *Murder in the Cathedral* depicts a medieval martyr, its matter found corresponding subjects in the many twentieth-century martyrs, most of whose names are unlikely to become known, this side of eternity, even to the church.

NOVELS AND THE CRITIQUE OF CONTEMPORARY CULTURE

Because it is essential for Christians to understand the spiritual effects of nihilism and to offer the antidote of words written, in Eliot's phrase, from "out of the centre of the silent Word,"[19] a spiritually rationalized avoidance of these texts is insufficient. Whether expressing directly the explicit atheism common in twentieth-century political ideology or the more subtle yet still pervasive forces of greed, lust and power that often serve as modern substitutes for religious transcendence and ethical action, thoughtfully chosen examples of the literature of social nihilism should be required reading within a curriculum of Christian literary studies.

A text often taught as the first modernist novel of the twentieth century, Joseph Conrad's *Heart of Darkness* (1902) is much more than simply a critique of European colonialism and the clearly corrupt African ivory trade.[20] Told through the first-person voice of Marlow, a subjective storyteller figure like so many in modern fiction, the novel more directly chronicles European disillusionment. Whereas many nineteenth-century Europeans had believed that "by the simple exercise of

---

[19]T. S. Eliot, "Ash Wednesday," in *The Complete Poems & Plays of T. S. Eliot* (London: Faber & Faber, 2004), p. 96.
[20]Joseph Conrad, *Heart of Darkness*, ed. Paul B. Armstrong (New York: Norton, 2005).

our will we can exert a power for good practically unbounded," that delusion was, in the twentieth century, replaced by a single note scribbled in the margins of an actual report from the African Congo: "Exterminate all the brutes." "All Europe contributed to the making" of the author of this report, a charismatic ivory agent named Mr. Kurtz. Marlow hears much praise of Kurtz as he travels up the Congo River into the heart of Africa, but the true referent of Conrad's title is Kurtz's darkened heart. Eventually witnessing the heads of "brutes" on stakes that surround Kurtz's inner station, Marlow cannot fathom the "impenetrable darkness" within Kurtz, nor can he fully appreciate the meaning of the dying man's final words as he looks into the abyss: "The horror! The horror!" At novel's end, back in Europe, Kurtz's fiancée begs to hear his last words, and Marlow, unable to bear reporting the truth, says, "The last word he pronounced was—your name." "I knew it—I was sure," she replies, but the scene leaves Marlow "in the pose of a meditating Buddha," ironically sure of nothing, perhaps, but evil, suffering and an overhead sky that seems "to lead into the heart of an immense darkness."

The darkness that descended on Europe in the form of World War I altered the course of colonialism but continued the advance of nihilism due to the massive loss of young life from the "progressive" technologies of modern warfare. In the words of one poet mortally wounded in the Great War, Wilfred Owen, its horror led to a loss of faith in an "old lie": "Dulce et Decorum est / Pro patria mori" ("it is sweet and fitting / to die for your country").[21] What other aphorisms could no longer be trusted? And where were the young people to believe in them? Virginia Woolf's experimental novel *Jacob's Room* (1922) paradoxically laments one young man lost in the War without ever introducing him, except through the reminiscences of acquaintances. Jacob's "role" as protagonist is thus defined entirely by his absence, signified finally by his empty room.

British life following World War I is lamented in Evelyn Waugh's *Brideshead Revisited* (1944), where the ancient country estate of the

---

[21]Wilfred Owen, "Dulce et Decorum Est" (1920), in *The Collected Poems of Wilfred Owen*, rev. ed. (New York: New Directions, 1965).

Marchmains serves as symbolic background for a study of aristocratic corruption and familial decay. Alcoholism, adultery and general unfaithfulness lead to predictable family breakdown, but out of this story Waugh, a convert to Catholicism, weaves a narrative of grace. The elderly Lord Marchmain has left for Italy, and his elder daughter Julia has separated from her corrupt spouse, Rex Mottram; meanwhile, Charles Ryder, friend to Julia's alcoholic brother, Sebastian, is also seeking divorce and wants to marry Julia. Rather than providing a romantic ending, Waugh has Julia choose against an unconsecrated marriage, and years later Charles too, revisiting the Brideshead private chapel, experiences a conversion. Despite personal and social human sin, corruption and pain, the book argues that God's purposes can only temporarily be thwarted.

Of course, the twentieth century was haunted not only by two World Wars but also by the rise of brutal forms of atheistic totalitarianism—Marxist communism on the left and pagan fascism on the right. Writing against both movements, important authors and texts satirized false utopian projects, exposed their lies and condemned their abuses. In 1940 Arthur Koestler's *Darkness at Noon* (1940) described the terrors of Stalin's mock trials in Moscow, while in the same year a memorable Christian contribution appeared in Graham Greene's *The Power and the Glory*, which depicts communist persecution of the Catholic Church in Mexico. Far from idealizing his "whisky priest" protagonist or demonizing the communist authorities, Greene presents the latter as socially responsible and the unnamed priest as craven and irresponsible. Yet, as with Waugh, the priest finally finds grace; out of his execution God makes of the padre's life a meaningful martyrdom and even, perhaps, a kind of saint's life.

Such politically induced challenges and horrors prompted a number of novels in which the clash of ideologies provides the fundamentals of plot and character development. In 1941 Rex Warner's *The Aerodrome* depicted the dangerous attraction of fascism in Great Britain, even as Hitler began a vigorous counterargument by dropping his bombs on London. Most famously, in 1945 George Orwell penned his political allegory *Animal Farm*, depicting the tyranny of totalitarianism, the irrational torture and dehumanization foundational to both communist and fascist regimes. In any world ruled by a "Napoleon," Orwell's final lines remind us, one can look "from pig to man, and from man to pig," but very soon it becomes "impossible to say which was which." Further unsparing depictions of German fascism later emerge both from victims and survivors of the War, as in Albert Camus's *La Peste* (translated as *The Plague* [1947]) and *L'Homme revolté* (*The Rebel* [1951]), Anne Frank's posthumously published *Diary of a Young Girl* (1952), and Elie Wiesel's *Night* (1960). Years later, other award-winning novels such as Thomas Keneally's *Schindler's Ark* (1982) and Anne Michaels's *Fugitive Pieces* (1996) continue to reflect on the horror and trauma of the Holocaust.

Finally, all Christian students should be aware of the extraordinary career and public witness of Russian novelist Alexander Solzhenitsyn, who drew on his own experience in Stalinist labor camps in *One Day in the Life of Ivan Denisovich* (1963).[22] Solzhenitsyn depicts the education of the title character by a fellow prisoner, the Baptist Alyoshka, who hides a Bible within his bunk and eventually tells him: "Look here, Ivan Denisovich, your soul wants to pray to God, so why don't you let it have its way?" (p. 195). Aloyshka further teaches him to pray not for "a package or for an extra helping of gruel," but rather "for the things of the spirit so the Lord will take evil things from our hearts" (pp. 196-97). For, he adds, "Paul the Apostle said: 'What mean you to weep and to break my heart? For I am ready not to be bound only, but also to die for the name of the Lord Jesus'" (p. 198; cf. Acts 21:13). Here, powerfully portrayed, is the enduring spirit of faith that ensures the tyrant's fall and the survival of both the individual human soul and the Christian church.

Solzhenitsyn's willingness to speak truth to power prompted him, at Harvard University in 1978, to insist that the modern West was, in many ways, as atheistic as communist Russia.[23] Though controversial, this speech provides an absolutely essential reminder that Western Christians must be self-critical of both tacit and explicit atheism: often

---

[22]Alexander Solzhenitsyn, *One Day in the Life of Ivan Denisovich* (New York: Bantam, 1969).
[23]Alexander Solzhenitsyn, "A World Split Apart," reprinted in *Finding God at Harvard*, ed. Kelly Monroe (Grand Rapids: Zondervan, 1997), pp. 95-102.

a tacit atheism operates under the guise of materialistic progress, hedonistic pleasure and philosophical relativism. In this respect Aldous
Huxley's *Brave New World* (1932) now appears an even more prophetic
text than Orwell's *Nineteen Eighty-Four* (1949).[24] Whereas Orwell depicted the capacity to enforce totalitarianism by technological means,
Huxley foresaw how technology could be used to manipulate human
nature so that people would not only accept but actually desire a totalitarian state, particularly if war, natural disaster or disease made it impossible to sustain participatory democracy.[25] Under such conditions,
how much will people give up in order to attain the motto of Huxley's
World State: "Community, Identity, Stability" (p. 19)? Most of the
novel presents the *means* by which such a state can be achieved—ge-
netic engineering, sleep conditioning, control of reproduction, manipulation of sexual desire through pornography, a constant supply of diversionary entertainment and, if all else fails, free distribution of a happy
drug called "soma." Only John the Savage, raised outside the World
State and one of Shakespeare's last readers, can question why these
technologies are necessary, or whether they are truly good. In chapters
sixteen and seventeen, World Controller for Western Europe, Mus-
tapha Mond, explains what the Brave New World has chosen to eliminate. First is "what people used to call high art," replaced now by art
made "out of practically nothing but pure sensation" (p. 219), for the
beauty inherent in writing like Shakespeare's causes one to experience
real pain and the hope for a better world, and so is incompatible with
Mond's version of happiness. Science, too, "is dangerous," so long as it
means the search for truth rather than the application of technology to
preordained ends; as Mond, a former physicist, admits: "all our science
is just a cookery book, with an orthodox theory of cooking that no-
body's allowed to question" (p. 224). Whether one's aim is beauty or

---

[24]Aldous Huxley, *Brave New World* (London: Grafton, 1977).
[25]See here Neil Postman, *Amusing Ourselves to Death* (New York: Viking Penguin, 1985), who
casts the distinction in this way: "What Orwell feared were those who would ban books. What
Huxley feared was that there would be no reason to ban a book, for there would be no one who
wanted to read one. Orwell feared those who would deprive us of information. Huxley feared
those who would give us so much that we would be reduced to passivity and egoism. Orwell
feared that the truth would be concealed from us. Huxley feared the truth would be drowned
in a sea of irrelevance" (foreword).

truth, Mond explains, "Ford himself" (a comical reference to the American automaker that runs throughout the novel) "did a great deal to shift emphasis from truth and beauty to comfort and happiness. . . . Universal happiness keeps the wheels steadily turning; truth and beauty can't" (p. 226).

Finally, religion, or any traditional concept of God, must also be rejected; Mond quotes Cardinal Newman at length, on how the normal aging process leads one away from sensual satisfactions and toward contemplation of eternity, of "absolute and everlasting truth," but then proudly proclaims that the Brave New World preserves "youth and prosperity" until sudden euthanasia, thus preventing contemplation of God (p. 231). Interestingly, Mond thinks that "there quite probably is" a God (p. 231). Like many moderns, however, he believes God "manifests himself" only "as an absence" (p. 232). To his credit, John the Savage sees through some of this argument, quoting *King Lear* to argue that the gods of Mond have "used [our] pleasant vices as an instrument to degrade [us]," but that objective value still exists; in the words of *Troilus and Cressida*, that stern parable against marital infidelity, "value dwells not in particular will," says the Savage, but rather "it holds his estimate and dignity as well wherein 'tis precious of itself as in the prizer" (p. 233). In other words, John knows that, outside of the World State's control, reality does exist, and he wants to know it even though it includes suffering. Mond offers "Christianity without tears—that's what *soma* is" (p. 235), but John replies: "I don't want comfort. I want God. I want poetry. I want real danger, I want freedom, I want goodness, I want sin" (p. 237). Paradoxically, John the Savage exhibits a Christian saint's willingness to die rather than live in a world without religious meaning and value. He is soon so overwhelmed by the painful death of friends and guilt-inducing experiences, however, that he commits suicide. One is left to ask: can human society as a whole do any better, or are we doomed to destroy ourselves by one means or another?

An important Christian response to this question appears in Walter M. Miller's 1959 novel *A Canticle for Leibowitz*.[26] Set in the future, after

---

[26]Walter M. Miller Jr., *A Canticle for Leibowitz* (New York: Bantam, 1968).

nuclear war, the novel's three-part structure represents a comical medieval period in which only monasteries preserve manuscripts, a "renaissance" in which knowledge is again applied to the creation of technology, and a "modern" period in which nuclear pollution and war again threaten humanity, and desire to avoid suffering again pushes many toward suicide or euthanasia. At the heart of the book is the ancient question of Genesis: can humanity eat of the tree of knowledge of good without also dying from evil? As secular scholars in the "renaissance" period urge knowledge for its own sake, the faithful monks read Scripture aloud, reminding readers of Satan's primary temptation—"you shall be as gods, knowing good and evil"—and insisting that Christians must read *ad lumina Christi* ("for the light of Christ").[27] In the "modern" age the faithful Abbot Zerchi echoes John the Savage in arguing that God allows pain in the world because without it there could be no courage or self-sacrifice. As political events spiral out of control and another nuclear holocaust becomes imminent, signs of God's grace and ability to preserve and create new life are revealed, and the monks themselves eventually fly into space to start a new colony where they can continue to worship the living God. As a whole, Miller's *Canticle* can be taken as a pessimistic warning that recurring human abuse of knowledge, technology and personal ethics must lead to the end of particular civilizations, but also a faithful affirmation that God retains his capacity to make "all things new."

One of the more remarkable recent dystopian novels in English is P. D. James's *The Children of Men* (1993).[28] James, a British detective novelist who became a Christian convert in the 1990s, references Psalm 90 in the title and quotes the same text in chapter 28 of the novel: "Lord, thou hast been our refuge: from one generation to another. . . . Thou turnest man to destruction: again thou sayest, Come again, ye children of men." Not simply a suspenseful page-turner, this is a story about the end of humanity—not through war or totalitarian oppression but through sudden and inexplicable mass infertility. As the novel begins, in 2021, we learn that no children have been born since the

---

[27]Ibid., pp. 192-93.
[28]P. D. James, *The Children of Men* (Harmondsworth, U.K.: Penguin, 1993).

"Omega" year, 1995. Among the many drastic consequences of this sudden loss of the young in society and consequent public orientation toward human extinction rather than any kind of future hope, is the emergence of a despotic government, whose power is supported by a corrupt ecclesial community. The last of the earth's children, now in their mid-twenties, the "Omegas" live in hedonistic irresponsibility while the elderly are forced to engage in mass suicide rituals called the Quietus. Then somehow, without explanation, comes a miraculous conception: a young woman named Julian flees the authorities to protect her unborn baby and after a harrowing escape eventually gives birth to a son. Her protector Theo quotes St. Paul in pledging "nothing and no one will separate us, not life nor death," as the evil authorities close in.[29] The book ends ambiguously, not with any certainty of a better future (or indeed of any kind of future), but with a baptism: "with a thumb wet with [Theo's] own tears and stained with [Julian's] blood . . . he made on the child's forehead the sign of the cross."[30]

CONVERSION AND CONTEMPORARY CHRISTIAN AESTHETICS

Although prophetic critique is important and necessary, it is vital also for Christian writers to develop aesthetic forms capable to some degree of affirming truths that can be known by reason or revelation. Among the best-known writers to do just that are the two founding fathers of twentieth-century Christian aesthetics, C. S. Lewis and J. R. R. Tolkien, fellow Oxford English professors, lifelong friends (despite some disagreements) and artistic collaborators within a conversation group calling The Inklings. Lewis in fact began his academic career as a confirmed atheist. According to his autobiography, *Surprised by Joy* (1955), Lewis ceased to believe in God after the death of his mother when he was eight, and eventually settled on a neo-Platonic but atheistic idealism.[31] However, through various childhood and literary experiences, Lewis had also experienced glimpses of beauty that produced a longing different from that for simple happiness or pleasure. In Longfellow's

---

[29]Ibid., p. 343; cf. Rom 8:38-39.
[30]Ibid., p. 351.
[31]C. S. Lewis, *Surprised by Joy* (New York: Harcourt Brace, 1997).

"Saga of King Olaf," for example, Lewis "heard a voice that cried, / Balder the beautiful / Is dead, dead," and the line filled him with what he later called, in a "technical sense," *joy* (German, *Sehnsucht*), a longing for eternal beauty that, in this world, almost feels like "unhappiness or grief" except that "anyone who has experienced it will want it again."[32] As a scholar Lewis loved classical myths that offered such joy, and he saw similarities with the Christian story but assumed this likeness to confirm that religion is just one of many fictions. Subsequent study revealed crucial differences, however, and after conversation with theistic scholars such as Owen Barfield, Hugo Dyson and Tolkien on the nature of myth—conversations partially recorded in Tolkien's poem "Mythopoeia" (1965)[33]—Lewis came to the view that Christianity is "perfect myth and perfect fact":

> claiming not only our love and obedience, but also our wonder and delight, addressed to the savage, the child, and the poet in each of us no less than to the moralist, the scholar, and the philosopher.[34]

Lewis's conversion bore extraordinary fruits for theological aesthetics. His nonfiction writings often spell out his distinctly Christian worldview and afford important conceptual clues to the major themes of his imaginative writing. For example, Lewis's famous argument (his "trilemma") that Jesus must be judged as either lunatic, liar or Lord, in *Mere Christianity* (1952), reappears in an imaginative world when the Professor in *The Lion, the Witch, and the Wardrobe* asks Peter and Susan to reconsider whether they believe Lucy or Edmund's account of whether or not Narnia exists.[35] Likewise, Lewis's clarification of the word *love* in *The Four Loves* (1960) is crucial to explaining why, in his *The Great Divorce* (1946), the loves of some souls lead them directly to God after death, while the loves of others prevent them from reaching him. Lewis's critique of materialistic approaches to education, human nature and religion in *The Abolition of Man* (1944), "Man or Rabbit"

---

[32]Ibid., pp. 17-18.

[33]J. R. R. Tolkien, "Mythopoeia," *Tree and Leaf* (Boston: Houghton Mifflin, 1989).

[34]C. S. Lewis, "Myth Became Fact," in *God in the Dock: Essays on Theology and Ethics*, ed. Walter Hooper (1944; reprint, Grand Rapids: Eerdmans, 1970), p. 67.

[35]C. S. Lewis, *The Lion, the Witch, and The Wardrobe* (London: Fontana, 1980), pp. 47-48.

(1946) and *Miracles* (1947) is crucial to understanding the conflict between characters in his space trilogy—*Out of the Silent Planet* (1938),
Perelandra (1944) and *That Hideous Strength* (1945)—in which a scientific materialist named Dr. Weston kidnaps Elwin Ransom, a philolo-
gist possibly modeled after Tolkien. Lewis's thoughts on "Second
Meanings" in classical myths and the Psalms[36] directly apply to potential interpretation of his complex reworking of the Cupid and Psyche
myth in his final novel, *Till We Have Faces* (1956).[37] The novel's heroine, Orual, blames the goddess Ungit, a dark version of Venus, for making her ugly; meanwhile, her beautiful youngest sister, Istra (in Greek,
Psyche), is sacrificed to Ungit's son, Cupid. However, Cupid truly loves
and has saved Psyche, as Orual briefly sees in trying to retrieve her
dead body from a mountain passage. Following a Greek Stoic philosopher named Fox, Orual becomes a powerful but lonely and unhappy
queen. After many years of creating a false face, Orual regrets her own
egotistical self-love and ceases to blame the gods, saying, "how can they
meet us face to face till we have faces?" (cf. 1 Cor 13:12). In a final vision, Orual, now renamed according to her real self as "Maia," is led by
the self-sacrificial love of Psyche to a vision of the divine. As "joy si-
lenced her," a "great voice" proclaims, "you also are Psyche," suggesting
that Orual is also beautiful, beloved and truly blessed by a good God,
though the purity of this vision leaves her unable to remain alive in the
world.[38] In a letter, Lewis described his Psyche "as an instance of the
anima naturaliter Christiana," the soul of a natural Christian, who leads
people "towards the true God," a key role within what he calls the "good
dreams" of classical mythology.[39]

Other short works not to be missed include "Meditation in a Tool
Shed" (1945), which simply but brilliantly illuminates the difference
between seeing experience from inside or outside, subtly suggesting
Lewis's sympathy for subjectivity but also his recognition of the need

---

[36]C. S. Lewis, "Second Meanings," and "Second Meanings in the Psalms," *Reflections on the Psalms* (Glasgow: Collins, 1961), pp. 84-91, 101-15.
[37]C. S. Lewis, *Till We have Faces: A Myth Retold* (Glasgow: Harper Collins, 1991).
[38]Ibid., pp. 317-18.
[39]C. S. Lewis, Letter to Clyde Kilby, February 10, 1957, in Clyde Kilby, *The Christian World of C. S. Lewis* (Grand Rapids: Eerdmans, 1964), p. 58.

for objectivity. *Preface to Paradise Lost* links Lewis's lament for the human tendency to be swayed by rhetoric rather than reason to the influence of Satan, which Milton so vividly portrays. Comical tone and spiritual seriousness define *The Screwtape Letters;* like Milton's Satan, Screwtape sometimes speaks truth in spite of himself, which affords lovely ironies for the reader; seeing things from the diabolical perspective is here both humorous and instructive:

> One must face the fact that all the talk about His love for men, and His service being perfect freedom, is not (as one would gladly believe) mere propaganda, but an appalling truth. He really *does* want to fill the universe with a lot of loathsome little replicas of Himself—creatures whose life, on its miniature scale, will be qualitatively like His own, not because He has absorbed them but because their wills freely conform to His. . . . Our war aim is a world in which Our Father Below has drawn all other beings into himself: the Enemy wants a world full of beings united to Him but still distinct.[40]

"On the Reading of Old Books" (1944) explains why the reading of ancient authors, especially Christian authors, helps us to avoid the common errors of our own times. *Experiment in Criticism* (1961) is a tour de force book-length essay whose primary purpose is to distinguish between attributes of a literary reader, who reads for the joy of entering into an imaginary world in which the true, good and beautiful are revealed in a pleasurable fashion, and the "unliterary reader" who reads merely for information, or in some other utilitarian fashion (e.g., so as to pass an exam). What he shows is that the unliterary reader is doomed to be disappointed on all counts by the impropriety of his approach. This text is indispensable reading for serious students of literature and the humanities generally. Finally, lest anyone think that Lewis regards himself as especially holy or self-righteous, his many flaws and even spiritual doubts are recorded in *Surprised by Joy* (1955), *The Problem of Pain* (1940) and especially *A Grief Observed* (1961), Lewis's elegy for his wife, Joy Davidman. Such reading prepares students better to appreciate the theological riches in his much better known children's fiction,

---

[40]C. S. Lewis, *The Screwtape Letters* (London: Geoffrey Bles, 1942), pp. 45-46.

even as it offers insight into the character of faithful scholarship and teaching of literature. Christians who find their vocation in this discipline should perhaps focus a little less exclusively on Lewis's fiction and literary apologetics, and more on imitating him in his scholarly rigor, linguistic competence and range of reading. When we have done this, then the impact of Christian worldview in literary study in our time will be much greater.

Lewis is a remarkably accessible Christian intellectual. Nowhere is this more evident than in his Chronicles of Narnia, Lewis's perennially popular series of seven children's books. These books do not constitute simplistic allegory but rather an analogical, "subcreated" world of talking animals and wicked witches in which moral and spiritual conflicts are played out. The lion Aslan, who incarnates the divine spirit that defeats evil, sin and death, is most obviously a Christ figure in the first published (and still most popular) book in the series, *The Lion, the Witch, and the Wardrobe.* Aslan's substitutionary sacrifice to save his new human friends is a complex enactment of the meaning of Christian atonement. As Lewis made clear in a letter to a child named Anne Jenkins, however, each of the other Narnia books also explores biblical themes. *The Magician's Nephew* recasts Genesis into the creation of Narnia and its corruption by the demonic Jadis; *Prince Caspian* shows the restoration of a true king after a period of political corruption; *The Horse and His Boy* depicts the presence of Aslan even among pagans who do not know him by name; *The Voyage of the Dawn Treader* comically presents the spiritual and physical journey of a bold, though diminutive saint, Reepicheep; *The Silver Chair* presents children, Jill and Eustace, who must faithfully interpret four signs from Aslan in order to defeat powers of darkness and rescue another Narnian ruler, Prince Rilian; finally, *The Last Battle* depicts the coming of an antichrist figure, an ape named Shift, who parodies Aslan before the distinction between a true and false god is made clear and a last judgment occurs, allowing past and present Narnians to travel "further up" and "further in" to Aslan's country. Notably, there is a last-minute convert from the enemy side, Emeth; his name is the Hebrew word for "truth." Wherever Lewis's imaginative fiction takes us, he always combines fascinating symbols with a disciple's insight into the redemptive work of Christ.

Many believe the same to be true of Tolkien's work. Certainly this devout Roman Catholic author accepted and lived the grace of Christ as fully as Lewis, but two main factors complicate Christian approaches to his highly complex mythology. First, like Lewis, Tolkien rejected simplistic attempts to read his fiction as allegory. Second, Tolkien placed his myths in historical time periods—divided into a First, Second and Third age—all long before the time of Christ. In what sense, then, can his works be said to be Christian? Clues come from his letters where, after stating that "I dislike Allegory," Tolkien immediately qualifies his remark by limiting it to "conscious and intentional allegory," and further adds that "any attempt to explain the purpose of myth or fairytale must use allegorical language."[41] Avoiding simplistic, one-to-one identification between Tolkien's fictional world and history, it is then still legitimate to speak of the Christian motifs or themes suggested by his myths, as when Tolkien's friend Father Robert Murray spoke of *The Lord of the Rings* having "a positive compatibility with the order of grace." Of Murray, who was later to concelebrate his funeral mass, Tolkien said that he was "more perceptive, especially in some directions, than anyone else," commended his conception of grace and stated plainly: "*The Lord of the Rings* is of course a fundamentally religious and Catholic work; unconsciously so at first, but consciously in the revision." Paradoxically, this revision involved a decision to "not put in, or have cut out, practically all references to anything like 'religion,' to cults or practices, in the imaginary world."[42] By avoiding clear reference to any mythical or historical religion, Tolkien created universal myths that, in a creative sense, function as Christian types in ways parallel to Lewis's reimagining of classical myths, or even of the Old Testament. Since Jesus is the Word with God in the beginning (Jn 1:1), there is on this view no truly pre-Christian period, but rather only a

---

[41]J. R. R. Tolkien, "Letter 131 To Milton Waldman" (1951), *The Letters of J. R. R. Tolkien*, ed. Humphrey Carpenter (Boston: Houghton Mifflin, 1981), p. 145.

[42]J. R. R. Tolkien, "Letter 142 To Robert Murray, S.J." (1953), in *Letters of J. R. R. Tolkien*, pp. 171-73. See also Father Murray's lovely sermon tribute to Tolkien, "J. R. R. Tolkien and the Art of the Parable" (1992), reprinted in *Tolkien—A Celebration: Collected Writings on a Literary Legacy*, ed. Joseph Pearce (San Francisco: Ignatius, 2001), pp. 40-52.

common "order of grace" by which the light of God often illuminates both the historical and imaginative worlds.

The prehistory of Middle-earth and of Tolkien's Third Age is recounted in the posthumously published *Silmarillion* (1977).[43] It includes a Genesis-like story of origins, in which the creator, named both Eru, "the one," and also Iluvatar, "the illuminator," joins with his angels (the Ainur), to sing harmony out of many disparate parts. There follows a Fall, caused by a proud Ainur, named first Melkor, then Morgoth, a Lucifer figure whose music distorts and attempts to destroy the song of others. The main story of *The Silmarillion* tells how first elves and then humans follow Melkor in becoming artists so enamored of their own creation that they forget its true source. In the collection's tragic, central story, Feanor the elf makes the precious stones, the silmarils, whose beauty derives from the divine light contained within them, but then he and his sons become so possessive of them and alienate their race from the Ainur, ultimately losing all freedom through their own self-destructiveness.

The Silmarillion's greatest heroes may be Luthien, an elf princess who forsakes immortality, and her husband Beren, a human who passes through horrific danger and suffering to regain one of the silmarils. Luthien's choice begins a line of elven characters who, in giving up immortality, mirror the willingness of the biblical Son of God to live and die as a human despite his own divine, immortal nature. The curse caused by Feanor persists throughout *The Silmarillion,* and Tolkien's account of the First Age ends with a warning that "the Power of Terror and of Hate, sowed in the hearts of Elves and Men," remains and "will bear dark fruit until the latest days."[44] Still more suggestively, we are told that regarding "the Doom of the World . . . One alone can change who made it."[45]

The Third Age is portrayed in *The Hobbit* (1937) and *The Lord of the Rings* (1954-1955), both of which include many allusively Christian images. Rather than being focused on elves, the narrative now becomes,

---

[43]J. R. R. Tolkien, *The Silmarillion*, ed. Christopher Tolkien (London: HarperCollins, 1999).
[44]Ibid., p. 255.
[45]Ibid., p. 264.

to use an expression from Tolkien's letters, "hobbito-centric," which implies "the ennoblement (or sanctification) of the humble."[46] The power of the evil one ring to corrupt and then dominate the once-hobbitish Gollum introduces a profoundly Augustinian reflection on the corruption of the human will and heart. And the biblical insight that "God hath chosen the foolish things of the world to confound the wise" (1 Cor 1:27), is reflected in the hobbit Frodo being chosen to carry the ring to Mordor: "neither strength nor wisdom will carry us far upon it. . . . [S]mall hands do [such deeds] because they must, while the eyes of the great are elsewhere."[47]

Though Frodo is far from a perfect hero and cannot be taken as a Christ figure in any allegorical sense, the cumulative pattern of good choices and providential actions that have affected his life allow him, his friend Sam and the world to be saved. Gollum, by contrast, shows the potential for cumulative choices to destroy one's power to choose, and a strong case can be made, as Tolkien himself implies in his correspondence, that he may be damned; on the other hand, the matter is "Goddes privitee,"[48] and Gollum's final action of destroying the ring, however unintended, may instead cause God to say, as does Frodo, "let us forgive him . . . here at the end of all things, Sam."[49]

In his essay "On Fairy-Stories" (1964), Tolkien coins the word *eucatastrophe* to describe praise for and assent to the tragicomic triumph of Christ on the cross, and argues that such an event or "turn" in "the true fairy-story (or romance)" offers "a far-off gleam or echo of *evangelium* in the real world."[50] The distinction between myth and history or literature and Scripture is always clear in Tolkien, but ultimately the joy to be found in both is akin, for "Christian joy, the *Gloria*," is the supreme story, "and it is true. Art has been verified. God is the Lord, of angels, and of men—and of elves. Legend and History have met and

[46]J. R. R. Tolkien, "Letter 181 To Michael Straight" (1956), in *The Letters of J. R. R. Tolkien*, ed. Humphrey Carpenter (Boston: Houghton Mifflin, 1981), p. 237.

[47]Ibid., p. 262.

[48]Ibid., pp. 233-34.

[49]J. R. R. Tolkien, *The Return of the King* (London: HarperCollins, 1999), p. 268.

[50]J. R. R. Tolkien, "On Fairy-Stories," in *Tree and Leaf* (London: HarperCollins, 1988), pp. 98, 64.

fused."[51] Ultimately, Tolkien's art is coherent in itself, yet also infused with a Christian vision of both art and life itself as not only redeemable but already redeemed. That joyful fact encompasses all time, both real and imagined, and promises hope for the future.

While Tolkien and Lewis expressed their distinctive Christian vision through fantasy, myth and fairytale, other contemporary Christian writers have chosen grittier fictive venues. Particularly outstanding has been some work by writers from the southern United States, whose audiences live within the religion-saturated "Bible Belt" but nevertheless suffer from the common modern maladies of nihilistic materialism and general and biblical illiteracy. In the view of one novelist, Walker Percy, for the modern southern Christian writer the fundamental challenge is: "How to proclaim the Good News in a society which never needed it more but in which language itself has been subverted?"[52] To take one example, Percy explains, the word "sin has been devalued to mean everything from slightly naughty excess" to "emotional unfulfillment" to "the loss of 'intersubjective communication'" or simply "the failure of creativity."[53] Underlying such obfuscation is metaphysical nihilism and a loss of faith in eternal realities that can infect Christians themselves. In the words of another major southern writer, quoted in the introduction to this book, "If you live today, you breathe in nihilism. In or out of the Church, it's the gas you breathe."[54]

Flannery O'Connor's fiction, especially her often startling short stories, confront this nihilism and seek to restore a New Testament understanding of Christian truth. Eschewing the often heretical platitudes thoughtlessly uttered by the outwardly pious, O'Connor instead puts gospel truth into the mouths of unlikely preachers, the despised, outcast, sometimes even violent folk assumed to be among "the least of [Christ's] brethren" (Mt 25:40). In very direct language that rebukes

---

[51]Ibid., pp. 65-66.
[52]Walker Percy, *Signposts in a Strange Land*, ed. Patrick Samway (New York: Farrar, Straus & Giroux, 1993), p. 322.
[53]Walker Percy, "Why Are You a Catholic?" in *Living Philosophies: The Reflections of Some Eminent Men and Women of Our Time* (New York: Doubleday, 1990), p. 168.
[54]Flannery O'Connor, "Letter to Elizabeth Hester," in *The Habit of Being: The Letters of Flannery O'Connor*, ed. Sally Fitzgerald (New York: Farrar, Straus & Giroux, 1979), p. 97.

both the South's learned liberal elite and its uneducated, often racist lower class, these characters represent the radical, existential challenge inherent in Christianity. In the famous story "A Good Man Is Hard to Find" (1953), for example, a serial killer named the Misfit entraps and is about to murder a southern family whose spiritual leader, their grandmother, offers the weakest of spiritual defenses: "Jesus, you ought not to shoot a lady. I'll give you all the money I've got!" The Misfit's motivations are not monetary, and he has his own views of her "Jesus"; if Jesus "raised the dead," the Misfit says, "then it's nothing for you to do but throw away everything and follow Him, and if He didn't, then it's nothing for you to do but enjoy the few minutes you got left the best way you can." To this challenge the grandmother feebly replies: "Maybe He didn't raise the dead."[55] The Misfit admits his own uncertainty, offering the familiar modern claim that he could not know unless he "had of been there," at which his demeanor changes, "as if he were going to cry." The grandmother, sensing their essential kinship, exclaims, "Why you're one of my babies. You're one of my own children!" At that utterance, the Misfit shoots her dead. The grandmother's sentiment here may or may not be sincere; in her final posture "with her legs crossed under her like a child's and her face smiling up at the cloudless sky," there is at least a potential image of redemption. But while we grasp the existential import of the Misfit's final judgment on her—"She would have been a good woman . . . if it had been somebody there to shoot her every minute of her life"—for then she might have taken both life and death more seriously—the Misfit's own nihilistic creed is also undercut by his own final words in the story: "It's no real pleasure in life."[56] O'Connor's seemingly clichéd title carries more than a hint of Jesus' assertion that "none is good, save one, that is, God" (Lk 18:19). And that God's judgment falls alike on the misfit and the ostensible pillars of polite society.

As Roman Catholics in the overwhelmingly Protestant South, both Percy and O'Connor could be said to be misfits in their own culture,

[55]Flannery O'Connor, "A Good Man Is Hard to Find," in *Flannery O'Connor: The Complete Stories* (New York: Farrar, Straus & Giroux, 1971), p. 132.
[56]Ibid., p. 133.

and both reflect profound uneasiness with the dominant spiritual ethos. The work of Baptist writer and rural Kentuckian Wendell Berry, whom *The New York Times* hailed as the "prophet of rural America," is, however, even more radically countercultural. A prolific poet, essayist and fiction writer, Berry offers a profoundly creational and incarnational Christian theology as the essential foundation for community. Equally opposed to the intrusions of socialist big government and the industrial farming techniques of big business, Berry fearlessly rebukes both the left and right wings of American political life, insisting on a personal, accountable, sustainable economy in a harmonious relationship to creation. Such ideas are expressed both in provocative essays and in short stories and novels rooted within the fictional geography of Port Royal, Kentucky, whose many vivid characters span multiple generations. The role of institutional religion is often understated in Berry's fiction, but a short-story cycle such as *Fidelity: Five Stories* is bound together by profound expressions of ordinary Christian faithfulness. The opening story, "Pray Without Ceasing," is a deeply moving novella in which narrator Andy Catlett delves first into "the great mystery we call time," but also "the greater mystery we call eternity."[57] Knowing from old newspaper clippings that his great-grandfather, Ben Feltner, was murdered by his closest friend, Thad Coulter, Andy goes to his always-praying Grandma Feltner. Among other things, he learns from her that her husband, Mat Feltner, with the help of others, had made peace between the Coulter and Feltner lines, and eventually allowed the marriage of Thad's cousin Marce Catlett and Bess Feltner, Mat's daughter, who became Andy's parents. The consequences of forgiveness, mercy and persistent prayer have thus, out of tragedy, provided Andy with the miracle of life, which he is then able to celebrate in a simple but joyful epiphany:

> I am blood kin to both sides of that moment when Ben Feltner turned to face Thad Coulter in the road and Thad pulled the trigger. The two families, sundered in the ruin of a friendship, were united again first in new friendship and then in marriage. My grandfather made a peace

---

[57]Wendell Berry, "Pray Without Ceasing," in *Fidelity: Five Stories* (New York: Pantheon, 1992), p. 3.

here that has joined many who would otherwise have been divided. I am the child of his forgiveness.[58]

"A Jonquil for Mary Penn" expresses the unaffected beauty of fidelity within the trials of a young marriage; "Making It Home" describes a soldier's restored faith and hope as he returns home after futile foreign wars; the title story is a long, complex account of a son's faithful commitment to a father who wishes to die in familiar surroundings rather than attached to monitors in an alien hospital. Finally, "Are You All Right?" shows two old friends faithfully searching for others lost in the forest during a flood. Kentucky's forests and fields may not be holy ground for everyone, but to Berry this natural habitat, his ancestral home, remains a place to be, in the words of one of his "Sabbath" poems, "lost to all other wills but Heaven's."[59] In novels such as *Hannah Coulter* (2004), *Jayber Crow* (2000), *A Place on Earth* (1967) and *Remembering* (1988), Berry has set a high standard for prophetic fiction in a postmodern age. His essays, including notably those collected in *Sex, Economy, Freedom and Community* (1992), and even his poetry, such as the countercultural *Sabbaths* (1987, 2002, 2006), have marked him out as a writer willing to critique cultural Christianity for its acquiescence in the destruction of Christianity's highest values. All of his writing, in its unflinching commitment to social, political, natural and theological realism, bears eloquent witness to his love of truth.

Three other contemporary American novelists are particularly worthy of the Christian student's thoughtful appraisal. Marilynne Robinson's Pulitzer Prize–winning *Gilead* (2004) is a tour de force achievement of Christian character and "voice," exploring lived Christian virtues in the light of experimental theological inquiry. It is one of the best-written novels of the past several decades in American fiction. Leif Enger's bestselling *Peace Like a River* (2002) and *So Brave, Young, and Handsome* (2008) reveal him to be a fine writer of both plot and character, whose own Christian worldview and lively sense of hope and love for the world will repay close attention. Ron Hansen is perhaps less

---

[58]Ibid., p. 59.
[59]Wendell Berry, "Sabbath Poem II, 1995," in *A Timbered Choir: The Sabbath Poems, 1979-97* (Washington D.C.: Counterpoint, 1999), p. 188.

well known than Robinson or Enger, but his novel about the life of the poet Gerard Manley Hopkins, *Exiles* (2008), and his *Atticus* (1996), a nice turn on the parable of the prodigal son in which a father goes looking for his wayward offspring, both reveal literary talent suffused with Christian literacy and are deeply expressive of an understanding of sacrifice. His collection, *A Stay Against Confusion: Essays on Faith and Fiction* (2001), is worthy to be read alongside Flannery O'Connor's *Mystery and Manners* (1969) as a fascinating prompt to Christian critical reflection on the art of fiction.

Distinctive Christian writing has also come from Canada, a markedly different physical and cultural landscape from that of the U.S. Writing almost exclusively from the rural Miramichi region of New Brunswick, but initially inspired by Dickens, David Adams Richards has for the past thirty years written novels that blend physical and historical realism to depict universal ethical problems. Since his award-winning fictional theodicy *Mercy Among the Children* (2000), and more recently in his personal prose credo *God Is,* Richards has sympathetically portrayed the power of Christian faith to ward off falsehood and violence, and affirmed the transcendent presence of God in his characters' lives. An even more catholic and biblical sense of God's providence pervades the work of Ontario-based writer and painter Michael D. O'Brien. The long, richly symbolic novels of O'Brien's Children of the Last Days series are to be compared not to the speculative apocalyptic fiction popularized in efforts such as the Left Behind books but rather to Robert Hugh Benson's *Lord of the World* (1908), Vladimir Soloviev's "A Short Story of the Anti-christ" (1900) and the epic, spiritually weighty novels of Russian and Eastern European writers. O'Brien explores the West's loss of faith and subsequent moral and spiritual decline, and offers hope for renewal through personal sacrifice, aesthetic creativity and intentional Christian community. O'Brien himself experienced a dramatic conversion after a visit to a mental institution for children convinced him of the immense significance of even the weakest human soul.

The Last Days novels center on one main family who, in *Strangers and Sojourners* (1997), migrate to Canada in the early twentieth century and settle in British Columbia. Surviving the linked dangers of secularism, pseudospiritualism and shamanism, a member of the family becomes a journalist committed to sharing religious and moral truth in *Plague Journal* (1999), but subsequent persecution leads into the incipient totalitarianism of *Eclipse of the Sun* (1998), a novel whose real target is not so much political institutions but rather the apparent lack of spiritual courage within the Canadian Catholic Church. The faithful work of a Polish immigrant priest, Father André, bears fruit in *A Cry of Stone* (2003), in which O'Brien tells the story of Rose Wabos, an orphaned native girl who becomes a mystic and painter with a special capacity for what she calls *"falling-into-seeing."*

Father André provides a link to the two novels set in Europe for which O'Brien is best known. *Sophia House* (2005), a prequel published as a sequel, recounts the formative World War II trials and aesthetic education of David Schafer, the young Polish Jew who will become Father Elijah in O'Brien's most famous novel. The spiritual power of *Father Elijah* (1996), which has appeal for both Catholic and Protestant readers, comes first from the profound interior prayer life of Elijah and his attempt to be obedient to the wisdom of "Dottrina," modeled directly on then Cardinal Ratzinger (now Pope Benedict XVI) and "the present Pope," John Paul II. Elijah's wisdom shines in an electrifying dialogue with Count Smokrev, a nihilistic, abusive figure from his Polish past, whose extraordinary conversion comes at the very center of the novel. Anna Benedetti, an Italian lawyer, is also converted under Elijah's pastoral influence, but both efforts are prelude to the attempted conversion of an unnamed European political leader about to fulfill the role of antichrist. O'Brien's "Apocalypse" unmasks spiritual deception and apostasy in a compelling way and celebrates the virtues of self-sacrifice and spiritual obedience, as well as the need for radical personal conversion: "Be with us now as we face our foe, That we might stand firm, And strengthen the things which remain."[60] O'Brien's *Island of the World* (2007), a love story set in twentieth-century Croatia, and *Theophilos* (2010), a historical novel set in

---

[60]Michael D. O'Brien, *Father Elijah: An Apocalypse* (San Francisco: Ignatius Press, 1996), p. 596.

the first century and focused in epistolary fashion on the Gentile to whom Luke the evangelist dedicates his gospel and the Acts of the Apostles, are each in their fashion eloquent expressions of a deeply thoughtful Christian worldview.

Poet Margaret Avison, with whom we end this brief account of recent writers of particular interest for Christian students of literature, commenced a long and distinguished career with the 1960 publication of *Winter Sun*. In 1963, after reading the Gospel of John, Avison converted to Christianity, and her 1966 collection *The Dumbfounding* expressed a new understanding of both human and divine nature. In "Person," human identity itself seems a prison, for "This door that is 'I Am' / seemed to seal my tomb"; somehow, though, "he passes *through*," the resurrected Christ leaving one "drenched with Being and created new." In this poem's companion piece, ". . . Person," Avison turns to the third person of the holy Trinity, addressing the common difficulty in speaking of the divine Person least accessible to our senses: "How should I find speech to you," she writes, "the self-effacing / whose other self was seen / alone by the only one" (1-4), or Christ. Avison's answer to this aesthetic and spiritual problem is a prayer that echoes Christ's farewell discourse, where our Lord prays "that they all may be one; as thou, Father, art in me, and I in thee, that they also may be one in us" (Jn 17:21); she asks God: "Let the one you show me / ask you, for me," "to lead *my* self, effaced / In the known Light, / To be in him released / From facelessness" (9-16). As the human person in the previous poem was imprisoned within the walls of the alienated self but redeemed by the spiritual movement of the physical Christ, here Avison almost parallels Lewis's final novel, asking Christ to send the Holy Spirit, to finally allow her to see God "face to face" (1 Cor 13:12).

In 2002, at age eighty-four, Avison's collection *Concrete and Wild Carrot* won the prestigious Griffin Poetry Prize, and thus offered more widely a new vision of the theological personalism discovered in her conversion. Her vision of the person of Christ is most clearly displayed in a series of four poems drawn from the Gospels. The first three, "On a Maundy Thursday Walk," "Uncircular" and "The Crux" recollect Christ's suffering, while "The Whole Story" bespeaks the "inexplicable

'Peace'" made possible only through his resurrection. In "Prayer of Anticipation" from the suggestively titled *Momentary Dark* (2006), Avison looks forward to meeting "Jesus, interpreter—more, / configurer of all." Her seasoned reflection, cast in the form of intercessory prayer, makes a fitting coda for this troubled period and is a worthy call to Christian writers and critics both:

> It is my best good
> to let you speak your
> remembered, translated,
> printed, painfully
> accessible word.
>
> Jesus, disclose
> your journeying for
> this day's avenues.

SUGGESTIONS FOR FURTHER READING

Barge, Laura. *God, the Quest, the Hero: Thematic Structures in Beckett's Fiction.* Chapel Hill: University of North Carolina Press, 1988.

Berman, Marshall. *All That Is Solid Melts into Air: The Experience of Modernity.* New York: Simon & Schuster, 1982.

Booker, M. Keith. *Dystopian Literature: A Theory and Research Guide.* Westport: Greenwood Press, 1994.

Detweiler, Robert. *Breaking the Fall: Religious Readings of Contemporary Fiction.* San Francisco: Harper & Row, 1989.

Ericson, Edward E., and Alexis Klimoff. *The Soul and Barbed Wire: An Introduction to Solzhenitsyn.* Lanham, Md.: Intercollegiate Studies Institute, 2008.

Ficken, Carl. *God's Story and Modern Literature.* Philadelphia: Fortress, 1985.

Gallagher, Susan VanZanten. *Postcolonial Literature and the Biblical Call for Justice.* Jackson: University Press of Mississippi, 1994.

Gillespie, Michael Allen. *The Theological Origins of Modernity.* Chicago: University of Chicago Press, 2008.

Hoffman, Frederick J. *The Imagination's New Beginning: Theology and Modern Literature.* London: Oxford University Press, 1971.

Hopper, Stanley Romaine. *Spiritual Problems in Contemporary Literature.* San Francisco: Harper & Row, 1957.

Howard, Thomas. *Dove Descending: A Journey into T. S. Eliot's Four Quartets.* San Francisco: Ignatius, 2006.

Jacobs, Alan. *The Narnian: The Life and Imagination of C. S. Lewis.* New York: HarperOne, 2008.

Joyce, Stanislaus. *My Brother's Keeper: James Joyce's Early Years.* 1958. Reprint, Cambridge, Mass.: Da Capo Press, 2003.

Kent, David A., ed. *Lighting up the Terrain: The Poetry of Margaret Avison.* Toronto: ECW Press, 1987.

Kramer, Kenneth Paul. *Redeeming Time: T. S. Eliot's Four Quartets.* Boston: Cowley, 2007.

Manganiello, Dominic. *T. S. Eliot and Dante.* London: Palgrave Macmillan, 1989.

Maritan, Jacques. *Creative Intuition in Art and Poetry.* Bollingen Series 35.1. New York: Pantheon, 1953.

Markos, Louis. *Lewis Agonistes: How C. S. Lewis Can Train Us to Wrestle With the Modern and Postmodern World.* Nashville: B & H, 2003.

Rosenthal, Peggy. *The Poets' Jesus: Representations at the End of a Millennium.* New York: Oxford University Press, 2000.

Rutledge, Fleming. *The Battle for Middle-Earth: Tolkien's Divine Design in "The Lord of the Rings."* Grand Rapids: Eerdmans, 2004.

Scott, Nathan, Jr. *The Broken Center: Studies in the Theological Horizon of Modern Literature.* New Haven, Conn.: Yale University Press, 1966.

Smidt, Kristian. *Poetry and Belief in the Work of T. S. Eliot.* London: Routledge & Kegan Paul, 1961.

Taylor, Charles. *A Secular Age.* Cambridge, Mass.: Belknap, 2007.

———. *Sources of the Self: The Making of the Modern Identity.* Cambridge, Mass.: Harvard University Press, 1992.

Weller, Shane. *Literature, Philosophy, Nihilism: The Uncanniest of Guests.* London: Palgrave Macmillan, 2008.

Wirzba, Norman. *Wendell Berry and Religion: Heaven's Earthly Life.* Lexington: University Press of Kentucky, 2009.

Wood, Ralph C. *Flannery O'Connor and the Christ-Haunted South.* Grand Rapids: Eerdmans, 2005.

———. *The Gospel According to Tolkien: Visions of the Kingdom in Middle-Earth.* Nashville: Westminster John Knox, 2003.

LITERARY STUDIES IN
CHRISTIAN PERSPECTIVE

He has made everything beautiful in its time.
He has also set eternity in the hearts of men;
yet they cannot fathom what God has done from beginning to end.

ECCLESIASTES 3:11 NIV

It will have been apparent to our readers long before now that we are strong proponents of the good that literary study can achieve at the heart of the humanities curriculum. But we do not, in saying so, mean to suggest that the academic discipline as it exists in many places—perhaps especially in private secular and public universities—is currently realizing its humane and liberating potential. In fact, literary study is in many respects in a decadent phase, decadence manifest in the aversion of many theorists to the necessary connection of fiction and poetry to truth, and explicit in the distortion, inversion and redefinition of language itself in many spheres of critical practice. Although we have left a liberal trail of clues to the map of such practices along our way, we do not propose here to review and critique schools of theory and criticism we judge to be substantially unprofitable. Once again, however, we do want to remind our readers that even these fashions are far from being as novel as they may advertise themselves to be.[1]

---

[1]Parts of this chapter have appeared in David Lyle Jeffrey, "Communion, Community, and Our

When Richard Rorty says that the essential postmodern theme is that "what is most important for human life is not what propositions we believe, but what vocabulary we use," he cites William James and Nietzsche, who he says have taught us "to give up the notion of truth as a correspondence to reality." Henceforth, he continues, the example of the pragmatists shows us that the power function in language is its real purpose, namely, "to help us get what we want."[2] This is a familiar idea to people with younger siblings or to parents with small children. When it becomes acceptable as adult discourse, the position of many a student trying to understand a literary theorist today is not unlike that of Alice trying to understand Humpty Dumpty:

> "There's glory for you!"
>
> "I don't know what you mean by 'glory,'" Alice said.
>
> Humpty Dumpty smiled contemptuously. "Of course you don't—till I tell you. I meant, 'there's a nice knock-down argument for you!'"
>
> "But 'glory' doesn't mean 'a nice knock-down argument,'" Alice objected.
>
> "When *I* use a word," Humpty said in a rather scornful tone, "it means just what I choose it to mean—neither more nor less."
>
> "The question is," said Alice, "whether you *can* make words mean so many different things."
>
> "The question is," said Humpty Dumpty, "which is to be master—that's all."[3]

Humpty's is a Nietzschean world, a calculus of deliberate antirealism and disdain for others in which truth can be dismissed with a subversive rhetorical flourish as "illusions about which one has forgotten that this is what they are."[4] But it is a world as old as the Gar-

---

Common Book: Or, Can Faustus Be Saved?" *Christianity and Literature* 53, no. 2 (2004): 233-46; also in his, "Tolkien and the Future of Literary Studies," *Tree of Tales: Tolkien, Literature and Theology*, ed. Trevor Hart and Ivan Khovacs (Waco, Tex.: Baylor University Press, 2007), pp. 55-70—in both cases included here by permission.

[2]Richard Rorty, *Consequences of Pragmatism* (Minneapolis: University of Minnesota Press, 1982), pp. 142, 150.

[3]Lewis Carroll, *Through the Looking Glass*, in *The Annotated Alice*, ed. Marin Gardner (New York: Bramhall, 1960), pp. 268-69.

[4]Friedrich Nietzsche, "On Truth and Lie in an Extra-Moral Sense" (1873), trans. W. Kaufmann, *The Portable Nietzsche* (1954; reprint, New York: Penguin, 1982), p. 47.

den of Eden, and its evasions are as questionable as those of Adam and Eve or Cain.

How should the Christian student of literature approach this aspect of reality in much critical discourse in the profession? Well, we have suggested that it is a good idea to begin by accepting reality as it is: our discipline is among the least well salted by cogent Christian contributions to critical thinking. About that much we must be willing to bear the reality. But we must equally refuse to abdicate responsibility, to acknowledge and uphold the eloquent witness of centuries of Christian writers who have tried to work out their own salvation in fear and trembling through careful artistry and imaginative response to Christian revelation. As intellectuals, our job is to try to tell the truth as best we are able by patient inquiry to discover it. Truth-telling is representing reality as it is, whether it gets us what we want or not (cf. Ps 15:2); whether descriptively, analytically or by those types of analogical utterances we call poetry, truth is possible to the Christian imagination to the degree that it has been formed by that One who is Truth.

It is the business of theology, not literary criticism, we might well think, to establish "the truths of faith." Yet it is imperative for a Christian intellectual in any discipline to live out personal faith in the light of Holy Scripture and sound theology. That Christianity is a revealed religion, and that the church has everywhere and always taught certain truths of faith, is a first principle; the authority behind our conviction is not in the strength or weakness of our conviction itself. There is a large and well-reasoned body of knowledge of which we may avail ourselves and in terms of which we may form a mature Christian intellectual identity. There is, as well, the witness of the Spirit in our hearts that lends a quiet confidence greater than deductive reasoning can by itself provide. This is one of the essential points made in that magnificent poem of biblical wisdom, the book of Job: we can be said to *know* what we cannot see (Job 19:25; cf. Heb 11). This is the kind of knowing referred to in 2 Timothy 1:12: "I know whom I have believed, and am persuaded that he is able to keep that which I have committed unto him against that day."

If we learn language by analogy, we also come to know truths of the human condition by analogy. After all, as Paul Ricoeur says, "characters in plays and novels are humans like us who think, speak, act and suffer as we do."[5] This makes of literary study a natural workshop for the formation in charity of Christian readers, and for a broader exploration through vicarious understanding of the nature of virtue and of the consequences of human choices with respect to vice as well as virtue. In this way literary study, as Walter Benjamin so eloquently argues in his essay "The Storyteller," is a means of acquiring wisdom.[6] Story as a means of wisdom is at the heart of Scripture itself, and nowhere more so than in the teachings of Jesus, surely the chief exemplar for Christian poets as well as critics. Finally, literature gives us access to a deeper understanding of beauty. This in turn, as the writer of Ecclesiastes suggests, leads us in more sensitive apprehension to reflect on the infinite source of beauty: "He has made everything beautiful in its time. He has also set eternity in the hearts of men; yet they cannot fathom what God has done from beginning to end" (Eccles 3:11 NIV). The yearning after beauty in us is hard-wired; our longing is after an eternal beauty we cannot by any words of our own or art of our own adequately capture—but we are created to follow the lineaments of this desire until, by means of our delight in creation and in the best of human creativity responding, we come at last to the One whom Hopkins has called "the true critic," the Judge of all. This Judge is to be feared more than any human judge, for he is flawless in his perception; he is the Alpha and Omega, beginning and end of all beauty, truth and good—being incarnate and yet *saecula seculorum,* the eternal God. Pursuing his beauty is, for a Christian, far from evasive and sterile aestheticism, for a Christian will recognize, with Vladimir Soloviev, the ethical imperative implied by such desire: "The aesthetically beautiful should lead us to *an actual improvement of reality.*"[7]

It would be possible for undergraduates in a Christian academic envi-

---

[5]Paul Ricoeur, *Oneself as Another* (Chicago: University of Chicago Press, 1992), p. 150.

[6]Walter Benjamin, "The Storyteller: Reflections on the Works of Nikolai Leskov" (1936), in *Illuminations,* ed. Hannah Arendt (New York: Schocken, 1968).

[7]Vladimir Soloviev, "Beauty in Nature," in *The Heart of Reality: Essays on Beauty, Love, and Ethics,* ed. and trans. Vladimir Woznink (Notre Dame, Ind.: University of Notre Dame Press, 2003), p. 30.

ronment to imagine professional literary study as a particularly gratifying occupation. It can be, and even the rigors of graduate study in normatively politically correct doctoral programs can provide many benefits to the intellectually honest and truth-seeking student. But no one should be misled into thinking, as Ernest Hemingway might say, that such a course of life is all "downhill skiing in powder snow." It is part of the job of teachers in the discipline to acknowledge contemporary challenges to students contemplating graduate school, and it is no contradiction to the enthusiasm teachers have for the literature to do so.

There is in many graduate programs a studied avoidance of pre–twentieth-century great texts; also, it should be acknowledged, there is widespread ignorance of the Christian worldview out of which they were written. But it is also true that many literature students lack sufficient background in the richness of the English language itself to fully enter into the world of such texts. While students who read this book are certainly better advantaged than the majority—or so we trust—they are precisely to that degree an "elite" among twenty-first-century readers. There is a broader cultural imperative, accordingly, for well-trained Christian scholars to take up leading roles in literary study. Properly prepared, they should have a great deal of value to say. It is conceivable that preservation in the curriculum of some great vernacular texts may even come to depend on such scholars. But to accomplish this, they will need to do what all scholars do who would preserve a great but unfashionable literature, whether for their own purposes or the common good of humanity. They will need first to read and teach with deep understanding the foundational literatures, including the Bible and its major traditions of exegetical and poetic commentary, among which subsequent literary works hold their own conversation. Not even teachers in confessional colleges can count on churches or departments of religion to have done this groundwork accountably.

Most scholars readily accept this sort of intertextual necessity—familiarity with foundational texts—for literature composed in other, nonbiblical religious contexts. There is continuing pertinence in Voltaire's observation concerning the crucial role of foundational books for understanding the literary cultures he identifies:

> The whole of Africa, right to Ethiopia, and Nigritia obeys the book of
> the Alcoran, after having staggered under the book of the Gospel.
> China is ruled by the moral book of Confucius; a greater part of India
> by the book of the Veda. Persia was governed for centuries by one of the
> books of the Zarathustras.[8]

For teaching postcolonial or world literature, few would argue with
Voltaire. Yet in our own guild, there has been for some time an extreme
scruple where the "book of the Gospel" and Western literature is concerned. Notably, professional aversion to our own traditional "govern-
ing" book is proving to be coincident with an ongoing crisis of identity
for English literary studies as a profession, an academic discipline, we
might note, far younger than classical studies, the study of oriental literature or any of the other core disciplines of the traditional university.

English literature became a university discipline only in the nineteenth century, and at least in part as a rejection of both classical and
religious foundations. The modernist character of our disciplinary genealogy is pertinent: though the famous headmaster Thomas Arnold of
Rugby remains memorable for the power of his proclamation of traditional Christian verities, most of his more famous students—such as
Arthur Clough and his own son Matthew—soon departed from the
senior Arnold's religious belief in order to embrace an ideal of culture
from which a living faith had been largely excised. The first professor
of poetry at Oxford to lecture in English rather than Latin, Matthew
Arnold, signaled the future of the discipline not only by focusing on
what he called "the modern element in literature" but by turning literary education itself toward social construction. Yet in his revolutionary
wish for the study of literature to provide an alternate clerisy and to
preserve reading of the Bible not for religious but for cultural purposes,
he exhibited an unstable tension that has bedeviled literary formation
in our guild ever since. For some who have pursued the profession as a
career, literary criticism has become a kind of substitute religion.

---

[8]François Voltaire, "Books," in *Philosophical Dictionary* (1764), ed. and trans. Theodore Bester-
man (London: Penguin, 2004).

Justification for the place of vernacular literary studies in the university depends on a commitment to teach more than simply rudimentary skills that, for the most part, would not once have obtained a passing grade at Rugby. As a new university discipline, literature's relative twentieth-century prominence has depended on successfully ascribing high, even quasi-religious ideals to an increasingly low and secular reading practice. The advertised function of the practitioner is to make culture itself more widely available (in Arnold one moves from reading Homer in the original to comparing English translations of Homer), but doing so ostensibly in search of a "grand style" expressive of a certain "nobility of the human spirit." If the poet "sees life steadily and sees it whole," Arnold thinks, then the well-read critic all the more so. As literature assumed the functions of religion among Arnold's successors, at least down to the New Critics and Northrop Frye, there was plenty of such high-sounding stuff for its professors to sell to college administrators, trustees and many students. Arnold's "perfecting of a national right reason" worked in nicely with the later "pooled social intelligence" of John Dewey and with numerous other identifications—of salvation with the state, and of literary merit with a never-to-be-ended quest for relevant, pragmatic and hence conveniently subjective "truth."

As we look over our shoulder, then, we can see how Thoreau's contention that the Greek and Roman classics are "the noblest recorded thoughts of man," the "only oracles which are not decayed," reflects an increasingly archaic secular piety that would not long persist after the founding of our discipline.[9] This reverence was never so fully extended in the modern university to biblical literature. For Matthew Arnold, enamored of Germanic biblical criticism, Goethe and the Romantics, traditional religion was already bankrupt; as one of his more famous dismissals puts it, "the strongest part of our religion to-day is its unconscious poetry."[10] Conscious poetry, especially of the Romantics, he reckoned to possess a "higher truth and a higher seriousness."[11] James Joyce

---

[9]Henry David Thoreau, *Walden* (Columbus, Ohio: Charles E. Merrill, 1969), p. 110.
[10]Matthew Arnold, "The Study of Poetry," *Essays in Criticism, Second Series* (London: Macmillan, 1908), p. 2.
[11]Ibid., p. 21.

simply echoes Arnold when Stephen, in *Portrait of the Artist as a Young Man*, refers to literature as "the highest and most spiritual art."[12]

These sentiments continued to be the prevailing secular pieties of our guild in America in the early 1960s. By the 1980s they too had been, of course, irrevocably interrogated, shaken down and in some considerable measure dissolved. There is much in the postmodern challenge to prompt the gratitude of Christian intellectuals, who will recognize that even in the careerism of the time there was a kind of unconscious idolatry. But the new revolutionaries were more than accidental secularists; among them a more candid apostasy was a requirement of the license to practice. Many were thoroughgoing iconoclasts: they worshiped no authority higher than the self. With few exceptions, their revolution has pretty effectively "done in" Arnold as a functioning authority, and, we might now suspect, the residual authority of most of the apostolic succession of his clerisy with him.

In much of the English-speaking world, the formal study of literature is in disarray. As English departments focus on books of the most slender claim to nobility of thought, let alone grandness of style, pressing rather for what is taken to be more marketable fashion and relevance, students have continued to disperse to majors in communication studies, media-telecommunications, journalism, technical writing, cinema criticism and cultural studies. Meanwhile, our discipline has acquired a popular notoriety for being the purveyor not of high and noble verities but of low and often trivial advocacies. Consequently, as the late Bernard Williams observed, even the primary literature itself has suffered from "some very reductive criticisms of traditional academic authority":

> If the canon of works or writers or philosophies to be studied, and the methods of interpreting them, and the historical narratives that explain those things, are all equally and simultaneously denounced as ideological impositions, we are indeed left with a space structured only by power.[13]

But such diminishment is hardly confined to the canonical status of

---

[12]James Joyce, *A Portrait of the Artist as a Young Man* (London: Jonathan Cape, 1942), p. 244.
[13]Bernard Williams, *Truth and Truthfulness: An Essay on Genealogy* (Princeton, N.J.: Princeton University Press, 2002), p. 8.

texts (as deans of humanities and provosts will attest). The loss of literary authority to an utterly reductive account, as Williams further observes, deprives the critics themselves of sufficient power to sustain their enterprise in a competitive environment within the university. Put more crudely: confident defenses of the status of literary study as an apprenticeship to wisdom had the advantage of appearing even to the unwise (e.g., administrators) as a species of learning probably deserving of some environmental protection; current rationalizations for literary study as a venue for avant-garde politics, competitive with the therapeutic social sciences, tend more quickly to lose fiscal traction. In American institutions of higher learning the overall number of English majors is sharply down, and with that trend so are the number of teaching positions.

In "The Decline and Fall of Literature," in the *New York Review of Books*, Andrew Delbanco reviews seven books on the subject and explains our loss of academic prestige as the corruption of a discipline that in its heyday had been an intellectual flagship for modernity, able to pride itself on replacing the narrowness of earlier Christian teaching by the broad liberality of inspired, Emersonian principles as discovered in secular literature.[14] Matthew Arnold likewise, as the discipline's first academic officer, was of course foundationally associated with the displacement of God and the Bible by modern literary criticism, consistently with the curricular exchange of "dogma," as he called it, for secular literature. Several recent jeremiads (including those Delbanco reviews) lament the loss of these secularizing exemplars and the absence of sufficiently powerful successors. Much like other notable Arnoldians, Northrop Frye included, and more recently the new-light Arnoldian Jonathan Culler, many of these critics—ironically enough—are now worried about a tragic falling away of literature as a discipline that they have helped to inspire, a flight away from literary works themselves toward newer theoretical dogmas so sectarian as to have marginalized literature as a discipline in the university. Delbanco is himself among those who cling to that perdurable Arnoldian apolo-

---

[14]Andrew Delbanco, "The Decline and Fall of Literature," *New York Review of Books* 46, no. 17 (1999).

getic by which the place of English literature has often been justified—
to wit, that without it the university would be "left without a moral
center."[15] But to read this cliché now, at least in the West, is to realize
just how outworn the old justification has become.

Astonishing as it may seem, the idea that secular English literature
can replace central religious texts as a moral compass has been persis-
tently employed in advertisements for the discipline for more than a
century. The rhetoric, typically unexamined, has become unthinking
and reflexive. In a 2002 presidential address to the Modern Language
Association, Stephen Greenblatt called for literary study to promulgate
the antireligion of naturalist materialism, and yet he himself displayed
a displaced religious fervor in almost every sentence of his address.
Greenblatt's final call was for a revival of a Lucretian pagan doctrine of
metempsychosis (soul return) in which frustrated literary critics reas-
sure each other that they are among the immortals and get to live on as
ghostly shades in the pages of their surviving academic work.[16] A reader
who remembers the grim consolation claimed by Brunetto Latini regarding the "men of letters" in Dante's hell, among whom he is num-
bered as one of those once "prominent" (*Inferno* 15.103-24), will wonder
at the unconscious irony of such a sentiment. This sort of rhetoric may
not derive from traditional religion, but it is nonetheless evidently a
species of substitute religious exhortation. Christian students of literature will, like Dante, not linger over such a sorry scene but press up-
ward to higher ground.

Worthy authority, notably, accrues to possession of, or capacity for,
truth of the high order that readers from Aristotle to Wordsworth to
Nietzsche ("poetry aims to be . . . the unvarnished expression of the
truth")[17] have associated with "great books." Whereas our modern discipline began with Arnold in the credo that religious truths had been,
in literature, supplemented by the "higher truths" of nature, we may
well have approached a survival limit for the guild with postmodernist

---

[15]Ibid., p. 35.

[16]Stephen Greenblatt, *Profession 2003* (New York: Modern Language Association, 2003), pp.
    4-7.

[17]Friedrich Nietzsche, *The Birth of Tragedy and Other Writings*, ed. Raymond Geuss and Ronald
    Speirs, trans. Ronald Speirs (Cambridge: Cambridge University Press, 1999), p. 41.

assertions that literature affords us no stable or shareable truths at all. In his provocative book *Truth and Truthfulness*, philosopher Bernard Williams argues for a profound reversal of what he calls the "deconstructive vortex":

> If the passion for truthfulness is merely controlled and stilled without being satisfied, it will kill the activities it is supposed to support. This may be one of the reasons why, at the present time, the study of the humanities runs a risk of sliding from professional seriousness, through professionalization, to a finally disenchanted careerism.[18]

The trajectory of Williams's argument is actually toward a reassertion of that uncommon sense we still call "common," of a revaluing of prereflective openness to truth in relation to language, even of a sort of "primitive trust" in such "virtues of truth" as "accuracy and sincerity," and the "pooling of information" as a common good.[19] There is more than a touch of Arnold here, but also an indication of a felt need for something more substantial.

This is precisely the point at which an informed Christian perspective can make a real contribution, and in such a fashion as to find allies amongst non-Christian critics. For example, Williams's reflections correspond to our own querying of the claim (now enshrined in critical dogma) that there are no longer sustaining common stories or grand narratives. Tolkien's trilogy, we have suggested, has become a significant counterexample of such claims. If we are thinking about the dissolution of the modern European socialist narrative there is, of course, a certain rhetorical relevancy to this postmodern assertion, whereas if we are thinking of, say, African literature, often devoted to recovering a national grand narrative, it makes almost no sense at all. Among writers in China, whose formal Marxist grand narrative has, despite ceremonial observance, also stuttered to a stop, many contemporary novelists have identified openly with religious story, particularly the Christian grand narrative. (Among the most prominent Christian novelists are Lao She, Xu Dishan, Bing Xing and Mu Dan.) There is even

---

[18]Williams, *Truth and Truthfulness*, p. 3.
[19]Ibid., pp. 49, 57.

a new Chinese literary style called "biblical" *(sheng jing ti),* whose characteristics are described as "objective, truthful, terse."[20]

Christian students will thus want to reckon with the vigor of Christian literary culture elsewhere; in parts of Africa, Asia and South America our own greatest older texts are now being carefully taught and reflected upon intertextually. But the pendulum may yet swing back here too, if only because the academic study of literature cannot much longer be sustained by the purveying of trendy ephemerality alone. To return to Williams:

> The need to make sense of the past reasserts itself. It is particularly so when the smooth order of things is disturbed by violence, if only to answer the questions "Why?" "Why us?" "Where from?" Communitarian politics (and, at the limit, renewed tribal wars) are one area in which the need is very much alive, and it appears, too, in the interest in current historical disputes. . . . The demand for an explicit and definite story about one's own people or nation is only one form of it, and that particular demand has been more urgent in some places than in others.[21]

Tolkien, it seems to us, might credibly be described as having made an attempt, through recovery of faerie, to respond to that urgent need.[22] But he is hardly to be blamed if his work was not, at least for the future hope for literary studies, in itself sufficient to provide a renewed contemporary foundation.

The present crisis for literary study has been long in the making: from a Christian perspective it might be seen as the outworking of a congenital defect, present at the birth of the discipline. From a secularist point of view it has been more natural to think of it as merely a state of temporary dis-ease, the etiology of which has been examined, belatedly, and with eloquent diagnostic acuity by critics such as George Steiner since the 1960s and Terry Eagleton, beginning in the 1980s. In his essay "To Civilize Our Gentlemen," Steiner's nominal occasion for alarm was

---

[20]David Aikman, *Jesus in Beijing: How Christianity Is Transforming China and Changing the Global Balance of Power* (Washington, D.C.: Regnery, 2003), p. 254.

[21]Williams, *Truth and Truthfulness,* pp. 262-63.

[22]His Andrew Lang lecture of 1939, published as "On Fairy-Stories," in *Essays Presented to Charles Williams,* ed. C. S. Lewis (London: Oxford University Press, 1947), pp. 38-89, provides a good view of the philosophy undergirding his fiction.

the proliferation of arcane doctoral dissertations and thin literary journalism, but his underlying targets were the failed "rational and moral
optimism" of I. A. Richards and Henry Sidgwick (which Steiner rightly
identifies as secondhand Arnold) and the aestheticism, however elegant,
of F. R. Leavis and Arthur Quiller Couch. Steiner's gesture toward
medicine for the ailing discipline targets only one symptom; however
much we affirm his notion of a multilingual courtesy toward other languages and literatures (and indeed we heartily recommend it), this gesture is by itself inadequate. Steiner asks, "Is it not as important for the
survival of feeling today . . . to know another living language as it was
once important for a man to be intimate with the classics and Scripture?"[23]
To this we would answer no—that these sources of common understanding are not equivalent in value. A secondary good cannot long be
sustained without the primary good from which it proceeds. For love of
the neighbor to be sustained, at least on the biblical view, it must grow
out of love for God with all our heart, soul and mind (Mt 22:37-40).
From this prior love, neighbor love obtains its true value, integrity and
credible modes of expression in whatever language lies mutually to hand.
A Christian will recognize that the most effective prompt to generous
neighbor love is a self-effacing and unrestrained love of a Being higher
than ourselves, and that, on all the evidence, alternatives for this transcendence have not long been effective.

For Terry Eagleton, a post-Catholic Marxist for whom the authority
of his new religion lay precisely in its ethical rather than aesthetic
claims, it was the failure of literary study following the 1960s to keep in
the vanguard of socialist reform that occasioned his greatest anxieties;
the "crisis" which he addressed was likewise a crisis of logical coherence.[24] For Eagleton, the turn from literature to cultural theory has
since then degenerated further into a socially endorsed yet entirely nar-
cissistic self-preoccupation in which "quietly-spoken middle class students huddle diligently in libraries, at work on sensationalist subjects

---

[23]George Steiner, *Language and Silence* (New Haven, Conn.: Yale University Press, 1998), p.
62.
[24]Terry Eagleton, *After Theory* (1983; reprint, London: Basic Books, 2003).

like vampirism and eye-gouging, cyborgs and porno movies."[25] Eagleton's wrath rises proportionately to his sense that professional literary study has fled from public and political purpose to radically anarchic self-absorption: "The emancipation which has failed in the streets and factories" he writes in *After Theory*, "could be acted out instead in erotic intensities or the floating signifier."[26]

These are but two late twentieth-century realizations that formal literary study, in its pretensions to substitute for religion, has lost sight of a common good and become incoherent. We could cite others. Among them, more recently, is Jonathan Culler, in *Profession 2003*. Culler's current project involves resuscitating the system of Northrop Frye (who was, of course, one of Arnold's most eminent twentieth-century disciples). Summarily, Culler now sees that our professional position is untenable if we are unable to maintain even so much as a common ideal of literary value. For a Christian it is difficult to disagree, however astonishing it is to reckon with Culler as the source of this appeal. His recommendation that we turn again to purely formalist concerns such as genre, mode and archetype, is in itself welcome, even necessary. But resurrecting Frye—which is to say, resurrecting Arnold with a dollop each of William Blake and Oscar Wilde—will not by itself restore intellectual respect for the discipline. The decline of literature within the literature curriculum has become more general, and what we ambiguously refer to as "cultural studies" has filled much of the emptied space. That one can satisfy distribution requirements in literature by courses in the "History of Comic Book Art" (Indiana), "Rock Music from 1970 to the Present" (Minnesota) or "Campus Culture and Drinking" (Duke) gives some sense of where recent Ph.D. topics in literature can lead the survivors of contemporary graduate programs. As George Steiner has suggested, in such academic contexts our reserves of cultural capital appear to be almost completely exhausted. It is perhaps not too much to say that English is a *discipline* that has "lost its story." The apparent loss, as we have suggested, was perhaps an inevitability following upon the choices made by our discipline's academic

---

[25]Ibid., pp. 2-3.
[26]Ibid., p. 29.

founders. What Matthew Arnold and others too faintly recognized in their gesture to acknowledge the Bible as background or foundation literature, while shearing it of its supernatural or theological significance, is that coherence in the inherently incoherent realm of creative expression depends on the possibility of periodic reconnection to a normative, anchoring central narrative. The story that has been lost is "our story," and if we have not lost it ourselves we can help others by bringing it back to the fore.

Steiner and Eagleton are types, respectively, of Kierkegaard's "aesthetic" and "ethical" man. Each laments but also remains locked into the Arnoldian legacy, despite ardent attempts to rise above it. We should empathize, but with a more self-examining circumspection. Steiner admits, correctly, that while "'Art for art' is a tactical slogan . . . pressed to its logical consequences it is pure narcissism."[27] Eagleton, while he recognizes the tactical advantage for radical social reform in coded discourse, is as appalled as Steiner at the loss of elegance and clarity in the wake of postmodern psychobabble. Each staggers under the professional burden of a discourse without rankable values, the Babel effect of a secular religion gone wrong on both truth and beauty, and whose acolytes, cheerless in their alternate fits of denial and despair, discourse incommensurably even with each other, let alone with an increasingly indifferent world. It is not surprising, on these accounts, that some are losing quorum in the classroom. In Christian liberal arts colleges and university environments across North America, meanwhile, the discipline is doing far better.

The parallels with the near-modern history of institutional mainline religion, in particular Christianity, are many—too many to explore here. The loss of any authority sufficiently transcendent to command a common allegiance and thus create a common discourse is but one of these parallels. It is no merely secular reflex, I think, when Steiner is made unhappy by that apparent permissiveness in the guild whereby "We can say any truth and any falsehood" and get away with it;[28] nor is it extrinsic to his radical left social purpose that Eagleton defends the

---

[27]George Steiner, *Real Presences* (Chicago: University of Chicago Press, 1989), p. 143.
[28]Ibid., p. 55.

idea of truth and objectivity as fervently, if not as cogently, as does Bernard Williams.[29]

Since at least the time of Aristotle, who asserted in his *Poetics* that fiction has about it an order of truth more universal than history, the hope for shareable truth has been indispensable for the social authority of literature.[30] One came to the theater at Athens because the truths made flesh on the stage were more than transient truths. This gave even to a dramatized *denial* of truth a terrible power to wound and heal. But just as with the religious plays of Aeschylus and Sophocles, Shakespeare and Marlowe, so for all literature that, in the end, bids to be taken seriously by the wider community of thoughtful minds: at bottom, the only guarantor of communal truth is transcendent truth; the only guarantor of authority is the near presence of an ultimate and abiding authority.

This is why Walker Percy speaks directly to the fatigued emptiness of much of Western literary culture when he says, "I take it as axiomatic that one should settle for nothing less than the infinite mystery and the infinite delight; i.e., God. In fact, I demand it. I refuse to settle for anything less. I don't see why anyone should settle for anything less than Jacob, who actually grabbed ahold of God and wouldn't let go until God identified himself and blessed him."[31]

To an almost overwhelming degree, literature in English has acquired both its historic identity and its cultural authority from the mystery of divine transcendence to which Percy refers; it is this transcendence which has authorized our sense of the power of the word, and its shadow which still haunts our consciousness with an unbidden conviction that fine literature may no more be reduced to mere semiotics than the quality of human life boiled down to mere chemistry or political formula.

"If no authority, then only power," says Williams.[32] Yet the political

---

[29]Eagleton, *After Theory*, pp. 103, 105.

[30]"Poetry therefore is a more philosophic and a higher thing than history: for poetry tends to express the universal, history the particular" (Aristotle *Poetics* 9.3, ed. Francis Fergusson [New York: Hill & Wang, 1961], p. 68). Cf. William Wordsworth, *Preface to Lyrical Ballads* (1802).

[31]From "Questions They Never Asked Me," in *Signposts in a Strange Land*, ed. Patrick Samway (New York: Farrar, Straus & Giroux, 1991), p. 417.

[32]Williams, *Truth and Truthfulness*, p. 8.

power some in our discipline have wrested from moral authority is proving to be a rather feeble order of power; just how feeble, perhaps especially in straitened economic circumstances, the next decade will likely tell more completely. Put positively, it seems to us that the best hope for literature as a secular discipline is for it to reacquire its access to a moral and rhetorical authority derived from at least a quest for truth; the rush to trade such authority for power has proved to be a very bad bargain indeed.

Meanwhile in communities of those who yet think there is truth and inquire after it, there remains more hope than despair, and accordingly, we believe, more hope for literature. That is because these communities know that for hope to persist there is required a postulate of self-transcending truth, and that correspondingly, in the words of novelist Leif Enger, "denying the truth is the beginning of death."[33]

Indeed, for those who yet think that truth has consequences, in time and out of it, there is, accordingly, an added obligation of neighbor love—to study the greats of many languages and to do so in a fashion richly affirmative of their relation to founding religious texts. An advantage to readers whose common treasure is the common Book, and for whom common prayer and a common sense that salvation is both desirable and not a purely individual matter, is that they can become confident enough in their own identity to take the ultimate concerns of others, past and present, a little more seriously. They should be able—if they have not entirely forgotten their calling—to give to our own older literature a comparably responsible treatment of its primary religious and moral as well as stylistic dimensions.

Matthew Arnold thought that the spiritual capital of Christianity would readily transmute at comparably high value to secular cultural capital, the prestige of its canons carrying over into a secular clerisy of the literate. Accordingly, he was happy for the grandiloquence of the King James Bible and Book of Common Prayer to persist, and even to echo in the prose of literary scholars. But after 150 years it is clear

---

[33]"Interview with Leif Enger, author of *Peace like a River*," interview by Mark LaFramboise <midwestbooksellers.org/site/wp-content/uploads/2008/12/peacelikeriver-interviewleif-enger1.pdf>.

that much of that capital has been used up. Arnold and his successors, we suggest, were simply wrong to think we could keep these stylistic virtues without the high order of spiritual reverence to which they were attached.

Readers of Marlowe's *Doctor Faustus* may remember how he was willing to go from half-truths through illusions about his own power to a kind of rabid incoherence in which he proved at last to have no power at all. Having rejected the undergirding fullness of the common Book, believing himself superior to it in knowledge, wisdom and mastery, he took up instead certain books of magic and necromancy, by which in his search for self-aggrandizement he anathematized to himself the "New Testament and the Hebrew Psalter." In the end, in that last horrible scene, as the clock strikes and the demons draw near, he cries out in vain, "I'll burn my books!" His attempt at reformation, however, came all too late. What the Renaissance audience could see (can a modern audience perceive this?) was that what he probably needed to do, at the very outset, was to tell "German Cornelius and Valdes," most emphatically, where to go.

Now it must be admitted that in literature, hell is full of notable academics. Among other memorable examples are Dante's Brunetto Latini, for his reasons, and Charles Williams's Professor Wentworth for his. What these denizens have in common is a lifelong practice of retreat from the common good, and of its concomitant, rationalizing away any sense of accountability to the truth of the other. Perseverant egoism and almost absurd levels of narcissism are, in each case, made possible by a disdain for self-transcendent, mind-independent reality. Particular rationalizations for this or that denial are often, of course, ingenious: what gives each catastrophic fall its tragic dimension is audience appreciation that "rationalization is the homage paid by sin to guilty knowledge."[34] The literate audience knows there was a choice.

Cogency depends on a common sense, a sense of objective value to which, communally, we may appeal. Language itself will not otherwise work. As Williams observes, "Children learn language in many ways

---

[34]J. Budziszewski, *What We Can't Not Know: A Guide* (Dallas: Spence, 2003), p. 19.

and in many different kinds of situation, but one essential way is that they hear sentences being used in situations in which those situations are plainly true."[35] In this respect also, "Except ye . . . become as little children, ye shall not enter into the kingdom of heaven" (Mt 18:3).

Can we bear the burden of obligatory clarity? It may not seem obvious to many of our contemporaries just how easy it is to make a pact with the devil, then all too belatedly to regret it. Perhaps too few now believe there is such a thing as a soul to lose. Yet, for our discipline, there surely is a "soul" to lose. What we suggest in this book is that the thoughtful and soundly prepared Christian student can help to restore to that "soul of the discipline" its power to choose for health. To wit: it may be that the fate of our profession still lies in our own power of decision—to want hope more than wanhope, to love health more than despair. This involves our willingness to locate literature in a real rather than purely chimerical notion of community—indeed, in a community across time and across many cultures—and yet to be open to the full reality of our own immediate community of learning as much as that of any metaphoric "professional" community. As Wendell Berry has it, community life is by definition a life of cooperation and responsibility. Christians in any walk of life, it seems to us, are obliged to embrace their responsibility to community more readily than others; hence, they can and should work to preserve all literature that encourages future hope and the common good.

Tolkien favored the recovery of faerie at least in part because he was intent on the happy ending, the potential of literature for consolation. His dislike of the drama was focused on tragedy (Nietzsche's preferred genre) because in it the very form of closure depends on a realized catastrophe.[36] One wonders how eucatastrophic works such as Shakespeare's *The Winter's Tale* or *The Tempest* might have been integrated into his thinking about the worth of drama as a genre. It seems to us improbable, however, that recovery of the religious power of great literature can be complete without an acceptance of the complementary

---

[35]Williams, *Truth and Truthfulness*, p. 45.
[36]Tolkien, *On Fairy-Stories;* cf. Nietzsche's *The Birth of Tragedy and Other Writings*, ed. Raymond Geuss, trans. Ronald Speirs (Cambridge: Cambridge University Press, 1999).

necessity of unhappy endings, Tolkien, Dame Julian of Norwich and T. S. Eliot's citation of her notwithstanding. In Christian theological terms the assurance that "all shall be well" does not mean that all shall be happy, any more than the proposition "God is good" requires as its equivalent, "just in the way we'd like him."

Let us be clear. We disagree with those who would make the case that literature can provide, even for a secular world, "an ersatz transcendence."[37] A Christian perspective accords with Eagleton's Marxist conclusion that "Works of art cannot save us. They can simply render us sensitive to what needs to be repaired."[38] We agree entirely with Jacques Maritain (against Arnold) that "it is a deadly error to expect poetry to produce the supersubstantial nourishment of man."[39] Virgil is a splendid guide, but he cannot lead us all the way. At the same time we firmly believe in the power of literature to enable our will to truth. We caution, however, that without intellectually accountable access to a full range of texts that encounter and explore divine truth, very many worthy literary guides to truth may go without understanding, and may eventually even be unread and unreprinted. That would be for far more than ourselves a great loss; it might also, perhaps irredeemably, further diminish the residual authority of our fragile discipline. In this context the task for Christians is clear; it is to take up what Tolkien called the work of "recovery." This work, we suggest, is for Christian literary critics a central part of our specific calling, and we believe that for both ourselves and for the wider culture in which we live it is a worthy and redemptive work. It is our hope that among those who read this book will be young intellectuals who will choose to make it their own work as well—that, to conclude with an apt injunction of our greatest storyteller and critic himself, more among us shall be as scribes "instructed unto the kingdom of heaven . . . [like] an householder, which bringeth forth out of his treasure things new and old" (Mt 13:52).

---

[37]Terry Eagleton, *Reason, Faith and Revolution: Reflections on the God Debate* (New Haven, Conn.: Yale University Press, 2009), p. 83.

[38]Ibid., p. 159.

[39]Jacques Maritain, *Art and Scholasticism* (London: Sheed & Ward, 1930), p. 29.

SUGGESTIONS FOR FURTHER READING

Barratt, David, Roger Pooley and Leland Ryken, eds. *The Discerning Reader: Christian Perspectives on Literature and Theory.* Grand Rapids: Baker, 1995.

Benjamin, Walter. *Illuminations.* Edited by Hannah Arendt. New York: Schocken, 1969.

Bergman, Susan. *Martyrs: Contemporary Writers on Modern Lives of Faith.* New York: HarperCollins, 1996.

Brown, W. Dale, ed. *Conversation with American Writers: The Doubt, the Faith, and the In-Between.* Grand Rapids: Eerdmans, 2008.

————, ed. *Of Fiction and Faith: Twelve American Writers Talk About Their Vision and Work.* Grand Rapids: Eerdmans, 1997.

Brown, David, and David Fuller, eds. *Signs of Grace: Sacraments in Poetry and Prose.* Ridgefield, Conn.: Morehouse Press, 1996.

Buechner, Frederick. *The Clown in the Belfry: Writings on Faith and Fiction.* San Francisco: HarperCollins, 1992.

————. *Speak What We Feel (Not What We Ought to Say): Reflections on Literature and Faith.* New York: HarperSanFrancisco, 2001.

Craig, David, and Janet McCann, eds. *Odd Angles of Heaven: Contemporary Poetry by People of Faith.* Wheaton, Ill.: Harold Shaw, 1994.

————, eds. *Place of Passage: Contemporary Catholic Poetry.* Ashland, Ore.: Story Line, 2000.

Contino, Paul, and Susan M. Felch. *Bakhtin and Religion: A Feeling for Faith.* Evanston, Ill.: Northwestern University Press, 2001.

Eagleton, Terry. *After Theory.* London: Basic Books, 2003.

————. *The Illusions of Postmodernism.* Oxford: Wiley-Blackwell, 1996.

————. *Reason, Faith, and Revolution: Reflections on the God Debate.* New Haven, Conn.: Yale University Press, 2009.

Esolen, Anthony. *Ironies of Faith: The Laughter at the Heart of Christian Literature.* Wilmington, Del.: ISI Books, 2007.

Felch, Susan M., ed. "A Seminar on Christian Scholarship and the Turn to Religion in Literary Studies." *Christianity and Literature* 58, no. 2 (winter 2009): 213-303.

Felch, Susan M., and Paul C. Vitz, ed. *The Self: Beyond the Postmodern Crisis.* Wilmington, Del.: ISI Books, 2006.

Hansen, Ron. *A Stay Against Confusion: Essays on Faith and Fiction.* New York: HarperCollins, 2001.

Hartill, Rosemary, ed. *Writers Revealed: Eight Contemporary Novelists Talk About Faith, Religion, and God.* New York: Peter Bedrick Books, 1989.

Hart, Kevin. *Postmodernism: a Beginner's Guide*. Oxford: Oneworld, 2004.

Hill, Geoffrey. *The Lords of Limit: Essays on Literature and Ideas*. New York: Oxford University Press, 1984.

Holberg, Jennifer L., ed. *Shouts and Whispers: Twenty-One Writers Speak About Their Writing and Their Faith*. Grand Rapids: Eerdmans, 2006.

Impasto, David, ed. *Upholding Mystery: An Anthology of Contemporary Christian Poetry*. Oxford: Oxford University Press, 1997.

Kort, Wesley A. *"Take, Read": Scripture, Textuality and Cultural Practice*. University Park: Pennsylvania State University Press, 1996.

Lamott, Anne. *Grace (Eventually): Thoughts on Faith*. New York: Penguin, 2007.

———. *Plan B: Further Thoughts on Faith*. New York: Penguin, 2005.

———. *Traveling Mercies: Some Thoughts on Faith*. New York: Anchor, 2000.

L'Engle, Madeleine. *Walking on Water: Reflections on Faith and Art*. San Francisco: Northpoint Press, 1995.

Lundin, Roger. *The Culture of Interpretation: Christian Faith and the Postmodern World*. Grand Rapids: Eerdmans, 1993.

Manganiello, Dominic. *"Ad Fontes:* The Vine and the Green Branch," *Religion and Literature* 41.2 (2009): 1-9.

Maritain, Jacques. "The Frontiers of Poetry." In *Art and Scholasticism*. London: Sheed & Ward, 1930.

Markos, Louis. *From Achilles to Christ: Why Christians Should Read the Pagan Classics*. Downers Grove, Ill.: InterVarsity Press, 2007.

Peterson, Eugene. *Take and Read: Spiritual Reading: An Annotated List*. Grand Rapids: Eerdmans, 1996.

Robinson, Marilynne. *Absence of Mind: The Dispelling of Inwardness from the Myth of the Modern Self*. New Haven: Yale University Press, 2010.

Steiner, George. *After Babel: Aspects of Language and Translation*. New York: Oxford University Press, 1975.

———. "To Civilize Our Gentlemen." In *Language and Silence: Essays on Language, Literature, and the Inhuman*, pp. 55-67. New Haven, Conn.: Yale University Press, 1967.

———. *Real Presences*. Chicago: University of Chicago Press, 1989.

Tolkien, J. R. R. "On Fairy Stories." In *Essays Presented to Charles Williams*. Edited by C. S. Lewis, pp. 38-89. London: Oxford University Press, 1947.

Wolfe, Gregory, ed. *The New Religious Humanists: A Reader*. New York: Free Press, 1997.

Yandell, Keith, ed. *Faith and Narrative*. New York: Oxford University Press, 2001.

EPILOGUE

One of the main things we have tried to show in this book is that Christian faith has, in its literary expression through the centuries, produced a distinct knowledge tradition with distinctive habits of mind. These habits of mind are most apparent to those readers who come to the study of literature with a readerly sensitivity formed by reading Scripture itself as, in effect, the high literature of a long and fruitful faith tradition mediated through shared experience and the exposition of the church. Even readers who do not share the religious faith of Christians need to have an appreciation of the literary character of both the Bible and its historic interpretation to "get inside" this tradition, to appreciate its distinctive feeling for the ironies of human existence, and to enter imaginatively into its essentially poetic manner of disclosure. But for those who accept, as a matter of faith, the historic character of the biblical texts, an appreciation for literary elements such as irony, paradox, metaphor and enigma is likewise necessary if one is to read wisely and well the full legacy of biblical and postbiblical literature.

Perhaps the chief value of a literary education grounded in the Bible as foundational text is the formation of an imagination wary of ostentatious reductionism of any kind. We do not mean to imply that the systematic theologians and form-critical scholars, or the modern advocates of literary theories that propose in some measure to replace them, do not have anything to contribute. Clearly they do. Just as the genuine rigor of analytical philosophy and historiography of the postmodern sort have excellent correctives to offer—precision in argument and counsels against naive or sentimental readings of important intellectual works in those spheres—so too with redaction criticism or structured theological analysis for scriptures both sacred and secular. Yet because of their predominant technical focus they tend to miss something of crucial importance to the character of the Christian imagination. This "something" we may regard as a dynamic truth of insight, variously captured by gifted writers who have written out of a deep understanding of the character and mode of intellectual engagement offered in the Bible itself. If there is one thing that both sacred and secular scriptures have to teach us, it is that we cannot do without *literary* understanding if we wish to conjure adequately with the most profound narratives of human experience, for the art of their expression is almost invariably part and parcel with the truth they have to communicate.

In Flannery O'Connor's brilliant short novel *Wise Blood* (1952), there is a character named "Onnie Jay Holy" who reminds us that the self-serving and often intellectually dishonest evasions of the oldest tempter in Christian literature are typically expressed as a desire to construe the divine voice as a voice very like our own. Onnie is speaking for folks who think of themselves as Christian readers, but are not, even when reading the Bible:

> You don't have to believe nothing you don't understand and approve of. If you don't understand it, it aint true, and that's all there is to it. . . . It's based on the Bible, friends. You can sit at home and interpit your own Bible, however you feel in our heart it ought to be interpited. That's right . . . just the way Jesus would have done it.[1]

Onnie Jay, a corrupt and dissolute former radio preacher, sadly reflects a view found not only among some contemporary televangelists but also in many a more innocent Christian. Too many Christians are formed less by the Bible itself than by essentially postmodern views about anything extrinsic to the self. To hold such views as Onnie Jay is, from the perspective of a legitimately *biblical* faith, in effect a blasphemous denial of the integrity of the holy writings. But to hold them with regard to literary works of *any* kind, including explicitly anti-Christian writings, is transparently transgressive of the right of an author to his

---

[1]Flannery O'Connor, *The Collected Works* (New York: Library of America, 1988), pp. 86-87.

or her own views. This selfish attitude is often encouraged by the way literature is taught in our lower schools. (A self-referential reading can seem charming in an eight-year-old child but is surely appalling in a forty-year-old teacher.) No text means just "whatever it means to me." A Christian is obliged to recognize this reflexive practice for what it is—a refusal to love our neighbors as ourselves. Moreover, whether applied to Scripture or to a secular text, it is inherently anti-intellectual.

Human judgments, including critical judgments, are always provisional. As the epigraph to this book declares in the words of Hopkins, there is only one "just judge" and one "just literary critic," and that is Christ. His singular judgment in respect of the Book of Life marks plainly the final limit to all provisional opinions whatsoever. It is nevertheless the responsibility of a literary critic who seeks to be Christian to try in this professional sphere to obey, however incompletely, the injunction of Christ: "Be ye therefore perfect, even as your Father which is in heaven is perfect" (Mt 5:48). This seems on any reading to be a tall order.

What might this worrying injunction of Jesus mean in the calling of literary critics? First, Christian critics will grow in maturity toward the "measure of the stature of the fulness of Christ" (Eph 4:13) to the degree that they recognize their own subjective partiality and the need for conversation with the whole community of interpreters. Within that community the Christian critic's job is above all to represent reality as it is, and to eschew the distortions of advocacy or of self-serving critical rhetoric: "self-justification" is no substitute for just judgment in interpretation any more than in the moral life. Christian critics must not be idolaters of either texts or authors; they will, as Alexander Pope puts it, carefully strive to "blame the False and value still the True."[2] At the same time, Christian literary critics will see every author and fellow critic, each of whom is to be considered in respect of their correspondence to truth, as a neighbor. This implies a charitable, self-effacing "reading" of the other, a reading determined on truth rather than on an opportunity to score rhetorical or political points. Finally,

---

[2]Alexander Pope, "Essay on Criticism," l. 406, in *Poems of Alexander Pope*, ed. John Butt (London: Methuen, 1965), p. 156.

Christian critics will, out of love for authors as neighbors, learn both languages and cultural signposts in such a way that it becomes possible to approach even that more limited standard of perfection commended by Pope:

> A perfect judge will *read* each Work of Wit
> With the same spirit that its Author *writ,*
> Survey the *Whole,* nor seek slight faults to find.[3]

Pope was just twenty-one, about the age of most of the students who will be reading this book, when he wrote these lines. He here sets us all a challenge, but it is a challenge we must take seriously if we are to contribute to literary studies in a Christ-honoring way.

We believe that disciplined and faithful students who do so will acquire resources to become better readers of Scripture itself, as well as of the rich and variegated tradition of literature that is so often, in effect, its midrashic commentary. To the degree this objective is realized, our philosophical foundations will be appropriately reflected in our critical practice.

---

[3]Pope, "Essay on Criticism," ll. 233-35, in *Poems of Alexander Pope,* p. 151.

Index of Authors and Anonymously Authored Texts

Scripture Index